Y0-AHV-494

CHICAGO PUBLIC LIBRARY
SULZER REGIONAL

R0 03108 37313

```
HT         Harmston, Floyd K.
321
.H365  The community as an
1983       economic system
```

17.95

```
HT         Harmston, Floyd K.
321
.H365  The community as an
1983       economic system
```

4/85 R00427 27305

DATE	BORROWER'S NAME	

CHICAGO PUBLIC LIBRARY
CONRAD SULZER REGIONAL
4455 LINCOLN A
CHICAGO, ILLINOIS

MAR 1985

© THE BAKER & TAYLOR CO.

THE COMMUNITY
AS AN ECONOMIC SYSTEM

THE COMMUNITY AS AN ECONOMIC SYSTEM

FLOYD K. HARMSTON
PROFESSOR OF ECONOMICS
UNIVERSITY OF MISSOURI, COLUMBIA

THE IOWA STATE UNIVERSITY PRESS / AMES

Figures 4.2, 4.3, 4.4., and 4.5 are reprinted from *Theory of Location of Industries,* by Alfred Weber, trans. Carl J. Friedrich, by permission of the University of Chicago Press. Copyright © 1968, University of Chicago Press.

Figures 4.7, 4.8, and 4.9 are from *Central Places in Southern Germany,* by Walter Christaller, trans. Carlisle W. Baskin. Copyright © 1966. Reprinted by permission of the translator.

Figures 4.10–4.22 are from *Economics of Location,* by August Lösch, trans. W. H. Woglom. Copyright © 1954. Yale University Press. Reprinted by permission of Gustav Fischer.

Figures 4.26, 4.27, 4.28, 4.29, and 4.31 are from *An Introduction to Regional Economics,* 2d ed., by E. M. Hoover. Copyright © 1971 by Alfred A. Knopf, Inc. Reprinted by permission of the publisher.

Figure 4.32 is from "Spatial Price Discrimination," by E. M. Hoover, in *Review of Economic Studies,* June, 1937. Reprinted by permission of the publisher.

Figures 4.34, 4.35, 4.36, and 4.37 are from "Location and Theory of Production," by Leon N. Moses in the *Quarterly Journal of Economics,* May, 1959. Copyright © 1959. Reprinted by permission of John Wiley & Sons, Inc.

Figures 4.38, 4.39, 4.40, 4.41, 4.42, and 4.43 are from "A Theoretical Framework for Geographical Studies of Industrial Location," by D. M. Smith, in *Economic Geography,* April, 1966. Reprinted by permission of the publisher.

Figures 5.3 and 5.4 are reprinted from *Transportation and Urban Land,* by Lowdon Wingo, Jr. Copyright © 1961. Reprinted by permission of Johns Hopkins University Press.

Figure 6.3 is from *Public Finance in Theory and Practice,* by Richard A. Musgrave and Peggy Musgrave. Copyright © 1973. Reprinted by permission of McGraw-Hill Book Company.

Figure 11.1 is from *Discrimination in Labor Markets,* eds. Orley Ashenfelter and Albert Reese. Copyright © 1973 by Princeton University Press. Reprinted by permission of the publisher.

Figure 11.3 is from *The Economics of Black Community Development,* by Frank C. Black. Copyright © 1977 by University Press of America. Reprinted by permission of the publisher.

© 1983 The Iowa State University Press. All rights reserved

Printed by The Iowa State University Press, Ames, Iowa 50010

No part of this book may be reproduced in any form, by photostat, microfilm, xerography, or any other means, or incorporated into any information retrieval system, electronic or mechanical, without the written permission of the copyright owner.

First edition, 1983

Library of Congress Cataloging in Publication Data

Harmston, Floyd K.
   The community as an economic system.

   Includes index.
   1. Urban economics. 2. Regional economics. I. Title.
HT321.H365   1983   330.9173   83-4355
ISBN 0-8138-0327-6

CONTENTS

Preface, vii

1 / THE COMMUNITY ECONOMIC SYSTEM, 3
   The Economic System, 3   Interaction of Economic Units, 4
   Relationship to Other Communities, 6   Summary, 19

2 / THE SYSTEM IN A BARTER ECONOMY, 23
   An Economy without Money, 23   How Money Might Change Things,
   33   Summary, 34

3 / THE COMMUNITY MULTIPLIER, 36
   The Local Economy, 37   Calculation of the Multiplier, 39
   Community Matrix, 47   Uses of the Model, 63   Intercommunity
   Impact, 63   Summary, 64

4 / THEORY OF LOCATION, 67
   Contribution of Von Thünen, Weber, Christaller, and Lösch, 67
   Summary, 98   Spatial Economics, 100   Summary, 126

5 / THE LOCATION DECISION, 130
   Role of Information, 130   Decisions Relating to Spatial
   Structure, 136   Summary, 149

6 / THE COMMUNITY AS A SUPPLIER OF GOODS AND SERVICES, 152
   Private vs. Collective Goods, 152   Revenue Sources for Communities, 167   Summary, 172

7 / ECONOMIC EFFECTS OF PUBLIC ACTION, 176
   Governmental Reaction to Spillovers in the Private Sector,
   176   Spillovers in the Public Sector, 178   Summary, 195

8 / ROLES OF PEOPLE IN ECONOMIC ACTIVITY, 198
   People as Consumers, 198   People as Consumers and Producers,
   207   Composition of Population, 216   Summary, 221

v

9 / CHANGE AS AN ECONOMIC PHENOMENON, 226
Role of Production, 226   Role of Money in Change, 247
Structure of Industry, 248   Economies of Size, 248   Diversification, 250   Role of the Firm in Change, 250   Governments and Change, 253   Other Social Systems and Change, 254
Dual Economy, 254   Summary, 260

10 / COMMUNITY DYNAMICS: GROWTH, DECLINE, STAGNATION, 264
Role of Innovative People, 264   Role of Money in Community Growth, 267   Problems Inherent in Growth, 269   Building of New Communities, 270   Growth vs. No-growth Controversy, 276
Differences in Communities in Urban and Rural Regions, 276
Summary, 278

11 / ECONOMICS OF INVOLUNTARILY FORMED ENCLAVES, 281
Some Economics of Discrimination, 281   Involuntary Enclave as a Community Economic System, 289   Solutions, 290   Summary, 293

12 / METHODOLOGIES USEFUL IN COMMUNITY ANALYSIS, 296
Community Structure, 296   Population Projections, 307   Summary, 312

13 / PROBLEMS AND OPPORTUNITIES, 315
The Household, 315   Information Revolution, 323   Energy, 323   New Products, 324   Summary, 325

Index, 327

PREFACE

This text is designed to be used at the senior or graduate level. It will be most useful in courses where communities of all densities are of interest. An attempt is made to identify those characteristics that are common to communities located in both urban and rural regions. Differences, engendered largely by the regional environments, are also discussed, where appropriate.

For the student of urban economics, this will serve as an introductory text, since urban problems tend to be related to specific kinds of communities. Many of the interactions among communities, as well as specific relationships, develop because of the close proximity found in urban areas. Even so, there are some marked differences among identifiable communities.

For the student of rural communities, this text may well be considered to be introductory to regional economics. As with urban regions, rural regions consist of communities. The greater distances involved are basic to differences in regional problems.

Students of community planning should find a good grounding in community economics important to them. It is hoped that this book will fill that need as well.

The mathematics in this text has been kept as simple as possible. Where proofs are deemed necessary, reference is made to appropriate sources.

Since there are so few texts that deal with community economics and since books of readings in this area are scarce also, an attempt has been made to cover most topics of interest. The book is designed to be used in a one-semester course. Extensive lists of references at the end of each chapter provide a resource for outside readings.

The author is indebted to his students over a period of a decade who have "endured" the material covered here in its various versions as it was developed and refined.

Floyd K. Harmston

THE COMMUNITY
AS AN ECONOMIC SYSTEM

CHAPTER 1

The Community Economic System

THE ECONOMIC SYSTEM

Economic activity can be viewed as developing within a geographic framework for which natural resources, physical configuration, and the matrix of technological conditions are given (Isard 1956, p. 2). Each geographical point within that framework is unique with respect to these influencing factors. Each such point is also isolated to some degree from all other points by the friction of physical distance or some other geographical factor.

Households, stores, factories, governmental units, and so on, are microunits within this pattern and function as producer and consumer. Each unit, as producer, produces more of certain goods and/or services than it consumes; as consumer, it consumes more of certain goods and services than it produces. The result is a system of exchange.

While each unit is unique in consumption and production abilities, these abilities change over time. Further, each unit is mobile to a degree and can move about in an effort to find the best situation to satisfy its desire for production and consumption. As it moves through time, within the constraints of the geographic frame, there is gravitation toward points where economic advantage exists. Greater specialization among producers results in increased production and the need for additional market outlets. Exchange systems become elaborate and specialized.

As resources are exhausted and technological change occurs, there are further rearrangements. Clusters of activity decline and disappear; others grow and expand. New clusters spring up where there were none before. Elaborate trading systems develop, dominate the scene for a time, then fade away. Instability is inherent in the system (Harmston and Lund 1967, pp. 4-5).

At any particular time, certain clusters of units can be identified. They and their internal and external systems of exchange make up "community economic systems." They are complex trading economies.

Groups of these elemental systems can be aggregated into larger economies or extended systems of production and consumption. These are called urban areas, metropolitan statistical areas, regions, and so on. Nations of the world are made up of such aggregations, many of the nations being rather simple combinations of communities.

Role of Common Economic Interest

A large degree of common economic interest within the cluster is indicated by the facts that considerable economic interchange occurs within each cluster and that these relationships tend to be rather intense, but interchange with units in other clusters tends to be less so. As we move from the theoretical structure into the complex real situation, economic interest becomes one key determinant in delineating a community economic system. This does not rule out the influence of other social factors as well.

Economic interest may be the result of employment in one or a few basic industries. It may be due to the type of economic self-sufficiency that develops around a common shopping center. It may be due to geographical location or spatial isolation. In short, it is due to the economic advantage of a particular point.

Community

A community can be defined as "a collection of microunits having common economic interests." The community plus the activity resulting from interaction of the units and their relationships to units outside the community make up the community economic system. The social and political factors that are important in community life are assumed to be manifested as part of the economic interests of the units.

INTERACTION OF ECONOMIC UNITS

Endogenous-Exogenous Relationships

Trading relationships among units within the community are referred to as "endogenous." Those with units in other communities are said to be "exogenous." Exogenous forces create basic income that circulates through the community in response to local activity. Any one unit may be responsible for exogenous and/or endogenous activity. For example, in one household unit there may be a nurse working at a local hospital and a machinist who commutes 30 kilometers to a large manufacturing community. The first is producing a service for local consumption; the second is exporting services to another community. Or a local bakery may sell half its product to local stores and half to a wholesaler who serves other communities. The bakery's activity would be endogenous; the wholesaler's activity would be exogenous.

Each producing unit requires certain inputs. These include raw materials, energy, semifinished goods, labor services, and other services. Some are resources available in the community, some are the product of other local microunits, and some must be imported from other clusters.

Input equals output for each unit. This rules out producing something from nothing; it also rules out waste. Hence, input must equal output for the system as well. For any given short-term period it is possible to identify the existing structural input-output relationships. These result from and describe the endogenous part of the system.

Imports Equal Exports

For purposes of explanation, it is necessary at this point to make an assumption that imports into the community equal exports from it. This is generally true in the long run. This assumption will be relaxed later when balance of payments problems are discussed, but for the moment, these will be ignored.

It is also necessary to recognize the difference between flows of goods and services and flows of funds. These are counterflows. The machinist exports labor service to the manufacturing center; in turn his or her income flows to the community in which he or she lives. The baker exports bread to the community in which the wholesaler is located. The wholesaler's payment flows into the baker's community.

There are types of flows that are not counterbalanced. Transfer payments, such as gifts or welfare payments, represent flows of money unrelated to the production and sale of goods and services. For any short run period, the flow of capital funds may also be in this category. Sometimes goods and services flow without counterflows of funds, although these are less likely events. For example, help to another community in case of disaster may include goods and services for which payment is not expected.

Community Multiplier

As basic income is introduced into a community, it begins to circulate, and in its circulation, it creates other activities. The effect of this circulation can be measured and is called a "multiplier" (Harmston and Lund 1967).

Chapter 3 discusses the multiplier in depth. The multiplier measures the extent of turnover of money in a community from the time it is introduced until it leaks out in various ways--as payment for imports, as a tax payment to a larger unit, or as a transfer payment. The size of the multiplier is dependent upon the input-output relationships existing in the community. Each economic unit has its pattern of payment relationships for any given moment in time. Thus, the amount of turnover of a given unit of basic income will depend upon the pattern into which it is introduced.

The income of the machinist may be spent for food, house payment, utilities, clothing, and a vacation for the family. The turnover of the machinist's money will be influenced by the input-output pattern of the grocer, the bank, and the utility company, and the fact that a portion is leaked to pay for a vacation in other areas. It is not just his or her family's input-output pattern that is important.

The income of the baker may be spent for flour and other ingredients (some may represent leakage in payment for imports), utilities, payrolls and profit, rent, debt payments and interest, local advertising, and so on. Thus, the turnover of the money received from the wholesaler will be influenced by input-output patterns of the baker, the local miller, the utility company, his or her household and those of employees, his or her landlord, the bank, the local newspaper, and others.

A community is variously affected by the flows of basic income it receives. Therefore, the overall multiplier provides only limited information about the community. Nevertheless, by its size it indicates the extent of interaction in the community.

RELATIONSHIP TO OTHER COMMUNITIES

The exogenous activities of a community represent its economic relationship with all other communities in the world. For some communities, relationships may be very extensive. For others, they may be restricted to the immediately available communities. These patterns are largely the result of relationships established by units within the community. To some degree, relationships are influenced also by general location.

Rural Communities

<u>Agriculture based</u>. To a large extent, a rural farm community is a reflection of the type of agriculture practiced within its confines. A ranching community in Wyoming tends to have patterns that are distinct from those of a farming community in Iowa. A subsistence agricultural community in Africa is different from a hacienda community in Paraguay, although both are in underdeveloped economies.

The most significant thing about rural communities is that they cover rather wide areas. Although the shopping center may be the point of common interest, the community includes all those who share this interest. Thus, a Wyoming rancher may travel 80 km to his shopping center and an Iowa farmer only 10 km, yet they may be equally members of their respective communities. A rancher with his own airplane may buy all of his goods and services from a large city 300 km away rather than one 80 km away, and for all intents and purposes be a member of the larger community. Interaction rather than distance is indicative of community membership.

In their relationships to other communities, rural communities present various patterns depending upon type of product and technical development of the society. As producers, they tend to export agricultural products. The distance they can ship these products depends upon perishability and types of transport available. Wheat

The Community Economic System

is easier to ship than lettuce or milk. In a highly technical society there may be a wide market for all commodities. In a less highly technical one, the market may be limited. Thus, community A, in a highly technical society, may ship its products in a nationwide market. It will tend to have a highly specialized agriculture. Community B, in a developing nation, may produce largely for local consumption, exporting some grains to communities within a limited distance.

Mining based. Rural communities may receive basic income from export of minerals. Some communities are strictly mining towns or oil towns. These have a temporary character about them, since their existence depends upon the supply of minerals available. Oil towns tend to boom during exploration and wither away afterward. The kinds of goods and services sold in a mining community are distinct.

Mining communities tend to buy large proportions of supplies from supply centers and to sell their products in large markets. In cases where rural communities have both mineral and agricultural bases, the local market for farm products is larger than usual, hence interaction is facilitated. But this is true of any community with a wide variety of economic activity.

Diversification of base. The addition of manufacturing to a rural community increases interaction. Whether or not it affects nearby communities depends upon where it gets its inputs. If it happens to be a shoe factory that buys leather from a tannery in another community, the effect will be direct. A factory that hires commuters from another community has a similar effect.

Location vis-à-vis other communities. Where rural communities are close together, they tend to compete, but the effects of such competition depend upon the friction of time (in a spatial context) and distance. If the mode of transportation is walking or bullock carts, the extent of influence of a shopping center is limited as are the community boundaries. If the mode is the automobile and truck with dirt roads, the boundaries are greatly enlarged, but not as extensive as with surfaced roads. Superhighways tend to extend boundaries even further.

Communities developed in an era of bullock carts that find themselves in an era of autos and surfaced roads are forced to amalgamate. Usually, this means that one will grow and others will die. The dominant position is not always assumed by the one in the center. The kinds of people found in a community affect the outcome as do other factors.

Problems. Problems of rural communities are related to spatial configuration. Agglomeration economies and diseconomies that arise from spillover effects caused by industries locating near one another are of minor importance. Most problems seem to be related to provision of adequate jobs for the local labor force, but others stem from population density and transition from agrarianism to industrialization.

Labor as a resource. The labor supply in a rural community tends to range from unskilled to skilled in only a few areas. Therefore, industry moving into a rural community must be low information base so as to use unskilled workers, must import its own skilled workers, or must enter into some kind of arrangement for upgrading nonskilled to skilled among the local supply. Often rural communities find that cooperation in the establishment of a technical school, designed with considerable flexibility in order to train workers for specific industrial jobs, helps with attraction of higher skill industries. This does not help, of course, if the problem stems from attitude toward work and productivity.

In underdeveloped areas of the world where there is a high birthrate, the proportion of the population below age fourteen tends to be high. These persons tend to be heavy consumers and low producers. Another heavy consuming group comprised of those age seventy and above is increasing in the advanced nations. Obviously, only the people in productive age groups can be considered as labor resources to any appreciable extent.

Out-migration also affects the availability of labor. Lack of opportunities in rural communities is a major reason for the worldwide phenomenon of migration to urban communities. Such migration is a drain on the resources of rural communities and lessens the impact of labor supply on development. Thus, it is a result of slow development and may be a cause as well.

Lack of density. Whereas most urban problems are related to density of population, many rural ones are caused by lack of it. For example, rural communities have pollution problems stemming from the handling of human waste. Sewerage plants are "lumpy" type investments requiring a considerable amount of resources. Often rural communities cannot afford adequate treatment plants, unless they receive subsidies from a higher governmental unit.

Public transportation of any kind is hard to maintain if the number of paying riders is too low. Thus, rural communities can have bus service if they can pay for much of it out of the public treasury. Other kinds of public services that usually require cooperation among urban communities cannot be enjoyed at all by rural ones. If a rural resident wants to go to a zoo or museum, it is necessary to go to an urban region.

Dual economy. The problems faced by most rural communities in the world stem from their dependency upon stagnant agricultural industries for their basic income. A dual society is one that is basically agrarian but is trying to move toward industrialization. Its problem is how to accomplish this when its agriculture is producing just slightly more than is needed for subsistence. This problem is dealt with in detail in Chapter 9.

Urban Communities

Urban areas are aggregates of communities within limited geographic boundaries. There are often great contrasts among them. The central business district tends to be made up of business, industrial, and governmental units and to be lacking in households. The central business district imports labor services from the suburb and exports other types of services as well as goods, some of which go to the suburb.

The suburban community tends to be made up of households, with a minimum of business, industrial, and governmental units. Often the only export from the suburb is labor service; local business exists only to serve the local market. This type of suburb has often been called a "bedroom community." The ghetto is also a labor export community with special problems.

Within the urban area there are also less specialized communities. These may have a fairly balanced economy of business, industry, households, and government. Even these communities tend to interact more strongly with nearby communities than is the case with rural ones.

The major difference between the rural and the urban community lies in the ties they develop with other communities. The factor of space is important in this context as are the types of economic organizations that arise under the two circumstances.

Problems. Because urban communities are physically close to one another, many spillover effects are experienced. Some of these are agglomeration economies that have an important positive effect. Some are agglomeration diseconomies that have negative effects. Crime, location of jobs, pollution, transportation, public services, and housing present problems to the urban area.

Crime. Problems of the urban ghetto communities tend to create problems for other urban communities as well. High unemployment among ghetto youth is not only a problem of wasted resources but one of negative social and economic impact if they turn to lives of crime. The nearby central business district is affected when use of the district for entertainment purposes at night is curtailed due to the likelihood of being mugged or even murdered. The criminal element rooted in the central city also contributes to crime within suburban communities. Thus, solution of economic and social problems leading to the development of criminal activity is of regional and not just community interest.

The same situation obtains where the ghetto is on the outskirts of the city as in most underdeveloped regions. In these areas, the problem has been approached by the erection of walls and other barriers and the employment of guards. These approaches provide protection, in a rather unsatisfactory manner, but they contribute nothing to the solution of the problem.

Ramsey Clark (1970, pp. 48-50) has noted that the FBI lists seven crimes in its "index of crimes": murder, forceable rape, aggravated assault, robbery, burglary, larceny (theft of over $50), and auto theft. Four are crimes against persons, and three are crimes against property. If one considers the violence that may accompany robbery as incidental, then four of them involve some form of property, and these make up 92 percent of the indexed crimes.

The index shows that in a year's time a U.S. resident has 1 chance in 400 of being a victim of a violent crime. But a black ghetto dweller has 1 chance in 80, and the resident of an upper-class white suburban community has 1 chance in 10,000. Robbery rates in inner-city communities are 10 times higher than in suburban communities and 35 times higher than in rural communities. Larceny rates are 5 times higher in urban communities (highest in the central business district) than in rural ones, and the rate of auto theft is 14 times greater. Crime, then, is quite largely a problem of central city communities.

From the viewpoint of costs and benefits, the person with the lowest skill level has the least to lose when considering crime. Assuming that two persons are contemplating stealing money from a bank and that both of them regard it as a "business" proposition (i.e., no feelings of stealing being a wrongful act), it is to their interest to know what will be the expected return above possible costs. A rational criminal would consider such things as the probability of being caught and convicted, the opportunity cost of spending time in jail (earnings foregone), legal costs, expected length of sentence, and effect of a criminal record on future earnings.

Suppose that a bank teller earning $10,000 per year and a janitor earning $3000 were to be the ones involved. The teller would steal by embezzlement and the janitor by other means. Let the probability of being caught be 50 percent, of being convicted, once caught, be 80 percent, and the average sentence be 10 years for stealing from a bank. What amount of money would each have to steal for costs to equal benefits? Let us suppose that the teller would be reduced to taking jobs paying $5000 but that the janitor could still earn $3000 after serving time. Each has an earning life expectancy of 40 years. We will ignore the time between commission of the crime and apprehension, assuming that if not caught, each will go on doing what he was doing before.

Costs (certain) of the teller would be $100,000 in foregone salary plus $150,000 of postprison salary reduction (we are ignoring raises here) or $250,000. For the janitor it would be $30,000. These must be multiplied by 0.8 x 0.5 = 0.4 to get the expected value of $100,000 for the teller and $12,000 for the janitor. To this must be added court costs and any other costs resulting from being caught. Further, costs have to be discounted to a present value. Since a dollar received today is worth more to us than one to be received a year from today, next year's dollar has to be discounted. Thus we say $PV = X_1/(1 + r) + X_2/(1 + r)^2 + X_3/(1 + r)^3 + \ldots + X_n/(1 + r)^n$, where PV = present value of the money flow, X_i = money flow for the ith year (i = 1, 2, ..., n), and r = the discount rate. The point is that, for a nonskilled person, the amount of money to be stolen in order to make these types of crime monetarily rewarding is considerably less than for a skilled worker. Most crimes involving property are small, which means they are carried out by people whose discounted costs are very low, owing to low possible earnings or very low perceived probabilities of being caught and convicted or both.

Criminal justice works on four interrelated areas that are calculated to increase costs of committing crimes: employment, detection and apprehension, prosecution, and detention. Employment affects the opportunity costs by increasing earnings possibilities for people who might be tempted to turn to crime. Detection and apprehension (including street lighting, police vehicles, communication systems, and surveillance systems) increase costs by increasing probability of being caught. Prosecution works on the probability of being convicted (it also increases costs of legal talent). Detention (including various rehabilitation programs) affects costs dependent upon severity of the punishment and effectiveness of rehabilitation.

Costs of committing crime can also be increased by making it harder to commit them. This works on costs in several ways. One is to increase the effort necessary; another is to increase probability of being caught. These procedures are also costly to society and involve better locks, stronger doors, burglar alarm systems, marking of property, neighborhood patrolling by citizens, citizen education, better planning of public facilities, and so on.

Costs to society of criminal activity include loss of production caused by perpetration of a violent crime, hospital and medical expenses, loss of future earnings where there is a permanent disability, value of property destroyed (property stolen is a loss to the individual but not to society), increased prices due to merchandise theft (this is offset somewhat by low prices charged for stolen merchandise), increased insurance rates, and the depredations practiced on legitimate businesses and people by organized crime.

The cost to society from organized crime includes higher prices for goods and services as a result of the use of illegal tactics to eliminate or control competition. Where labor unions are infiltrated, workers are often robbed of pension money. Gangs often blackmail businesses into buying low quality merchandise at high prices. Corruption of police and other law enforcement officers adds to costs of local enforcement and lowers its effectiveness. Elimination of criminal activity turns these values into benefits. The costs then become the actual costs of operating police forces, judicial systems, and deterrent and punishment systems, plus any costs assigned to prevention, such as the furnishing of jobs and training to youth.

Location trends. In the more advanced economies certain forces have been at work, including the impact of the automobile, which have resulted in movement of manufacturing and many types of low skill service jobs away from the center of the city to communities on the outskirts. At the same time, many white-collar and professional or technical jobs, all of which require high information bases, have tended to remain. This means that the central business district must import workers from suburban communities. Meanwhile, low information base ghetto workers are cut off from industries where they have chances for employment, by the friction of distance. This is made even worse by lack of public transportation systems between ghettos and the new industrial locations.

Separation of labor-exporting communities from location of jobs causes a great many of the basic problems of urban regions. While inaccessibility of low skill jobs adds to poverty in the ghetto, the need for higher information base workers to commute to jobs in the central city creates transportation problems in the whole urban area. In addition, use of automobiles for commuting is one of the main sources of air pollution.

Pollution. Pollution may be defined as discharge of effluents at such a level as to overload environmental capacity. One reason pollution becomes a problem more readily for communities in an urban region is that there are so many more people per unit of environment. Pollution does not limit itself to any kind of economic, political, or social boundary. Hence, it is one of the major agglomerative features of the region.

Pollution is also related to standard of living. Certain kinds of pollution are related to poverty. For example, a community of shack dwellers on the edge of a city, having no sanitary facilities, creates human waste pollution that impinges upon other communities in the region. Other kinds of pollution occur because of people's ability to consume large volumes of goods. Thus, ending up as trash in affluent societies are metal, glass, and paper containers that could be recycled if conditions were right. Wet garbage is enhanced if people are above the subsistence level in use of food.

As the concentration of population increases with respect to area of land utilized, a larger proportion of goods that are not consumed, and by-products of production that cannot be sold are going to be discharged into a smaller proportion of the natural environment (air, water, and land). This is one of the major agglomeration disadvantages that may be very important in forcing economic activity out of urban and into rural regions.

A major difficulty in solving the pollution problem is that the environment is free. No one charges directly for its use. There are no property rights, in general, so far as the air is concerned, and only limited rights are exercised with regard to water: hence, their use becomes everyone's business--which has long been noted as no one's business. Of course property rights do not, by themselves, guarantee freedom from pollution. Communities often have to take action against owners of land who use it in such a way as to impinge upon their neighbors, à la the cartoon character Moose Miller or a junk dealer who fails to conceal his yard.

Pollution becomes a problem when the cost to society outweighs the benefits of the activity creating the pollution. If eliminating pollution means closing down a factory and throwing several thousand people out of work, society must decide which is the greater evil. The space program has shown that it is possible to have a system where all wastes are recycled. But this is a very expensive procedure, and the benefits from clean air may not match the costs.

Freeman, Haveman, and Kneese (1973, p. 80) have noted that control of pollution competes with production of things of value for scarce resources. Thus, too much pollution may be balanced by too much pollution control if the things of value foregone are of greater worth to society than the amount of pollution decrease. If one person is made better off and no one else is worse off, we have a gain, in terms of Pareto Welfare, for society as a whole. But suppose one person's gain results in someone else being made worse off. Then society has to decide, by means of some types of criteria, if those who gain are in some sense more deserving than those who lose. The economics of the situation is discussed in Chapter 8.

In general, the solutions selected by society will vary depending upon whether or not the problem is so pervasive as to require an immediate solution. Short run approaches usually involve finding ways to ration uses of the environment, such as requiring firms to meet certain emissions standards with existing equipment. This may entail finding alternate sources of inputs that contribute less pollution materials but are more costly.

Where a problem can be controlled temporarily or where it is not serious enough to require immediate action, long-term solutions, usually involving the use or development of new technology, can be utilized. However, unless polluters are being charged or are in imminent danger of being charged the costs associated with pollution, they are not likely to look for long run solutions.

Where the short run solution involves cutting back on production, the communities in the region will be faced with two types of demand for compensation, that of the workers laid off and that of the producer for foregone production. If the benefits are great enough, use of subsidies in this case may be justified.

One of the major questions in analyzing the impact of pollution is, "How do you measure the benefits of cleaning up a polluted situation?" In general, we consider effects of pollution on people to be most important of all possible effects. Direct observable effects of pollutants, such as carbon monoxide, sulfur dioxide, oxides of nitrogen, hydrocarbons, and particulates, vary from irritating to deadly. Only occasionally, usually during an inversion of airflow, will there be direct fatalities from air pollution. But that does not mean there will be no effect on people's health. So far, no one has been able to determine the actual impact, therefore, there is no basis for determining the benefits.

Even if researchers were to uncover statistically significant relationships between some measure of air quality and mortality rates, there would be a number of problems. For one thing we do not know how to measure the value of a human life, so we do not know what value to place on increased life expectancy. For another, air quality varies among areas within the urban region and people are mobile. Thus, a person might live in a community where pollution is low and work in one where it is high. Researchers are struggling with these problems and have managed to make some rather general estimates, error terms of which are probably quite large.

Aside from its effect on people directly, it is obvious to all of us that air pollution corrodes metals, erodes stone, kills trees, and damages crops. Some of these damages can be assessed quite readily. The impact of this type of pollution on land values is harder to determine.

Benefits from cleaning up water resources can also be identified quite readily for certain uses, such as swimming, fishing, and industrial consumption, since it is possible to find out how much people would pay for clean water in these cases. Other more esthetic benefits are harder to quantify.

Noise pollution also presents problems when one attempts to assess damages. The fact that rock music fans actually pay to have their hearing reduced by noise indicates some of the peculiar situations to be encountered.

Transportation. Transportation problems also tend to be at their worst in the older and more central urban communities. This is due directly to the fact that they were designed before the automobile became a factor. Consequently, both the volume of traffic to be generated and the need for parking facilities were not anticipated.

Congestion causes communities to consider the possibilities of rapid transit. Traffic congestion is a classical queuing problem, which means that there are certain times and/or places where resources are insufficient for the demand placed upon them. The usual approach to such a problem is to ration resources in some way.

A street or stretch of highway becomes congested at the point where the addition of one more car will cut down the rate of increase in number of trips per hour that can be made. At that

TABLE 1.1. Relationship of speed, density, and flow of cars

Speed km per hour	Number of cars per km	Total km traveled per hour
88	150	13,200
80	200	16,000
72	250	18,000
64	300	19,200
56	350	19,600
48	400	19,200
40	450	18,000
32	500	16,000
24	550	13,200
16	600	9,600
8	650	5,200
1	700	700

point, marginal social costs become greater than marginal private costs for use of the roadway, although both are rising.

Let us assume that for every 50 cars added to a particular stretch of highway, there is a resultant 8 km per hour decline in average speed traveled. The legal speed limit is 88 km per hour. As shown in Table 1.1, the number of total kilometers traveled will increase until 350 cars are using the highway segment, and the speed is 56 km per hour. Beyond that point, there will be a decline to the point of bumper to bumper traffic where cars are just barely moving.

Assume the operating cost for the average car is $0.093 per km and that this increases $0.006 for each decrease of 8 km per hour in speed. Assume also that the average occupant values his or her time at $10.00 per hour. At 88 km per hour the total cost of driving a car is $0.2066 per km. Thus, up to 150 cars can be accommodated at this cost, hence marginal cost below that number is 0. At the point of bumper to bumper traffic the cost increases to $6.314 per km. Marginal cost at that point is $4.972 per km.

Marginal costs and marginal benefits are illustrated in Figure 1.1. Marginal private costs (MPC) and marginal social costs (MSC) are the same up to the point where the addition of one more car reduces the number of total kilometers traveled in an hour. Beyond

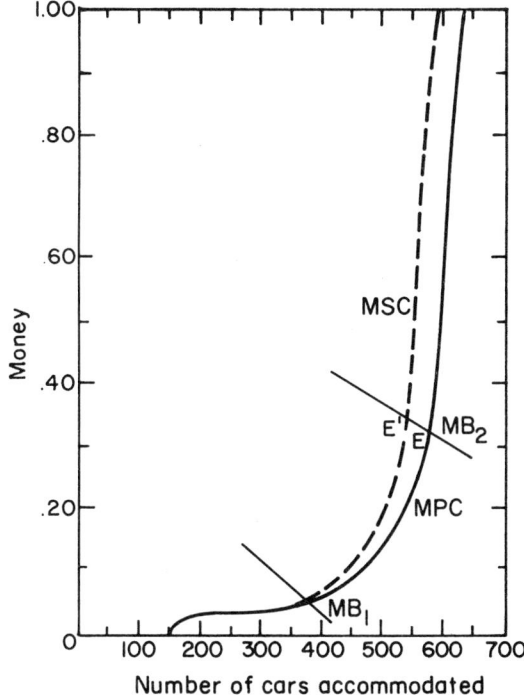

Fig. 1.1. Marginal costs and benefits from use of a highway.

that point, the cost to society is even greater than the cost to individuals. There are aggregate diseconomies, in other words.

If MB_1 represents trips to the grocery store and MB_2 trips to work, we see that people going shopping are not likely to use the highway when it is congested. Going to work is another proposition. However, at approximately a concentration of 550 cars, marginal benefits and marginal costs are equal (point E). For any greater concentration, it would not be worthwhile for drivers to use the highway at that hour, unless they were willing to pay more than they were getting in return. From the point of view of society, it would be better if they would stop using it at a lesser congestion point (E'). So long as roads are public goods, drivers will not stop entering the highway until their marginal costs catch up with their marginal benefits. If society wants to stop them before that, a system of rationing would be necessary. The queuing, of course, occurs only twice each day, thus rationing would be necessary only at those times.

Theoretically it should be possible to get drivers to stop entering at point E by adjusting private costs by $0.012 per km to bring them up to the social costs. This could be done by instituting a toll for a given stretch of road and certain hours of the day. If it were 10 km long the toll would be $0.12. Cost of administering the toll would have to come out of receipts; the objective would be to relieve congestion, not make money for the government.

However, consideration would have to be given to alternative routes that would be used by those cars whose drivers chose not to use the main highway. If, by discouraging its use, some other streets became equally congested, the whole idea would be self-defeating. On highways with several lanes of traffic, it is possible to help the situation by increasing capacity for the peak period. Center lanes can be made one-way traffic into the central business district in the morning and out at night. Even with this arrangement, however, it is possible for congestion to occur.

Another approach would be to set up a pricing system that would encourage formation of car pools. A toll system might be set up, for example, charging a toll of $2 for a car containing one person, $1 for two people, and zero for three or more. If this resulted in one-fourth less cars on the highway, a significant increase in total kilometers traveled during peak hours would be achieved.

One of the problems involved in using prices as a vehicle for rationing is difficulty of determining both private and social marginal costs and benefits. However, if experimentation is allowed (by starting with a fee known to be too high and gradually lowering it), the point of equilibrium between marginal social costs and benefits can be found.

— An often suggested solution for congestion in urban regions has been the building of rapid transit systems. The advantage to this type of solution, if it works, is that pressure is relieved on roads as well as parking facilities. But there are also some major problems involved with this alternative. First, the time queues are there regardless of the kind of transit used. Facilities adequate to meet peak demand will be over capacity for the remainder of the day. As with all peaking problems, charges have to be made that will enable recapture of the investment. But, whereas most peak situations lend themselves to the imposition of peak demand charges, this situation does not. Cost of using public transportation has to be below the cost of using automobiles, and this includes some discounting of the auto cost due to psychic factors (convenience, prestige, flexibility, time, privacy, and so on).

Second, in order to pay out, rapid transit has to serve large numbers of people. Therefore, it cannot serve all of the communities in the urban region, since the traffic potential along most of the corridors would be inadequate. Further, movement of industry out of the central business district may result in its being dispersed. This makes it almost impossible for rapid transit to give adequate service from all the labor exporting to importing communities.

Problems such as this are essentially the same whether rapid transit is by bus or train. The major differences come with flexibility and basic investment. Buses can use freeways and are somewhat more flexible. But they still face the time queuing and density problems. Another factor that works against success is that in most labor exporting communities people have investments in automobiles and will continue to keep them, even if they use rapid transit.

The general conclusion has to be that rapid transit is, at best, a partial solution to the congestion problem in urban regions. The automobile is both the cause and the basis for the solution. Because of the dynamic nature of community economies and the intense interactions among them, solutions must be kept as flexible as possible. Whenever a major investment in facilities is required, a top consideration must be a possibility of change.

The individual community in an urban region has an intense interest in having adequate transport communication with other communities, particularly those with which its people have intense linkages or are likely to develop such linkages in the future. However, it cannot provide the service itself. There has to be some unit that can operate at a regional level, in order that the overall pattern can be considered. This could be a transport district, state highway commission, road district, or whatever. When such exists, the problem becomes one of getting adequate community input to the planning process. Communities expecting to receive adequate transport service will see to it that they have good representation on advisory councils to the transport authority.

Other public services. There are other areas where cooperation among urban communities is necessary for efficiency in the dispensing of public services. A zoo, museum, opera house, sports complex, convention center, or major park is located in one community, but costs as well as benefits spill over to all communities in the region. Likewise, school districts may need to span several communities. Sewer and water districts may also be needed for most efficiency. Thus, cooperation may extend for the entire region to special districts, each of which spans a limited number of communities.

These cooperative efforts result in complex revenue raising arrangements. Where the service can be paid for by the users such as is the case with water, sewerage, and garbage collecting utilities, there are no major problems. But where taxes must be imposed, a consensus is necessary. In that case taxation and other problems become important. (These will be discussed in Chapter 6.)

The general result is that citizens of any urban community may find themselves working with several layers of local government, some of which are limited to their community, some of which involve contiguous communities, and some of which are regional. Rural communities have this situation to some degree also, but the complexity and intensity of relationships are quite different.

The chances are good for inefficiencies to develop in such a situation. There needs to be a certain amount of expertise among citizens who work with these entities. Since most citizens would rather not be bothered, adversary relationships between citizens serviced and entities doing the serving may disappear.

Housing. Problems of urban communities would not be completely discussed without consideration of the housing problem. Since it is largely poverty related, most of the factors of importance are discussed in Chapter 11. However, since inadequate housing is so conspicuous and may well have spillover diseconomies for communities that do not have the problem directly, its solution will often involve all communities in the urban region.

Housing services flow from an edifice that has certain quantity and quality considerations marking it as adequate, more than adequate, or inadequate. Among quantity measures are size of lot and dwelling unit; number of people served per square meter; number of rooms; number of bathrooms; presence of water (hot and/or cold); and communications facilities, such as a telephone. Among the quality measures are structural characteristics, landscaping, quality of neighborhood, location, type and adequacy of public services, and socioeconomic status of the neighbors.

In looking at a dwelling unit from the viewpoint of inadequacy, structural characteristics are usually the first considered. Welfare of the occupants is considered to be endangered by a unit with falling plaster, sagging or leaky roof, holes in the foundation, loose boards on the porch, sagging floors, storm damage, leaking basements, low quality original construction, and lack of plumbing. Crowding, in terms of number of square meters per occupant, is also considered important.

Of course, for the most part, such conditions are the result of inadequate income. The only possible solution is to somehow increase the funds available for housing. This can usually be done most expeditiously with some kind of public action. Rental supplements may be used to enable people to live in adequate units, providing such units can be found.

Publicly owned housing is often used. Here the major problem is one of maintenance. If the information bases of the people provide them with an understanding of the relationship between adequate care and maintenance of the structure and their own welfare, the housing unit will be successful. But where this is not the situation, vandalism, neglect, and indifference will raise maintenance costs astronomically. Lack of adequate social leadership among residents of housing units may be an important factor, since leaders tend also to be teachers of social values.

Public ownership becomes the only viable alternative when private ownership results in spillover effects that are uncontrollable, such as littering, vandalism, and landlord indifference. Since value of a dwelling is related to quality of the neighborhood, as neighborhood quality declines, marginal benefits to any one landlord for keeping up property declines. In inner-city communities, high property taxes that are needed to keep up services also work against adequate maintenance. Necessary high rents result in crowding by poor people who are sharing space. The prospect of neighborhood deterioration spurs the landlord to try to recover the investment rapidly. Eventually this may lead to abandonment of the property, since no one wants it.

Urban renewal has been used in the United States and elsewhere to improve neighborhoods in central city communities. Unless combined with construction of adequate additional housing, however, it can cause as many problems as it solves. Generally speaking, urban renewal changes land utilization in an inner city community from residential to commercial. Thus, the character of the community changes from labor export to labor import, which is a very drastic change. But when a ghetto community has reached the point of deterioration where abandonment of buildings is the next viable alternative, drastic measures are in order. Urban renewal has a definite role to play here.

In cities of the developing world, where slums exist on the outskirts rather than the inner core, short run solutions to housing problems entail public housing effort of some sort. This requires a substantial revenue flow that many countries do not have. Long run solutions could only come from raising personal income.

SUMMARY

Communities develop because there is some common economic interest that brings various kinds of economic units to one geographic location. These units create the community economy through their interaction with one another. This interaction is more intense within the community than with units outside the community. These clusters of units and their internal and external systems of exchange make up community economic systems.

Trading relationships within the community are said to be endogenous. Those with units in other communities are exogenous. Exogenous forces create basic income that circulates within the community in response to local linkages. These local linkages create a multiplier effect in the sense that a dollar of basic income creates more than a dollar of local economic activity. The multipliers can be calculated to reveal local impacts of various changes in exogenous flows due to economic factors, public policy, and so on.

In general we can classify communities according to intensity of relationships to other communities. Rural communities have less intensive intercommunity ties than do urban communities. These relationships can be shown to help explain differences in opportunities and problems faced by the individual community.

The character of community economic systems is also influenced by the major sources of basic income flows.

REVIEW QUESTIONS

1. What is meant by the word "microunits"?
2. How do their actions result in a system of exchange?
3. How do communities result from mobility of economic units?
4. What are some of the factors affecting growth and subsidence of communities?
5. How does common economic interest operate to form economic units into a community?
6. What is a community economic system?
7. What is meant by the words "exogenous" and "endogenous"?
8. Show how the same economic unit might be producing for sale in a local and an export market.
9. Distinguish between flows of goods and services and flows of money.
10. What is a transfer payment and how is it different from other money flows?
11. What is meant by the concept of a community multiplier?
12. How do input-output patterns influence multipliers?
13. What does the size of the multiplier indicate?
14. How does the type of agriculture influence the character of a rural community?
15. What is the most significant difference between a town serving farms and one serving mines?
16. How does diversification change the character of a rural town?
17. How do communities located closely in a rural area affect one another in a society of rapidly changing technology? In a "backward" area?
18. Describe community types in an urban region.
19. What seems to be the major problem found by rural communities?
20. Why is the labor supply of most rural communities limited in capability?

The Community Economic System

21. What can be done about it?
22. How do spillover effects among communities in an urban region work in the case of crime?
23. Why does crime affect the central business district so heavily?
24. What proportion of indexed crimes involves some form of property?
25. What chance does a U.S. resident have of being the victim of a violent crime?
26. How does this vary by place of residence?
27. What costs and benefits do criminals have?
28. Does it make any difference what the criminal's opportunity costs are with regard to the money value of the crime?
29. What are the four areas emphasized in criminal justice and what is the overall objective?
30. What impacts have locational trends among urban communities had on urban problems?
31. What is pollution and when does it become a problem?
32. Is there a difference in pollution problems of an affluent versus a less than affluent society?
33. How do short run solutions of pollution problems differ from long run ones?
34. When might subsidies be used in solving pollution problems?
35. Why is it difficult to assess costs and benefits for pollution problems?
36. Why are transportation problems worse in central urban communities than in other urban communities?
37. What is meant by the statement that traffic congestion is a typical queuing problem?
38. How are queuing problems usually solved?
39. How do congested highways affect trips made for different purposes?
40. Why should marginal social costs take precedence over marginal private costs in solving traffic problems?
41. How does society stop entry at the point where marginal benefit and marginal social costs are equal?
42. Discuss three possible solutions for a traffic problem, excluding rapid transit.
43. Is rapid transit a viable solution to traffic problems in urban regions?
44. Why are there problems with provision of several types of public service in urban regions?
45. How are housing services usually appraised?
46. In what ways may housing problems be solved?
47. Which of these ways seem to offer the best solutions?
48. How does taxation affect housing in inner-city communities?
49. Does it make any difference in trying to solve housing problems, whether the ghetto is in the inner or outer parts of the urban region?

REFERENCES

Clark, R. 1970. *Crime in America*. New York: Simon & Schuster.
Downs, A. 1969. Housing the urban poor: The economics of various strategies. *American Economic Review* 59:646-51.
Edmunds, S. W. 1976. Environmental cost trade offs. *Pittsburgh Business Review* 45:8-10.
Freeman, A. M. III, R. H. Haveman, and A. V. Kneese. 1973. *The economics of environmental policy*. New York: Wiley.
Harmston, F. K. 1969. Use of an intersectoral model in developing regional multipliers. *Annals of Regional Science* 1:1-7.
Harmston, F. K., and R. E. Lund. 1967. *Application of an input-output framework to a community economic system*. Columbia: Univ. of Missouri Press.
Isard, W. 1956. *Location and space economy*. New York: Wiley.
Meyer, J., J. Kain, and M. Wohl. 1965. *The urban transportation problem*. Cambridge, Mass.: Harvard Univ. Press.
Vickery, W. 1963. Pricing in urban and suburban transport. *American Economic Review* 53:452-65.

CHAPTER 2

The System in a Barter Economy

AN ECONOMY WITHOUT MONEY

Two counterflows are important in looking at community economics: the flow of goods and services from economic units to other units within and without the community and the counterflows of money. Because we measure real wealth in money terms, we tend to make our analysis in money terms as well. But the really important flows are in terms of real wealth.

In order to orient ourselves properly with regard to real flows and to introduce ourselves to a complex world with a simple model, we can consider an economy that had no money and no written language yet developed a fairly sophisticated economic system. This community flourished at about 8000 B.C. on the Anatolian Plateau at a spot designated by anthropologists as Catal Mound. Details on the community are from a report by Mellaart (1964). It was also discussed by Jacobs (1969, p. 24) as "New Obsidian." We shall call the community Catal for convenience.

Catal was built along a stream on a plain about 160 km from an outcrop of obsidian that had superior qualities for the manufacture of arrow points, spear points, and mirrors. Location away from the source of material added considerably to costs, but this was perhaps offset by superiority of the site from a security standpoint. Apparently, transport of the raw material was by porter. Although the people had donkeys, they seem to have used them for food rather than as beasts of burden. Transportation expenses including the cost of security would have covered thievery losses and policing costs.

Since the products of Catal were exchanged widely throughout the Mediterranean Basin, there must have been a marketing system. One possibility was a periodic trading "powwow" with hunters and gatherers coming with hides, stones, seeds, and other items to trade for the products of Catal. For security reasons, this gathering might have been at some distance from the community itself.

The Community at Catal Mound

The community covered 13 ha (the largest Neolithic site known), and was organized into several specialized areas: residential, sacred, and workshop. It had an extensive economic development, specialized crafts, rich religious life, developed artistic culture, and social organization. Despite lack of a written language, there were maps of the community on the walls of the area that apparently served as a seat of government. These people could have been the first community planners.

Buildings in the community were close set, rectangular with roof openings, and were constructed of a standard size mud brick. This made them impervious to marauders, but highly vulnerable to fire. Thus, concentrated land use was related to security. Each residential area had a storehouse with grain bins, mortars for dehusking, and querns for grinding grain. Although work on clothing may have occurred, there is no evidence that any other type of economic activity was carried on in the individual residences.

Security costs as well as the usual Von Thünen-type relationships (see Chapter 4) were probably responsible for the fact that all farming appears to have taken place immediately outside the walls of the center. The community utilized peas, lentils, and bitter vetch in addition to naked six row barley and hexaploid free threshing wheat--grains that were introduced into Europe one to two thousand years later. The people also purchased or garnered wild nuts, fruits, and berries.

Further evidence of the importance of security costs is indicated by the handling of livestock. Although the people apparently utilized the lands further away from the center for grazing, as would be expected, they corralled their livestock near the center for protection at night. Domesticated sheep, cattle, goats, and dogs were in the livestock inventory. They also purchased or hunted wild cattle, red deer, wild sheep, asses, boars, and leopards.

Male dress included a loincloth or a leopard skin fastened with a bone hook and possibly a cloak of skin fastened with antler toggles. The women wore sleeveless bodices and jerkins of leopard skin with fringed or string skirts with the ends of the strings weighted with copper tubes. Bone pins were used for fastenings. Women and children wore necklaces, armlets, bracelets, and anklets made of beads and pendants of stone, shell, chalk, clay, mother-of-pearl, copper, and lead. They used cosmetics and admired themselves in mirrors of polished obsidian.

Men used maces with polished stone heads and had obsidian arrowheads and tips for javelins and spears. Their daggers were finely designed flint with chalk or bone handles and were carried in leather sheaths.

Foods were kept in baskets and finely carved wooden bowls and boxes. Grains were stored in bins made of clay brick. Pottery lined baskets were used to carry water from the nearby stream. The people were expert weavers, turning out fine textiles of wool and hair.

A Hypothetical Economy

Since archeologists found no sign in either the residences or the shrines of any economic activity except preparation of food, the many products used had to have been imported or produced in the workshop area. Considerable evidence of import activity is found in the fact that raw materials necessary for the arts and crafts were not available within a reasonable distance of the community. Flint knives were probably also imported.

An intricate trading economy can be envisaged, operating without either a monetary unit or a written language. Salisbury (1962, p. 212) argues that discrete sets of values, each dependent upon different value scales, develop in these societies and provide a simple mechanism for maintaining the standard of life and, at the same time, allocate status and power in the society. Firth (1967, p. 18) states that a broad scale ranking system is often used in nonmonetary societies. Some things are just not traded for certain other things.

Without a standard of value or medium of exchange the process of trading is complex. Markets either do not exist or tend to be intermittent. Exchange tends to be largely man to man. Gabel (1967, p. 51) has noted that trade seems to have been more likely to develop on a large scale in terms of either raw materials or artifacts. Extensive trading in stone products occurred in Europe during the Neolithic period.

One might conclude, therefore, that the extensive distribution of Catal products was based on methods satisfactory to their customers. Specialization is indicated particularly in trade goods such as arrow, javelin, and spear joints. Mirrors may have enjoyed a more limited market, being largely a vanity item. Some type of communal distribution to Catal households is also indicated.

Intracommunity relationships. If we assume that most of the products used by Catal households were produced in the community but outside of the residential area, we can identify a large number of activities that fall into industry categories.

The production of sheep, goats, and cattle constituted a livestock industry. The herders were specialists who drove the stock to nearby grazing lands and brought them back to the safety of the settlement at night. Dogs may have been used in this endeavor.

The production of wheat, barley, peas, lentils, and vetch took place in fields near the town. Women and children were used in this endeavor as well as some men. Small plots could have been assigned to a household or farming could all have been communal. The land itself, however, was community owned. This was the agricultural industry.

Possibly the most important raw materials industry was the mining of obsidian. For security and specialization reasons the manufacturing of obsidian products by persons other than miners took place at some distance from the source of material or in the community center workshops.

The movement of materials to the center was the job of porters. These may also have been miners, but in each of the endeavors they would carry out a different function. Since miners and porters were subject to raids from roving bands of hunters, securing of the area around Catal during the daytime was essential. This was also important to the livestock industry. Thus, a standing army was necessary.

In the manufacturing segment a number of fairly broad specialties could be identified including weaving of cloth, basket and mat weaving, brick making, carpentering and joining, wood carving, obsidian knapping, toolmaking, mirror and bead making, tanning, bone working, smithing, and artwork.

The economy of the community consisted of the basic household units, a livestock industry, a farming industry, a mining industry, thirteen manufacturing industries, a trading industry, religious services, and government.

Some definite patterns of interaction among these sectors is immediately discernable. The obsidian miners and porters furnished the major material input for obsidian knappers and mirror polishers. The latter furnished the trade goods for the traders. Weavers of cloth obtained their basic material from the livestock industry. Boxes were constructed by the carpenters and joiners and turned over to the wood-carvers for further processing. Toolheads were obtained from obsidian knappers and fitted with wood or bone handles by the toolmakers. The livestock industry supplied hides to the tanners and bones to the bone workers. Households were suppliers of labor and management, essentially as in modern economies. The priestesses took care of religious and medical needs of the households. Government provided the standing army for protection as well as much of the coordination and management expertise for the community. Every sector was dependent upon other sectors as markets for its goods and services.

Import relationships. Assuming that the advantages of specialization were such that the people of the community did no hunting or gathering on their own, major import items would include leopards (prized for clothing); wild cattle; red deer; wild sheep; wild asses; wild boars; wild nuts, fruits, and berries; cosmetics; copper and lead; stone, shell, chalk, and mother-of-pearl for beads and pendants; stone mace heads; flint daggers; and wood for boxes, tool handles, and heating.

Economic man. The argument is frequently made that men in primitive societies cannot be placed in the category of "economic man," since it is said they do not react logically as we would define logic in the Western technological world. The logic that man in his attempts to maximize his own welfare succeeds in maximizing welfare for others does not seem incompatible with the situation at Catal, even though the actions may have been more communal than individual.

The very fact of an obvious attempt to specialize in certain areas of endeavor indicates a concern for efficiency and for maximizing. If maximum welfare for that society consisted of living a secure life, with adequate food and clothing, and enough outward adornment to set them apart as individuals, these people had attained it with one major exception. The exception was fire, which apparently was the factor that caused their downfall. It was also the factor that preserved their site for archeologists.

Heterogeneity in the labor force. One of the most important lessons to be learned from a study of this community is the folly of assuming homogeneity in the labor force. The expertise attained by any civilization is a direct result of heterogeneity in the labor force. Since labor is the most important input to production, an assumption of homogeneity dooms a model from the beginning. Thus, even in a primitive society, if any diversity in production is to be achieved, some people have to be more productive, have greater expertise, than others.

That this was true in Catal seems obvious from the number of different arts in which people were expert. This required a very select group of people.

Distribution. Anthropologists recognize several methods by which goods and services are distributed. One method is the gift. In some societies anything admired must be given as a gift. In others, the gift is simply a way of avoiding haggling, and compensation in terms of another gift of equal value is expected. Another method is barter either at a marketplace or individually. This involves a matching of goods or services.

Still another is the communal method. Each producer turns goods over to the chief who distributes according to need, social prestige, and other criteria. Every society seems to have some form of communal distribution to provide for the unfortunate.

What form of distribution might one expect in Catal? Little evidence of differences in living quarters indicates a communal-type system. But if there were social strata, the priestesses probably held a major spot. The shrines to the major goddess were decorated more ornately than other areas.

But the society lived in a male oriented world, the world of hunters. Its major items of export were designed largely for hunters. Further, production took place outside the household. These factors indicate male involvement in manufacturing to a large degree. A male with expertise might be expected to demand payment in accordance with his productive ability.

An example. As an example of some of the intricacies that might develop if the producer did his own distribution, consider the situation of a knapper whose products were arrow points. Suppose his wife and children also worked a small plot of ground, producing wheat. The household would be furnishing labor services to two industries (a not uncommon occurrence in today's society as well).

The arrowhead producer would have certain costs to meet. He

would owe the mining industry for his obsidian; he would owe the carpenter and brick maker for upkeep on his work space; he would have taxes due the chief; and contributions to the priestess to assure blessings on his work. To pay for these things he would have his supply of arrow points.

In addition there would be certain costs of his household that he would have to pay in arrow points. Some would go to the livestock industry, some to the weaver for cloth, some to the basket maker, and so on. The rest would go to the trader where he would be paid in imports of various kinds. His wife and children would have trade goods in terms of wheat in excess of their needs.

Each of these transactions would necessarily require meetings between buyer and seller, but there was no marketplace in the layout of the town center. If one existed, it was outside the walls. A communal distribution system may have been used in which all producers took their excess to a trader and received in return what they needed. This would amount to a dictated price system.

This community was fairly self-sufficient; there were a great number of interrelationships. The expertise indicated by the items produced suggests that few people were expert in many lines of work. Thus the arrowhead knapper would be dependent upon many others in the community, such as the maker of knapping tools, the brick maker and carpenter for upkeep of work space, the obsidian miners and porters for raw materials, the priestess for blessings, and the trader for his market.

If the trader sensed an increase in demand for arrowheads, he would pass this information on to the arrowhead makers who would plan for more production. This would increase demand for labor, for obsidian, and other items such as bone tools. These increases would be reflected in increased activity in the input industries.

If the community had underemployment among its men, the effect would be to give many of them more work, consequently, more goods and services to consume. But if the labor force were working to capacity, the increased demand would have to be ignored unless immigration could be encouraged to create a larger work force.

Growth of the community at a given level of affluence, resulting in part from imports, would depend upon expanding demand for the export items. The impact of such expansion would be in multiplier form, and size of the multiplier would depend upon interrelationships in the community.

It is important to note that even in as simple an economy as that at Catal, the amount of interaction soon becomes astronomical. For instance, as the arrowhead maker disposes of his product and obtains the goods and services his family needs, he runs into a myriad of transactions. The herder (meat producer) may have no use for arrowheads but wants some new beads for his wife, so the arrowhead maker may have to trade for beads, then for meat, and so on.

In order to gain some understanding of the economy it is necessary to simplify. Otherwise, the model is too large for ready comprehension. Assume that the Catal economy consists of the following nineteen economic units:

The System in a Barter Economy

1. *Households* are the source of all labor and management services and are the ultimate recipients of all consumables. In addition, certain specific goods and services are produced within the living area, notably baked goods and other grain-based products, food preparation in general, and probably some clothing.

2. *Traders* are the major risk takers. It is their job to exchange the export goods of the community for needed imports. This means finding and developing markets, relaying needs, and bargaining. They are forced to go outside the security pattern of the community in order to carry on their commerce. They also establish the price system.

If ten arrowheads bought a tiger in the hunter's camp and it cost five arrowheads for the porters to carry it to Catal, the price at Catal might be thirty arrowheads or twenty-five arrowheads and a spear point. The difference is payment for risk and the trader's service. The traders are the ones who know how many arrowheads are worth a tiger, so that any wandering hunter who brings one into Catal will have to deal with them and cannot charge more than fifteen arrowheads plus an allowance for the risk factor. If the trader's margins become too large, there will be an incentive for others to arrange deals directly with the hunters. Thus, trading is a unique profession, requiring men of courage and cunning and is probably highly rewarding when things go right.

3. The priestesses take care of both *religion* and medicine for the community. They preside over shrines, make sacrifices to the chief goddess to assure ample harvests, and minister to the ill. They may be paid from income of the household.

4. *Government* exists for the purposes of protection and order. In order for activities, such as mining, agriculture, and livestock production, to be carried on outside the town wall, the general area has to be kept relatively secure. One expects some sort of taxation of the producing units to be utilized in paying for these services.

5. Herders take care of cattle, sheep, and goats (*livestock*) accompanying them to pastures in the daytime and returning them to secure corrals near the town at night. They are producers of meat, hides, bones, tallow, wool, and hair. Meat and tallow go to households for consumption and are paid for by the surplus of these households that would have been obtained from the occupations of the workers and/or their trading of worker's surplus for other goods. The other products go as inputs to manufacturing: hides to the tanners, wool and hair to the weavers, bones to the toolmakers. They likely are paid in products of these industries that they then consume or trade.

6. *Farming* may be limited to small plots. Perhaps each household has one that can be operated by those in the household who are not employed on jobs requiring full-time attention and special skills. This helps explain the storage bins and processing equipment for grain found in the homes. The legumes raised may also go for food. Under these conditions, there is a minimum of trading in farm products. However, specialization in particular crops should not be ruled out.

7. Since obsidian weapons and toolheads are the major specialty of Catal, there is a heavy dependence upon obsidian *mining* for raw material inputs. One would expect the miners to be paid in products of the knappers and mirror makers that they sell to the traders for imports and local goods or use to trade directly with other industries.

8. The *porters* are needed particularly to carry obsidian to the town and to serve the traders in carrying exports and imports between Catal and other communities. They may be paid in obsidian goods or whatever trade goods the traders have in stock.

9. The *construction* workers—carpenters, joiners, and bricklayers—have the responsibility for new additions to the town and for the maintenance of existing structures. They may also subcontract work for wood-carvers. Their medium for payment varies, depending upon the resources of their customers. They produce their own bricks, but wood may be imported, since they are in a treeless area.

10. The *knappers* manufacture arrow, javelin, spear, and ax heads. Their main customers are the traders, but they supply the toolmakers as well, and probably have to trade some of their product to others in the community, such as miners and porters. Their major inputs are labor and obsidian.

11. *Toolmakers* are major procurers of the bone that is used to manufacture many tools, toggles, and fasteners. Stone is used for knapping tools. They also put handles on imported mace heads. Wood is probably imported for this purpose, although bone is an alternative. Payment for their products is greatly varied, since they do business with most other units in the community and probably sell to traders for export.

12. Cutting and polishing obsidian *mirrors* is probably one of the community's foremost manufacturing industries. Labor, obsidian, and polishing materials are major inputs. Sales are to local households and to traders for export. Payment media vary widely. Polishing materials are imported, and mirrors can be traded for them.

13. Weavers manufacture three different types of *textiles*. Wool is a major input, and possibly some goat hair. The products probably have both a local and an export market. Payment media vary.

14. Some of the input material for *basket and mat making* is obtained from agriculture and the local environment. Much of it may also be imported. Wandering tribes of hunters have access to reeds and heavy swamp grasses that can be gathered and traded. The market is largely local households, workshops, and shrines.

15. Material used for *bead making* has to be imported. The bead makers are highly skilled and have developed a drilling tool that will drill a very small hole exactly through the center of the stone bead. This is probably largely an export industry, although there is a limited local market.

16. Hides and skins of wild and domestic animals, imported tree bark and fruit are the material inputs of the *tanning* indus-

try. The tanned hides and skins are used largely for clothing in local households.

17. The wood used in *wood carving* has to be imported. Local households are the major market for wooden boxes, which are probably put together by carpenters and joiners before the carving is done. The quality of work is high and an export market certainly is a possibility.

18. *Cooper and lead* are imported and worked up by smiths into ornamental tubes and pendants. The market is probably local.

19. Pigments used by the *artists* are imported. Painting is done on the walls of homes and shrines. Sculpturing is limited to religious objects. The market is local.

Interaction of these nineteen economic units is shown in Table 2.1. Sectors providing goods and services directly to all other sectors are placed at the bottom of the table. Since the household sector provides all labor and management, it necessarily has close ties to all sectors. Household to household relationships occur because of goods and services produced and consumed there. Since traders handle imports and since each sector utilizes imported goods, that sector provides goods to all others, including itself.

TABLE 2.1. Intracommunity trading relationships

Selling Sectors	3	6	16	18	12	15	19	13	17	7	8	5	10	11	14	9	4	2	1
3 Religion																			x
6 Farming																			x
16 Tanning																			x
18 Copper, lead																			x
12 Mirrors																	x	x	
15 Bead making																	x	x	
19 Artists	x																		x
13 Textiles	x																x	x	
17 Wood carving	x																x	x	
7 Mining					x						x								
8 Porters									x								x		
5 Livestock							x						x						x
10 Knappers										x	x	x		x		x	x	x	x
11 Toolmakers	x	x		x	x	x	x	x		x				x	x	x			
14 Basket/mat making	x	x	x	x	x	x	x	x	x	x	x	x	x		x	x	x	x	x
9 Construction	x	x	x	x	x	x	x	x			x	x	x	x	x	x	x	x	x
4 Government	x	x	x	x	x	x	x	x	x	x	x	x	x	x	x	x		x	x
2 Traders	x	x	x	x	x	x	x	x	x	x	x	x	x	x	x	x	x		x
1 Households	x	x	x	x	x	x	x	x	x	x	x	x	x	x	x	x	x	x	x

Note that what has been done here is to divide the economic functions, not necessarily the labor force. If the same man quarried obsidian, carried it to Catal, and did some knapping, he actually had three jobs. This sort of thing happens today, also, in the case of moonlighting. It is assumed that Catal carried specialization far enough, in its attempt to produce quality products, that each person worked in limited areas.

Relationship to Other Communities

Relationships to other communities are assumed to be carried on through the traders, giving them, after households, the most intracommunity relationships. All nonlocal inputs must be bought from them and all exports go through them.

They probably dealt with wandering hunting groups who killed wild animals and collected wild nuts, fruits, berries, and seeds. Any surplus could be traded for Catal's arrowheads, spear points, beads, and so on. Thus, instead of spending time manufacturing arrowheads, the hunters could devote all their energies to hunting and looking for other food. Under the assumption of specialization, this should have increased everyone's productivity.

Undoubtedly the Catal traders established relationships with mining communities from which they brought red ocher, blue azurite, green malacite, and galena for cosmetics, and precious and semiprecious stones for beads and inlays.

The result of Catal's trading effort--the demands that increased as efficiency at home increased--would have been more individual productivity throughout the region. As the other communities developed, their increased demands would be felt in Catal as well.

The development of successful trading systems as shown by Catal is not dependent upon the development of a monetary system. Further, the community interrelationships that result in a multiplier effect from increased export demand exist in a barter system as well. The inflow of materials in payment for obsidian articles constitutes a basic income. These become trade goods that can be circulated to increase production of other goods, including obsidian itself. The barter system can lead to economic growth.

Economic Growth

Certainly, the growth of Catal was due also to a good supply of innovative people, and innovation is the basis for all growth. But innovative people also need an environment in which they can test and improve on their ideas. Once an idea is shown to be successful, the establishment of a work place, tools, and a marketing system become necessary. With these in place, new ideas need to be fostered to bring about added productivity and products.

Innovation that results in new products, including new tools, comes as a result of technological skill. This type of information allows its possessor to recognize that improvements are possible, gives him the ability to design the new product and the skill to see it carried into production.

To continue growing the next step for Catal beyond the point at which we examined it would have been the introduction of pottery making and beyond that better utilization of metals. An innovation in transportation would have been using asses as beasts of burden rather than for food. An innovation in trade would have been finding an item that could act as a standard of value and a medium of exchange.

Capital Investment

Capital consists of tools, machinery, buildings, animals, and

The System in a Barter Economy

so on used in creating other goods. The capital utilized in this economy was of a very low order. There were no machines and no animals used for power or transport. The community invested its resources in land, animals for food and fiber, buildings, and simple tools. Any expansion would require choices concerning consumer goods that may or may not have been difficult. A great deal would depend upon the extent of capacity utilization. If bone hooks and antler toggles were needed and the decision was to produce tools instead, a significant sacrifice would be indicated. But if the bone workers were only partially employed, increased production of capital goods may have involved little or no social cost. A reasonable plan would call for tool production during slack periods. The same would apply to expansion and upkeep of workshop areas. However, this would require forecasting increases in demand for manufactured goods, a delicate operation in any society.

The usual assumption of increased capital, at the expense of consumer goods, is that slack periods are not considered to be a factor. It also overlooks the fact that in technical societies capital goods are not usually produced by the same plants producing consumer goods. In the Catal society they would be.

HOW MONEY MIGHT CHANGE THINGS

Suppose some innovative people at Catal were to realize suddenly that everything could be valued in terms of arrow points of a given size. Now, it would not matter that the herdsman had no need for more arrow points. He could accept them knowing that he could trade them for a tiger skin.

Trade within the community would be greatly facilitated and the time saved could be utilized for more production, a fuller life, or whatever. If this concept could be extended to the trade area, trade would flow smoother and faster. And since the recipients would not be using them anyway, why not use a small copper facsimile of an arrow point with the chief of Catal's crest and his guarantee that it could be redeemed for the real thing?

Now the traders could start to specialize. Some could be importers and some exporters. They could travel further in search of new things or in promoting local products. But accompanying this new freedom comes another need, the need to keep track. A merchant finds that he can make as many marks on a clay tablet as he has copper arrows and this helps him. Counting begins and a written commercial language is not far behind.

There is no basic theoretical difference between a community operating by barter and one with a monetary system. Under both conditions, there is a local and a nonlocal market to be supplied. Under both the community gives strength to specialization and fosters trade.

But a monetary system makes trade efficient. It serves as a basis for use of arithmetic and a written commercial language, and these lead to further gains in efficiency and new innovations. With a monetary system, it is possible to actually explore the interrelationships that exist in an economy, since all activity can be reduced to a common denominator. But we must recognize that there is a fundamental difference between a flow of funds and a flow of goods and services.

In the Catal society, a flow of exports was matched by a flow of imports. Their flows were necessarily matched at all times. In a monetary economy the outflow of exports is matched by an inflow of money (or credit, which is essentially the same thing). And an outflow of money is matched by an inflow of imports. Thus, money flows add two dimensions to trade--and are in opposite directions to the flows of goods and services.

The use of money also means one more item to keep in balance. Money must be available when it is needed if trade is to go smoothly. It also must be available for expansion of facilities. And it makes it possible to develop imbalances in trade in short run situations.

Money makes the price system possible. It was noted previously that a primitive-type price system could develop even in a barter community (some items could be compared in terms of others, such as tigers in terms of arrowheads). But this is far from being able to price everything and to have differences in price of any magnitude. Price differentials can make significant differences in the way community systems operate.

SUMMARY

There are no basic theoretical differences between the operation of a community economy with a barter system and one with a monetary system. But the latter is more efficient, more complex, and has more problems involving time relationships.

Major economic factors to be noted in the development of Catal are:

1. Location near an exploitable raw material
2. Recognition that the material was a resource
3. Recognition that there was an economic advantage to be gained from location and specialization in fashioning obsidian products
4. Willingness to act to use the advantage
5. Ability to develop further specialization
6. Innovation in developing new products
7. Development of a marketing and exchange system
8. Willingness to invest by giving up consumption goods
9. Interaction among the sectors, a multiplier effect

If one were to analyze an economically viable community in the modern world, many of these same attributes would be found.

Another important consideration is that people of Catal had to deal with the friction of space. They must have recognized the cost, in resource terms, of having to market their product over a wide area. They were also obviously aware of the fact that their product was lighter than their raw material. As indicated previously, communities develop in geographic space, and spatial elements have profound effects on their economic character.

These aspects of communities can best be understood after considering the principles presented in the next section.

REVIEW QUESTIONS

1. What were the major economic factors affecting development of the Catal economy?
2. How do the various goods produced in the Catal economy support and compete with one another?
3. How do imports affect production?
4. Does specialization in Catal affect other societies with which it comes into contact? Explain.
5. What were some of the spatial costs encountered in this primitive society?
6. How would this community have gone about developing supremacy in the manufacture and distribution of obsidian products?
7. What products would be identified as "export" and which as "import" in this community?
8. Which products of the community were largely used within it?
9. What major ingredients of the growth process might one identify in this community?
10. Explain the development of capital goods in this simple economy.
11. How would it differ from that in a modern technical society?
12. How would the use of one of its products as a medium of exchange have changed the Catal economy?

REFERENCES

Firth, R. 1967. General comment. In *Themes in economic anthropology*, ed. R. Firth, pp. 1-10. London: Tavisstock Publications.
Gabel, C. 1967. *Analysis of prehistoric economic patterns*. New York: Holt Rinehart and Winston.
Jacobs, J. 1969. *The economy of cities*. New York: Random House.
Mellaart, J. 1964. A neolithic city in Turkey. *Scientific American* 210:94-104.
Salisbury, R. F. 1962. *From stone to steel: Economic consequences of a technological change in New Guinea*. Melbourne, Aust.: Melbourne Univ. Press.

CHAPTER 3

The Community Multiplier

In Chapter 2 we have noted the sales and purchase relationships that could exist among producers of various products in a very simple economy. These relationships are called linkages. In terms of production, linkages are most important in the form of real goods and services. Multipliers developed from that type of data would reflect the amount of production (in real units) required from each sector to meet a one unit change in demand for an export good, such as arrow points. Of course, in the case of Catal, the data are not available.

In a twentieth-century community, the data would likely be in monetary terms. This has the disadvantage that two factors are involved, each of which has its own separate function. That is, prices are subject to market forces, whereas inputs of goods and services are dictated to a large degree by technical requirements of the production process. Thus, a change in value of inputs may be due entirely to price changes yet be interpreted as change in the input ratios.

But there are also advantages in using the value approach. The most obvious one is that it provides a common denominator so that comparisons can be made among sectors. This is very important for development of a community multiplier. In the case of an economy like that of Catal where money values are not available but real values are available, sectoral multipliers, which measure impact on each sector separately, are all that can be developed. Where money values are used, the multipliers can be added to obtain multipliers reflecting impact on the whole economy. Thus, the analyst can see the impact on both the individual sector and any combination of sectors deemed to be of interest.

The community multiplier reflects the turnover of basic income received from sources outside the current local economy. These sources may be the result of exports of goods and services to other communities, investment of savings or borrowed funds in new capital, transfer payments from higher governmental units, expenditures by higher governmental units for local payrolls and purchases, expenditures by visitors from outside the community, and gifts from nonresidents to local people. While an aggregate community multiplier can be developed to reflect impact of a monetary unit received from any of these sources, it is not very useful in analysis. Therefore, it is best to consider a set of multipliers developed for sectors set up in such a way as to make them as homogeneous as possible.

It would be physically possible to develop multipliers for every economic unit, i.e., each household, store, etc., but this would be costly and not very practical. In addition, since units have linkages with only a few other units, the matrix would contain many zeros, which is not desirable from a mathematical point of view.

For those analysts concerned with the effects of price differences, data for each of the homogeneous sectors can be adjusted by dividing by a price index. Thus, if multipliers were desired for a span of years to see how production linkages had changed, the effect of price changes could be eliminated leaving only changes in local production relationships.

THE LOCAL ECONOMY

A community is composed of economic microunits that produce and consume goods and services. As a producer, each microunit creates more of some things than it consumes. As a consumer, it uses more of some things than it produces. Each, then, has need of trade with other units to rid itself of its surplus and fill its deficits. The products of some units require rather wide markets. For others the community itself is a sufficient market.

In general, units within a community have fairly intense interactions. Thus the local economy is easy to define, since it is these economic and other social interactions that give a community its character. Economically local actions are at one and the same time sales and purchases. Many units will also have sales and purchase relationships with units in other communities or with outside entities such as a governmental unit operating above the local level or an outside firm. Purchases from outside firms are called imports. Imports and exports, along with other relationships with units outside the community, are said to be exogenous to the local economy. Local interrelationships are called endogenous.

Technical vs. Local Inputs

Land, labor, and capital provide services for production of goods and services and are called factors. All of the factor service needed by a unit would be referred to as a technical requirement, but the local economy may provide only part of this requirement. Likewise, materials and other goods and services used are technical but may be only partially supplied from local sources. Technical inputs reflect total needs of an operation. Local inputs are those needs supplied from local sources. Technical inputs are both exogenous and endogenous. Local inputs are strictly endogenous. It is these latter inputs that are important in community economics.

Monetary Turnover

Exogenous activities create flows of funds into and out of a community. While the funds are in the local economy, they pass from hand to hand creating new business, personal income, and tax revenues. The extent of this turnover depends upon integration of the local economy, that is, the intensity of linkages among economic units. If an industry buys all of its inputs in the local market, we say it has strong linkages. Multiplier size depends upon the strength of linkages.

Turnover and Integration

As an example of the development of multiplier strength, let us assume that on a western desert, where there is no settlement, a rich deposit of uranium ore is discovered. Further, suppose that within 10 km there is a stream of water. Thus, the basic elements exist for a mining and processing industry.

Introduce into this geographic area the Apex Mining Company, which will begin operations as soon as (1) the overburden is removed and (2) a mill is built to process the ore. Operating with exogenously obtained investment funds, Apex lets bids to Target Construction Company and Super Duper Uranium Mill Company. Assume that all personnel must commute from Riverside, 25 km away.

At this point there is a community consisting of three units, but it has no economy because it has no local inputs. Now assume that an enterprising person decides to drill a well and strikes a good supply of sweet water that he or she uses to set up a trailer park; and an electric company decides not to miss out on a coming bonanza and runs in a line. With these facilities provided, personnel of the mining and construction companies move in. The community now has five business units and X number of households. There is a slight turnover of money, but the linkages are quite weak and the multiplier is very small. Basic income is coming from investment funds but it flows back out again almost as soon as it arrives. About everything has to be imported.

As business opportunities become apparent, businessmen from a large town 100 km distant investigate and one of them starts running a mobile grocery store into the community. But his driver-salesman lives in the other community and nothing is purchased locally, so this operation adds nothing to dollar turnover; it is just another form of import. Eventually, the merchant erects a building and establishes a branch store there hiring local people as clerks; now his operation is part of the local economy and contributes to a local multiplier.

Such a multiplier would continue to be quite small until additional units are added. Units that increase integration, such as a dairy, add an additional layer of activity. As the community grows, more layers are added and increase dollar turnover.

CALCULATION OF THE MULTIPLIER

In order to develop a model that will allow an examination of the complex interrelationships existing in a community, it is necessary to assume that input patterns and sources of supply for any microunit are somewhat stable over time and for varying levels of output. This assumption allows the analyst, in effect, to hold time constant for purposes of analysis. This leads to an induction that the proportion of total inputs coming from inside the community economic system (local inputs) will remain constant over the short run, regardless of total input (or output).

The units operating in the local market may be producing for any one or both of two markets, export and local. An independent increase or decrease in the local market is not possible in the short run, since this market is determined by local input requirements. These are now hypothesized to be a constant proportion of total output. However, the export market is not so restricted and can vary at will.

Input-Output Model

The model that allows us the best picture of an economy is the input-output model developed by Wassily Leontief (1966). It has been especially adapted for use in analysis of communities by Harmston and Lund (1967). The following explanation is quite simple; more detail is given in Chapter 13. To acquaint us with its basic principles, let us begin with the simple situation of a closed economy, one that does not trade with any other community.

A closed economy. A very simple economy is made up of a farmer, a grazier, a miller, a baker, a weaver, a tanner, a leather worker, an iron smelter, and a blacksmith. The farmer produces hay, wheat, and barley; the grazier produces meat, milk, hides, and wool; the miller produces flour and cereals; the baker produces bread and pastries; the weaver produces cloth; the tanner produces leather; the leather worker produces shoes, gloves, and harness; the smelter produces iron; the blacksmith produces implements, shoes for animals, utensils, and hardware. Each of these producers has a household to maintain, so must earn profits from his or her operation. These profits are used to buy consumption goods.

The objective of this economy, as with all economies, is the production of consumption goods. But in trying to accomplish this, each unit will use the products of other units. Some units will produce mostly these "intermediate goods" and some will produce mostly consumption (final demand) goods.

Let us now construct an interactions table (Table 3.1) by detailing the sales of each unit to each of the others and to consumption or final demand. Sales are shown across the rows and are known as "forward linkages." Down the columns, these same figures represent purchases or "backward linkages," and are designated such because they are the "inputs" to production. Profits represent returns to the operator for his or her labor and land use. The other inputs, then, are the intermediate products referred to above.

TABLE 3.1. An interactions table

Sales:	1	2	3	4	5	6	7	8	9	X_D	Y_i
Purchases	Farmer	Grazier	Miller	Baker	Weaver	Tanner	Leather worker	Smelter	Black-smith	Final demand	Total sales
1 Farmer	2	8	10	1	1	1	1	1	1	4	30
2 Grazier	2	2	2	2	5	6	2	2	2	15	40
3 Miller	1	3	3	17	1	1	1	1	1	1	30
4 Baker	3	4	3	3	3	3	3	3	3	12	40
5 Weaver	2	2	2	2	2	2	2	2	2	7	25
6 Tanner	1	1	0	0	1	2	18	0	1	1	25
7 Leather worker	5	6	2	2	2	2	2	2	2	15	40
8 Smelter	1	0	0	0	0	0	0	2	16	1	20
9 Blacksmith	8	5	4	3	2	2	3	1	2	5	35
Profits	5	9	4	10	8	6	8	6	5	...	285
Y_j Total	30	40	30	40	25	25	40	20	35	...	285

The Community Multiplier   41

To generalize Table 3.1, let us designate the interactions data as x_{ij}, the final demand data as X_D, and the total value of production as Y_i for the rows and Y_j for the columns. Thus x_{11} = 2, x_{12} = 8, x_{13} = 10, etc.; while x_{21} = 2, x_{31} = 1, x_{41} = 3, etc.; and x_{D1} = 4, x_{D2} = 15, x_{D3} = 1, etc.; Y_1 = 30, Y_2 = 40, Y_3 = 30, etc. Note that $Y_i = Y_j$, or the value of sales, is used up in purchasing inputs. Purchase of capital goods is treated as though they were used up in a single season, hence they can be treated in the same way as any other input.

Generalization allows us to explain the steps necessary for development of the closed economy model. In this economy people are concerned with producing enough additional consumption goods to take care of their children and grandchildren. But to do this, they have to produce a lot of intermediate goods. Note on Table 3.1 that a total product of 285 is required to provide profits to buy 61 of consumption goods, so 224 represents the intermediate goods produced and used in production, or a ratio of nearly 4 to 1. So, if they want to increase consumption goods 1 unit, total production has to go up by considerably more than 1 unit.

The input-output model provides a means for determining what this increase will mean in terms of required increases of production for each sector. The first step is the development of an A matrix of "input coefficients." We define $a_{ij} = x_{ij}/Y_j$ where i stands for row and j for column. Thus a_{11} = 2/30 = 0.067. (See Table 3.2.)

TABLE 3.2. Input coefficients (A) matrix

Purchases	1 Farmer	2 Grazier	3 Miller	4 Baker	5 Weaver	6 Tanner	7 Leather worker	8 Smelter	9 Blacksmith
1 Farmer	.067	.200	.333	.025	.040	.040	.025	.050	.029
2 Grazier	.067	.050	.067	.050	.200	.240	.050	.100	.057
3 Miller	.033	.075	.100	.425	.040	.040	.025	.050	.029
4 Baker	.100	.100	.100	.075	.120	.120	.075	.150	.086
5 Weaver	.067	.050	.067	.050	.080	.080	.050	.100	.057
6 Tanner	.033	.025	0	0	.040	.080	.450	0	.029
7 Leather worker	.167	.150	.067	.050	.080	.080	.050	.100	.057
8 Smelter	.033	0	0	0	0	0	0	.100	.457
9 Blacksmith	.267	.125	.133	.075	.080	.080	.075	.050	.057

By use of some elementary algebra, we see that $x_{ij} = a_{ij}Y_j$, so if $Y_i = \Sigma x_{ij} + x_{Dj}$ then $Y_i = \Sigma a_{ij}Y_j + x_{Dj}$ and $Y_i - \Sigma a_{ij}Y_j = x_{Dj}$. Since $Y_i = Y_j$, $Y_j(1 - \Sigma a_{ij}) = x_{Dj}$. This tells us the situation for one row of the matrix, but it is true of every row, so it is true of the whole matrix. If we let Y stand for all $Y_i = Y_j$, A stand for all a_{ij}, X_D stand for all x_{Dj}, and the identity matrix (I) for 1, then we can express the above formula as

$$Y(I - A) = X_D \qquad (3.1)$$

In short, we must subtract the A matrix of input coefficients (Table 3.2) from an identity matrix of the form

$$\begin{bmatrix} 1 & 0 & 0 \\ 0 & 1 & 0 \\ 0 & 0 & 1 \end{bmatrix}$$

which is a matrix with ones on the diagonal and zeros elsewhere. Table 3.3 is an $I - A$ matrix. Note that $1 - 0.067 = 0.933$, $1 - 0.050 = 0.950$, $1 - 0.100 = 0.900$, etc., or that we have large positive ratios on the diagonal. All off diagonal values are negative because they are subtracted from 0.

TABLE 3.3. The $[I - A]$ matrix

	1 Farmer	2 Grazier	3 Miller	4 Baker	5 Weaver	6 Tanner	7 Leather worker	8 Smelter	9 Blacksmith
1 Farmer	+.933	-.200	-.333	-.025	-.040	-.040	-.025	-.050	-.029
2 Grazier	-.067	+.950	-.067	-.050	-.200	-.240	-.050	-.100	-.057
3 Miller	-.033	-.075	+.900	-.425	-.040	-.040	-.025	-.050	-.029
4 Baker	-.100	-.100	-.100	+.925	-.120	-.120	-.075	-.150	-.086
5 Weaver	-.067	-.050	-.067	-.050	+.920	-.080	-.050	-.100	-.057
6 Tanner	-.033	-.025	0	0	-.040	+.920	-.450	0	-.029
7 Leather worker	-.167	-.150	-.067	-.050	-.080	-.080	+.950	-.100	-.057
8 Smelter	-.033	0	0	0	0	0	0	+.900	-.457
9 Blacksmith	-.267	-.125	-.133	-.075	-.080	-.080	-.075	-.050	+.943

Now we are explaining X_D in terms of Y. So, if X_D changes, what happens to Y? We want to obtain Y from our formula. If we multiply the left side of (3.1) by $(I - A)^{-1}$, we get $Y \cdot 1$ and if we multiply the right side by the same value we obtain $(I - A)^{-1} X_D$ or

$$Y = (I - A)^{-1} X_D \qquad (3.2)$$

This is what we have been aiming for.

Table 3.4 is an inverse or multiplier table obtained by inverting $(I - A)^1$. It tells us that if we want to raise production of farm products by 1 unit for use in consumption, the farmer is required by the linkages (interactions) in the economy to produce 1.402 units, the grazier has to furnish 0.415 units, the miller 0.405 units, and so on. If we assume that all measurements are in money, then we have a common denominator and can add all of the multipliers. If the money unit is called a dollar, then we can say that a $1 increase in production of goods for consumption from sector 1 requires $3.94 in intermediate goods or a total of $4.94. This multiplier represents the intensity of local linkages. It is high because the local people do not buy anything from other com-

TABLE 3.4. The multiplier $(I - A)^{-1}$ matrix

	1 Farmer	2 Grazier	3 Miller	4 Baker	5 Weaver	6 Tanner	7 Leather worker	8 Smelter	9 Black-smith
1 Farmer	1.402	0.531	0.715	0.462	0.346	0.383	0.348	0.351	0.363
2 Grazier	0.415	1.375	0.424	0.363	0.481	0.558	0.444	0.385	0.405
3 Miller	0.405	0.429	1.496	0.794	0.364	0.397	0.374	0.390	0.403
4 Baker	0.492	0.467	0.516	1.444	0.436	0.474	0.451	0.474	0.489
5 Weaver	0.322	0.289	0.337	0.290	1.283	0.307	0.293	0.310	0.319
6 Tanner	0.343	0.320	0.292	0.237	0.273	1.340	0.723	0.236	0.277
7 Leather worker	0.503	0.479	0.451	0.373	0.366	0.401	1.373	0.384	0.396
8 Smelter	0.389	0.291	0.340	0.268	0.226	0.248	0.244	1.322	0.741
9 Blacksmith	0.665	0.536	0.618	0.494	0.421	0.461	0.455	0.390	1.434
Total	4.936	4.717	5.189	4.725	4.196	4.569	4.705	4.242	4.827

munities to use in their production, so there is no leakage from the economy.

Another important fact about this model is that labor services are not assumed to cause any multiplier effects. This is because we have balanced profits off against local final demand and profits include payment for labor. In order to apply this model to an open economy like a community, we have to make some changes.

Multiplier concept. To clarify the concept of multiplier, which can be elusive even when examining a very simple economy, this section will look at the concept apart from the mathematics involved. The basic matrix algebra concerned can be found in any linear algebra textbook.

Let us begin by looking at an overall multiplier for a given economy. We start by assuming that certain units in the economy—the export sector—sell all of their products to buyers in other communities. Let us further assume that all other units—the domestic sector—dispose of their products in the local market, that is, they sell to one another.

The domestic sector produces both goods and services for local households, and goods and services that become inputs to production in the export and domestic sectors. Let us assume that the household members only work within the community. They do not commute to other communities. Let us also assume that workers do not commute from other communities to this one.

Now, if we know the gross value of production by each sector, domestic and export, we can calculate an overall multiplier that will relate the impact of inflows of dollars paid for export on the local economy. That is, suppose exports were worth $10,565,-000.00 and the value of domestic production was $24,299,500.00. We calculate the multiplier relationship 24,299,500/10,565,000 = 2.30. So we say that for every dollar of export, the local economy will produce $2.30 in the domestic sector. This is called an indirect effect, or an indirect community multiplier. We could also calculate an overall community multiplier covering all production in the economy by adding together the value of production of both the export and domestic sectors (i.e., $24,299,500 + $10,565,000 = $34,864,500, and 34,865,500/10,565,000 = 3.30). We say that for each dollar of export, the entire local product would increase by $3.30. This is called the direct and indirect effect.

How do we use these multipliers? Suppose we know that the volume of some export goods is going to decline so that the value of exports will be reduced to $9,565,000. We can quickly estimate that the domestic volume will decline to $21,999,500 and total product of the economy will decline to $31,564,500. On the other hand, suppose we know that a new export industry is going to locate in the area and that it will produce $1,500,000 of goods. This will raise the export value to $12,065,000. Assuming the new industry will buy about as much of its inputs from domestic producers as the other exporters, we would expect the domestic product value to increase to 2.3 × $12,065,000 = $27,749,500 and total community product to 3.3 × 12,065,000 = $39,814,500.

These overall community multipliers are useful for measuring overall effects. However, they do not allow one to analyze the effect of change in any particular industry. Suppose that the new export industry had a local purchase pattern considerably different from that of other exporters, the overall multiplier would be too aggregated for an accurate appraisal. The introduction of new kinds of export industries into an economy may place demands on the local economy that can be determined only after they have been operating for a while. An overall multiplier will not allow for adequate analysis of this situation.

A matrix approach, with industries aggregated into sectors that are as homogeneous as possible, provides a model that produces multipliers at many levels of operation. Suppose it were important to know how a new industry would impact on local utilities, for example. An intersectoral model would provide a multiplier for the direct and indirect effects on utilities by industries in the new industry's group. Or if it were a completely new industry, so there was not an existing sector for it to fit into, the purchase patterns could be assigned to appropriate sectors and the impact of each of these changes on the utilities could be measured and summed.

Multipliers are very useful tools, whether you want a little information, such as an overall multiplier provides, or a lot of information, to be gained from an intersectoral model.

The community open economy model. In community economics, the basic income flows (or flows of new money) are largely received from exports of goods or services to other communities and sales to higher governmental units. Transfer payments (welfare, Social Security, and the like) will also generate local economic activity, although they do not involve direct production of goods or services.

In this section we will show the mechanism by which these flows of basic income generate local economic activity. We do this by explaining the derivation of the model and relating it to exports (as a surrogate for all exogenous sales).

To keep our discussion as simple as possible, let us assume that all basic income enters the community in payment for exports.

The Community Multiplier

We also assume a restricted situation with three industry sectors, a household sector, and sales of goods to export. Let x_{ij} be interactions data, x_{i4} be household expenditures, x_{4j} be household income, E be value of exports, I be value of imports, and $Y_i = Y_j$ be value of production. Then we have

$$\begin{array}{c c c c c c c c}
 & \multicolumn{4}{c}{\text{Buying Sectors}} & & & \\
 & 1 & 2 & 3 & x_{i4} & E & Y_i & \\
\text{Selling} & & & & & & & \\
\text{Sectors} & & & & & & & \\
1 & x_{11} & + x_{12} & + x_{13} & + x_{14} & + E_1 & = Y_1 & \\
2 & x_{21} & + x_{22} & + x_{23} & + x_{24} & + E_2 & = Y_2 & \\
3 & x_{31} & + x_{32} & + x_{33} & + x_{34} & + E_3 & = Y_3 & (3.3) \\
x_{4j} & x_{41} & + x_{42} & + x_{43} & + x_{44} & + E_4 & = Y_4 & \\
I & I_1 & + I_2 & + I_3 & + I_4 & = F & & \\
Y_j & Y_1 & Y_2 & Y_3 & Y_4 & & & \\
\end{array}$$

The value F is a total that assures total imports will equal total exports. Thus, our model is in equilibrium. It is called a general equilibrium model because the whole economy is in equilibrium. In contrast, the partial equilibrium models used in most economic analysis allow only certain things that the analyst is interested in to be in equilibrium.

The enclosed part of (3.3) represents the endogenous segment, i.e., local interrelationships. Inclusion of x_{i4} means that local consumption is considered an input to the production of factor services. In the closed economy model it was not considered as an input at all. The endogenous part contains the local linkages among economic units. It gives us a picture of the local community economy as it exists at a particular moment in time.

The values on the diagonal (x_{11}, x_{22}, x_{33}, and x_{44}) represent the amount of each sector's product that it uses itself in further production. We can call these intrasectoral relationships. The other values are interrelations with other sectors so they can be called intersectoral relationships.

To arrive at the community multiplier matrix, we follow the same procedure as with the closed economy model, except that now the change in final demand is in the export sector. That sector identifies flows of new money into the economy, and the import sector represents leakage of money from the economy. These trade relationships mean the economy is open. An open economy is heavily dependent on events in other economies. It is also one in which trade and specialization are very important. The law of comparative advantage begins to work among trading communities, and they tend to specialize in certain kinds of goods and services.

There are certain assumptions basic to the use of the model. One of these is that $Y_i = Y_j$, or that output consists of all the inputs necessary to produce it. This rules out any waste. Another assumption is that input from inside the economic system will remain constant for any short run period or that the relationship between x_{ij} and Y_j will not change during the period in which we are interested; this is called constancy of the input ratios. A third assumption is that exports in total equal imports in total (F).

Recall the input ratio $a_{ij} = x_{ij}/Y_j$ and that we derive the A matrix (3.4) from it.

$$A = \begin{bmatrix} a_{11} & a_{12} & a_{13} & a_{14} \\ a_{21} & a_{22} & a_{23} & a_{24} \\ a_{31} & a_{32} & a_{33} & a_{34} \\ a_{41} & a_{42} & a_{43} & a_{44} \end{bmatrix} \quad (3.4)$$

The values on the diagonal (a_{11}, a_{22}, ...) represent propensities of sectors to obtain input to production from within the sector. That is, if the sector were agriculture, use of hay to feed livestock would be the basis for this type of ratio. The off diagonal values represent propensities to trade for inputs with other sectors in the community.

Again we define $Y_i = \Sigma_{j=1}^{4} a_{ij} Y_j + E_i$ or in general terms, since $Y_i = Y_j$, we have

$$Y = AY + E \quad \text{or} \quad Y(I - A) = E$$

$$[(I - A)^{-1}(I - A)]Y = (I - A)^{-1}E$$

$$Y = (I - A)^{-1}E \quad (3.5)$$

We now have our community multiplier matrix, or the $(I - A)^{-1}$ values.

$$M = \begin{bmatrix} m_{11} & m_{12} & m_{13} & m_{14} \\ m_{21} & m_{22} & m_{23} & m_{24} \\ m_{31} & m_{32} & m_{33} & m_{34} \\ m_{41} & m_{42} & m_{43} & m_{44} \end{bmatrix}$$
$$M_1 \quad M_2 \quad M_3 \quad M_4 \quad (3.6)$$

The M_j are total sectoral multipliers obtained by adding, i.e., $\Sigma_{i=1}^{4} m_{ij} = M_j$.

Viewing the system in terms of money flow, every community takes part in certain export activities for which it receives an inflow of new money. These may be called "basic activities" and the inflow "basic income." Upon being introduced into the community, the basic income works its way through many hands before leaking out to pay for imports, taxes, etc. In this process "secondary activity" is produced that results in "secondary income." One dollar of basic income thus produces more than one dollar of economic activity.

COMMUNITY MATRIX

In analyzing a community, it would be possible to construct a matrix showing the purchase and sales relationship of each microunit to every other one in the system. But most microunits have links with only a limited number of other units, so our table would be very large and would have a lot of zeros in the cells. A more logical approach is to aggregate the microunits into sectors as homogeneous as possible and practicable, given the information we have available. If a sector were constructed from microunits that were exact duplicates, the sector would have the same ratios as the units. Of course, such a degree of homogeneity is impossible to attain, but it can be a goal in setting up the sectors.

Since our model is in equilibrium, sectors can purchase no more inputs than can be used in production, which rules out the building and use of inventories in the endogenous part. This assures Hawkins-Simon conditions, that is, input requirements from any sector for production in that and all other sectors cannot be greater than the amount produced in that sector. Thus all propensities (a_{ij}) will have values less than one. They result in a matrix of multipliers that reflects relationships of each sector to every sector (including itself) in the original community matrix. These multipliers are independent and can be added to create an overall multiplier for each sector in the economy.

Adding Endogenous and Exogenous Sectors

In most communities, the local government sector is regarded as part of the local economy. It produces services needed by local people; its revenues are tied, to a considerable degree, to local economic activity. This sector can be added to the endogenous part of the model in the same way the household was added in (3.3). Its expenditures will then be considered as local inputs to production of government services. The services will be considered part of the local product.

In addition to payment for imports, funds can leak from a local economy as payment of taxes to a higher government (such as state, provincial, or federal), as contributions to depreciation accounts and savings, and as transfer payments from local sectors to those in other communities. These values become part of the exogenous payments section of the model.

Exports may be in the form of sales to travelers as well as wholesale services to outside firms in addition to physical shipments of goods. Often an analyst will want to show these separately. Part of final demand may consist of sales to higher government entities. Although they perform local services, the decisions concerning their activity are made outside the local community, and they are generally considered to be outsiders so far as local economic activity is concerned. Sales to investment are also treated as exogenous sales for two reasons: (1) investment is a reentry of savings into the economy, and (2) investment is "lumpy," that is, it occurs in large amounts one year and small amounts the next. A sector for this is usually designated in the final demand section of the table as "sales to local investment." However, the endogenous portion of the model will carry construction, industrial machinery, and other sectors for capital goods industries. These sectors will "export" to the investment sector, which will also import some of its needs.

Since the world is dynamic but the model is static, one must take into account that some produced goods will go into inventory and some sales will come out of inventory in any given year. This is done by an inventory adjustment column in the final demand segment of the model. A positive value in that column indicates that goods have gone into inventory; a negative value indicates that they have come out of inventory. Thus, the total value shown reflects only the current production for the period. In small communities, inventories are often negligible and can be ignored.

An Actual Community Matrix

Table 3.5 is based on an actual community of 15,000 persons that was studied two times, five years apart (Harmston 1962). The material in this table consists of actual purchase and sales data for the latter time. Microunits in this community were aggregated into fourteen sectors. Exports were assigned to five exogenous sectors and imports to two.

The largest sector, oil and gas production and refining, is not as homogeneous as would be wished. It should have been considered as a minerals production sector and a manufacturing sector. But here one runs into the practical problem of disclosure, which has to be avoided in order to get cooperation from industry in supplying data. Aggregation was necessary in order to avoid disclosing data on the refinery. Consequently the purchases by this sector from itself were rather large. The sector also had a large purchase of transportation services; it purchased a large amount of personal services from the household, and it used large amounts of utility goods and services. Sales of the sector went largely to export. Within the community it sold gasoline to local wholesalers. Each sector in the table can be examined in a similar manner by reading purchases down the columns and sales across the rows.

The household sector's income includes local returns on investment as well as payments made for personal services. Thus, it represents payments for labor services as well as for locally owned land and capital. The result of local household expenditures is a large component of the overall community multiplier. Some analysts prefer to run two tables: one with the household outside revealing only the relationships among other units, and one with it inside to catch the Keynesian effect, or the impact of household purchases on business and industry multipliers. For most community analysis this is unnecessary. Since labor services constitute the largest input in the economy, most of the household expenditures can be considered input to the production of such services.

Basic income flowed into this particular community from a number of identifiable sources. We justify using state and federal government as a source (through transfer payments to sheep ranchers and households, road construction contracts, payrolls, and revenue sharing with the local government) because it represents a flow similar to the others. The argument is sometimes made that since these expenditures are offset by taxes paid by local units, they should not be considered basic income. However, the inflow of funds affects economic activity in the community. The fact that it flows out again is not germane, since that must happen under all conditions. It is what happens between its introduction and its outflow that is important. Money received from any source has essentially the same type of effect, and the size of that effect varies with the sector through which it is introduced. Eventually the money leaves as payment for imports or taxes, as gifts, or possibly as loans.

An *A* matrix. Table 3.6 contains the actual input coefficients calculated from data in Table 3.5. Since sales must balance with purchases, the input ratios sum to 1. Five of the sectors have propensities to import over half of their inputs. Several others have high propensities in that direction.

Using column 1 for illustrative purposes, the heavy purchases of local oil for the refinery show up clearly as do the heavy payments made for transportation services and utilities. Payrolls, royalties, and profits paid to local people show up in the heavy propensity to purchase from the household sector. Over half the value of the industry's product goes to pay state and federal taxes, and to buy goods and services produced outside the community, including payments to outside stockholders.

A sector with a heavy leakage factor will show a lower multiplier than a sector with a light one. This is because the first round of spending carries the most punch. Subsequent rounds are weakened by leakage itself.

This *A* matrix tells the analyst what will be the initial impacts of a change in basic income. It says nothing about subsequent rounds of spending. These are summarized in the multipliers, but they do not fall out directly from this table.

Table 3.5. Interindustry table, Carbon County, Wyoming, 1959 ($1000s)

Sales	1 Oil & gas prod. & refining	2 Other minerals	3 Manufac- turing	4 Agricul- ture	5 Transpor- tation	6 Communi- cation	7 Utilities	8 Retail	9 Services	10 Finance	11 Whole- sale
1. Oil & gas production & refining	8,304.3	...	1.5	...	4.6	...	73.8	...	...	...	807.8
2. Other minerals	...	...	...	...	66.1	...	...	0.5	...	...	...
3. Manufacturing	1.0	0.7	11.7	...	0.5	1.6	44.5	820.3	94.8	31.8	...
4. Agriculture	...	...	272.4	1,183.2	179.7	...	...	35.6	0.1	...	...
5. Transportation	2,646.7	3.9	430.0	616.8	1.5	11.1	13.7	251.7	44.6	1.5	47.7
6. Communication	21.2	12.0	12.4	7.4	22.2	1.2	3.4	80.9	85.2	8.4	6.5
7. Utilities	1,664.7	1.5	43.2	44.2	68.5	18.7	3.7	225.4	156.2	4.9	9.5
8. Retail	10.6	2.7	74.2	1,312.3	26.7	...	31.4	216.2	126.8	6.1	22.7
9. Services	185.6	12.4	115.5	545.5	30.6	17.1	49.4	201.7	259.0	19.0	44.7
10. Finance	0.1	0.2	99.0	38.5	19.1	16.2	31.1	133.7	143.0	113.4	29.4
11. Wholesale	118.4	3.7	147.3	236.0	136.3	...	128.3	3,543.1	302.6	1.6	...
12. Rentals	17.1	0.1	14.5	132.7	39.4	5.8	9.9	297.2	165.5	16.8	11.6
13. Construction	114.7	0.3	304.8	154.7	1.8	...	414.7	84.3	365.5	19.4	118.5
14. Household	4,292.3	181.0	2,096.9	3,671.0	5,355.9	340.7	371.0	4,183.9	3,109.8	920.5	774.9
15. Local government	628.1	16.5	17.6	312.3	281.5	58.7	52.8	432.2	137.5	40.8	104.0
16. State & federal government	1,094.4	107.5	580.0	721.2	204.8	33.1	55.4	552.6	115.8	48.5	1329.4
17. Imports	17,942.1	53.2	367.0	482.3	212.1	138.0	2,508.8	13,243.7	911.1	1,047.9	2,126.5
Total purchases	37,041.3	395.7	4,588.0	9,458.1	6,651.3	642.2	3,791.9	24,303.0	6,017.5	2,280.6	5,433.2

Table 3.5. (continued)

	Purchases					Final demand				
Sales	12 Rentals	13 Contruction	14 Household	15 Local government	16 State & federal government	17 Travelers & truckers	18 Oil well drilling	19 Mineral exploration	20 Other export	Total sales
1. Oil & gas production & refining	...	52.9	...	...	...	...	...	...	27,796.4	37,041.3
2. Other minerals	...	15.6	...	...	...	...	...	...	313.5	395.7
3. Manufacturing	103.5	...	231.6	26.0	...	...	...	4.5	3,215.5	4,588.0
4. Agriculture	...	...	...	...	630.4	...	...	...	7,156.7	9,458.1
5. Transportation	0.1	70.5	202.4	...	3.0	232.2	20.4	25.2	2,028.3	6,651.3
6. Communication	0.1	26.4	300.1	...	16.3	6.1	5.2	19.8	...	642.2
7. Utilities	19.7	21.2	1,429.7	7.4	6.8	...	7.1	9.8	...	3,791.9
8. Retail	43.7	216.3	14,917.4	57.1	6.0	3,989.7	26.6	17.6	3,020.5	24,303.0
9. Services	22.2	272.1	2,095.1	235.5	1.1	1,213.6	8.6	80.9	810.0	6,017.5
10. Finance	139.0	43.2	1,407.0	33.4	0.1	10.7	7.6	0.8	...	2,280.6
11. Wholesale	4.3	171.3	...	48.5	63.6	...	5.9	23.8	439.3	5,433.2
12. Rentals	...	42.9	65.8	107.7	6.5	...	1.6	0.3	...	829.3
13. Construction	84.4	1,211.1	2,157.0	1.6	2,240.5	...	...	1.1	4,251.0	12,313.7
14. Household	301.5	3,190.8	82.4	789.9	3,430.3	...	134.7	1,116.7	182.6	35,393.6
15. Local government	78.9	44.3	342.6	1,656.7	1,226.3	...	1.4	92.1	...	3,867.6
16. State & federal government	23.8	90.6	4,116.7	59.6	23.1	...	5.5	699.1	...	9,861.1
17. Imports	8.1	6,844.5	8,034.8	844.2	2,207.1	...	199.5	1,263.1	...	58,445.0
Total purchases	829.3	12,313.7	35,393.6	3,867.6	9,861.1	5,452.3	424.1	3,354.8	49,213.8	221,313.0

Table 3.6. Input-output coefficients (a_{ij}), Carbon County, Wyoming, 1959

	1 Oil & gas prod. & refining	2 Other minerals	3 Manufac- turing	4 Agricul- ture	5 Transpor- tation	6 Communi- cation	7 Utilities
1. Oil & gas production & refining	.2241	...	.0003	...	.0007	...	.0195
2. Other minerals	...	...	...	...	.0099	...	...
3. Manufacturing	...	.0018	.0026	...	.0001	.0025	.0117
4. Agriculture	...	...	.0594	.1251	.0270	...	...
5. Transportation	.0715	.0099	.0937	.0652	.0002	.0173	.0036
6. Communication	.0006	.0303	.0027	.0008	.0033	.0019	.0009
7. Utilities	.0449	.0038	.0094	.0047	.0103	.0291	.0010
8. Retail	.0003	.0068	.0162	.1387	.0040	...	.0083
9. Services	.0050	.0313	.0252	.0577	.0046	.0266	.0130
10. Finance	...	.0005	.0216	.0041	.0029	.0252	.0082
11. Wholesale	.0032	.0094	.0321	.0250	.0205	...	.0338
12. Rentals	.0005	.0003	.0032	.0140	.0059	.0090	.0026
13. Construction	.0031	.0007	.0664	.0164	.0003	...	.1094
14. Household	.1159	.4574	.4570	.3881	.8052	.5305	.0979
15. Local government	.0170	.0417	.0038	.0330	.0423	.0914	.0139
16. State & federal government & imports	0.5139	0.4061	0.2064	0.1272	0.0628	0.2665	0.6762
Sum	1.0000	1.0000	1.0000	1.0000	1.0000	1.0000	1.0000

52

Table 3.6. (continued)

		8 Retail	9 Services	10 Finance	11 Wholesale	12 Rentals	13 Construction	14 Household	15 Local government
1.	Oil & gas production & refining	...	...	...	.1487	...	.0043	...	...
2.	Other minerals	.0037	.0158	.0139	...	.1248	.0013	.0065	.0067
3.	Manufacturing	.0015	...	...	...	...	...	...	...
4.	Agriculture	.0104	.0074	.0007	.0088	.0001	.0057	.0057	.0019
5.	Transportation	.0033	.0142	.0037	.0012	.0001	.0021	.0085	.0148
6.	Communication	.0093	.0260	.0021	.0017	.0238	.0017	.0404	.0609
7.	Utilities	.0089	.0211	.0027	.0042	.0527	.0176	.4215	.0086
8.	Retail	.0083	.0430	.0083	.0082	.0268	.0221	.0592	.0125
9.	Services	.0055	.0238	.0497	.0054	.1676	.0035	.0398	.0278
10.	Finance	.1458	.0502	.0007	...	.0052	.0139	...	.0004
11.	Wholesale	.0122	.0275	.0074	.0021	...	.0035	.0019	.2042
12.	Rentals	.0035	.0607	.0085	.0218	.1018	.0984	.0609	.4284
13.	Construction	.1722	.5168	.4036	.1426	.3636	.2591	.0023	...
14.	Household	.0178	.0229	.0179	.0191	.0951	.0036	.0097	...
15.	Local government								
16.	State & federal government & imports	0.5676	0.1706	0.4808	0.6362	0.0384	0.5632	0.3436	0.2338
	Sum	1.0000	1.0000	1.0000	1.0000	1.0000	1.0000	1.0000	1.0000

The _I - A_ matrix. The next step toward calculation of the community multiplier matrix is to subtract from 1. Since an identity (or unity) matrix has 1s on the diagonal and 0s elsewhere, and since all a_{ij} have values less than 1, the result is another matrix with positive values on the diagonal and negative values elsewhere. Table 3.7 carries values derived by subtracting the values in Table 3.6 from an identity matrix.

The inverse. The final step is calculation of the multiplier itself. The theoretical basis for this multiplier is essentially the same as for the Keynesian multiplier. The major difference is that Keynes thought that Say's law applied to all units except the household. That is, he assumed all units but the household spent all of their income in the economy being analyzed.

In any community, few units spend all they take in within the economy. When the economy is described by a matrix, the chances are even greater that they will not spend all of their income with other local units. Thus, the assumption is substantiated that propensities to spend by all economic units within a community will be less than 1. This assumption forms the basis for the community multiplier. By inverting the _I - A_ table a new matrix is developed.

Each m_{ij} is a multiplier representing the effect upon a given sector of the circulation of one unit of basic monetary income through the economy. These intrasectoral and intersectoral multipliers are independent, hence additive, and can be combined to give the overall effect of a monetary unit introduced through a given sector (M_j). An overall multiplier indicative of the effect of all basic income can also be calculated directly from the data given in Table 3.5.

Such an overall multiplier is useful for measuring overall trends from year to year. It has serious limitations in analyzing the causes of the trends. The multiplier table is one of the most useful devices an analyst could hope for in analyzing community economic systems. However, it represents the endogenous part of the community economic system and tells nothing of exogenous happenings. Forces causing change in the basic income of a community have to be assessed with other tools.

The resultant inversion of the matrix in Table 3.7 is given in Table 3.8 and reflects direct and indirect activity per dollar of export. Each value in this table represents the effect of circulation of a dollar of basic income through the economy. The multipliers for sectors 1 through 13 have been combined to give a multiplier for the business and industry sectors. By adding those for local government and the household, an overall multiplier for each sector could be obtained.

The effect of increased exports would be as follows. Using column 1 of Table 3.8 as an illustration, suppose there were an increase in export of gasoline of $1000. This would increase the

The Community Multiplier 55

local market demand, which can be measured directly from the table. By comparing with the data from Table 3.6, one can get an idea of the impact of turnover beyond the first round. These comparisons are shown in Table 3.9.

The data in the total column show the results of circulation of money expended by the exporting industry and by its suppliers. It is noticeable that many sectors that had no direct input relationships (or very weak ones) with the basic industry received substantial amounts of business through turnover of the basic income. The amount of business increased from $1348.70 to $1822.50 for sector 1 in the turnover process beyond the first round of activity.

Personal income received by the households through that sector showed an increase from $115.90 to $351.50 and local taxes from $17.00 to $37.80. The overall multiplier for sector 1 increased activity from $1481.60 to $2211.80. Thus, the community economy generated $1211.80 of gross income in addition to the $1000.00 received from the added export.

There are activities that bring basic income to a community through purchases from several sectors, but that are not identified by the model as part of the economy's export base. The travel industry and nonlocal government are the most noticeable sources of unidentified income. The impact of such a source is not difficult to determine.

Suppose that Carbon County were to receive $2100 from travelers in one day, and it was desirable to know just what the community gained. Further, suppose that the money was spent in the following way: $100 for transportation, $1000 in retail stores, and $1000 for services.

Impact is determined by multiplying 100 by the multipliers in column 5 of Table 3.8 and 1000 by those in columns 8 and 9. The resultant values are given in Table 3.10. It is often a surprise to people who do not consider themselves part of the tourist industry to find how much of their local market depends upon it indirectly.

In this case the business multiplier from tourist trade is 4356.32/2100.00 = 2.0744, the multiplier for personal income is 0.6042 and for tax revenue 0.0433. These multipliers reflect the purchase patterns of the tourists as well as the interrelationships of tourist oriented sectors with the rest of the economy. If an analyst were particularly interested in the tourist industry, he or she would want to design the model to pick out sectors that are particularly oriented toward that activity. The retail sector might be disaggregated to reveal activities of cafés, grocery stores, souvenir stores, and gasoline service stations. The service sector might reveal those of lodging and recreation services.

An important point for any analyst setting about to analyze a community is to design a model so that the most important sources of basic income can be analyzed in sufficient detail. In the case of this particular community, income from truck drivers was impor-

Table 3.7. Matrix $(I - A)$, Carbon County, Wyoming, 1959

		1 Oil & gas prod. & refining	2 Other minerals	3 Manufac- turing	4 Agricul- ture	5 Transpor- tation	6 Communi- cation	7 Utilities
1.	Oil & gas production & refining	.7759	...	-.0003	...	-.0007	...	-.0195
2.	Other minerals	...	1.0000	...	...	-.0099	...	...
3.	Manufacturing	...	-0.0018	.9974	...	-.0001	-.0025	-.0117
4.	Agriculture	...	...	-.0594	.8749	-.0270	...	...
5.	Transportation	-.0715	-0.0099	-.0937	-.0652	.9998	-.0173	-.0036
6.	Communication	-.0006	-0.0303	-.0027	-.0008	-.0033	.9981	-.0009
7.	Utilities	-.0449	-0.0038	-.0094	-.0047	-.0103	-.0291	.9990
8.	Retail	-.0003	-0.0068	-.0162	-.1387	-.0040	...	-.0083
9.	Services	-.0050	-0.0313	-.0252	-.0577	-.0046	-.0266	-.0130
10.	Finance	...	-0.0005	-.0216	-.0041	-.0029	-.0252	-.0082
11.	Wholesale	-.0032	-0.0094	-.0321	-.0250	-.0205	...	-.0338
12.	Rentals	-.0005	-0.0003	-.0032	-.0140	-.0059	-.0090	-.0026
13.	Construction	-.0031	-0.0007	-.0664	-.0164	-.0003	...	-.1094
14.	Household	-.1159	-0.4574	-.4570	-.3881	-.8052	-.5305	-.0979
15.	Local government	-.0170	-0.0417	-.0038	-.0330	-.0423	-.0914	-.0139

Table 3.7. *(continued)*

	8 Retail	9 Services	10 Finance	11 Whole-sale	12 Rentals	13 Construction	14 Household	15 Local government
1. Oil & gas production & refining	...	...	...	-0.1487	...	-.0043	...	...
2. Other minerals	...	...	...	...	...	-.0013	...	...
3. Manufacturing	-.0337	-.0158	-.0139	...	-0.1248	...	-.0065	-0.0067
4. Agriculture	-.0015	...	...	...	...	...	...	...
5. Transportation	-.0104	-.0074	-.0007	-0.0088	-0.0001	-.0057	-.0057	-0.0019
6. Communication	-.0033	-.0142	-.0037	-0.0012	-0.0001	-.0021	-.0085	-0.0148
7. Utilities	-.0093	-.0260	-.0021	-0.0017	-0.0238	-.0017	-.0404	-0.0609
8. Retail	.9911	.0211	-.0027	-0.0042	-0.0527	-.0176	-.4215	-0.0086
9. Services	-.0083	.9570	-.0083	-0.0082	-0.0268	-.0221	-.0592	-0.0086
10. Finance	-.0055	-.0238	.9503	-0.0054	-0.1676	-.0035	-.0398	-0.0125
11. Wholesale	-.1458	-.0502	-.0007	1.0000	-0.0052	-.0139	...	-0.0278
12. Rentals	-.0122	-.0275	-.0074	-0.0021	1.0000	-.0035	-.0019	-0.0004
13. Construction	-.0035	-.0607	-.0085	-0.0218	-0.1018	.9016	-.0609	-0.2042
14. Household	-.1722	-.5168	-.4036	-0.1426	-0.3636	.2591	.9977	-0.4284
15. Local government	-.0178	-.0229	-.0179	-0.0191	-0.0951	-.0036	-.0097	1.0000

Table 3.8. Direct and indirect activity, Carbon County, Wyoming, 1959 (per dollar of export)

	1 Oil & gas prod. & refining	2 Other minerals	3 Manufac- turing	4 Agricul- ture	5 Transpor- tation	6 Communi- cation	7 Utilities
1. Oil & gas production & refining	1.3056	0.0136	0.0218	0.0250	0.0233	0.0148	0.0313
2. Other minerals	0.0011	1.0003	0.0013	0.0011	0.0103	0.0004	0.0003
3. Manufacturing	0.0103	0.0208	1.0257	0.0310	0.0303	0.0268	0.0192
4. Agriculture	0.0041	0.0026	0.0737	1.1488	0.0344	0.0034	0.0019
5. Transportation	0.1009	0.0220	0.1130	0.0119	1.0205	0.0313	0.0120
6. Communication	0.0056	0.0393	0.0134	0.0129	0.0173	1.0126	0.0045
7. Utilities	0.0775	0.0403	0.0523	0.0521	0.0667	0.0723	1.0144
8. Retail	0.1530	0.3047	0.3772	0.5195	0.4896	0.3585	0.1126
9. Services	0.0448	0.0996	0.0902	0.1516	0.1138	0.1080	0.0403
10. Finance	0.0200	0.0382	0.0669	0.0548	0.0620	0.0725	0.0230
11. Wholesale	0.0410	0.0633	0.0996	0.1189	0.1045	0.0652	0.0546
12. Rentals	0.0058	0.0094	0.0151	0.0302	0.0193	0.0196	0.0066
13. Construction	0.0528	0.0787	0.1578	0.1196	0.1177	0.1051	0.1512
Total business and industry multiplier	1.8225	1.7328	2.1080	2.2774	2.1097	1.8905	1.4719
14. Household income	0.3515	0.6936	0.8198	0.8306	1.1273	0.8275	0.2353
15. Local government revenue	0.0378	0.0645	0.0352	0.0714	0.0751	0.1168	0.0241

58

Table 3.8. (continued)

		8 Retail	9 Services	10 Finance	11 Whole-sale	12 Rentals	13 Construc-tion	14 Household	15 Local govern-ment
1.	Oil & gas production & refining	0.0082	0.0257	0.0100	0.2007	0.0192	0.0137	0.0197	0.0200
2.	Other minerals	0.0003	0.0005	0.0002	0.0003	0.0006	0.0016	0.0004	0.0005
3.	Manufacturing	0.0444	0.0437	0.0314	0.0080	0.1532	0.0125	0.0325	0.0275
4.	Agriculture	0.0055	0.0044	0.0029	0.0013	0.0120	0.0016	0.0037	0.0029
5.	Transportation	0.0195	0.0250	0.0118	0.0182	0.0285	0.0140	0.0197	0.0145
6.	Communication	0.0075	0.0255	0.0112	0.0049	0.0124	0.0079	0.0152	0.0112
7.	Utilities	0.0262	0.0714	0.0325	0.0253	0.0700	0.0239	0.0627	0.0508
8.	Retail	1.1442	0.3689	0.2596	0.1220	0.4209	0.1993	0.5493	0.3618
9.	Services	0.0404	1.1298	0.0667	0.0363	0.1173	0.0657	0.1209	0.0812
10.	Finance	0.0255	0.0764	1.0849	0.0208	0.2258	0.0271	0.0648	0.0509
11.	Wholesale	0.1730	0.1195	0.0455	1.0226	0.0845	0.0347	0.0909	0.0884
12.	Rentals	0.0166	0.0395	0.0148	0.0059	1.0137	0.0096	0.0141	0.0104
13.	Construction	0.0439	0.1659	0.0727	0.0577	0.2317	1.1521	0.1181	0.2966
	Total business and industry multiplier	1.5552	2.1142	1.6442	1.5240	2.3898	1.5637	1.1120	1.0167
14.	Household income	0.3100	0.8461	0.6001	0.2716	0.8340	0.4210	1.2979	0.6965
15.	Local government revenue	0.0295	0.0539	0.0362	0.0310	0.1257	0.0173	0.0332	1.0224

TABLE 3.9. Impact of increased exports of $1000 in gasoline (in dollars)

Sector	First round	Total
Export	1000.00	1000.00
Oil and gas local	224.10	305.60
Other mineral	...	1.10
Manufacturing	...	10.30
Agriculture	...	4.10
Transportation	71.50	100.90
Communications	0.60	5.60
Utilities	44.90	77.50
Retail	0.30	153.00
Services	0.50	44.80
Finance	...	20.00
Wholesale	3.20	41.00
Rentals	0.50	5.80
Construction	3.10	52.80
Total Business and Industry	1348.70	1822.50
Household income	115.90	351.50
Local tax revenues	17.00	37.80
All sectors	1481.60	2211.80

TABLE 3.10. Gains from $2100 in tourist expenditures (in dollars)

Sectors receiving gains	Transportation	Retail	Service	Total
Oil and gas	2.33	8.20	25.70	36.23
Other minerals	1.03	0.30	0.50	1.83
Manufacturing	3.03	44.40	43.70	91.13
Agriculture	3.44	5.50	4.40	13.34
Transportation	102.05	19.50	25.00	146.55
Communication	1.73	7.50	25.50	34.73
Utilities	6.67	26.20	71.40	104.27
Retail	48.96	1144.20	386.90	1580.06
Services	11.38	40.40	1129.80	1181.58
Finance	6.20	25.50	76.40	108.10
Wholesale	10.45	173.00	119.50	302.95
Rentals	1.93	16.60	39.50	58.03
Construction	11.77	43.90	165.90	221.57
Total business	210.97	1728.20	2114.20	4356.32
Household income (personal)	112.73	310.00	846.10	1268.83
Local government (tax)	7.51	29.50	53.90	90.91

tant, since there was a superhighway through the area. Reference to column 17 of Table 3.5 reveals that in 1959, travelers and truckers purchased goods and services from 5 of the sectors in the community system. The total business and industry resulting from these activities is shown below. Only business impacts are shown here because they are of most interest to analysts. Personal income impacts can be shown by using household multipliers (sector 14) and local government revenues by using government multipliers (sector 15).

Sector	Purchases	Multiplier	Total Business generated
Transportation	232,200	2.1097	489,872
Communication	6,100	1.8905	11,532
Retail	3,989,700	1.5552	6,204,781
Services	1,213,600	2.1142	2,565,793
Finance	10,700	1.6442	17,593
Total	5,452,300	1.7038	9,289,571

The Community Multiplier   61

If one could assume a similar purchase pattern in subsequent years, the multiplier of 1.7038 would be a useful planning tool. This same approach can be utilized in analyzing the impact of transfer payments and any other sources of basic income not directly identifiable by sector.

It was indicated previously that leakage from a community (the propensity to import), as measured by the leakage ratio, has an impact on the size of multiplier for a sector. One would expect that there would be a distinct correlation between low multipliers and a high leakage factor.

Again utilizing the data for Carbon County, the ratios from row 16 of Table 3.6 can be compared to the business and industry multipliers for Table 3.8. This comparison is shown in Fig. 3.1. Although there is not a perfect negative correlation between the two, the general relationship is evident.

The leakage coefficients of supplying industries will have some effect. For example, if a sector with a high leakage factor also has strong relationships to a sector with a very low leakage factor, the multiplier of the first will tend to be comparatively high, and that of the second will be lower than it would be without this link.

One of the problems encountered in using the community multiplier matrix to analyze the system is that the system itself

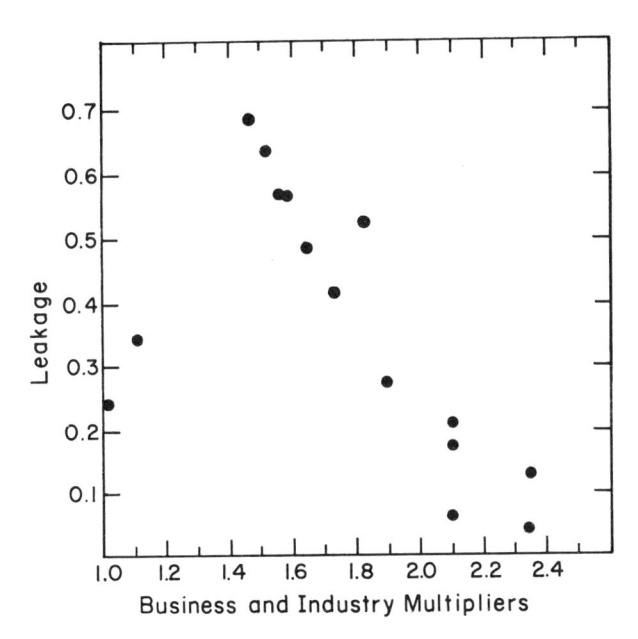

Fig. 3.1. Comparison of leakage coefficients from Table 3.6 and multipliers from Table 3.8. Leakage occurs from exogenous payments such as imports, savings, and payments to state and federal governments.

changes over time. A model constructed at time t may not contain useful multipliers for time $t + 5$ (five years on). This is where the analyst must be able to appraise the general trends in the community with an expert eye. However, in general, economies tend to be fairly stable.

In the case of Carbon County, a study had been conducted in 1954. During the ensuing five years two major events had a significant effect on the multipliers. One was the discovery of uranium and its development as a major part of the mining industry. The other was the introduction of heavy state expenditure for construction of a portion of Interstate Highway 80. The impacts of these changes on the multipliers can be seen in Table 3.11. It is obvious from this tabulation that the economy changed very little. Aside from the mining, construction, and government sectors, multipliers developed in 1954 were still fairly representative of the situation five years later.

TABLE 3.11. Business and industry multipliers, Carbon County, Wyoming, 1954 and 1959

Sector	Multipliers 1954	1959
Oil and gas production and refining	1.8287	1,8225
Other minerals	1.5621	1.7328
Manufacturing	2.1228	2.1080
Agriculture	2.2091	2.2774
Transportation	2.1126	2.1097
Communication	1.9088	1.8905
Utilities	1.5118	1.4719
Retail	1.6224	1.5552
Services	2.1567	2.1142
Finance	1.6608	1.6442

This illustrates a fact that is very important in the use of community multipliers: aside from rather extreme situations, which are usually easily spotted, small local economies tend to change very slowly. This is not necessarily true of larger areas, however. There are many reasons why small community economies change slowly. One is that certain patterns of interchange develop that do not change because they involve inertia, personal friendships, fear of losing quality of an input, and/or adjustment of one sector to the input requirements of another sector. Another is the factor of transport cost: some inputs cannot be imported. Another is related to cost of production: some inputs must be imported because it costs too much to produce them locally. Analysts always need to take into consideration size of the community and other factors that may affect interrelationships.

Drastic changes in price level, especially when there are significant differences in price change among the sectors, will change the ratios. Where this is a problem, models should be adjusted to the price level of one year; that is, if comparison is being made between 1954 and 1959, perhaps the 1954 table should be expressed in 1959 dollars.

USES OF THE MODEL

The intersectoral model emphasizes the complex interrelationships that exist in a community, and provides a methodology for analyzing them. One of the most frequent applications is for analyzing the two major ways that communities change economically.

One of these is a change in exports. If an existing industry changes its exports, the effect will be felt in the community in proportion to the size of the industry's multiplier (which reflects the strength of its interrelationships in the community). Introduction of new industry will also increase exports, and loss of an old industry will decrease them. In these latter cases, the multiplier itself may be affected somewhat.

Communities also change economically by increasing or decreasing the multiplier effect. Multipliers are increased through several procedures. One is to decrease the propensity of an industry to import, often referred to as "import replacement." This is somewhat misleading in that it indicates a decline in overall imports that is not possible. It is possible, though, to shift the kinds of things imported. If a local industry that has been importing a major input finds a local source, its propensity to import declines. But the new supplying industry may import just as much as its customers did. Yet the multiplier will increase because of greater integration--one more firm through which the money may circulate. Any situation that increases a unit's propensity to import will have the opposite effect. When a community is declining, the propensity of its inhabitants to go to other communities more often for goods and services, for example, accelerates the decline.

Assessing Impact

Another use of the multiplier is in assessing the possible impact of adding or subtracting an industry from an economy. If a new industry were to be attracted to a community, it may be of value to have some idea what the impact might be. In general, industries that will establish the strongest interrelationships will contribute the most. Impact can be measured by extracting from the firm some estimates of possible annual purchases from each of the existing sectors.

When a local government is planning special tax concessions or the construction and leasing of facilities, it is a good idea to know what might be expected in terms of local revenue generation from the firm's operations.

INTERCOMMUNITY IMPACT

Extending the multiplier concept to more than one community is often of value. Where there are strong trading relationships among communities, a major change in one may have important effects on the others. It is often useful to know where these effects will be felt.

The construction of an intercommunity model is similar to that for the community. As an example, suppose there are two communities with strong interrelationships consisting of three sectors each. A mock-up of the interindustry transactions matrix is given in Table 3.12.

TABLE 3.12. Mock-up of interindustry transactions matrix

Purchases		Community A sales			Community B sales			Other sales	Total sales
		Sector 1	Sector 2	Sector 3	Sector 1	Sector 2	Sector 3		
A	Sector 1	10	20	10	15	25	10	10	100
	Sector 2	5	30	50	5	0	10	0	100
	Sector 3	10	20	10	25	25	0	10	100
B	Sector 1	5	15	20	10	20	15	15	100
	Sector 2	0	5	10	25	5	30	25	100
	Sector 3	30	10	0	5	20	10	25	100
Other areas		40	0	0	15	5	25	85	...
Total		100	100	100	100	100	100	...	600

Such strong interrelationships among community systems mean that an event in one is likely to have significant effects on certain units in the other. The analyst must be aware of such relationships in order to do an intelligent job. It is also often important to know if an imminent development in one community is going to have a strong impact on units in another community, even where such relationships are not evident in the existing structure.

An intercommunity model may also be of use in measuring the impact of policy that affects an entire region. Government actions resulting in low cost power, for example, may result in the location of new industries that may have strong ties to units in a number of communities in an area. Or, an environmental policy for a region may have unexpected results because of the ties existing among units in the various communities.

The multipliers resulting from an intercommunity transactions matrix have the same theoretical base as for a single community. However, the result for the model in Table 3.12 is actually four sets of multipliers: two showing interrelationships within each of the communities and two showing A to B and B to A relationships. Calculation of the multiplier matrix involves the same steps as those illustrated for a single community, that is, the a_{ij} are calculated by dividing the x_{ij} by the y_j. This matrix is then subtracted from a unity matrix and inverted.

SUMMARY

Economic units within a community have intense interactions that define a local market. They also have ties to units outside of the community that result in export and import of goods and services. Funds flow into a community either in exchange for exports or as transfers. These constitute basic income for the local economy. The impact of basic income may be large or small depending upon the integration of the community. The more hands through which the money passes, the higher the effect.

Multipliers can be calculated to measure the effect of dollar turnover by making a few simplifying assumptions. These multipliers are fairly stable over time, unless drastic events occur. Even then the major impact is upon the sectors through which the changes are transmitted.

Actual calculation requires the compilation of a transactions table showing existing sales and purchase relationships among the units within the community. This is usually done by aggregating units into sectors as homogeneous as possible, the major reasons being restricted resources for research and the fact that the additional information is usually not really needed for a meaningful analysis.

Input ratios are calculated from the transaction table. These are then set in a matrix and subtracted from an identity matrix. The resulting matrix is inverted to obtain a matrix of multipliers, each of which measures direct and indirect impacts of change in the basic income on the individual sectors. The multipliers can be added to reveal effects on larger aggregates of sectors or the economy as a whole. There are many uses for community multiplier matrices, ranging from analysis of the existing structure to measuring possible impact of a hypothetical or expected development. Multipliers can also be established to measure the impact of changes on intercommunity relationships.

NOTE

The $(I - A)$ matrix is inverted in the same way as any other matrix. Since inversion may not be well understood by the reader, we offer the following explanation: In elementary algebra a value is the inverse of another if when the two are multiplied the result is 1; thus $(1/a)a = a/a = 1$. In matrix algebra a square matrix A^{-1} is the inverse of another square matrix A (both $n \times n$ matrices) if $A^{-1}A = AA^{-1} = I_n$. Or we can say that an inverse exists if two matrices are commutative and both products are equal to a unit matrix of the same order.

The procedure for finding the inverse of a matrix is as follows:

1. Replace each element of A (a_{ij}) by its minor. [Elements of $(I - A)$ are treated the same way.]
2. Divide each element of this new matrix by the determinant of A.
3. Transpose this last matrix to obtain A^{-1}.
4. Check to see that $AA^{-1} = I_n$.

REVIEW QUESTIONS

1. How does intensity of economic interactions affect a community?
2. What major assumption must be made in order to produce a model that will allow an examination of complex interrelationships?
3. What effect does this assumption have on the concept of the local market?
4. Does it affect the concept of the export market?
5. Explain the various parts of the intersectoral model reflecting endogenous and exogenous relationships.
6. How is the A matrix derived from this?
7. Show how the multipliers are derived from the A matrix.
8. Why would it not usually be wise to construct a community matrix reflecting interrelationships of individual economic units?
9. The intersectoral model equates imports with exports. How can the local economy be larger than these figures?
10. Do you see any similarity between the structural relationships shown for Catal in Table 2.1 and the intersectoral relationships shown in Table 3.5?
11. How are these two tables different?
12. What do each of the sectoral multipliers show?
13. Why is it possible to add these multipliers?
14. How would one determine impact on a community from expenditures by tourists?
15. What effect does leakage have on size of multiplier?
16. In what two aspects can a community grow?
17. Of what value might an intercommunity model be?

REFERENCES

Chenery, H. B., and P. G. Clark. 1959. *Interindustry economics*. New York: Wiley.
Harmston, F. K. 1962. *A study of the resources, people and economy of Carbon County, Wyoming*. Cheyenne: Wyoming Natural Resource Board.
———. 1969. Uses of an intersectoral model in developing regional multipliers. *Annals of Regional Science* 11:1-7.
Harmston, F. K., and R. E. Lund. 1967. *Application of an input-output framework to a community economic system*. Columbia: Univ. of Missouri Press.
Leontief, W. 1966. *Input-output economics*. New York: Oxford Univ. Press.

CHAPTER 4
Theory of Location

The objective of economic activity is to provide goods and services to people in the form and at the time and place they are desired. Thus, we refer to material, temporal, and spatial aspects of the productive process. Economics of the community is heavily dependent upon spatial economic theory, since, in the final analysis, it is spatial differences that define communities. The usual economics text does a reasonably good job of treating material and temporal concepts. The same cannot be said of spatial concepts, however. The following, therefore, is groundwork in this area.

The role of time in the productive process for products, such as wine and cheese, and in defining as durables goods used over time is well known. Not so well known is the role of transportation services in the productive process and the movement of goods to places where needed. An almost direct parallel is found in warehousing that conveys goods over time, and transportation that conveys goods over distances. Movement of goods through time is paid for in terms of storage costs. Movement of goods through space is priced via the transport rate. Thus, the idea, so often used in analysis of investment opportunities, of discounting from some terminal point to a present one, is both a temporal and spatial phenomenon.

Frequently, spatial and temporal phenomena become intertwined. For example, if a machine breaks down and a spare part must be shipped from some distant city, a premium may be paid to have it delivered by a certain date. The freight rate thus takes on a temporal character. A part of the differential in freight rates by air vs. by barge lies in the time needed for delivery of the material. There are also spatial differences in interest rates, related to interregional flows of money.

CONTRIBUTION OF VON THÜNEN, WEBER, CHRISTALLER, AND LÖSCH
Most spatial economic concepts are related in some way to the

work of four men: J. H. Von Thünen, Alfred Weber, Walter Christaller, and August Lösch. The following is a discussion of their major basic concepts.

Von Thünen

German-born J. H. Von Thünen published his ideas in a book, *The Isolated State*, in 1826. The following model drawn from early chapters helps to illustrate his concepts:

> Imagine a very large town, at the center of a fertile plain, which is crossed by no navigable river or canal. Throughout the plain the soil is capable of cultivation and of the same fertility. Far from the town, the plain turns into an uncultivated wilderness which cuts off all communication between this state and the outside world.
> There are no other towns on the plain. The central town must, therefore, supply the rural areas with all manufactured products, and in return it will obtain all its provisions from the surrounding countryside.
> The mines that provide the state with salt and metals are near the central town which, as it is the only one, we shall call simply "the town."
> The problem we want to solve is this:
> What pattern of cultivation will take shape in these conditions, and how will the farming system of the various districts be affected by their distance from the town? We assume throughout that farming is conducted absolutely rationally.
> It is on the whole obvious that near the town will be grown those products which are heavy or bulky in relation to their value and which are consequently so expensive to transport that the remoter districts are unable to supply them. Here, also, we find the highly perishable products, which must be used very quickly. With increasing distance from the town, the land will progressively be given up to products cheap to transport in relation to their value.
> For this reason alone, fairly sharply differentiated concentric rings or belts will form around The Town, each with its own particular staple product.
> From ring to ring the staple product, and with it the entire farming system, will change; and in the various rings we will find completely different farming systems.

This was probably the first economic model employing the concept of partial equilibrium. By assuming all other factors were either unique to this state or completely uniform, Von Thünen was able to isolate transportation costs as a function of distance, a most important concept in spatial economics. (See Fig. 4.1.)

Utilizing data based on his own operations, Von Thünen was able to illustrate the impact of transportation costs on prices of grain and on land rents. In his model he used rye that would be used as horse feed in hauling the grain to town and back. Other

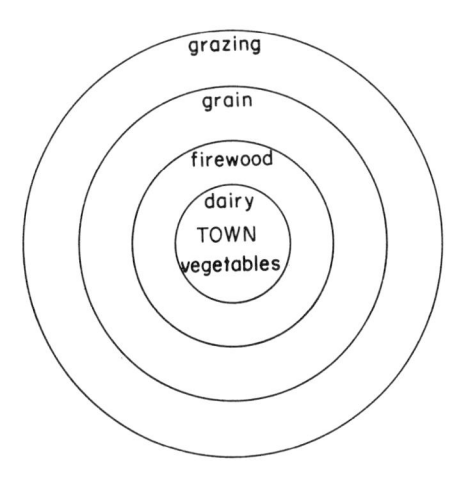

Fig. 4.1. Von Thünen's rings.

transport costs included time of teamsters and depreciation on the wagon. These were also equated in terms of rye. At some point (which he considers to be 80 km from town), it would cost all of the rye to get it to town. At that point the price would be zero.

At some point prior to this, price would equal cost of production, exclusive of use of land. At that point, land rent would be zero and the outer limit of the ring in which rye should be produced would be reached. Von Thünen acknowledged that a rise in the price of rye in the town would mean some rent would be paid for land and that the ring would expand outward. A price decline would have the opposite effect. But these effects were minor compared to the overall effect of transport cost (Von Thünen 1826, Chap. 5A). Therefore, one would expect the price of land to be higher, the closer one came to the town. This concept has been basic to most models and explains differences in land costs as one moves away from or closer to the center of a city.

Von Thünen's definition of land rent was "that part of farm revenue left after deduction of the interest on value of buildings, timber, fences and all other valuable objects *separable from the land*, that portion, which pertains to the land itself" (1966, p. 18). The combined return on land and improvements he called "estate rent." This definition of land rent is important, since location influences value of land, but value of improvements is more closely related to marginal return from their use.

Another aspect of Von Thünen's work has proven to be important even though it seems rather trivial in the context in which he developed it. This was his pricing system for town-produced manure. Since, in those days, manuring was the only known way of replacing nutrients, he was concerned with the amount farmers in the first ring could afford to pay for manure produced in the town. His argument was that those farmers near the town could afford to pay more, by the amount of transport cost, than those further away. At some point the cost of transport would equal the value of the manure and the price would be zero. This is the basis for basic laws of spatial markets that we shall discuss later. We can say, at this point, that any good that has a given free on board (FOB) price at the point of origin will be sold at different prices as the buyer's location varies from that point. The difference will be in terms of the cost of moving it. This applies whether the seller or the buyer pays the cost of transport. The location prices are then cost, including freight (CIF).

Weber

Alfred Weber was concerned with the problems of industrial location (1971, pp. 122-24). He began his analysis with an acceptance of the Von Thünen concept of price differentials being due to transport costs. Thus, he assumed constant labor and material prices and asked, "How would transport cost influence distribution and to what places would industry be attracted?" Ostensibly, the answer should be to those locations that have the lowest cost of transportation, considering movement of both raw materials and products. The question of interest now becomes, "How do we determine these lowest cost locations?"

He began with the following basic assumptions:

1. The firm operates in a perfectly competitive market.
2. The location of all materials is given.
3. The situation and size of flows of consumption are also given.

He defined the basic factors determining transport costs as weight and distance. By costs, he meant total amount of goods and labor absorbed in effecting the shipment. He was aware of the fact that other factors influenced transport costs, but he felt they could all be expressed in terms of weight and distance by adjusting the information.

Weber's Law. Weber's definition meant that lowest cost would be where there was a minimum of tons per kilometer during the processes of production and distribution. Since the company would not control the place of consumption, it would consider choosing sources of materials in such a way as to minimize tons per kilometer to place of consumption of the final product. Assuming the firm used two materials and produced a product to be consumed at one point, the relationship could be shown as a triangle. This has become known as the "locational triangle" and is the basis of the Moses model, in particular, that we shall discuss later.

In order to develop this concept, Weber resorted to mechanics, specifically Varignon's Frame, that demonstrate a parallelogram of forces. One may envision a graduated disk upon the edge of which are three rollers with horizontal axes. Over each roller runs a cord to which weights are attached. The inner ends of the cords are tied together. Furthermore, assume two local materials are used in making a product and that one-half ton of one and three-quarters ton of the other are required to produce one ton of product. These weights represent the force with which the center of the string (which represents location of the plant) would be drawn toward each one.

Thus, given weight $a_1 = 3/4$, $a_2 = 1/2$, $a_3 = 1$, we can show that this is a triangle whose sides are straight-line segments with length proportional to the force (Fig. 4.2A). That is, if an equilibrium has been established among the three forces, and the three straight-line segments are laid out in proper direction and length, a closed triangle results. This triangle is defined interior to the overall locational triangle, and it defines certain angles (α_1, α_2, and α_3).

Now, if the sides of the locational triangle are taken as bases, triangles are defined utilizing α_1, α_2, and α_3 as apex angles, and circles are transcribed about each of these triangles (Fig. 4.2B), their common intersection will identify proper location of the processing plant (point P). The general statement, then, is that so far as transportation is concerned, the process of determining location is a struggle among the various corners, particularly between the corner where the product is consumed and those where the material is furnished.

The determining factor is not the proportion of the weight of the material used to weight of the product, but the proportion of the weight of localized material (anything nonubiquitous) used to weight of the product. This Weber defined as "material index" (MI) of an industry. Thus $MI = (W_1 + W_2)/P$, where W_1 = weight of the first material, W_2 = weight of the second material, and P = weight of the product. The locational index of an industry (LI) depends

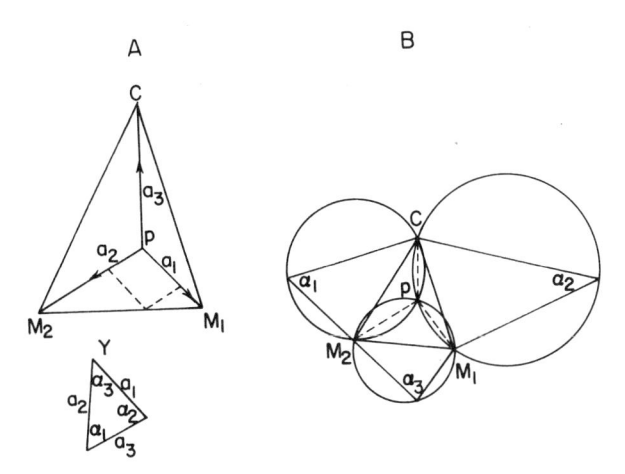

Fig. 4.2. Determination of location for processing plant.

upon this material index. Location weight of an industry is $MI + P$ and $LI = (MI + P)/P$. When $MI = 0$, $LI = 1$. When $MI = 1$, $LI = 2$. When $MI \leq 1$, the industry will locate at the point of consumption. If $MI > 1$, the pull is toward the materials. A ubiquitous material always favors location at the consumption point. For example, soft drinks, oxygen, sand, and gravel tend to be produced where used because their main ingredients of water, air, rocks, and sand tend to be found everywhere. If materials were pure (not weight losing), production would also be at the point of consumption.

Choices among materials. Where there are several deposits of the same material of comparable quality, cost of transportation will determine the one utilized. If more than one material is used, that combination of locations will be chosen that results in the lowest transportation costs.

Orientation of an industry. For a given large consumption center, there may be several locational figures with essentially the same cost indices. In this case, there will be several points from which the product can move. If the market is large enough, it may even be supplied from points with different transportation cost indices, with those having the lowest enjoying an advantage. (See Fig. 4.3A.) Where material deposits are too large for the nearest market, they will serve other points of consumption (Fig. 4.3B). They would appear as the center of locational figures grouped about them. Those materials used most would have a stronger locational pull than those used least.

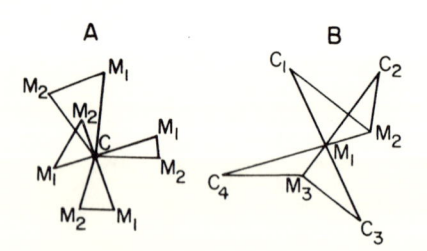

Fig. 4.3. Different suppliers to one market and one supplier to different markets.

Thus, for this model, the only factor influencing location is the industry's material index as determined by the technology of various producing units. The index is affected most by weight losses of localized materials used and weight of ubiquities. Weight loss increases the material index; increased use of ubiquities decreases it.

Impact of transport rates. Weber was aware of the fact that transport rates were important in location decisions. In order to accommodate them (and other factors working in the real world), it was necessary to abandon two major assumptions: (1) weight and distance are the only factors determining costs of transportation, and (2) costs of transportation are always uniform and conform to only one method of transportation.

Rate variations alter competitive relationships among material deposits that can shift the optimal location point. (Price changes for a material may limit area of choice, but only freight rates shift the optimal point.) However, for any given set of rates related to a particular location figure, the material index would still be important in locating the optimal point. (An optimum is the most that can be attained because constraints keep us from doing everything we would like to do.) Some factors affecting rates that should be considered in applying the theory are bulkiness of either material or product, value per unit of weight, and increased rates for shipment in small quantities.

Nonuniform transport rates result from transport systems being made up of parts that cooperate technically but otherwise act as independent units. Also, they do not follow straight lines, so the choice of location can only be an approximation of the ideal. Railways with their adjuncts, the waterways, connect the actual materials location to consumption centers. Hence, the transport patterns that need to be considered in location decisions are those of the rail network. The water routes represent shortened distances and cheaper rates, provided they can be used.

Material deposits that are in position to use these shortened routes have an advantage over deposits that cannot use them. This may cause a considerable change in the optimum plant location. For example, in Fig. 4.4A, the deposit M_2 is nearer C (the consumption point) than is M_2'. If there were no waterway, point P would be chosen. But the waterway makes it cheaper to ship from M_2' to P' and to transport the product to C. In contrast, in Fig. 4.4B, deposit M_2 also lies closer to C than does M_2', but the locational triangle makes use of the waterway possible. Location at P' in the triangle $M_1 M_2 C$ would have lower transfer costs than at P in $M_1 M_2' C$.

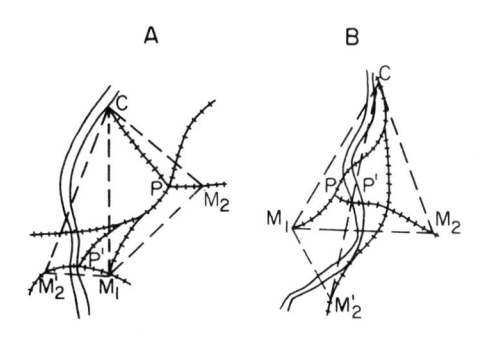

Fig. 4.4. Processing locations in transport networks.

Price differences. According to Weber, price differences themselves never change location within the triangle very much; they simply shift competitive conditions among material deposits that are equal in other respects. In other words, low priced materials have larger spheres for utilization than do higher priced ones.

Labor orientation. Having established these general concepts for location of manufacturing industries, Weber introduced another factor that he considered to be important in location. He allowed labor costs to vary and deduced that they cause industry to deviate from its transportation-oriented location. The extent of the variation was determined by the ratio between the cost of labor per metric ton of product (the labor index) and the total weight of all goods transported (the locational weight). This ratio was the "labor coefficient." His general rules were (1) location of manufacturing industries is determined by the material index; and (2) an industry deviates from its transport locations in proportion to the size of its labor coefficient.

To Weber's initial three basic assumptions concerning location he added three more regarding labor.

1. It is assumed that the area is covered by several fixed labor locations that are not influenced by other locational tendencies of industry.
2. The wages of each branch of industry are "fixed" and the amount of labor available at the price is unlimited.
3. Services are not inputs to the manufacturing process.

Weber defined an industrial process as consisting of four steps: (1) securing the location for the enterprise and the fixed capital to be used in it; (2) servicing the raw and semifinished materials and energy sources; (3) the manufacturing process; (4) the shipment of the product. He considered steps 1 and 2 to be primarily material costs and steps 3 and 4 to be labor costs.

Weber's general law holds that every point of lower labor costs (whether due to lower wages or greater productivity) constitutes an economic center of attraction that tends to draw industry away from the point of minimal transportation cost to itself. In order to take advantage of lower cost, the plant has to actually locate there.

The increased transport costs that result have to be offset by decreased labor costs. To understand the theoretical significance of this, it is necessary to introduce it into a model emphasizing minimal transport costs. A basic assumption of this model is that deviations from a point of minimum transport cost can be in any direction. Further, in every direction there will be points at which the added transportation costs will be equal. These points can be connected by lines that form closed curves and are called "isodapanes," meaning of equal cost.

The isodapane concept may be illustrated as follows. Assume a point of lowest transport cost (P_0) within the locational triangle (Fig. 4.5). Around this point there are numerous closed curves

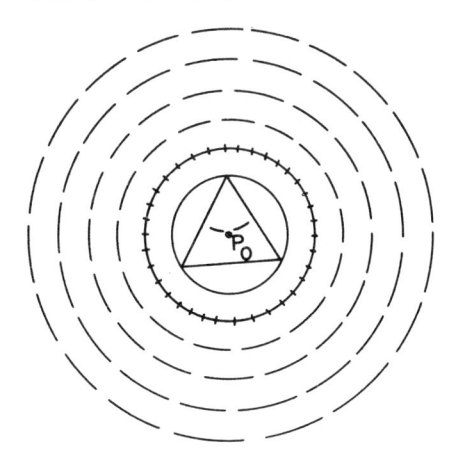

Fig. 4.5. Isodapanes.

each of which represents an equal increase in transport cost above that at point P_0. For every point where labor is available there is an isodapane that indicates the amount of labor cost saving necessary to offset the additional transport cost. On a few of these the trade-off will be equal. These are critical isodapanes. A labor location lying on an isodapane outside the critical one will have economies less than the added transport cost. Thus, a labor location on a lower isodapane will be attractive to industry; one on a higher one will not.

Agglomeration. The other major contribution made by Weber dealt with agglomeration, or the result of spillover effects of industries located closely together upon one another's cost structures (Weber 1971, pp. 122-24). It was Weber's contention that cost of transport and labor are interregional in nature; all other costs are intraregional; that is, they have only local effects. The two facets of the latter are agglomerative and deglomerative effects. An agglomerative factor is defined as an "advantage" (lower cost) that results from production being carried on at one place by many plants. A deglomerative factor is an advantage resulting from decentralization. These will be considered in more detail later. Although Weber's agglomeration concept is considerably more limited than is commonly accepted, his was the basic idea.

Christaller
    In contrast to Von Thünen, who studied the relation of the location of various types of agriculture to population centers, and Weber, who studied the impact of transportation, labor, and agglomeration on the location of industry, Walter Christaller studied an entire spatially oriented economic system (1966). And where they ignored many economic and social factors, he incorporated political, social, and geographic factors into his analysis.
    He began with a general observation that neither the number,

size, nor distribution of towns can be explained by natural geographic advantages. Highly favorable locations can be found where no towns have developed and towns can be found in highly unfavorable geographic locations. It was his conclusion that towns exist because there is a demand for the things towns have to offer.

Theory of central places. Christaller compared human communities to the physical phenomenon of the crystallization of mass around a nucleus; in other words, he noted that there is a centralistic order in all things. Towns were established to be and perform as the centers of regions with the exceptions of towns bound to a particular land area (areally bound); those tied to a specific material resource, a harbor or road (point bound); and places settled for religious or whimsical reasons.

This centralization takes place because a town serves a market area, and market areas are related to the kinds of goods and services provided. There are hierarchies of places. Places that provide lower order goods and services are lower order places. To express it another way, goods and services that are commonly used do not require large market areas, hence can be provided in small markets. People will not travel far to get a loaf of bread or a container of milk, under ordinary circumstances, because these can be made available in the smallest hamlet. Since enough people want them, they can be offered by small stores. As goods are added that smaller proportions of the population will buy, the market must expand in size so there will be enough demand to make offering them economical. These higher order goods are generally in the luxury rather than necessity category.

The importance of a place is, then, related to the market size requirements of the goods and services it provides. A place deserves the designation of "center" if its inhabitants have professions that are bound by necessity to the central location. Thus a medical center may have brain surgeons, but since very few people have their brains operated on, this center would have to serve a very large population. In contrast the smallest places in the region may have clinics with physicians' assistants staffing them; the next larger may have small hospitals and several general practitioners, a few general surgeons, and so on. There are, therefore, "central goods and services" and "dispersed goods and services." The first are offered at a few points to be consumed by inhabitants of many points, and the latter are offered and consumed at many points.

The region served by a central place (of whatever size) is called the "complementary region." The size of this region depends upon the range of the highest order good offered at the place. The range of a good is the greatest distance a dispersed population is willing to go in order to obtain it. But distance has to be expressed in economic terms. Economic distance is determined by freight costs, insurance and storage, time and loss of weight in transit, and--where people are the items moved--costs, time, and discomforts of travel.

Every central good or service has its characteristic range,

Theory of Location

the outer limit of which is determined by the distance from a central place beyond which it cannot be purchased. Let us assume, for example, that there are only three goods in the world. One of these is a basic necessity, and people will never travel more than 5 km to obtain it. A second is a near necessity but people will travel 15 km to obtain it, if they have to. The third is a luxury that few people can afford, so it takes a large population to find enough buyers. Those who want and can afford it will not travel more than 40 km to get it.

The last has to be offered by a place that can serve a very large area. We call this an A place. The A place also sells the other two goods up to their limit. That is, it sells a 5 km good up to that limit, so it is surrounded by C places that sell only that good, hence have a very small market area. It is also surrounded by B places that sell 15 km goods, as well as 5 km goods, so B places are also surrounded by C places.

The most efficient area for a firm, from a market standpoint, is a circle--assuming a perfectly flat plain with equal access everywhere and evenly distributed population. But in order to serve all the customers, so that there will be no areas uncovered, the circles for each place must overlap. It is assumed that competitors will split the overlapped area giving the complementary region the shape of a hexagon. In Fig. 4.6 the overall market area

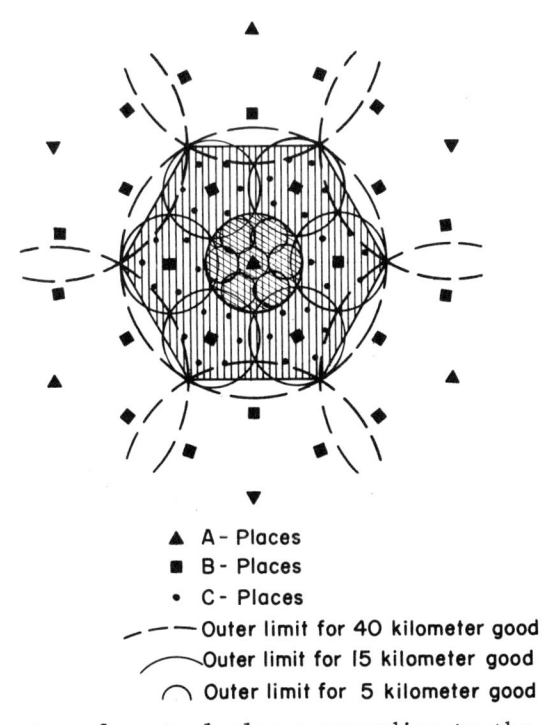

▲ A - Places
■ B - Places
• C - Places
― ― Outer limit for 40 kilometer good
⌒ Outer limit for 15 kilometer good
⌒ Outer limit for 5 kilometer good

Fig. 4.6. A system of central places according to the market principle.

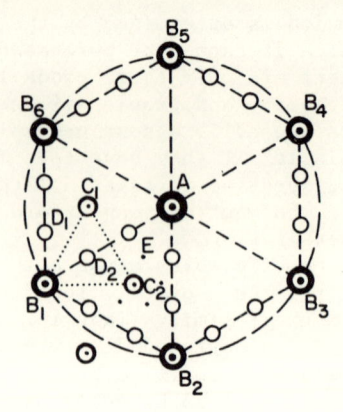

Fig. 4.7. Triangular and hexagonal form of location.

of the A place is the larger shaded area. That of the B place the smaller shaded area and of the C place the smallest hexagon. Details are left off all except those places in the center of the diagram to emphasize this idea.

The general form that emerges can also be shown in terms of lines connecting the various central places. This establishes a triangular relationship between the A place and each of the B places. That is, in providing the 40 km good, the A place serves its own territory for up to 15 km plus those of places B_1 and B_2 (Fig. 4.7). The same triangular arrangement occurs with each pair of B places. In turn, the B places have triangular relationships to C places (B_1 with C_1 and C_2) and C places to even smaller D places (C_1 to D_1 and D_2).

The formation of marketing regions as a result of these triangular hexagonal relationships are shown in Fig. 4.8. Geographers have found patterns similar to this in undeveloped regions where transportation systems have not been built. If only the principle

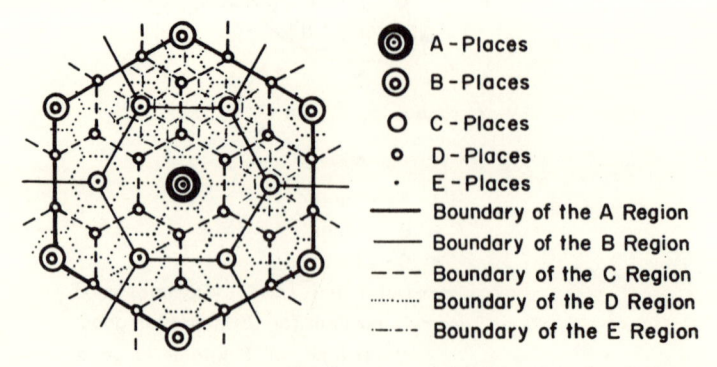

Fig. 4.8. Marketing regions in a system of central places.

of efficient marketing were of significance, if there were no barriers to movement, and if people were distributed fairly evenly over space, this is how the various-sized communities would be distributed.

According to Christaller, then, there are always a large number of places of the lowest order, a smaller number of the next higher order, a still smaller number of the next higher order and so on, with a very few of the highest order. Every central good and service has its characteristic range with an outer limit determined by distance from its central place. Beyond this distance economic factors, such as transport cost, preclude its being purchased without moving to another central place.

Lower limits. Lower range limits play a significant role in determining the types of goods that will be offered. For example, if a certain good needed a population larger than could be provided within 40 km from A (its minimum range limit would be higher than the upper range limit of A), it would not be offered in that region at all. One would have to go to an even higher central place to obtain it. It was Christaller's contention that certain key goods, with lower limits higher than some norm for like goods, could cause weak development of central places that could not offer them as often as they should for the best welfare of people in the region. On the other hand, if the lower limit should be lower than normal, goods that were offered at B places could now be offered at C places. This would strengthen the C places at the expense of the B ones.

What sets lower limits? Usually they are set by the number of units sold (not necessarily kilometers of distance), the range of possible distribution (which would be influenced by transport rates), and the social, cultural, and professional structure of the population. Hence, in a densely populated, wealthy, and highly cultural industrial region, there would be more central places of higher order than in one lacking these attributes. These factors plus transportation networks and political factors cause alterations in patterns. So the marketing principle fits only a theoretical model showing, in a rational and favorable state, the most efficient system for distribution.

Transportation principle. The marketing principle is considered to be the most efficient way of distributing goods, assuming that the Von Thünen concept holds--a flat plain with no obstacles to movement in any direction and a population evenly distributed over the plain. This situation could only exist in a very special situation. In most cases, there would have to be a distribution system of some kind. The most obvious kinds are railroads and highways. But transportation systems affect location also. Thus, even if an area were to develop its distribution of communities on a purely market principle basis, the introduction of transportation systems would change things.

From a transportation point of view, it is necessary to have the largest possible amount of freight and the most direct route possible. Whether or not a place would be served by a railroad, for example, would depend upon its location with regard to other places of like size and the amount of freight it could generate. A railroad from one A place to another, passing through a region where there are a number of low order places that generate little freight, would be a straight line such as 1 in Fig. 4.9. In this case, both B places (2 and 3) are off the line. But 2 generates sufficient traffic so that a main line connects it to two A places, whereas 3 is served only by a secondary line from the regional A place.

In another section of the region we have two main lines designed to pick up freight from C, D, and E places en route to an A place (4 and 6), while a B place (5) is again served by a secondary line that also serves two D places. This bypassing of the B place could contribute to its reduction in rank and the enhancement of rank of the C places on the main lines. In a third section of the region, we have two B places on main lines. In the one case (7) a C place shows itself to be important enough to warrant main line service, whereas in the other, two D places have this honor (8). Main line traffic in these cases does not involve relationships with other A places, hence importance of the B places would be enhanced. In a fourth instance (9), a B place is serving as a transport node to pull the route away from a straight-line A to A route. Goods (or passengers) could be transported to either of two A places from this point.

In all of these regions we can see the potential impact of the transport system on development of the various types of central places. Some of the C, D, and E places not served by main lines are served by secondary lines. Others are served by branch lines and still others are not served. If we extend this analogy to highways as well as railroads, the impact becomes even more obvious. Good transportation adds to the growth possibilities of a place and poor transportation increases the chances of demise. The

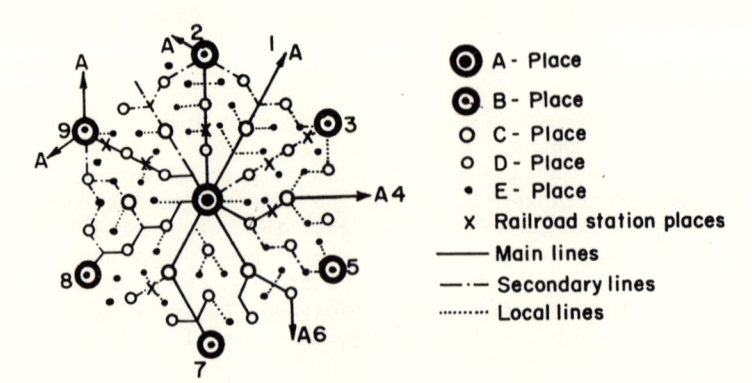

Fig. 4.9. Traffic routes in a system of central places.

economic principle of transportation is to satisfy as many transport needs as possible with minimum cost. Where transportation is inferior, activities tend to shift to superior routes. Over time, therefore, the transport system changes the configuration from a spatial one, best illustrated by nested hexagons, to a linear one.

According to Christaller (1966, p. 275), "The traffic principle states that the distribution of central places is most favorable when as many important places as possible lie on one traffic route between two important towns, the route being established as straight and cheaply as possible . . . the central places would thus be lined up on straight traffic routes which fan out from the central point." Even where straight-line routes are not possible, linear relationships will develop. One would expect movement toward a most favorable distribution, even though it is never achieved exactly.

Separation principle. Christaller conceived of a third principle that may help explain location under certain circumstances. It is particularly applicable in explaining location of older places in countries where there was considerable insecurity at the time of their founding. It also helps explain the influence of administrative centers such as capital cities. The separation principle, also known as the administrative principle, results in a spatial ordering consisting of a capital place surrounded by a wreath of satellite places of lesser order, where certain government functions are carried out, and a thin population toward the edge of the administrative district.

The central idea is the creation of districts of practically equal area and population. The most important place will lie in the center of the district. Since the borders are thinly populated, the distribution of places will seldom be hexagonal. In most countries, there are administrative influences, but seldom such strong ones as to overwhelm the impact of marketing and transportation principles. However, in studying the lower court districts in Germany, Christaller found that several different systems, each containing six or seven towns, prevailed. In his enunciation of the separation principle he stated that the number of central places necessary to provide central administration services fits a rule of three in a somewhat altered fashion; that is, three places of B importance may be related to an A place.

Dynamic processes. Christaller viewed his models as static, hence subject to change in a dynamic world. Of all the possible processes that would modify the picture, he selected eight as important: population changes, demands for and supply of the central good, production costs and technical progress, changes in natural endowments of a region, the effect of traffic, variability in range of central good, the dynamic aspects of a system of central places, and the business cycle.

Population changes that increase the numbers of people outside the higher order places tend to weaken them, but movement toward them gives them added strength. Changes can also occur with shifts in occupations, age distribution, income and social structure; their impacts will differ depending upon their influence on demand for central goods. Population declines, by decreasing potential markets, tend to decrease the importance of centers. In addition to changes in demand caused by population factors, there can be changes in supply of goods and changes in people's tastes over time that influence their price elasticity responses. These will influence growth and decline of the centers furnishing the goods. In general, increases in price levels tend to strengthen and decreases tend to weaken central places.

Christaller maintained that a central good with relatively high capital cost would be necessarily of a higher order requiring a large market. Further, these costs are subject to drastic changes as technology changes, subjecting the higher order places to greater variations than those of lower order. Wages tend to perform two functions; as income, they affect overall demand, and as costs, they affect prices. They are usually lower in the lower places than in the higher ones, giving some advantage to the higher order places. Land rents are highest in the places of higher order, which is related to higher concentration of people, greater investment, and higher wages.

Technical progress increases people's productivity, hence their wages. It contributes in that way, as well as through changes in capital, to growth of central places.

Natural endowments can be changed by exhaustion, new discoveries, new information making previously useless materials useful, and erosion. Since growth of higher order central places tends to be related to overall productivity in a region, resources can be very important.

Lower transportation costs mean greater profits and more money to be used in buying higher order consumption goods. Good transportation makes acquisition of these goods easier as well as making greater diversity of purchases possible. Transport-oriented concerns such as location of railroads, highways, crossroads, and other modes, and development of airfields, canals, and ports are important to community location and to development of different sizes of communities. The automobile and improved highway quality have had striking impacts on location, not noted by Christaller.

Christaller named four main factors influencing the range for a central good. First is size and importance of the central place. In a large, important central place, many different kinds of central goods can be offered that make it worthwhile for people to go there from considerable distances. If a place decreases in importance, it is usually because fewer goods are being offered. Second is price willingness of the purchaser. Since price paid consists of that paid directly plus cost of travel to the purchase point, if a person's price willingness declines, his willingness to travel for the good will also decline. Third is subjective economic distance. This includes anything that will influence cost of movement over space, such as changes in fares and freight rates; security; technology of cargo handling; changes in types of transportation; such subjective factors as tastes, income distribution, ideologies; and relative importance of time. The fourth factor is type, quantity, and price of a good. Some goods can only be offered if a large enough population can be served, since only a few people need them. If quantity of goods offered changes, the distance people will travel to get them also changes. Likewise, price changes may influence whether or not people go to a higher center to obtain certain goods.

Dynamic aspects of a system of central places are often determined by the principle having the greater impact. Imagine an isolated country whose pattern of central places was established according to the marketing principle. Now, let it be penetrated by a rail line and have its ports improved. As the system develops, certain places will increase and others decrease in importance. Or let there be a political division of territory such that B places formerly attached to an A place are now cut off; then some C places may grow to take their place. Or suppose a country decides to make a capital city out of a small town. This will cause a whole system of central places to develop.

Christaller maintained that despite the observed short-run nature of business cycles, they had long run consequences. Certain kinds of activity during a boom period result in added capital capacities. Further, these are not evenly distributed over space, so they give emphasis to certain places. Also their influence on employment and price levels are different at different periods of the cycle. Other factors also influence employment and price levels. Some communities are little affected by downturns in business cycles because of the kinds of basic industries they have acquired, while others find their economy responds immediately to cyclical factors in the region, the nation, or even the world.

Lösch

August Lösch was the first to discuss the broad aspects of spatial economics in a book, *The Economics of Location* (1954). He was concerned not with things as they are, but with the question, "What is a rational location decision?" He identified two basic types of market area: market areas of supply and market areas of demand. He pointed out that Von Thünen's model was based on areas of supply and that location of types of agricultural production had been analyzed largely from that viewpoint. In contrast, he felt that areas of demand played a larger role in location theories concerning nonagricultural location.

Isodapanes and isovectures. One of Lösch's major contributions was in his modification of Weber's model. He accepted Weber's definition that an isodapane is a line connecting loci of equal cost for a given ton per kilometer combination; but he added freight rates for transport from and to a certain place. They become the basis for construction of isodapanes. In Fig. 4.10, the solid lines Lösch calls isovectures. Each of them represents costs

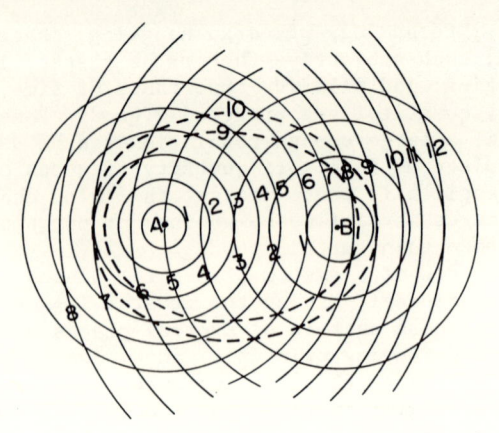

Fig. 4.10. Use of isovectures to construct isodapanes.

in monetary terms. That is, those around point A represent 3 tons shipped at costs of 1, 2, 3, etc., monetary units and those around point B represent 2 tons shipped at a cost of 1, 2, 3, etc., monetary units. Where they overlap, they determine a given amount or total cost; that is, isodapane 10 forms through intersection of isovecture 6 from A and 4 from B, 7 from A and 3 from B, 8 from A and 2 from B, 9 from A and 1 from B, and so on.

It is easy to see that Lösch thought very little of Weber's locational triangle. Rather, he felt that a method was needed that would allow for as many shipment points as possible. Each pair of points would have isodapanes. Thus, if there were four, a very complex set would result with many intersections where freight costs would be equal. They would be good location sites; it would not be necessary to draw circles around triangles to attain this.

Principle of substitution. Despite his aversion to the triangle idea, Lösch was intrigued by the Varignon Frame. To this he applied Predöhl's principle of substitution (1952, p. 306) that states, "An optimum location is somewhere in the vicinity of the point where the sum of freight increases in production is balanced by the sum of freight decreases in inputs."

Assuming freight rates proportional to distance (that is, no differentials because of type of goods shipped), he imagined four possible cases. The first related to weight ratios. If, on the frame, the weight on one of the threads is greater than the sum of weights on the others, the center of the string will move to the point where the string attached to the large weight enters the frame. As an example, he cited a situation where 3 tons of ore plus 1 ton of coke produces 1 ton of pig iron. The optimum location point is where the iron ore is produced. In the case of beer, where all inputs are relatively light except for water, which is ubiquitous, the tendency would be to locate as close as possible to the market, since no one wants to ship water very far (not even Rocky Mountain spring water).

The second case had to do with relative position of the various possible locations. Even if the weight on one string is not absolutely dominant, the optimum location would tend toward the entry point for the string having the greatest weight, since the resultant would be greatest for the one with shortest string length (heaviest weight). (A resultant is a sum of vectors or lengths of the strings.) Thus, if the product were heavier than the inputs, location would be drawn toward the market.

The third case assumed that weights can be expressed in terms of cost, that is, high transportation cost for a material tends to draw location toward it. Transport networks have nodes that have the advantage of being a shorter distance from all points of interest than any other point in the area because movement has to be over the network that coincides at the node. The nodes have certain cost advantages. Sometimes they favor raw material sites, sometimes the market, but often they are neutral.

The fourth case was a continuation of the third, since it concentrated on one aspect of cost found at the node. Where it is necessary to shift from one mode of transportation to another (railroad to steamship), if transshipment costs are high, the node may be optimal for production. This is particularly true where increases in line-haul costs are less than decreases in terminal expenses.

Agglomeration economies. Lösch considered Weber's work on agglomeration to be of special interest. Transport nodes possess one type of general agglomeration economy. Lösch considered community location to be related not only to the hierarchy of goods developed by Christaller but also to agglomerative forces. He identified the four general types of concentration shown in Fig. 4.11. A true network has no agglomerative advantages; each plant serves a certain market area. A real agglomeration occurs either as a restricted network or as a cluster within a small area. Market ar-

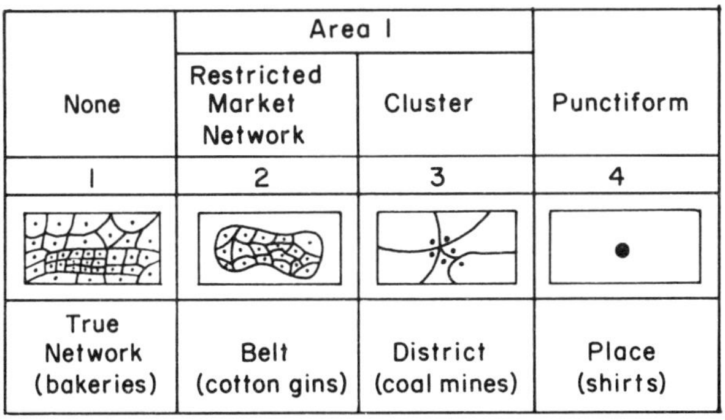

None	Area I		
	Restricted Market Network	Cluster	Punctiform
1	2	3	4
True Network (bakeries)	Belt (cotton gins)	District (coal mines)	Place (shirts)

Fig. 4.11. Concentration of locations.

eas for both of these remain separated but lie close to one another. Market areas of restricted networks tend to surround the producer, whereas clustered producers have areas extending outward from a center. The fourth type, punctiform, occurs when all producers locate in one place. Thus, the market area is the same for all.

Town settlement. Lösch defined a town as "a punctiform agglomeration of nonagricultural locations" (p. 68). In most towns, there are specific characteristics related to one of three types of agglomeration: (1) an especially large enterprise, (2) a collection of similar enterprises, and (3) an agglomeration of dissimilar enterprises. A large enterprise locates at a place in order to take advantage of large scale production of one or several products. Obviously, the place has to have some peculiar advantage for this type of operation.

Similar enterprises locate together

1. So that buyers can have a wide selection of goods
2. To take advantage of external economies, such as a large labor market, more efficient suppliers of other goods and services, and mutual stimulation
3. Because of availability of a key raw material or intermediate product input
4. Because they have direct ties to their customers, that is, printing plants must be in frequent contact with their clients
5. Because it allows access to a larger market for their products
6. Because certain government agencies with whom they have frequent contact are located there
7. Because the place has certain transportation advantages that are important to the industry or industries, for example, good terminal facilities
8. Because there are enough differentiations among them that they complement one another

Dissimilar enterprises agglomerate because

1. There are advantages in having large numbers of firms producing a large amount, regardless of kind of product.
2. There are advantages in having a variety of products available for the buyers; costs are lowered and demand is strengthened.
3. Firms having different cyclical variations can operate more efficiently if they are located together, since one will be high while another is low, thus giving some stability to an otherwise unstable situation. Where labor can shift easily among the industries, for example, a stable labor force is achieved.
4. Diversity tends to draw abler people to a location.
5. Certain support industries are adaptable to a wide range

of customers. In order to exist, they need this broad market. The recipient industries, in turn, are benefited by having them available. This is a sort of symbiotic relationship.

6. To a degree, industries create their own markets by drawing people to a particular place. Thus, the more diverse the industrial mix in an area, the better the market for everyone.

Sometimes different enterprises will agglomerate by chance without any particular agglomerative advantage. These types may be caused by governmental decree or simply orientation toward an administrative center; orientation by main roads, which confers advantage apart from those of agglomeration; the fact that there are advantages in being located at certain distances from other groups.

Towns develop for a large number of reasons, many of which may be lost in antiquity. Some firms may choose a location simply because the originator lives there. However, there must also be some economic advantage if a community and a particular economic structure are to persist.

General locational patterns. Lösch states that not every location is amenable to analysis or manipulation. "There is a reason in things preserving them from chaos and, as a rule without any human assistance whatsoever. . . . It is not true that man must supply the world with an organizing principle. . . . Nature works according to laws, but man acts according to his idea of laws. . . . as to economic equilibrium this means that in order to guide his activities he needs insight into the condition of this equilibrium" (1954, pp. 68-84, 92-100). The equilibrium of location is determined by two fundamental tendencies: that seen from the standpoint of the individual firm, affected by industrial struggle from within, and that seen from the standpoint of the economy as a whole, affected by competition from without each firm. An individual chooses a location in such a way as to achieve highest profit as a producer and/or the cheapest market as a consumer.

Lösch's model had five basic conditions that he believed must be fulfilled to give meaning and permance to spatial order of the economy. They were (1) location of an individual must be as advantageous as possible; (2) locations must be so numerous that the entire space is occupied; (3) in all activities open to everyone, abnormal profits must disappear; (4) areas of supply, production, and sales must be as small as possible; and (5) at the boundaries of economic areas, it must be a matter of indifference to which of two neighboring locations people will go to buy. (The boundaries are indifference lines.) These conditions do not guarantee that the best location for production will be the best for consumption. Where there is free competition, the best location for consumption of industrial goods is also the best for production, but this is not true of agricultural or mineral products.

Shape of market areas. In the section of his book concerning shape of market areas, Lösch made some of his most important contributions to location theory (1954, pp. 105-38).

Demand cone. Assume that materials are evenly and adequately distributed over a wide plain, that population and other factors are also homogeneous, and that everyone lives on regularly distributed self-sufficient farms. Now, suppose one of the farmers decides to manufacture pots and pans. How large will the market be?

Suppose all of the farm families have the same demand function D (Fig. 4.12). Suppose P_1 is the price charged by the new manufacturer of pots and pans at his place of business, and Q_1 is the amount that would be bought by any one family providing it was not necessary to travel to obtain it. If the price were P_1', the quantity Q_1' would be taken.

But the families do not live at the point of production in general, and the price they will pay is $P_1 + RD$, where R is the transport rate and D is the distance the customer lives from the production point. In other words, the amount actually paid is the price at point of production plus cost of transportation, or a CIF price. Since $P_1 + RD > P_1$, except at the origin, the amount purchased by each family is some value Q_k ($k = 2, 3, \ldots, E$), purchased where $P_1 + RD = P_k$ and where $Q_k < Q_1$. The result is a cone of demand for each FOB P value. These are illustrated in Fig. 4.13 for FOB prices P_1 and P_1', $P_1' > P_1$.

Rather than adding the demand curves directly, as is done in spaceless economics, it is necessary to add volumes of the cones. The resultant industry demand function faced by this regional monopolist is shown in Fig. 4.14. The volume of a cone is equal to the area of the surface times the path of its center of gravity. To get the industry demand curve, it is necessary to calculate the volume of each cone existing at each FOB price. When these are

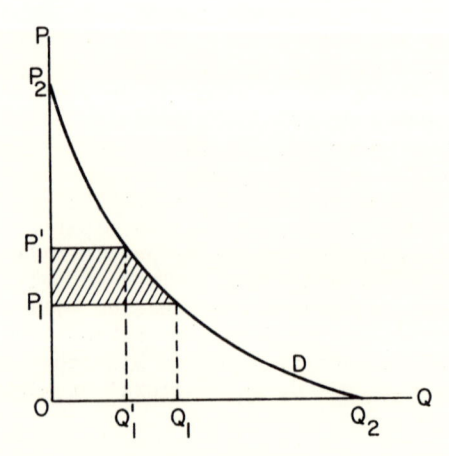

Fig. 4.12. Individual demand function of families.

Theory of Location   89

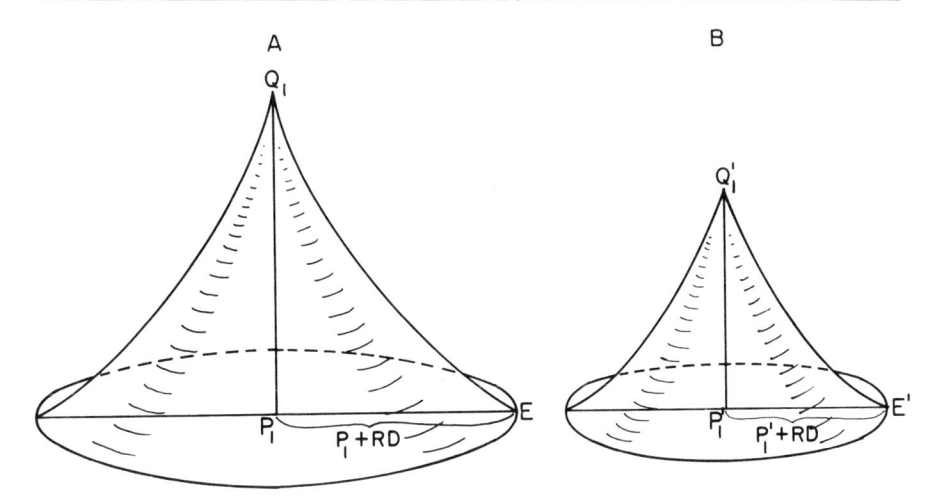

Fig. 4.13. Demand cones for different prices.

charted a total demand curve (D) that is concave to the origin is derived.

Upon this we also draw a planning curve (C) that gives average cost at which any given amount can be produced. The manufacturer of pots and pans can only operate if the demand and cost curves intersect. The largest amount that can be produced and sold is OM and the smallest amount is ON. If OM were to be decided upon, this would be the volume of the appropriate demand cone for price P.

Lösch pointed out that the demand cone defines a market area as a circle, but that if there were no overlap of market areas among spatial monopolists (each serving a single market), some of the people in the plain would not be served. These are in the in-

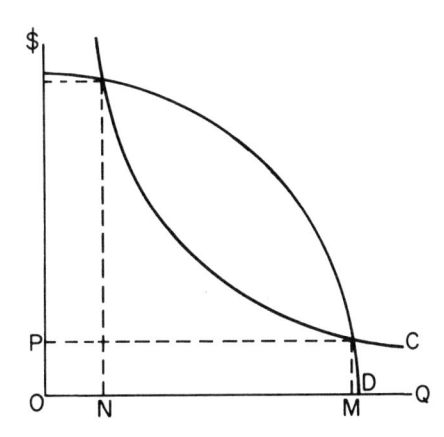

Fig. 4.14. Total demand for pots and pans.

A   B   C

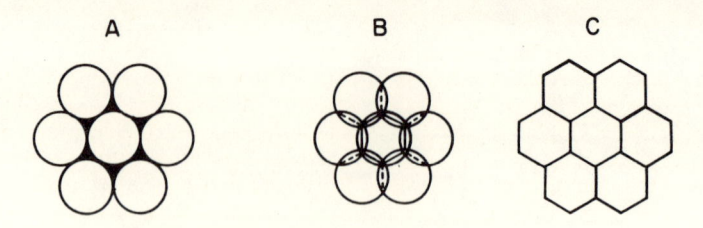

Fig. 4.15. Market area spacing.

terstices shown in Fig. 4.15A. In order for all people to be served, under the assumption of a homogeneous distribution of population on a flat plain, the circles would have to overlap (Fig. 4.15B). But if they overlap, who is to serve whom in the overlapped area? The argument is that it would be split evenly, creating a hexagonal pattern (Fig. 4.15C).

This means that total demand for each producer is actually less than would be indicated by a demand function derived from the volume of cones. Lösch developed a formula to measure this, but it is of little interest to most of us. His major conclusion is that "the honeycomb is, therefore, the most advantageous shape for economic regions" (1954, p. 112).

Where populations are concentrated in certain places, each distribution center (A_1) will serve only some of the settlements with many of its goods. This brings up the question of optimum spacing between suppliers. According to Lösch, the law is, "The distance between two enterprises of the same kind is equal to the distance between the settlements supplied times the square root of their number" (p. 112). Assuming other settlements to be supplied are located equidistant from A_1 (distance a), the smallest number of settlements to be served, including A itself, is three (Fig. 4.16A). That is, even if it supplies itself and all six other settlements with some goods, it will have competition from at least two other supply centers (B_2 and B_3), hence could be expected to supply one-third of the needs of each customer area. In this case

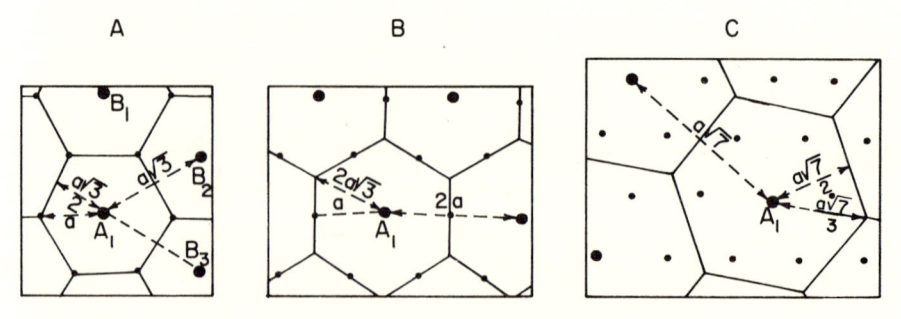

Fig. 4.16. Three smallest market areas.

Theory of Location 91

the market area is $a^2 3\sqrt{3/2}$ and the distance between supplying centers is $a\sqrt{3}$.

Where the settlements are not located at the corners of the hexagons but somewhere along the sides (perhaps on transportation routes), the distance from A is still a (Fig. 4.16B). But now it is further between supply centers (say, $2a$) and A_1 receives demand equal to three other settlements plus its own. The distance between market towns is $2a$ or $a\sqrt{4}$. In this case, where the boundary among market areas extends beyond settlements in the immediate vicinity (Fig. 4.16C), A_1 has to supply all the needs of seven settlements. Now the distance between suppliers is $a\sqrt{7}$. Lösch called these $K = 3$, $K = 4$, and $K = 7$ market patterns.

A location at center of gravity is one that makes access to all points of sale advantageous either from a time or cost of transport viewpoint. It is not in an original settlement, meaning it has very little local market. Lösch's illustration is a location among three establishments, rather than at one of them. For this particular case, the necessary shopping distance would decline from a to $0.58a$. He argues that this would be the only factor affected, since the number of points to be supplied would be the same and the distance between points of supply would remain the same. This implies that if one supplier selects a center of gravity rather than a settlement, all others will also. He offers no proof for this. The concept of gravity as a locational factor has been developed into "gravity models" by other locational economists.

The argument so far has produced the conclusion that the hexagon is the only suitable shape for market areas, that there are a limited number of sizes and orientations, and that a most favorable area is uniquely determined for each commodity. But, since there are more products than market sizes, the same area will be optimum for several goods. Each of these goods can vary in possible shipping areas, hence in sales volume. Only the geographic limits of the area are fixed. Thus, goods whose market areas are equal would be classed together.

Since all interest lies in the market areas themselves, and since it has been established (Fig. 4.15) that areas of the same size lie in immediate contact, a honeycomb pattern extends over the whole area being considered. That is, development of a composite central place network is accomplished by superimposing all of the possible hexagonal nets in such a way that each has at least one center in common (Fig. 4.17A). The nets are then rotated so as to organize the production centers as nearly as possible into linear clusters that integrate the notion of the traffic principle (Fig. 4.17B). The latter, Lösch contended, fits the pattern of many metropolitan areas, such as Indianapolis and Toledo, shown in Fig. 4.18.

These agglomerations of locations were the same as Christaller's central sites. Note that only the patterns shown in Fig. 4.16B and 4.16C can be rotated under the assumption of discontinuous settlement. That is, Fig. 4.16A is fixed in place by the mar-

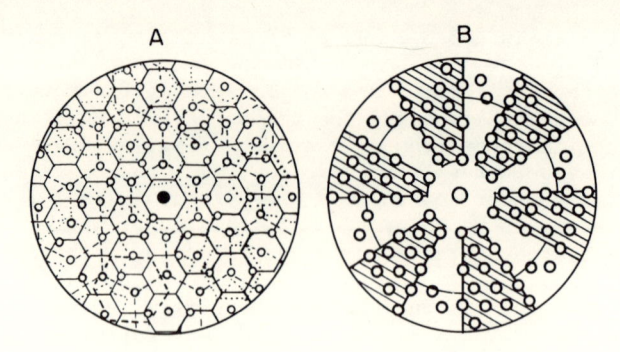

Fig. 4.17. Theoretical pattern of an economic landscape.

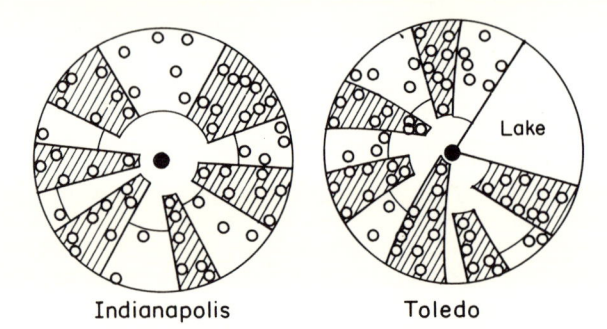

Fig. 4.18. Pattern of economic landscape for two areas.

ket pattern; once the pattern for any particular market size is established, the hexagon corners defined by settlements tend to be fixed in place. But the others are not and can be rotated within certain limits.

Where the centers of several market areas coincide, the distribution of these agglomerations tends to occur with considerable regularity. Lösch postulated that small agglomerations tend to be found at distances $\sqrt{3}a$, $3a$, and $2\sqrt{3}a$ from each other, while medium size ones are $6a$, and large ones, $12a$ apart. Note that Lösch's system results in a more continuous hierarchical distribution of centers than does Christaller's.

In Fig. 4.19, Lösch has shown how these distributions would coincide with major transport routes, assuming perfectly flat terrain. Sites that are centers for distribution of large numbers of commodities tend to lie on the major routes (heavy black lines). The broken lines connect sites that are centers for the smallest number of commodities. The amount of commodities distributed by sites along heavy lines is twice the number and along thin black lines is 1 1/2 times the number on the broken lines. This distribution of regional transport networks, then, constitutes an economic landscape. From one metropolis extends a market area and

Theory of Location

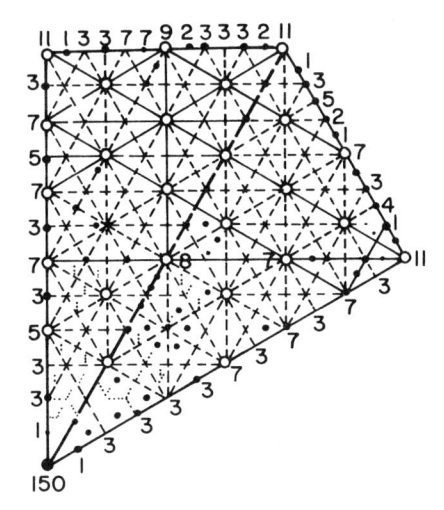

Fig. 4.19. Transport lines in an ideal economic landscape.

smaller competing centers in a concentric fashion. As distance from the metropolis increases, sizes of the larger centers also increase.

Lösch noted that political geography is usually such that certain small regions are combined into larger administrative districts. (This is especially true of Europe.) Two of these are shown in Fig. 4.20. The $K = 4$ structure is one in which every town of any rank dominates three towns of next lower rank. In the $K = 7$ structure, every ranked town dominates six lower-ranked towns.

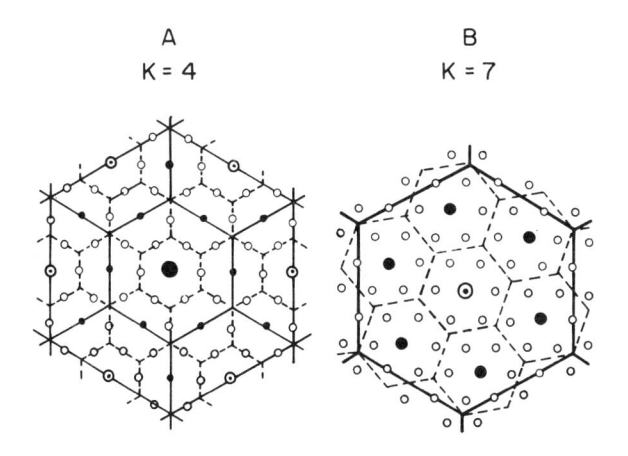

A
$K = 4$

B
$K = 7$

Fig. 4.20. Regions with equal structure.

Some new factors. Lösch (1954, pp. 139-210) recognized the influences of a number of economic, spatial, social, and political factors affecting location that would modify his models.

Local differences in price. Once free of the concept that demand is all concentrated in one place, we recognize the fact that the sums of demand functions in various areas are going to be different. First, there will be a difference in price due to freight costs between areas. Second, the price actually paid by a customer will depend upon the attitude of the seller toward absorbing freight costs. Third, there may be geographic differences in elasticity of demand. Lösch felt these were interrelated. As he stated it, "The individual demand in respect to the CIF price is more elastic than the individual demand as a function of the corresponding FOB price ($\varepsilon_1 > \varepsilon_2$). . . . The reason is that a certain percentage change in the FOB price causes a smaller percentage change in the corresponding CIF price, whereas the absolute change is the same in both" (1954, p. 141). That is, CIF price > FOB price.

Where one is comparing differences in demand among areas, each of which is served by a different seller, the same principle with respect to elasticity holds. If the differences in FOB prices between the two centers equals the total freight cost between them, demand with respect to current FOB prices becomes less elastic as distance increases. This is because the prices are not really competitive and the buyer cannot substitute one product for the other.

If freight costs are absorbed, prices remain competitive, and elasticity of demand with regard to current FOB prices becomes more elastic with increased distance. Thus, demand near a supplier is likely to be less elastic than demand further away. This makes it possible for the supplier to discriminate against local customers by absorbing freight costs. (For proof of this, Lösch uses E. M. Hoover's derivation [1937, pp. 182-91].)

However, if we assume a homogeneous linear demand function, the demand cone will approximate the demand for a particular seller at a particular FOB price, and demand by customers away from the local market will be one-third that of local customers. (Lösch attributes this to the fact that the volume of a cone equals the area of its base times one-third its height.) Thus, if population were concentrated around the seller, local customers would not only be more numerous, their demand per unit would be three times greater (in the limiting case). Lösch admits that the limiting case seldom holds, but insists demand per customer in the local area is larger than demand further away.

Since local demand is relatively inelastic, price changes would have smaller impact locally than in the remainder of the region. A price rise, for example, might reduce the size of the circle by elminating the fringe customers, but may not affect local demand at all. This is because customers away from the supplier's location always pay more and are more sensitive to price changes than are local customers. Thus, if an entrepreneur were concerned about

Theory of Location

losing customers on the fringe of the market area, he or she might not raise the price to them.

Lösch concludes that where there is competition for markets away from a supplier's location, the tendency will be to lower the price by absorbing part of the freight cost. As a matter of fact, with linear demand curves, it turns out that sellers can maximize profits by absorbing exactly half of the transport cost. This is illustrated in Fig. 4.21. In Fig. 4.21A there are linear demand curves D_1, D_2, D_3, accompanied by three marginal revenue curves MR_1, MR_2, and MR_3. These represent demand for a product produced at a given point with customers located i units apart. Since all customers are drawing on the same supply, the marginal cost is constant for all units supplied (M, MC).

The seller can maximize profit by selling the amount to each customer determined by the intersection of the appropriate MR and MC curves. The first demand curve represents that of customers near the supplier, the second that of customers i units from the supplier, and the third, those located $2i$ units away. Thus, at the seller's location, Q_1 units are sold at a price of P_1; at the first site away, Q_2 will be sold at a price of P_2; at the second, Q_3 will be sold at a price of P_3. The profit curves attached to each of these transactions are shown in Fig. 4.21B. The line drawn between M and $\hat{P}_1$ is the same length as the segment of D_1 from $\hat{P}_1$ to N, hence the triangle $MN\hat{P}_1$ is isosceles and the line segment $\hat{P}_1 L = MN/2$, $\hat{P}_2 R = MS/2$, and $\hat{P}_3 U = MT/2$. But $MN - MS$ is cost of movement over distance i times some rate r. So $ir = t$ = total cost of movement from the seller to buyers at the second point. The difference in price at that point and at the seller's home is $P_1 - P_2 = \hat{P}_1 L$

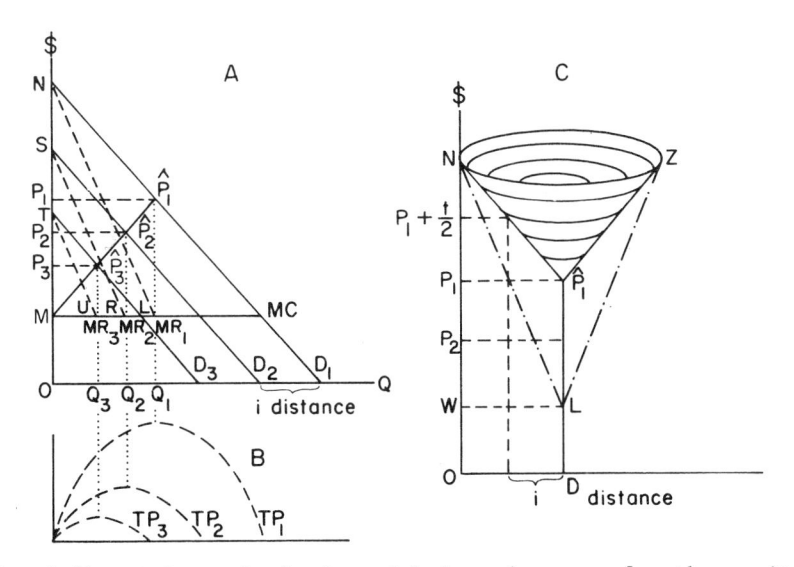

Fig. 4.21. Price calculation with demand curves for three sites.

$- P_2R$ (since MC is constant) $= (MN - MS)/2$. Hence the difference in price paid by the customers at point 2 is $P_1 - (t/2)$.

The remainder of the argument is in Fig. 4.21C. The cone represents transport cost in every direction from the seller's location. Again $\hat{P}_1 L$ is shown as the difference between the price at that point and the marginal cost; the profit lines LN and LZ represent marginal cost plus transport cost. Customers i distance away pay $P_1 + (t/2)$, in short, they absorb half the transport cost and the seller absorbs the other half. So the seller will charge price P_2, which is $P_1 - (t/2)$, and the buyer will pay $P_2 + t = P_1 + (t/2)$.

The cross section of the traffic funnel, if no monopoly profit were taken and a uniform factory price at the level of variable costs were charged, would be NLZ. If one unit were sold at every point on the line OD, variable production costs would be the area $OWLD$, transport costs WNL, and $LN\hat{P}$, the contribution to fixed costs and profit. But, as seen in Fig. 4.21A and Fig. 4.21B, there is a maximum amount of profit to be made at certain points on the demand curve, namely those at which marginal revenue equals marginal cost. This turns out to be at $P + (t/2)$ for each of the sites.

Local product differentiation. Product differentiation works against spatial monopoly by causing markets to overlap. There are very few goods that are strictly homogeneous. Thus, people tend to prefer certain goods over certain others and will spend additional money to obtain them. Thus, Lösch concludes that differentiation tends to intensify competition, rather than reduce it.

Freight rates. Public regulation of freight rates brings noneconomic factors into the picture. Rates may be designed, for example, to give advantage to certain regions or to certain goods. Further, graduated tariffs amount to discrimination in the pricing of transportation. For short distances, these tariffs lie above, and for long distances, below, those that would be charged without graduation, such as a tariff proportional to distance. These differences affect the size of market areas.

What is the relation between sales areas of two places shipping the same product under different freight rates? First, the product with the lower rate is going to have a market somewhere. Even if the competitor produces its product cheaply enough to displace the first product in its own market, given a large enough market, eventually $P_1 + R_1 D$ will fall below $P_2 + R_2 D$ ($P_2 > P_1$, $R_1 > R_2$). Second, the sales area of the place with the higher tariff will be surrounded by that of the other (Fig. 4.22). Note that $P_1 + R_1 D$ is lower than P_2, hence can take over that market, yet $P_2 + R_2 D = P_1 + R_1 D$ at D_1; and also note that the higher priced commodity establishes a market completely surrounding that of the lower priced one. How rapidly this occurs depends upon the relative rates for the two products and the FOB prices.

If there are upward and downward movements in freight rates with no discrimination, size of market area will be affected. Lower rates mean lower CIF prices that mean higher demand per customer

Theory of Location 97

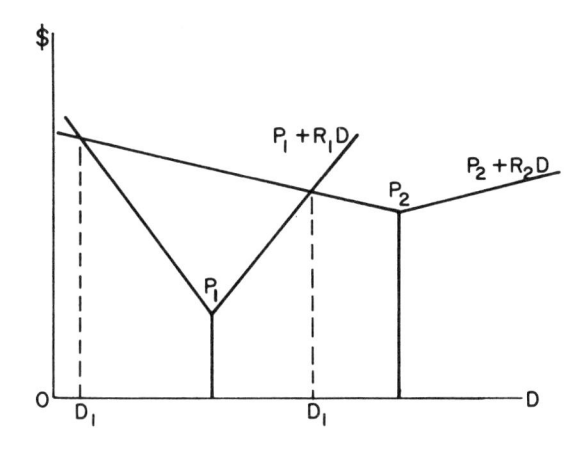

Fig. 4.22. Effect of high freight rate on market of low cost industry.

and smaller necessary sales area. It also means that possible sales area might be increased, since prices are lowered everywhere. However, it must be kept in mind that all producers are likely to be affected equally by the change. Thus, all may simply share in an expanded market on the same basis as before. If the industry is competitive, the extra profits earned will entice new operators into the field. They may be more efficient than the old ones, owing to more up-to-date equipment, and have lower costs that may force some old operators out of business.

Natural differences. Having developed his model on the basis of uniformity in endowments, Lösch relaxed many of these assumptions to see how differences in natural and human resources impact on economic activity. These impacts come through differences in productivity. That is, regions have different endowments, hence different capabilities. Changes can also occur in these endowments if some of the differences, as in topographical features, are not so pervasive and fixed as to limit types of possible orientation. Where this is not the case and changes occur slowly, drastic interference with economic orientation is not to be expected. Quick changes in endowments, hence in productivity, cause problems; agriculture, forestry, mining, and fishing are most vulnerable.

Accessibility can make a difference. Natural obstacles and assets have a great deal to do with where transportation is available. An adequate transport network is essential for major economic activity.

Nodal points are of special importance in the transportation picture. As Lösch pointed out, they are usually preferred locations for industry and trade. This is especially true where there is transfer from one type of transportation to another.

Societal differences may enter in. In general, the more capable people have the largest markets. But there are many factors affecting capability, one of the more important of which is culture. In some societies consumption is rigidly determined; in others it is completely free. In some societies entrepreneurs have to live with an extended family system that works against efficiency, since each member must share earnings with the others.

Political differences are often present. Political boundaries are not necessarily the same as economic ones. However, political reality and economics may move in the same direction. Lösch lists seven similarities.

1. State and regional economies may have the same capital or central city toward which other cities and traffic routes are oriented.
2. Where central cities exist, they tend to be located as centrally as possible.
3. There is a tendency toward equal size in both central cities and capitals.
4. Size depends upon development of transportation and of production techniques. Places must be of adequate size to continue in existence; economics through markets, political systems through power. If they exceed this size they become rich and powerful.
5. Boundaries of states and certain economic landscapes cut through regular market networks, thus resulting in economic losses.
6. Boundaries separate the various orders; enclaves and exclaves tend to be inefficient, since they either enclose or exclude certain people.
7. Influence of centers lessens toward the periphery. Capitals and their immediate surroundings differ more sharply from each other than do border regions.

He also lists four dissimilarities.

1. Political frontiers tend to be more rigid than do economic boundaries.
2. Economic boundaries separate through price differences. Political boundaries separate by customs, duties, laws, language, community sensitivity, insecurity, and destiny.
3. Political frontiers are more sharply defined than economic boundaries. Economies tend to overlap, to change as profit opportunities change, to regard distance as an important factor. Political boundaries are usually changed only by war.
4. Goals of men as economic activists and political activists are quite different.

Differences in natural and human resources have a recognizable impact on economic activity (pp. 210-12).

SUMMARY

The works of Von Thünen, Christaller, Weber, and Lösch are basic to most spatial economic concepts. These four thinkers introduced such a variety of concepts that many of them have required years of work by other analysts to assimilate them into the body of theory.

Von Thünen was a pioneer economic analyst and thinker who lived in the late eighteenth and early nineteenth centuries. Some concepts found in his works include marginalism, partial and total equilibrium, separation of short- and long-term and an improved definition of rent. In the spatial area, he developed the concept of crop zones, agricultural intensity, and location of agricultural activities with regard to markets. His idea of rings has been used extensively in developing the concepts of market structure, community layout, and land use. He was responsible for the concept of land rent as negative transport cost. He also discussed the impact of costs of production and price of the end product on rents.

Weber addressed the question, "What causes a given industry to move from one location to another?" Where Von Thünen assumed location given and type of production to be determined, Weber assumed branch of industry given and location to be determined. His analysis was based upon three factors: cost of transportation, cost of labor, and forces of agglomeration. The first two were regional and the last one was local in nature. The major distinction was that transportation cost was basic to location of industry, and cost of labor and agglomeration forces worked in opposition to transport cost.

He introduced labor orientation and agglomeration into the picture by means of isodapanes, the locus of points having common transport costs at some distance from a minimal point. If savings due to labor costs and/or agglomeration economies at a particular point are equal to or exceed transport costs of a given isodapane, industries will be attracted to that point. Weber felt that only industries with high value added would gain cost advantages from agglomeration.

Unlike Von Thünen or Weber, Christaller looked at an entire spatially oriented economic system. Where they ignored many noneconomic factors, he incorporated political, social, and geographic factors into his analysis. His modification of market areas from circular to hexagonal has been of special interest, as have his ideas concerning market, transportation, and administrative principles. He was the first to suggest the idea of central places.

Lösch synthesized the ideas of the other three men and added a number of his own to develop the first volume on economics of location. He felt that analysis of agricultural production could best be handled by Von Thünen's approach based on market areas of supply; but market areas of demand were best for theories concerning nonagricultural location.

Lösch introduced four methods for determining points of minimum transportation cost. The first, discussed by Weber, consisted of the locational triangle and the superimposing of other triangles based on exterior angles along its sides. The second was the mechanical model also used by Weber. The third was Weber's model with the addition of isovectures, defined as lines representing equal per unit freight rates for transport to and from a certain

place. They were used to construct isodapanes. The fourth method
was Predöhl's principle of substitution that states that an optimal
location is somewhere in the vicinity of the point where the sum of
freight increases in production is balanced by the sum of freight
decreases in inputs. Lösch interpreted "freight increase" so that
it could be either material weight or freight cost.
    Assuming no differentials in freight cost because of goods
shipped, he cited four cases: the first related to weight ratios;
the second had to do with relative position of various locations;
the third dealt with substitution in established transport networks; the fourth had to do with cost of transshipment. Lösch also
considered the effect of the combination of production and freight
to be lowest when freight costs were high, and highest where
freight costs were low. It was his feeling that profit was really
the best criterion for determining location, but that its use leads
one away from theoretical models. However, where it is possible to
assume stability in revenue flow, models based on cost produce near
optimum solutions.
    Lösch defined a town as "a punctiform agglomeration" of nonag-
ricultural locations. The town has to have peculiar advantages
causing enterprises to want to locate together. He discussed reasons that similar and dissimilar firms would want to agglomerate.
    In his discussion of the shape of market areas, Lösch devel-
oped the concept of a demand cone, based on ideas of circular market areas from Von Thünen and Christaller. This resulted in a total demand curve that, combined with a cost curve, determines the
amounts that can be sold profitably. From the demand cone he went
on to show the reasoning behind Christaller's hexagons, particularly, he demonstrated how hexagonal figures could be used to explain
spacing of settlements. In so doing he used a different orientation from that of Christaller's central cities pointing out that
orientation could be on the basis of markets, transportations systems, or administrative districts. From the hexagon, he developed
the idea of the honeycomb, and from that, the net.
    On local differences in price, Lösch maintained that demand of
customers who pay FOB prices tends to be inelastic but that of customers who pay CIF prices tends to be elastic. But where freight
is absorbed, prices are competitive over distance. Product differentiation, according to Lösch, works against spatial monopoly by
causing markets to overlap. Thus, a practice that conveys monopoly
power in spaceless situations tends to mitigate it once space is
considered.

SPATIAL ECONOMICS

Law of Market Areas
    The concepts of Von Thünen, Weber, Christaller, and Lösch are
basic to most of the work done since. The concept of market areas
is important. A "market" may be a place or a context in which buyers and sellers exchange goods and services. In spatial economics,

Theory of Location

special attention is given to the market as a place. In ordinary economics, everything is sold at the same place at a given price. Equilibrium is attained in such a market when supply equals demand. Where a homogeneous good is sold in more than one spatial market, demand (d) and supply (s) may be balanced in each one, but there will be no equilibrium among the markets until prices have adjusted so that the differences are equal to transport costs. Thus, in Fig. 4.23A each market has local equilibrium where $s_1 = d_1$ and where $s_2 = d_2$; but because there are major differences in price levels, the local equilibriums are unstable. There will be movement of the commodity from the first region (the one with lowest price) to the second. Supply in the first will decline to s_1' and will increase in the second to s_2'. This second set of local equilibriums will also be unstable and adjustments will continue until the situation shown in Fig. 4.23B is attained, at which point we say a stable spatial equilibrium is established. Equilibrium is attained among markets when the difference in price between any two of them is equal to the cost of transportation between them. This is illustrated in Fig. 4.23 where T_{12} represents transport cost between markets 1 and 2. The other requirement for equilibrium among markets is that the amount exported from them must equal the amount imported to them. This model is somewhat simplis-

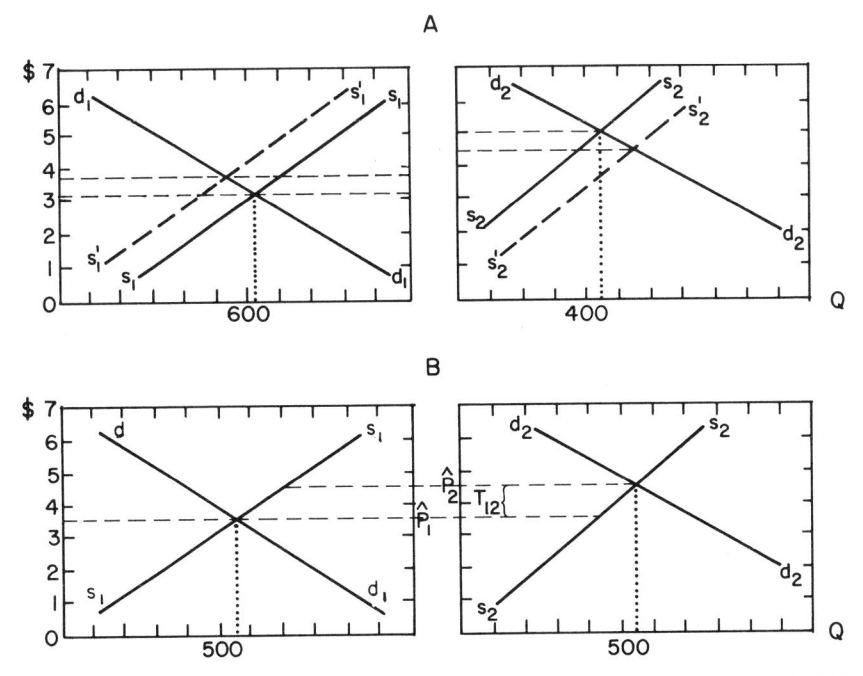

Fig. 4.23. Equilibrium (A) in two separate market areas and (B) between two market areas.

tic, yet is useful for explaining one important fact: when a good is sold from one position to people who live at other places, the FOB price pertains only to people who live right where it is sold. For all others the price is $P + RD$, where P is the FOB price, R is the cost per unit of distance from the residence of the buyer to that of the seller, and D is the distance. This concept is basic to Lösch's demand cone discussed earlier. Remember, for each FOB price there is a separate demand cone. When the volume of each cone is plotted against the different FOB prices, a demand curve is formed. Given Lösch's assumptions, demand for a good is a direct function of its price at the seller's location and an inverse function of cost of transporting the goods. The goods, in this limited model, cannot be sold beyond some limit set largely by transport costs.

So far, we have discussed markets as though there were only one seller; but under most circumstances there will be more than one, and we must be aware of the mutual spatial repulsion among competing sellers. Sellers compete for strategic locations; the locations of any one firm with regard to the overall market is affected in important ways by the location of other firms selling like goods, their pricing policies, and the transport rates.

<u>Effect of change in price and transport rate</u>. Assuming that producers use FOB pricing on their homogeneous goods, that there are no barriers to trade (aside from distance), and that there are two geographically separated sellers X and Y, each surrounded by many buyers, we need to know: (1) the size and shape of the market area of each seller, and (2) how the territory will be divided among the sellers.

Let us call the external consumption points z_i. Let the cost of movement be the freight rate times distance from any z and the seller. Let P_x and P_y be the FOB prices, R_{xz} and R_{yz} be the freight rates, and D_{xz} and D_{yz} be the distance. If the consumer at point Z buys from X, the overall price paid is $P_x + R_{xz}D_{xz}$. The consumer would be indifferent between the two sellers (or shopping areas) when

$$P_x + R_{xz}D_{xz} = P_y + R_{yz}D_{yz} \tag{4.1}$$

This, then, forms a boundary between the two sellers. It also may determine the boundary between two communities for that commodity, assuming one seller in each community.

Rearranging (4.1) gives

$$R_{xz}D_{xz} - R_{yz}D_{yz} = P_y - P_x \tag{4.2}$$

Dividing through by R_{xz} gives

$$D_{xz} - (R_{yz}/R_{xz})D_{yz} = (P_y - P_x)/R_{xz} \qquad (4.3)$$

Let $R = R_{yz}/R_{xz}$ and let $P = (P_y - P_x)/R_{xz}$, which may be positive or negative depending upon the relative prices. Then (4.3) may be expressed as

$$D_{xz} - RD_{yz} = \pm P \qquad (4.4)$$

This formula defines a family of hypercircles, known as Descartes's Ovals, whose mathematical feature is that one curve represents the locus of all points that have a ratio of distance from two fixed circles equal to a constant. This concept, known by Lösch, was developed by Frank Fetter (1924, pp. 520-29). From (4.3) and (4.4), it is seen that the size of the market tributary to X depends not only on the relative prices at the two markets, but also the ratio of the freight rates and the ratio of differences in price to the freight rates.

Statement of the general law. The boundary between two areas tributary to two geographically competing markets for a homogeneous good is a hypercircle. At each point of this circle, the difference between cost of transportation from each of the two markets to that point equals exactly the difference between market prices. On either side of the line freight rate and price differences are unequal. Since the price at the seller's location applies to everyone in the market area, it is depicted in Fig. 4.24 as a line. For a given R_{xz}, cost of transport will increase with movement in all directions from the seller, hence the funnel-shaped relationship in the figure. The illustrations in the first part of Fig. 4.25 are also funnel shaped, but since only two sellers are considered, a limited portion of the funnel is of interest so only a cross section is depicted.

The amount of area involved in each market and the shape of the curve marking the boundaries depends upon both the relationships between R_{xz} and R_{yz} and P_x and P_y. In Fig. 4.25A the spa-

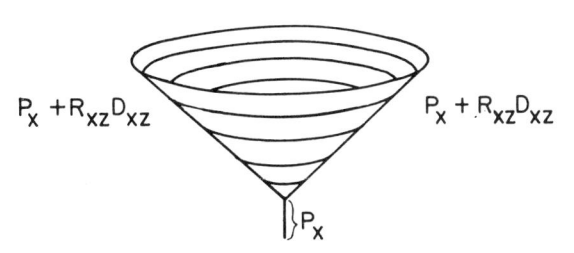

Fig. 4.24. Price plus transport cost.

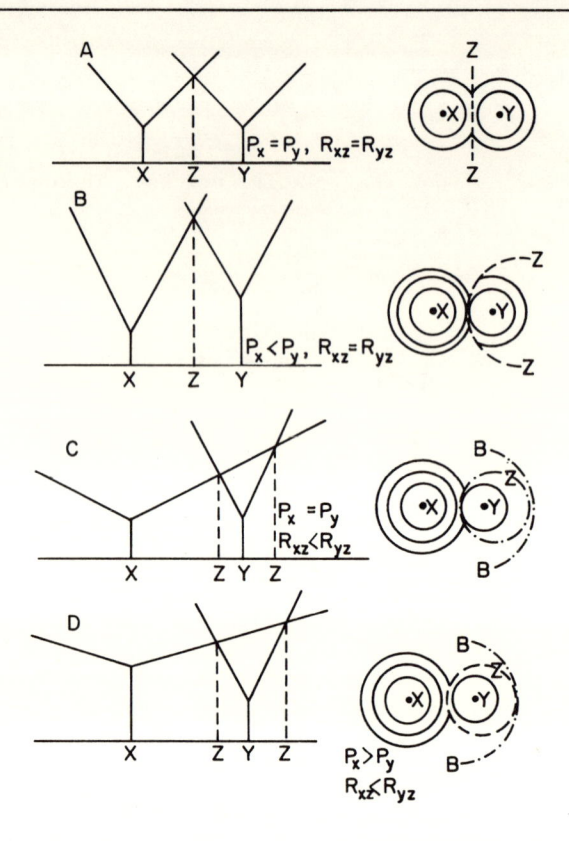

Fig. 4.25. Varieties of hypercircles.

tial relationships are equal and intersect at a point equidistant from both X and Y. In the second position of the diagram, these relationships are shown to form a straight line.

In Fig. 4.25B freight rates are equal but prices are not. The lower price received by X at its home allows for an invasion of Y's territory, the intersection in the first part of the diagram. The curve marking the market boundaries becomes one part of a hyperbola. In Fig. 4.25C prices at the centers are equal, but A has an advantage in that its freight rate is lower than Y's. The spatial price for X's goods is such that Y can only match it within a small range from its center. The market demarcation line becomes a circle. Firm Y has the alternative of living with the situation or attempting to change it by lowering prices. In Fig. 4.25D the situation where Y has lower price than X gives more elbowroom but does not change the overall configuration. Thus the power of freight rates in market demarcation is illustrated.

The curves Z represent points of indifference defined by (4.1) for the various consumers located along them. In Figs. 4.25C and 4.25D there is a further boundary for $X(B)$ that marks the points

Theory of Location 105

where the spatial price reduces demand to zero. This boundary surrounds both X's and Y's market areas.

Freight rate dominance. The same general pattern obtains when a high cost industry has a freight rate advantage that enables it to limit market areas of its competitors. This is known as freight rate dominance and is depicted in Fig. 4.26.

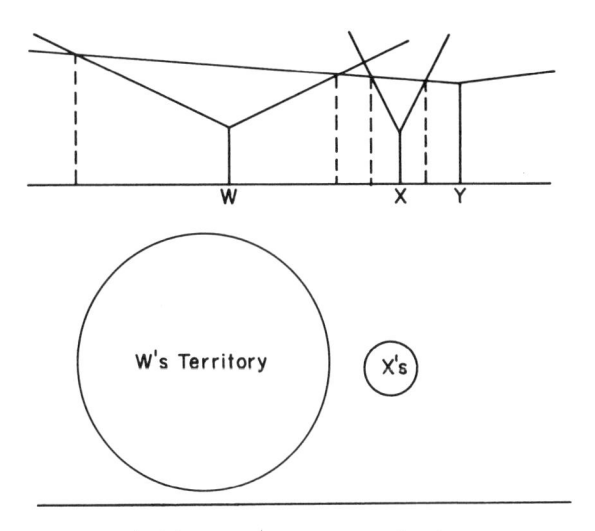

Fig. 4.26. Freight rate dominance.

Here the dominating firm is Y and despite higher on-site costs, it is able to sell below W and X everywhere except within certain boundaries where lower costs give these firms the advantage. Note that the market territories in these cases are circles. The higher costs incurred by Y might be due to terminal costs that were then offset by lower costs of transfer per ton kilometer. This limits the market in the immediate vicinity but produces an advantage up to the limit where freight rates eventually raise the spatial price to the point where competition can again enter the picture. But the competition will be someone other than W and X.

One firm, several plants. Another type of spatial pattern occurs when market areas are arbitrarily delineated. Assume completely standardized output of one product with equal costs, hence equal FOB prices at each plant, and equal rates (costs rising linearly with distance). Assume also that the decision maker wishes to assign markets among the plants in the most efficient manner. Then, between any two sellers' locations will be a "natural boundary" defined in the Löschian manner (that is, it bisects the overlap portion of circular market areas). Where more than two sellers are

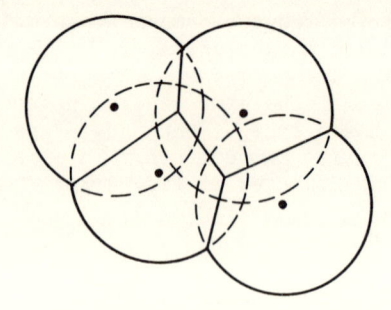

Fig. 4.27. Branch units of a single firm.

involved, the market areas will be as indicated in Fig. 4.27 with each manager enjoying a cost plus transport advantage up to the dividing lines, which are indifference loci. Assuming the firm enjoys monopoly advantages in other contiguous areas, the portion of each area where there is no possibility of substitution is circular.

Market overlap. In the above analysis, we have assumed standardized products that result in clearly defined market areas developing naturally due to each seller's ability to supply at lower delivered prices than competitors. In order to bring our theory closer to explaining the nature of the world (as all good theory is supposed to do), we must recognize that clear lines of delineation on market areas do not exist. This is due to practices in pricing that involve freight cost absorption. Transport costs can be absorbed by many different agencies including governmental agencies, the agency making the transfer, the buyer, and/or the seller.

Governments subsidize transport costs by maintaining highways, waterways, railroads, airports, and so on, at less than full cost to the users. The influence on market boundaries depends upon access of sellers to systems carrying greater subsidies. For example, if waterways are subsidized more heavily than railroads, those firms located at lake or river ports may have an advantage and be able to move into other sellers' markets. Commercial areas of government may also absorb costs involved in marketing their services,

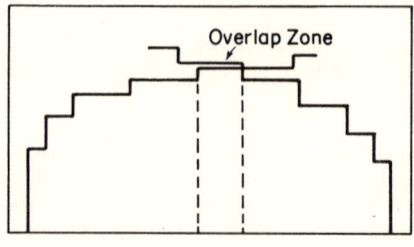

Fig. 4.28. Market area overlap owing to rate schedule bracketing.

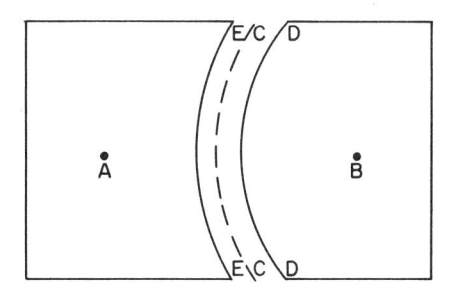

Fig. 4.29. Influence of differentiation of market boundary.

as does the U.S. Postal Service. One-way transfer agencies absorb costs for certain sellers by setting up uniform rates over certain geographic zones. This causes overlapping of market areas as shown in Fig. 4.28.

Where there is differentiation of the product (perceived differences whether real or not), buyers absorb transport costs by insisting on buying brand A even if it involves an extra trip to points further away. Thus, in Fig. 4.29, the natural boundary may be CC, but buyers who think A's product is worth more than B's will move their boundary to DD and those who favor B will move theirs to EE. Since at any one location there are likely to be both kinds, the boundary becomes a belt within which considerable overlap occurs.

Sellers often absorb part of the cost. Lösch proved that, under certain circumstances, absorption of one-half the cost of transport leads to an optimum position. This is easily done where the seller has a monopolistic position in the home market. Uniform delivered prices result from this type of situation, especially if the home market is rather large.

Market Types

We have been discussing markets as though there were one kind. In fact market structure falls into a variety of types under both spatial and spaceless concepts. The two extremes of market structure from the seller's side are polypoly (competition) and monopoly, and from the buyer's side are polyopsony and monopsony. Since most analysis is carried on from the point of view of the firm as a seller of its product, most discussions use the seller classification. We will begin there.

Nonspatial types

Perfect competition. A market is polypolistic if products of each firm compete with those of some identifiable group and each seller in the group considers his or her production to be an unimportant part of the overall market. If we add to this the requirements of a completely homogeneous product, completely homogeneous sellers, absolute independence among sellers, perfect knowledge of market information, perfect flexibility of prices, and perfect mobility of resources (but excluding absolutely free entry into the market for sellers), we have perfect competition. This concept stresses short run phenomena. If free entry is added, it becomes long run in nature, since entry involves investment. For further discussion of perfect competition, see Machlup (1952, pp. 102-12).

Imperfect polypolistic and monopolistic competition. Imperfect polypolistic and monopolistic competition are designations used interchangeably, but there is a conceptual difference. If differentiation is allowed in either the product or the seller, the market is imperfectly polypolistic. If we add free entry, the market is monopolistically competitive. The difference is in the demand curves faced by a firm under perfect and imperfect polypoly. In the first case the curve has zero slope, in the second it has some, but not much, slope downward.

Perfect monopoly. Under perfect monopoly there is only one seller whose demand curve is the total curve for the industry. This curve slopes downward and will have more slope than in the case of monopolistic competition. The product has no viable substitutes, except in the sense of one expenditure being part of all expenditures, in which case every good is a substitute for every other good.

Oligopoly. Oligopoly includes all market structures between monopolistic competition and pure monopoly. Under it there are only a few sellers. If few becomes two, it may be designated as duopoly, but this is not theoretically significant. Probably the most important characteristic of oligopoly, in addition to fewness of numbers, is the awareness each has of the actions or possible actions of the others.

Oligopoly may be organized or unorganized, but determining which class a particular group fits into is not easy. If there are only five firms in an industry, and one of them is larger than the others, it stands in a good position to exert price leadership. If it does this vigorously and brings the others under its influence, the industry can be understood to be organized to a degree. If it sets up an industry association that it manipulates to keep the others in line, it is even more organized. If it gets the others to sign an agreement splitting up the market, it has a cartel, and can be said to be organized.

If one abstracts from space and considers relationships among firms, assuming all are located in the same general area, the facts that there are few firms in the market and that each of these firms has considerable clout results in a peculiar type of demand function. Each firm must take into consideration the reactions of each of the rival firms in setting its policies. The industry demand curve faced by all of the oligopolists has a downward slope. Each firm maneuvers to claim a portion of the demand at a price that will guarantee an adequate profit. Once these positions are estab-

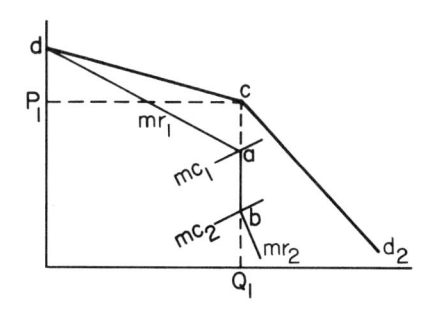

Fig. 4.30. Spaceless kinked demand curve.

lished, each firm faces a peculiar type curve, the kinked demand curve (Fig. 4.30).

Figure 4.30 depicts an oligopolist's position at price P_1 in the situation where all rivals are located in one place. The portion of the demand curve (d to c) reflecting the quantities that would be taken at prices higher than P_1 has fairly high elasticity (small slope) that means if prices were raised, consumers would react by cutting back on purchases. This would be compounded if rivals hold prices at P_1. Since an oligopolist would not expect rivals to follow with a price increase, such an increase is highly unlikely on the part of any of them. On the other hand, an oligopolist would expect rivals to follow a price decrease. The lower part of the demand curve (d_2) is less elastic than the upper part (d_1) because of this.

The result of this situation is that the marginal revenue curve (change in total revenue for each change in price) slopes downward from d to a (mr_1) has a discontinuity from a to b and downward slope beyond b (mr_2). This means the most efficient point for operation of the firm would be at Q_1 regardless of its cost position, high at mc_1 or low at mc_2. Thus, stability of pricing is to be expected in oligopolistic industries.

Spatial types

Perfect polypoly. Where price is functionally related to distance, there can be no perfect polypoly. When sellers and buyers are dispersed, each seller has some monopoly power over those customers located close by. In the discussion of the law of market areas, relationships between two spatially separated sellers were considered, but the implication was that there were others nearby, making demarcation of boundaries complex. These firms might be viewed as imperfectly polypolistic or monopolistic competitors but never as purely or perfectly competitive. Where quantity demanded is expressed as the volume of a cone, elasticity changes with changes in price.

Imperfect polypoly. Imperfect polypoly requires homogeneity in the distribution of both resources and population, which results in hexagonal market area patterns. The pattern that would persist, according to Lösch, would be the one yielding zero profits. (That is, profits in an economic sense. Costs thus include the opportunity cost of using factors, and returns on capital equal to the next best earning opportunity are not included in profits. So a firm could operate indefinitely with zero profits.) But even if resources and people were evenly distributed at the beginning of a development, over time certain spillover effects would occur that would attract sellers (and perhaps buyers) to one another. This would make competition impossible due to market control. In other words, market structure would tend toward oligopoly.

Oligopoly. Spatial considerations magnify the importance of kinked demand functions, since discontinuities develop when rivalry arises from distant sources of supply. The spatial curve is actually composed of three sections. The top section is highly elastic; attempts to raise price on the part of one oligopolist would lose the market if rivals did not follow. The bottom section may be highly inelastic if rivals follow, or elastic if they do not. The center section is a compromise toward which all oligopolists are drawn because of possible rival reaction to movement either toward the top or toward the bottom. In Fig. 4.31 it is assumed that there are two spatially separated oligopolists with initial identical prices P_{1x} and P_{1y}. The market area boundary for each (area of customer indifference) is at B_1, assuming transport costs from both X and Y to B_1 are the same. The spatial price ($P + RD$) at that point is B_1C_1.

Suppose X has a group of nearby buyers with relatively inelastic demand so they will not reduce purchases if he raises the price. He raises his price to P_{2x} to take advantage of this situation. Now Y considers her customer demand and decides to follow but not all the way. She raises her price to P_{2y} ($P_{2x} > P_{2y}$). The market area boundary now shifts to B_2. Since transport rates have not changed, line $P_{2x}C_2$ has the same slope as $P_{1x}C_1$ and $P_{2y}C_2$ has

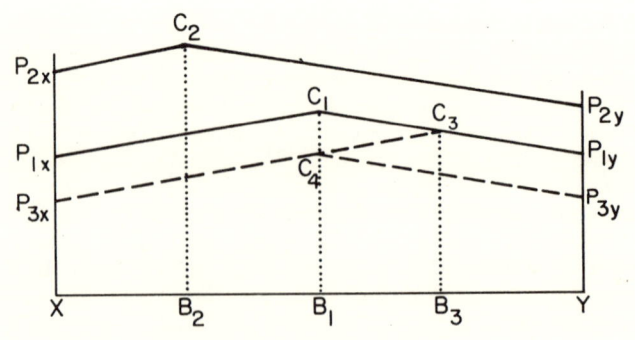

Fig. 4.31. Demand curve of spatial oligopolists.

Theory of Location

the same slope as $P_{1y}C_1$. Thus, C_2 is defined and X forfeits sales in the area from B_2 to B_1 to Y.

There would be a strong incentive for X to lower his price to the P_{2y} level. This would give both oligopolists more revenue than they were getting before but would move the market boundary back to B_1. In this case the reaction of rival Y to follow a price increase partway has limited the action of X but has actually resulted in a price increase for both. Where there are more than two spatially separated oligopolists, there is considerably more uncertainty with regard to a rival's responses. This is a primary reason for spatial oligopolists to try to split the market as evenly as possible. In this range each seller has certain freedom to act without inviting retaliation.

In general, the same result will occur if rivals follow a price decline. Suppose X's nearby buyers have elastic demand and are thus sensitive to a price decline. He lowers his price to P_{3x} hoping to increase his total revenue. There are now two alternatives for Y: she can hold her old price and forfeit some of the market whose boundary would then be at B_3, or she can follow. If she follows by lowering her price to P_{3y} ($P_{3y} = P_{3x}$), both firms will retain the same market share at a lower price. If demand in both areas were highly elastic, both firms would increase their total revenue. If demand is inelastic in Y's market, total revenue will decline for her.

In the preceding analysis, it is assumed that customers pay a spatial price that includes the full cost of transport. If demand schedules at the various markets are linear, however, we remember from the discussion that sellers can maximize profits by systematically discriminating against the nearer markets and absorbing exactly half of the transfer costs. If oligopolists absorb half the cost, this means prices at the seller's site will be higher, giving the PC curves in Fig. 4.31 half the slope. Those customers nearby will be subsidizing those further away. This will not detract from the tendency to split the market.

The many uncertainties and fears of losses explain why price stability is so common when there is oligopoly, spatial or nonspatial. Once rivals have established a pricing policy they tend to stay with it. However, competition on nonprice characteristics is common. In a spatial sense transport costs are part of pricing policy. But differences in servicing, advertising to try to win customers in a rival's territory, and other such activities are engaged in rather freely, if there is no collusion.

Collusion among spatial oligopolists occurs frequently, as when all of the barbers in a community belong to the barbers' association. The association decides $3.50 is the price of a haircut and no matter where one gets a cut, that will be the price. Further, no barber will change the price to entice more business. Competition can only take place in other areas of service. The barbers are spatial oligopolists in the sense that there are a small number, each is aware of possible retaliation for going against the rule, and they are separated spatially from other competition.

Collusion can also occur over space. That is, several manufacturers of a common good located in communities at large distances from each other can collude. This is most likely to occur if one of them is strong enough to act as a leader. The leader may indicate, by actions, the price schedule the others are to keep. Or the leader may dictate through an association that may issue a manual containing suggested prices.

Although it is rather unimportant today, the basing-point pricing arrangement was formerly in wide use in the United States. Basing-point pricing is a rather rigid pricing mechanism followed by all firms in an industry. Under this system, the price charged in any community would be the FOB price at the basing point plus cost of transportation from that point. Thus, regardless of the actual point from which the goods were shipped, the same transport charge would be made. This would guarantee that prices were the same regardless of their origin.

Nonspatial kinked curves are especially applicable where firms are located in the same general area. This explains pricing policies with regard to one another, but it fails to explain pricing policies of agglomerated oligopolists with regard to other rivals. Assume three large firms agglomerated at a point with rivals some distance away (Fig. 4.32). Assume further that they are at the center of the population distribution so that turnover is higher than at D and E. Also assume lower costs for the agglomerated firms and prices equal for A, B, and C and lower than those at D and E. The latter have some control over local buyers owing to cost of travel to the center so long as A, B, and C do not absorb freight. But suppose there is free delivery from the center, then the price differentials in favor of D and E are limited.

Free delivery means discrimination against people in the center and in favor of those in D's and E's territories. So long as A, B, and C maintain center prices below those of D and E, inner ring buyers cannot act against the discrimination by buying from D and E even if the latter also give free delivery.

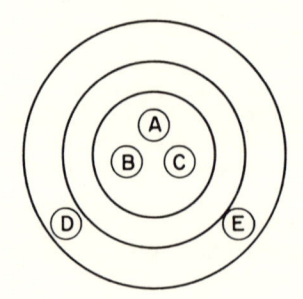

Fig. 4.32. Agglomerated oligopolists.

The firms at the center would have, in effect, a protected market and would act in concert if a price change were called for, even though there may be no formal collusion possible. These firms would tend to be larger than those of the fringe because of the population agglomeration advantage. The fringe firms would be able to serve only a small and rather select clientele for whom they would perform services not possible by A, B, and C.

Agglomeration Economies and Diseconomies

Agglomeration economies and diseconomies have important influences on the spatial pricing of goods and services. This is particularly true when the structure of industry is other than competitive, as is the case generally. Pricing policies in firms with some monopoly power are heavily influenced by costs that are in turn heavily influenced by the various economies and diseconomies associated with agglomeration.

The reasons for three firms locating in one place are to be found in the complexities inherent in the exchange of goods and services. Once we move away from simplified models containing homogeneous goods, single firms, and stereotyped customers, these complexities become readily apparent. Part are due to economies existing because units locate near one another. Since they are external to the unit, they are referred to as "external economies." They develop for a large number of reasons. For example, due to high overhead certain health services for the elderly may be very expensive if provided for only a few, but may be reasonably priced if a large number use them. The agglomeration of elderly people at one place thus produces economies that are external to each one, but internal to the group.

This would be a type of immobile economy, since it would not occur unless all of the elderly were located in one place. Economies like that also occur when certain firms of a like kind locate in one area. For an individual firm, having customers located nearby creates certain economies internal to the firm by making its internal operation more efficient.

Agglomeration economies can be divided into four classes: transfer economies; economies internal to a unit; economies external to a unit, but internal to the industry to which it belongs; and economies external to the industry.

Transfer economies. Transfer economies occur most generally because transportation networks exist. Transport networks are of various types including railroads, highways, trails, canals, rivers, and airways. There are many aspects to transportation, particularly where the automobile is concerned. For example, households experience a savings in transport costs (both in time and money) by frequenting shopping centers. This allows shopping for many items on one trip. The fact that these savings occur increases the number of households who want to participate. The larger market makes it economical for additional stores to locate there, or for existing ones to expand. Thus economies internal to the store result from economies internal to the household. For certain types of goods, shoppers like to make comparisons. Thus, certain transfer economies also result when furniture stores or automobile agencies locate near one another. These are somewhat different from economies related to a shopping center. In the one case economies occur because of lack of diversity and in the second because of it.

Transfer economies also occur because of transportation systems, including terminal facilities. Industrial firms, having widely dispersed markets, often will locate at transport nodes. Having a variety of systems available creates certain economies. For example, one place may have rail, highway, waterway, and air transport available. These are there because of certain fortuitous circumstances, but also because they are needed. There is, therefore, a cyclical relationship between supply and demand. Internal economies are available to the firm because facilities were built to serve other firms as well. Many of these economies result from specialized loading and unloading equipment that the firm could not afford on its own.

Transfer economies also occur when proximity allows direct transfer of output from one unit to another as input. For example, a steel fabricator located next to a steel rolling mill can have hot steel transferred directly, eliminating the need for reheating. Other savings occur when there are several successive states of processing in one area, such as an aluminum extrusion plant located near an aluminum plant. In this case the savings are in avoidance of loading, unloading, and movement costs, and are reflected in spatial prices of the input goods.

Internal economies of scale. Whenever agglomeration economies make it possible for a plant to operate on a larger scale, or in a more efficient manner, the economies are internalized. That is, they are reflected in the firm's costs. Increasing returns to scale means that if inputs are doubled, output will more than double. This is to be contrasted with constant returns, where production changes in the same proportion, and decreasing returns, where it declines. Another way of stating this is to say that the industry enjoys decreasing costs as quantity increases or that its costs remain constant or that they increase. Agglomeration contributes to decreasing costs by making it possible to obtain larger amounts of input at lower prices or to market larger amounts of output on some preferable basis, for example, concentration of customers at one spot.

Ways that costs are reduced. One way that size makes possible lower costs is by allowing greater specialization in the division of labor. It is common knowledge that specialization leads to efficiency to a considerable degree. Firms generally begin operations on a small basis. Under those circumstances, people tend to handle a number of different operations. Time is wasted in moving from one kind of work to another and one seldom has a chance to become proficient at anything. When the size of plant reaches a certain level, it is possible to begin breaking up the production and distribution processes into parts. This allows people doing each job to continually work at it, thus saving transfer time and building greater dexterity. Such specialization also allows coordinators to make more efficient use of differences in skill, aptitudes, and talents. The management process itself may also be helped by being broken into areas of specialization, such as finance, personnel, marketing, production, procurement, and maintenance.

Economies of scale result in lower costs, so long as the extra cost necessary to establish departments and other divisions of skills is more than offset by greater efficiencies. It is supposed that operations of a certain size are more efficient than those smaller or larger, since in the one case, efficiencies of specialization will not be fully realized and in the other case, cost of coordinating excessive division of labor more than offsets the advantages.

Automation also may mean lower costs. When a man is given a more efficient tool and learns to use it to its full potential, production necessarily increases. The same concept applies when the tool is a machine. Since most large capital goods come in certain sizes, a firm may gain internal economies by expanding to make use of larger and/or more sophisticated equipment. This is true only if the extra costs of the equipment, and better-trained personnel to operate it, are more than offset by value of increased production.

So long as the acquired equipment is operated by people it is called automation; when it is operated by a computer and/or other sophisticated devices, such as radar or laser, it is called cybernation. In a cybernated plant the only human operators may be those who monitor the computers and other controlling machines. These persons are necessarily highly trained and well paid. Again, lower per unit cost is the justification for making the necessary investment and incurring higher overall costs.

Paradoxically, a firm may reach a size that allows it to obtain greater efficiency by subcontracting certain of its processes to outside firms. Agglomeration economies make this possible by attracting to an area firms with like input demands. This gives the outside contractor a good market in which to operate and makes these services available to all firms in the area. Increased efficiency through specialization cuts costs for contracting customers. The firm making use of these services finds its costs are favorably affected, providing it has enough volume to hold per unit transfer and other costs down as well as to get volume prices from the contractor.

Every firm enjoying internal economies of scale is heavily dependent upon the coordination skills of management to keep costs down. It is an unusual situation when capacities of all types of equipment, buildings, people, and all other factors in the production process have the same optimum levels of production maximization and cost minimization. Further, each part of the production

and distribution process is likely to have its own optimum level of operation.
It is management's job to organize all facets of the plant or firm in such a way as to optimize overall operations. This often means less than optimum levels of other units or processes. Where a firm finds that optimal production and distribution levels are higher than optimum manageable size, it may turn to disintegration of processes or it may be ripe for merger with a firm having greater management talent. By disintegrating it can take advantage of management talent of contractors. By merging, it can beef up its own stable of talent.

Economies of scale to the firm, internal to the industry. If many firms in the same industry locate plants at one point because of economies of scale external to each plant, this is a most efficient point for the industry. Generally, these economies are related to spatial pricing of key inputs. Specialized service firms may be able to charge considerably less if they operate in a large rather than small market. Thus, a firm specializing in repair of looms could serve several textile mills. Once it is established, it becomes economical for other textile mills to locate nearby. All mills would gain from the lowered service charges. Some other types of external economies, internal to a given industry, include (1) those requiring a large input that would lower waste disposal costs, (2) presence of a large pool of labor trained in skills peculiar to the industry, (3) possibility of interaction among research and development staffs, or (4) the presence of key subcontractors.

Economies of scale external to several industries. Costs of production for several nonrelated industrial units may also be affected because all of them locate in one general area. These include transport costs and a large and flexible labor force trained in skills useful in more than one industry. The presence of specialized industrial, commercial, financial, and public services could also be important.
Many of these economies result because units are located in communities that in turn are located near other communities, as in an urban region. These are often called "urbanization economies." A set of urban communities tends to draw specialized industries that would not be attracted without a large market readily available. In turn, their presence makes it possible for firms using their services to save time and money by settling in the same general area.
These types of service (discussed later as hierarchical-type industries) include specialized repair functions that can serve many different kinds of plants, equipment and space rental, warehousing, lawyers, accountants, engineers, business consultants, advertising, investment brokers, power, and cultural activities that lower costs of enticing management skills. Units enjoying these types of scale economies are especially difficult to entice into rural communities, since input costs are higher there.

Agglomeration diseconomies. Agglomeration is not always advantageous. Some disadvantages stem from diseconomies of scale for an industry. If an industry becomes too large in one place, it may be necessary to reach too far for additional materials. Wages may be pushed too high because the union has more leverage in one place than in several.

Other types of diseconomy may be unrelated to scale but be of considerable importance. Land values may get too high because of heavy demand. Congestion on roads and highways slows traffic and causes problems for people trying to get to work. Pollution may make it necessary to clean air and water before use. Public services may break down if there are too many households or other units. Sewers may get overloaded; water supplies may fall short; energy supplies may not be sufficient; all of these can cause prices of inputs to rise.

Role of Transport Cost in Plant Location

Transport cost is only one factor in determining plant location. In many cases it is not the most important one. Yet it is important often enough that its role deserves a place in spatial microtheory. The cost of an input to a firm, located at the site of the input, will be the FOB cost at the point of production, or in the case of labor, at point of residence. At any other spot it will be higher due to cost of movement. When there are several inputs, management must locate the plant where overall input costs will be lowest. This may mean locating away from the lowest cost point for any one input.

Under conditions where such things as personal and subjective considerations, processing costs, location of competitors, and other factors affecting location can be ignored or held constant, choice of location site can be said to depend on transport costs. This is especially true when the freight and total cost ratio is high, and when it varies widely among different sites. Under these conditions the maximum profit point is often the one where transport cost is minimized. If the market for the product of a plant and the source of its major inputs are spatially separated, vertical dispersion of locations results.

Inputs fall into two general classes: limited in distribution and ubiquitous. In the case of ubiquitous inputs, high transport costs often limit market areas to be served from a plant. Thus the number of cement plants, utilizing fairly ubiquitous limestone, is usually limited to the number needed to serve the immediate area. As new markets develop, new plants are opened. Plants utilizing water as a major input (such as producers of bleaches, soft drinks, and malt beverages) are probably even more likely to build for a local market. Plants utilizing nonubiquitous inputs may be oriented toward the market if cost of shipping the product is higher than the cost of shipping the input. Plants may be materials oriented if the opposite situation holds.

When plants are materials oriented, it may be because overall transport costs vary more widely than other costs among various sites, and/or materials tend to lose considerable weight during conversion to the plant's product, and/or freight rates on materials tend to be higher than on the product. But when plants are market oriented, it may be due to the fact that the product is perishable, and/or the product weighs more than its major material inputs, and/or freight rates on products tend to be higher than on materials, and/or fluctuating demand causes inventory problems that are less costly with location close to the customer.

<u>A simplified model</u>. Assume a plant using one material input that is available at point X, converts by a simple one-stage process into a product that can only be sold at Y. Transport costs are of two kinds, cost of bringing the material to the factory and cost of taking the product from the factory to Y. (See Fig. 4.33.)

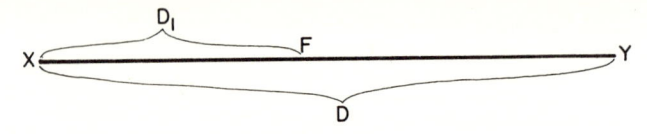

Fig. 4.33. One material, one market.

Let D_1 be the distance from X to factory F and D be the distance from X to Y. Assume transport cost per kilometer for enough material to make one unit of product c_m and per kilometer unit transport cost for product c_p. Let C be the total transport cost per unit. Then $C = c_m D_1 + c_p(D - D_1) = D_1(c_m - c_p) + c_p D$. One would expect the plant to be located where C is minimized, ceteris paribus. Suppose $c_m > c_p$, the coefficient of D_1 is positive so the manager will locate the plant at X. If $c_p > c_m$, the coefficient of D_1 is negative and the plant will locate at the market.

<u>Moses model</u>. The Moses model was developed to show that profit maximization is a function of properly adjusted output and input combinations, location, and price (1958).

The case of two inputs and variable rates. Assume two transportable material inputs (M_1 and M_2) used to produce a single output that is sold at a single market point (C). Let the distance between the location of M_1 and C be designated a and the distance between M_2 and C be designated b. The angle included between these lines is θ (Fig. 4.34).

We now fix the distance from C to the locus of production (whatever it may be) at the value h. Thus, h becomes the radius of a circle. However, we are only interested in the portion of the circle that runs from I to J within the locational triangle, since the location of the materials and the market preclude locating a production point outside it. Fixing the radius simplifies the

Theory of Location 119

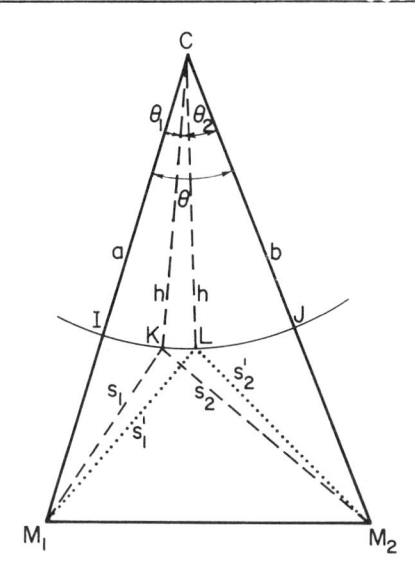

Fig. 4.34. Locational problem.

problem. Now all attention can be paid to the impact of materials movement.

Note that this is basically Weber's locational triangle. Moses has modified it to fit into a partial equilibrium problem in which the distance the final product is to be shipped is held constant. This distance defines an arc (cutting the triangle at I and J) along which all points are possible production locations. The cost of movement of the product is thus constant, a ceteris paribus condition.

Let s_1 be the distance from M_1 to a production site K and s_1' be the distance to another site L. Likewise s_2 is the distance from M_2 to K, and s_2' is the distance from M_2 to L. Let r_1 be the transport rate for material M_1, and r_2, the rate for M_2; and let P be the FOB price and $\hat{P}$ the CIF price of the inputs. Then $\hat{P}_1 = P_1 + r_1 s_1$, for the delivered price of material M_1 and $\hat{P}_2 = P_2 + r_2 s_2$ for the delivered price for M_2 to point K. Prices at L would be $\hat{P}_1 = P_1 + r_1 s_1'$ and $\hat{P}_2 = P_2 + r_2 s_2'$.

The ratio $(P_1 + r_1 s_1)/(P_2 + r_2 s_2)$ is the slope of an iso-outlay line (amount paid out is equal everywhere) relating to the point K. Likewise $(P_1 + r_1 s_1')/(P_2 + r_2 s_2')$ is the slope of an iso-outlay line relating to L. Since $s_1' > s_1$ and $s_2' < s_2$, the slope of the line for L will be greater than that for K. Each locus on the arc has such a line whose slope is defined by a ratio of delivered prices. Where prices and/or transport rates change, each locus will have a set of iso-outlay lines each defined by given values.

In Fig. 4.35 the iso-outlay line associated with production at point I, on the a leg of the triangle, is designated AB; the iso-

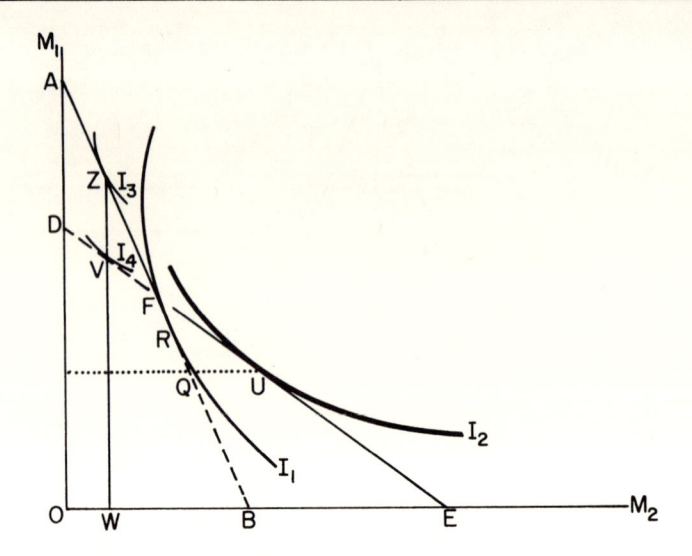

Fig. 4.35. Locational optimization.

outlay line DE is associated with J on the b leg (Fig. 4.34). These lines are tangent to two isoquants, I_1 and I_2, representing different levels of production, $I_2 > I_1$.

Point F represents a point of cost equality between the loci. The AF portion of line AB is tangent to the isoquant (I_3) at point Z, and the DF portion of DE is tangent to a lower isoquant (I_4) at point V. Since this relationship holds for all of the pre-F portions of these lines, the locus I (Fig. 4.34) has an advantage in that region. In contrast, FB lies below FE, hence would be tangent to lower isoquants, giving the advantage to J for this region of the illustration. The advantage at point Z over point V stems from the fact that location at I would allow the use of more M_1, which has a low delivered price, and the same amount of M_2 to produce the higher quantity I_3. The same argument could be applied to point U vs. point Q where more M_2, which has a lower delivered price to J than does M_1, is combined with the same amount of M_1 to produce the higher quantity I_2.

Here we are assuming (1) that M_1 and M_2 are substitute materials, (2) that their FOB prices are comparable, and (3) that one does not have a sizeable freight rate advantage over the other. These assumptions are built into the iso-outlay lines. We also assume that larger production of the end product would not result in too little revenue because of its influence on the price.

If each of the loci on the arc were compared in like fashion to each of the others, lines similar to AFE would be developed for each pair. Thus, the advantage or disadvantage of each point with regard to particular isoquants would be revealed. The combination would produce a smooth curve with each point on it showing a particular combination of M_1 and M_2 that the firm could purchase at a

Theory of Location 121

given location (considering the size of operation allowed by the basic firm budget plus transport rates and base prices of the two inputs). This curve may be called the iso-outlay curve.

The iso-outlay curve tells us that if continuous substitution between inputs is possible (that is, every point on the curve is a possible choice), then it is possible to find an optimal combination of inputs for each locus on the arc. Therefore, this curve is the result of an optimizing process. The optimal points will define a locus of location where the iso-outlay curve is tangent to the highest possible isoquant.

In Fig. 4.36 iso-outlay lines have been constructed for eight sizes of operation. Operation size is determined by tangency of the overall budget with an isoquant. Optimal location is then determined by tangency of the iso-outlay curve with that isoquant. The shape of the iso-outlay curve is determined by price and freight rates for the two inputs. For example, if the iso-outlay curve were determined by only two points and for the price and freight rate relationships shown in Fig. 4.35, and if the operation size were to produce at the amount defined by isoquant I_3, then location would be at I. But if production were to be at the amount defined by I_2, location would be at J.

Larger budgets make greater production possible; hence, as budgets increase they define optimal points on higher isoquants. Suppose management wishes to produce at the level of isoquant I_7 (Fig. 4.36). The iso-outlay curve ZZ' represents the constraint on budget that would be required, and point P defines the volumes of M_1 and M_2 that would be needed in order to maximize profits. Point P also defines a particular location along the arc IJ of Fig. 4.34. Thus, the firm would choose the location at which the ratio of delivered prices (slope of the iso-outlay line) would equal the slope

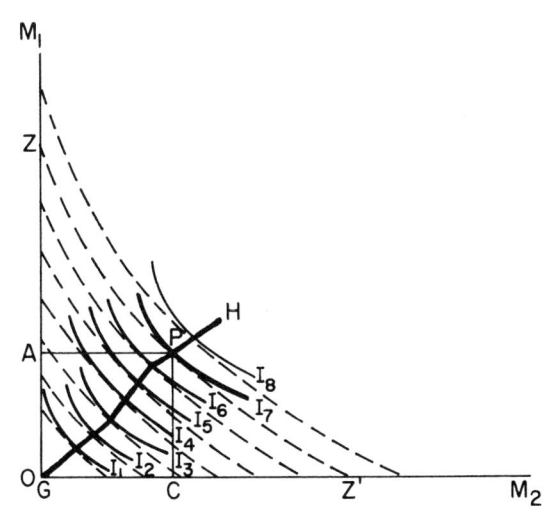

Fig. 4.36. Optimal locations with different budgets.

of the I_7 isoquant. At this point, it would utilize OA units of M_1 and OC units of M_2. Total expenditure of these inputs would be at a minimum. Line GH traces an expansion path for the firm, each point of which identifies both a location along the arc IJ and a combination of inputs that are optimal in terms of profit maximization.

Spatial cost curve. To this point, only transport costs have been considered, but they are not the only costs that vary over space. In this section all spatial costs will be considered.

The usual type of economic cost curve holds location fixed and indicates how costs vary with level of output. The spatial cost curve assumes that once level of production is determined it stays constant and shows how costs of production vary over space, under those circumstances. Basic costs are those incurred in the usual procedure of producing goods; to these are added the locational costs incurred in moving factors to the actual plant location. These are the costs considered in the Moses model, plus such things as differences in costs of labor, power, or even costs of capital that occur among geographic areas.

The spatial cost curve is really an iso-output curve because it assumes no change in basic operations, that is, the solution is for one isoquant, thus all emphasis can be placed on changes in per unit costs that result from factors affecting location decisions. The Moses model gives us some explanation for the U shape of the curve. There are multiple locations that are feasible in a spatial context with the possibility that there may be more than one least cost point.

As indicated in the Moses model, if the level of output changes, a new cost curve is required and the least cost location is likely to change. Economies of scale (agglomeration economies) may cause the curve to shift downward for higher isoquants, thus expanding the area within which location options are possible. Where economies of scale are not neutral among locations, then it is possible for different-sized plants in the same industry to have different least cost locations.

Effect of taxes and subsidies. Communities often try to attract industry by giving subsidies. Governments often use both taxes and subsidies as a means of influencing location. The effect is to shift the cost curve up and down. In Fig. 4.37 both types of shifts are shown. The shaded areas reflect the size of tax or subsidy.

In the area $BCB"C"$ the object is to cause a plant to settle in either areas BX_1 or CX_2. This is done by imposing a tax sufficiently high to cause an actual loss (area above AR) if the plant is placed between B and C. The areas BX_1 and CX_2 now become the feasible areas for location. In the area $DED'E'$ the objective is to attract industry to an area completely outside its possible range by giving a subsidy that has the effect of lowering the cost curve for that particular area. The new least cost location would

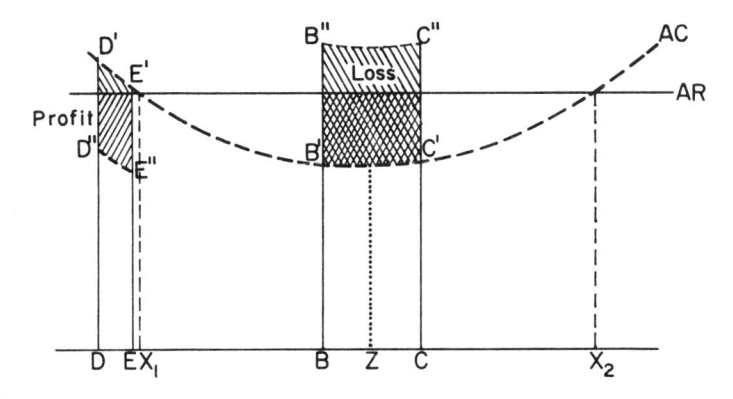

Fig. 4.37. Effect of tax and subsidy.

be E. This type of subsidy must be permanent unless something happens to actually lower the cost curve for that plant.

Effect of differences in managerial skill. Where units face differences in skills of managers, a different spatial cost situation evolves for each firm. The highly efficient manager has a much wider range of location choice than a less efficient one. This is shown in Fig. 4.38.

In that figure, AC represents the average situation in the industry. Within the industry, unit S can produce at 10 percent below average cost of the industry and unit T at 10 percent above. The space cost curve for unit S (ACS) gives it a possible profit, anywhere between MS_a and MS_b, that is much wider than for the average firm ($M_a - M_b$). That for firm T (ACT) gives the firm only a little area of possible profit, $MT_a - MT_b$.

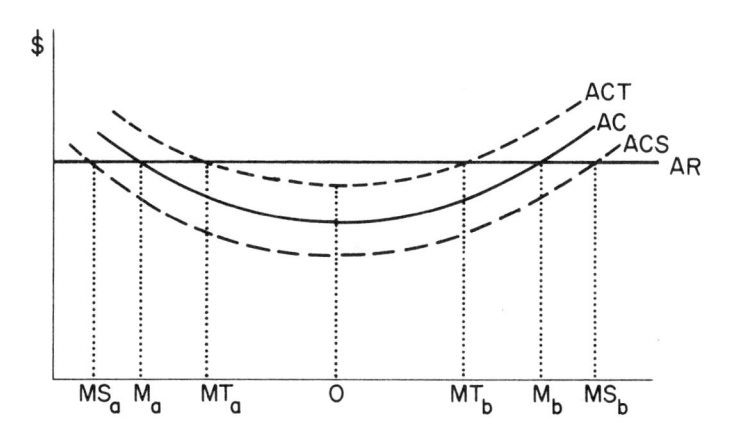

Fig. 4.38. Effect of differences in entrepreneural skill.

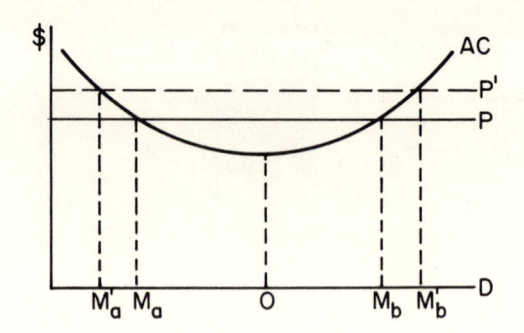

Fig. 4.39. Effect of change in price.

Effect of change in price. The effect of a change in price on locational possibilities is given in Fig. 4.39. The original price line gives a margin for decision from M_a to M_b. Raising the price increases the margin to $M'_a - M'_b$. The point of maximization stays the same as long as the change in price is uniform in space. Lowering the price would compress the margin for decision.

Effect of change in cost of a factor. Suppose a unit uses two factors of production each of which can be purchased at particular points (A and B) at $10 for each unit of output. The cost for B declines over a considerably greater distance than does A, and A rises over a much larger area than does B, but both spatial cost curves are U-shaped. A total cost curve (ATC) is derived from the factor cost curves ACB and ACA. According to Fig. 4.40, it costs about $2 per unit to ship both inputs to the optimum location point O. Assume the product can be sold for $30 no matter where the plant is located. The limits of profitability are at M_a and M_b. Optimum profitability is at O.

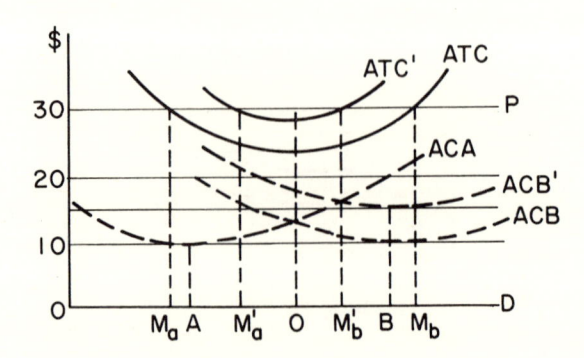

Fig. 4.40. Change in the basic cost of one factor of production.

Theory of Location

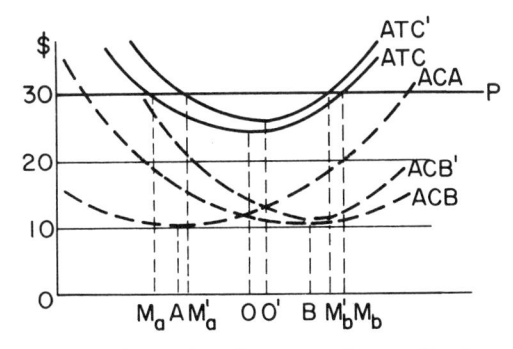

Fig. 4.41. Change in locational cost of one factor of production.

Assume factor B has a price increase at the source to $15. This causes an increase of $5 in the cost of each unit of output. The new cost curve for factor B is ACB'; optimum profitability is still at O, since it still costs $2 to ship the material, but limits move in to M_a' and M_b'. Alternatives are now extremely limited.

Effect of change in freight rate. Assume cost of moving B from its source increases by $1 because of increased freight rate. A new ACB' is plotted and a new ATC' (Fig. 4.41). The result is not only a contraction in the limits but a shift in the optimum location from O to O', which is closer to source of factor B. Thus, although a change in price of an input changes margins only, a change in freight rate affects both margins and optimum points.

Effects of a simultaneous change. Assume the process by which factor B comes into being has a technological breakthrough that results in the base price being halved. At the same time freight rates are renegotiated resulting in a halving of the locational cost. The new cost curve ACB' is below the old one. (See Fig. 4.42.) The new total cost curve is ATC'. Margins have widened

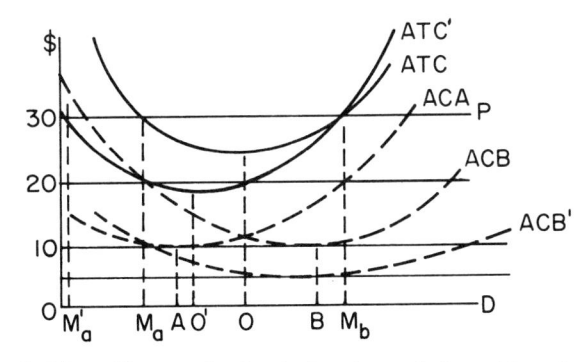

Fig. 4.42. Change in both basic and locational cost.

from (M_a, M_b) to (M'_a, M_b) and the optimum point has shifted toward the source of factor A whose locational pull is now stronger.

Replacement of a high locational cost factor with a ubiquitous one.
Assume input B is coal, the cost of which increases away from its source. Because of development of a huge hydroelectric project, large amounts of electricity become available. This can be purchased at $14 per unit of product anywhere the manager decides to locate; the cost curve (*ACE*) is a straight line. Note that the cost of coal at its source is $10 per unit of product. Between points R and S coal is cheaper than electricity. The cost curve for energy, from whatever source, follows the *ACE* curve to R, the *ACB* curve to S, and the *ACE* curve beyond S. This is reflected in the *ATC'* curve as well, since it corresponds to *ATC* between R and S. The general effect of introducing electricity is a widening of the margins of choice by moving M_a to M'_a. M_b is not affected. Thus, the shift is in favor of factor A, with the new optimum for location of production at A. (See Fig. 4.43.)

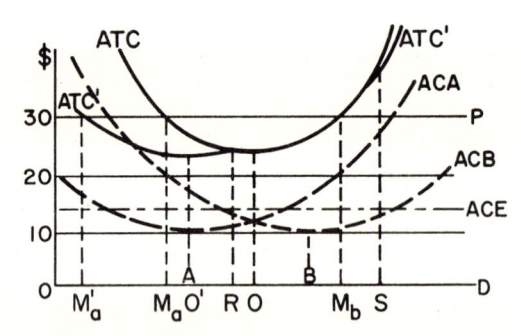

Fig. 4.43. Replacement of a spatially variable factor by a ubiquitous one.

SUMMARY

Microtheory explains economic behavior of individual decision-making units. When applied to the impact of space, it considers decision making under circumstances where the units are either spatially separated or where space has an impact on the decision itself. Since the same general concepts are used for the analysis of the impact of space, as for spaceless economics, the latter are given a place in the discussion.

The basic problem of scarcity is generally assumed to be solved by the price system, when it operates efficiently. Pricing over space is somewhat different from pricing in a spaceless society. Under definitions used in the analysis, a market may be considered either as a context or a place. In spatial economies, it is regarded as a place. Equilibrium is a balancing of market forces. Partial equilibrium is an analytical device by which only certain items are allowed to vary. Comparative statics is a method for stopping the processes so they can be studied, and dynamics is the study of the processes by which equilibrium is achieved. Under general equilibrium analysis all market forces are expected to achieve a balance, thus an equilibrium among market areas involves balance between supply and demand in each market as well as a balancing of supply and demand among markets.

The general law of market areas states that the boundary between two areas tributary to two geographically competing markets for a homogeneous good is a hypercircle. It demonstrates the significance of transport rates in determining market power of individual sellers. Other types of configurations result when one firm serves several market areas with a plant in each, when political entities use rate scales that bracket causing a zone of no advantage to various sellers, and where product differentiation causes people to cross market boundaries.

Market structure also influences spatial pricing. It is most obvious in the case of oligopoly. Since space confers monopoly power, it rules out the possibility of perfect competition, even if all of the usual assumptions were satisfied. A spatial duopoly will lead to each seller absorbing half of the transportation cost. Where oligopolists agglomerate, they tend to combine against rivals from outside the immediate area. Agglomeration economies are manifested in those internal to a firm that contribute to scale economies, those internal to an industry but external to the firm, and those external to the industry. There are also diseconomies resulting from agglomeration.

Location of an industry is heavily influenced by factors that influence its costs. Transportation costs for inputs and products are important as are other factors, such as coordinational skills, labor costs, and public policy.

REVIEW QUESTIONS

1. What are Von Thünen's contributions to spatial economics?
2. How did Weber build on Von Thünen's concepts?
3. Why did Weber begin his analysis with all things held constant except transportation?
4. What was the rationale behind his locational triangle?
5. How did he handle transport rates?
6. How do transportation systems impact on his locational triangle?
7. Discuss Weber's analysis of the impact of labor costs using the isodapane idea.
8. Why did Weber think agglomeration and deglomeration would affect location?
9. Discuss Christaller's concept of central places.
10. Show how Christaller utilized basic Von Thünen concepts.
11. How do traffic routes alter the distribution of towns based on the marketing principle?

12. How does government change distribution based on the marketing principle?
13. In what way did Lösch improve on the isodapane idea?
14. Lösch used Varignon's Frame differently from Weber. What was the difference?
15. What were Lösch's ideas about town settlement?
16. Show how Lösch used ideas of Von Thünen and Christaller to develop the demand core and market networks.
17. Distinguish among $K = 3$, $K = 4$, and $K = 7$ market patterns.
18. How did hierarchical distribution of centers differ under Lösch's system versus that of Christaller?
19. What is Lösch's argument about freight cost absorption?
20. How did Lösch feel that freight rates affected market areas?
21. What other factors did he feel were important in location?
22. What is the general law of market areas?
23. How does this law explain freight rate dominance?
24. What are some of the other factors that affect location of plants with regard to complementary or competitive plants of the same type?
25. Why would spatial oligopolists tend to split their market and absorb half of the transportation cost?
26. How do interactions differ when oligopolists are spatially separated vs. those that are agglomerated?
27. Discuss the various kinds of agglomeration economies and show how they affect location.
28. Using the Moses model, show how a company might move toward an optimum location where costs of transporting materials and budgets are the major constraints.
29. Using the spatial cost curve, show how each of the following affect location:

   a. subsidies
   b. taxation
   c. entrepreneurial skill
   d. change in price of the product
   e. change in price of one material
   f. change in the freight rate for one material
   g. replacement of a high locational cost material with a ubiquitous one

REFERENCES

Christaller, W. 1966. *Central places in southern Germany*, trans. C. W. Baskin. Englewood Cliffs, N.J.: Prentice-Hall.
Fetter, F. 1924. The economic law of market areas. *Quarterly Journal of Economics* 39:520-29.
Hoover, E. M. 1937. Spatial price discrimination. *Review of Economic Studies* 5:182-91.

Lösch, A. 1954. *The economics of location*, trans. W. H. Woglom. New Haven: Yale Univ. Press.
Machlup, F. 1952. *The economics of sellers' competition*. Baltimore: Johns Hopkins Press.
Moses, L. 1958. Location and the theory of production. *Quarterly Journal of Economics* 72:259-72.
Predöhl, A. 1952. Das standart problem in der wirtshaftstheorie. *Weltwirtschaftliches Archiv* 21:306.
Smith, D. M. 1966. A Theoretical Framework for Geographical Studies of Industrial Location. *Economic Geography*, Apr.
Von Thünen, J. H. 1826 (Hamburg)/1966. *The isolated state, part I*. Trans. C. Wartenberg. Elmsford, N.Y.: Pergamon Press.
Weber, A. 1971. *Theory of the location of industries*, trans. C. Friedrich. New York: Russell & Russell.

CHAPTER 5
The Location Decision

Most communities are concerned about growth and development so that decisions made by business people regarding the location of plants and other facilities are important to them. We have discussed many of the factors affecting location under an implied assumption that management knows all the pertinent information needed to make decisions. Since most location decisions are made with regard to investment, they are long run in nature. This means they are made with certain perceptions of the future in mind. This brings the decision maker face-to-face with the problem of uncertainty.

ROLE OF INFORMATION
   The amount and quality of information available to a decision maker defines the amount of uncertainty involved. Adequate, accurate information creates a situation of certainty. If the future can be known perfectly, good location decisions should be expected of a rational decision maker. But, the future can very seldom be known with certainty, hence most location decisions must be made under conditions of uncertainty.
   There are two types of uncertainty. Absolute uncertainty implies the availability of no reliable information at all. Risk implies the existence of some information so that the decision maker can choose among alternatives on some sort of rational basis. A decision maker will try to operate under conditions of risk, rather than absolute uncertainty, and will devote resources to the collection and analysis of information.

Types of Information Needed
   Location decisions require seven types of information (Serck-Hanssen 1970) revealed by the following questions:

   1. What alternatives are available?

The Location Decision

2. What possible states of nature will have to be faced?
3. What factors will affect the states of nature?
4. What would be the consequences of each alternative for a given state of nature?
5. What are the probabilities of each state of nature occurring?
6. What strategies are available?
7. What choice criterion is to be used in solving the problem?

Alternatives. In every location decision more than one alternative is possible. There are alternatives regarding regions within which to locate. This may involve a region of the world, such as a continent. It may involve a country within a continent. It may involve the region of a country, or a particular part of a larger region, such as a state, province, or urban area. It does involve the community where the operation actually settles.

The process of collecting information regarding alternatives can be very costly. Usually a large amount of secondary data will be needed, much of which can be gathered from sources such as censuses and administrative reports of governmental agencies. Where secondary data do not suffice, primary data collection may become necessary. Since these procedures are costly, communities can enhance their chances of being chosen by assuming some of this chore.

Types of data needed include market data, such as population size, age distribution, per capita income, income distribution, and transport networks; production information, such as size and skill level of the labor force, existing wage rates for various skill levels, productivity of workers (including attitudes), degree of unionization, work stoppage history, location of possible raw materials or semifinished inputs, possible industrial and commercial sites (including available buildings); local financial assistance, such as the issuance of industrial development bonds to construct buildings, transportation freight rates, time distance to various markets; and the transport alternatives, such as railroads, trucks, barge, and air; agglomeration factors, such as the kinds of business and industry already in the area and community attitudes toward growth.

The one thing communities have to avoid in providing such information is the tendency to exaggerate, or provide inaccurate information aimed at enhancing the local image. This is known among location specialists as "chamber of commerce" data. Communities providing this kind of data often find it has not even been considered.

States of nature to be faced. A state of nature is a situation beyond the control of the firm. It can include such things as weather patterns, terrain, water supplies, business cycles, governmental decrees, and actions of rivals. The decision maker collects information that enables him or her to put a probability value on each state of nature that may be faced. There are three ways of assigning probabilities: the Laplace, historical, and Bayesian approaches. The Laplace principle states that when nothing is known, every event is equally likely. Historical probability is based on experience gained from past trends and experiments. The Bayesian approach is based on opinions. These will be discussed in more detail later.

Factors affecting states of nature. It is a mistake to assign probabilities to states of nature without considering the fact that something may change the state itself. A change in governmental philosophy, the eruption of a volcano, pollution of the atmosphere, depletion of underground water supplies, social policies that affect business cycles, and changes in birthrates and death rates are a few of such factors. New states of nature may arise that must be dealt with.

Consequences. These are sometimes called payoffs. They are values assigned to each action. They may be positive or negative depending upon the situation. Usually actions with negative consequences are avoided. Collection and analysis of information leading to the establishment of possible consequences is very important in decision making. This is where a lot of resources are likely to be used. The criteria problem, to be discussed later, is especially important here.

Probabilities for each state of nature. Since states of nature are beyond control of the firm, they are the major sources of uncertainty. Decision making under complete uncertainty is almost impossible, so the decision maker will assign some kind of probability to each identifiable state of nature. The problem lies in getting and properly processing the required information. Raiffa (1970) has indicated that the first question to be faced is, "What would perfect information be worth?" In short, how much money can one afford to spend in perfecting one's information? If perfect information would be worth $50,000, this places a limit on what one would want to spend trying to perfect it.

If the decision is made that it is not worthwhile to collect information about an absolutely uncertain situation, then the decision maker can consider each state of nature to be equally likely. Where historical or experimental data are available, the probability of a given state can be obtained directly. Where such data are not available, but it is possible to get the opinions of knowledgeable people, Bayesian approaches can be employed to develop estimates of probabilities for each state of nature.

Possible strategies. A strategy is a decision rule for choosing actions to be taken. One frequently used strategy is to choose that action with the highest expected value (EV). An example would be the following payoff matrix:

	States of Nature		
Actions	I	II	EV
A_1	50	30	38
A_2	45	35	39
Probability	.4	.6	

The expected values are obtained by weighting the payoff for each possible action by the probability for each possible state of nature. In this case, the highest expected value would be for action A_2. The strategy would lead the decision maker to choose an action with only a slightly larger payoff than the other possible alternative, but uncertainty has been decreased somewhat.

Criteria. The criteria problem is important in decision making. In order to make reasonably efficient decisions or even to rank preferences, a decision maker must be able to identify proper criteria by which to measure the relative merits of alternative courses of action and to distinguish preferred vs. nonpreferred combinations of consequences. McKean (1958, Chap. 2) has identified a number of areas where the criteria problem becomes acute.

Problem of suboptimization. A decision to locate a plant would seem to be a fairly straightforward thing. But there are many aspects to such a decision that require separate analyses. For example there may be many inputs of material to consider and transportation costs may vary by the item.

Under these circumstances, analysis often has to be broken into categories for it is impossible to examine everything at once. Part of the decision may require an arbitrary type of criterion. Another part may require acceptance of the status quo. Still another may require drastic changes in basic functions. Whenever this type of situation exists, a firm runs a risk of suboptimization. That is, a danger exists that criteria adopted at a lower level may be unrelated to higher level criteria. This means that strong pressure must be brought upon subunits to gear their location decisions to overall objectives of the firm.

Another type of suboptimizing problem arises from choosing inconsistent criteria. A common one is to attempt to maximize gain while minimizing cost. Maximum gain is infinitely large and minimum cost is zero. If one manager tries to optimize by maximizing gain and another by minimizing cost, the subgoals will be in conflict. The criteria are not consistent. Making these criteria consistent would result in striving for some overall goal, such as maximizing profits. Thus, suboptimization would have to be eliminated.

Neglecting spillovers. The action of one company, in selecting a site for a plant, will often affect gains and costs of the other firms. These have been referred to before as agglomeration effects or spillovers. Criteria must include these factors for an accurate location decision. When several firms are moving at about the same time, rivals' actions must be given probabilities, and the decision criteria must take into consideration the spillover effects of their moves. Community leaders interested in economic development should be aware of these factors, good and bad. Where spillovers are favorable to location of a firm, they should be emphasized. Where they may be detrimental, the dangers involved in trying to entice both firms to the same general location should be explained.

Handling of sunk costs. A decision to relocate should not be influenced by the amount invested in existing facilities at an old location. Where a plant has become obsolete, the relevant cost is the amount necessary to bring it up to the same condition as a new plant of adequate size; the amount already invested is irrelevant. Often community residents become upset when they see a company abandon an old plant that seems to be in good physical condition. But the criteria selected for the decision making should recognize the irrelevance of sunk costs.

Allocation of joint cost of a multiproduct venture. Where a plant produces more than one product, as is often the case, location decisions may involve moving product lines. Where costs for individual products can be identified, they are called "separable costs." All others are "joint costs." Some people argue that joint costs should be allocated on an equitable basis among purposes and projects. But this contributes nothing to good decision making. Good economic theory tells us that the present value of total benefits ought not to be less than the total cost of the project and that present value of benefits from each product ought not to be less than the total separable costs related to that product. A decision to move one of the product lines would involve either its selling below separable costs and/or the ability to lower the separable costs at another location, without lowering the overall efficiency of the first plant.

Some types of decision criteria. Where the analyst has no history or experience to apply to analysis in setting probabilities of occurrence of a state of nature, he or she must improvise. There is no really satisfactory solution for a completely uncertain situation. Therefore, while many people have suggested approaches such as maximin minimax, minimization of regret, and use of the Laplace criterion, it is up to the analyst to find some way of logically attaching a probability to each potential state of nature. The Bayesian approach is the only good criterion for this problem (Hirshleifer and Riley 1979).

Let us assume, for example, that all acts, states of nature, and consequences are known. The problem, then, is to work out estimates of probability for the states of nature. But the analyst knows the information is poor. How can it be improved?

He or she must begin with the current information. Let Π_s be the initial belief as to the state of the world; this includes all known states of nature. Information can, then, be acquired [that is, one of a known set of possible messages $M = (1, 2, \ldots, m)$ can be received] that will lead to a revision of Π_s. Let Π_{sm} be the revised probability belief, $Pr(S|M)$ be the probability that state S is true given that M is true, and $Pr(M)$ be the probability that M is true. Other symbols will be quite similar. The revised probability will be determined by Bayes's theorem (5.1),

$$\Pi_{sm} = Pr(S|M) = Pr(M|S)Pr(S)/Pr(M) = q_{m.s}\Pi_s/q_m \qquad (5.1)$$

where q_m is the probability of receiving message m and the conditional probabilities are $q_{m.s}$. These are related by (5.2).

$$q_m = \sum_{s=1}^{S} q_{m.s}\Pi_s \qquad (5.2)$$

Figure 5.1 illustrates the Bayesian recalculation of probabilities on the basis of a given message m where given states of the world are on a continuum from 0 to some upper limit S. The prior information, Π_s, indicates that there is a greater probability for a high state than a low one (an intense recession vs. a mild one). A message is received that indicates a much higher probability for the smaller value of S ($q_{m.s}$). The analyst has considerable confidence in the prior information, but is influenced by the latter so that the new distribution, $\Pi_{s.m}$, contains elements of both.

The greater the amount of confidence an individual has in prior information, the less time and effort will be given to collecting additional information. The value of informational actions is based essentially upon the expected utility to be gained from shifting to better choices among a set of terminal actions. This model demonstrates a well-known fact, that we tend to judge and assess new information on the basis of information we already have available to us. Thus, a person's ability to utilize information is not only a function of the amount, timing, and accuracy of the information, but also of his or her ability to interpret it.

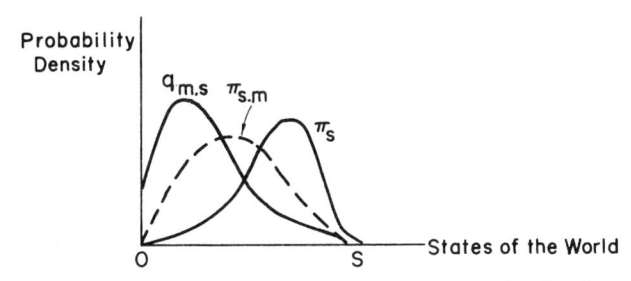

Fig. 5.1. Bayesian probability recalculation.

The way information is used is also important. Once it becomes available, several alternative ways of reaching a goal may be determined, and they all may seem, at first glance, to be equally attractive. In order to make choices, the list of alternatives has to be organized and ranked. Both ranking and final choice of a solution may be heavily influenced by the way the decision maker interprets the information. To a community leader interested in luring a new plant to the area, the procedure used in making location decisions may appear obscure. Perhaps an understanding of problems faced by those making location decisions would be of value. A good manager will always decide in ways he or she feels will help the firm achieve its overall goals. This may or may not fit in with goals of a given community.

Importance of the location decision to community economics. An economy exists because funds flow into it from trade with other communities. This trade tends to be highest with certain kinds of industry. Therefore, the location of these industries in the community is important to its well-being as well as its growth.

Basic-type industries often develop in the hometown of the founder. But they remain there only if the situation is favorable to their growth and development. If not they move elsewhere. Success in one location will likely lead to expansion, sometimes with branch plants. Branch plants are often located to give better service to a market, to exploit a new material source, to take advantage of low cost labor inputs, or one of the other factors affecting the location decision. The whole gamut of economic development activity at the community level is related to the location decision.

DECISIONS RELATING TO SPATIAL STRUCTURE

Most theories having to do with the structure within communities and urban regions are extensions of the ideas of Von Thünen, Weber, Christaller, and Lösch. However, we must recognize the importance of historical factors, such as technological level of the founding society, and the role of defense in original design. These factors are particularly important in older areas of the world. Primitive communities were often laid out with defense the main consideration and access purely secondary. Many of these structures are still in evidence. Attempts to modernize are often frustrated by the necessity to destroy much of the infrastructure to gain room for movement.

Von Thünen's concept was developed during a era when walled towns were still important. Yet his model was based on a market town, with economic factors dominant. Perhaps this explains why it has proven so useful. The central idea of the model is still generally accepted. Activities compete for space, and this competition results in an efficient allocation.

Minimization of Function Cost

A basic hypothesis to most spatial structure models is that

The Location Decision   137

organization of the community reflects attempts by units to overcome the "friction of space." Distance stands as an impediment to interaction and must be overcome if an effective community is to be realized. The costs are in the form of transport and rent. Under this hypothesis, the optimal site for an activity is the one that furnishes a desired degree of accessibility at the lowest cost. An efficient transport system results when distance has been overcome and activities are located in the proper places. Corollary to this, where activities are distributed over space, the system is inefficient. As Fales and Moses (1971, p. 49) have noted:

> The technology that formed the nineteenth century city is not the technology of our age. The motor truck freeway, and interstate highway have reduced the cost of intraurban goods transport. They have reduced the need for physical proximity between manufacturing firms that use each other's products as inputs and have given them greater freedom in location. In addition, the service sector is much more important in today's cities than it was in the last century. These changes mean that an effort to explain locational patterns of industries and households in modern cities might well need different variables and a more complicated approach. . . . Intraurban variations in wage rate and labor supply functions might well prove to be more important in such a study.

It must be recognized that many communities in the world have not advanced beyond the plans for a nineteenth century city. Many of these are in underdeveloped areas, but many communities in technically advanced areas are still trying to readjust. This is particularly true of inner-city communities. For these the Von Thünen-based models still have some value.

Concentric zone theory. According to the concentric zone theory, a community grows in five concentric zones: (1) the central business district, (2) the transition zone where business and industry encroach on residential areas, (3) a zone consisting of independent workingmen's homes, (4) a zone of better residences, and (5) a commuter's zone. These zones can be thought of as occupying approximate circles radiating outward (Fig. 5.2A).

In this theory, as the community grows, each zone extends its area by invading the next one. If the community's population declines, outer zones remain stationary, but those next to the central business district recede toward it, creating slight problems. The economic explanation is that friction costs consist of transport costs plus rent and that the dual of the minimization of friction costs is maximization of rent (transport costs = negative rent).

Each unit occupying a piece of land receives a value equal to what it is willing to pay in rent. If a household, this would be explained as utility; if another type unit, as marginal product. If conditions are competitive, bidding for land will insure that

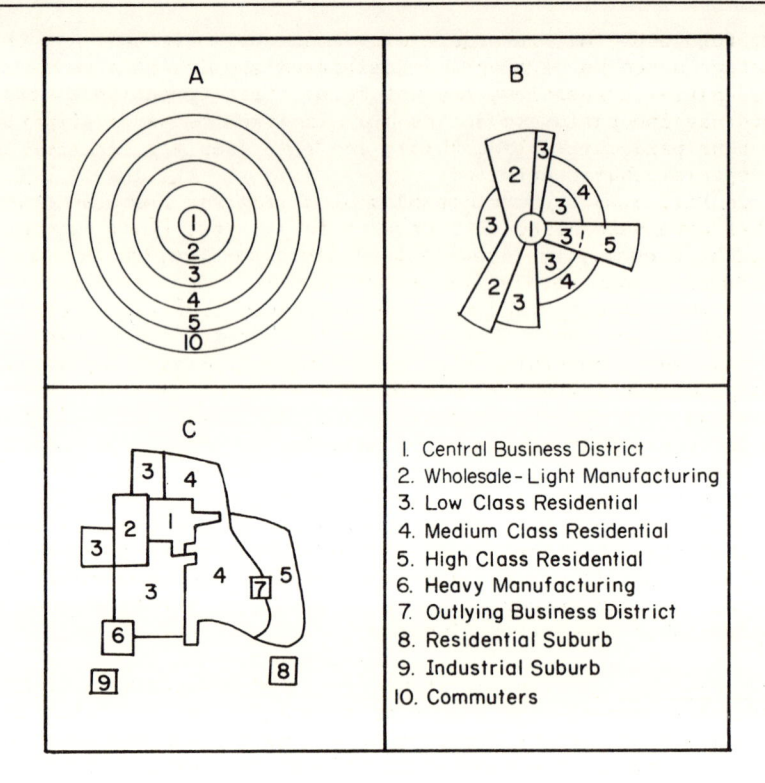

Fig. 5.2. Generalized internal structure of communities.

each site is devoted to its highest and best use. This results in an orderly pattern of land use.

As an urban region develops, many communities branch off from the original configuration. Thus, we find many ghetto communities where multiple housing consists of old mansions that once graced a particular zone of the city when it was first formed.

Sector theory. A somewhat more refined application was made by Homer Hoyt (1939) in his theory of axial development. According to this idea, growth takes place along main transportation routes (lines of least resistance) to form corridors, in a somewhat star-shaped pattern, of like land use. The community is thought of as originating as a set of circles, with the central business district maintaining its circular shape. Similar types of land use originate near the central business district and move outward along the transportation corridors. Thus, expansion takes place in only limited parts of the concentric circles (Fig. 5.2B).

A number of explanations are given for this. Among them are that concentric circles apply only to a restricted concept of a uniform flat plain, traversed equally well in all directions. However, topography may interfere with concentric circles; and transportation networks develop and activities are drawn to them. Further, spatial assumptions may not hold: free competition seldom exists; agglomeration economies and diseconomies may be important (the rent paid may reflect this); and some uses may require sites with special characteristics.

In Fig. 5.2B, a corridor of wholesaling and light manufacturing has developed along a route, possibly a rail line, running through the community. Low- and middle-class residential areas have developed in earlier times and tend to remain as the community grows. The different income classes tend to live in rather distinct areas, but there is a downward rent gradient extending outward and, where possible, people take advantage of it. The high quality residential areas tend to pull certain types of growth with them along the fastest transport routes and toward open country. Certain types of growth, such as shopping centers, also influence directions of growth of the upper-class area. Nevertheless, growth of a zone tends to be in the same general direction over time. Eventually, if an urban region develops, certain communities will form that have characteristics derived from certain sectors. For example, a high income bedroom community may be the culmination of movements along transport routes. Other kinds of communities may form from what was left behind.

Single nucleus, no circular structure. The structure illustrated in Fig. 5.2C reveals the impact of square surveys but maintains the same general concept of development around the central business district. This is the type of configuration one might find where a railroad is located near the central business district.

Multiple nuclei. The concept of the three previous explanations is that communities develop around a single nucleus, usually the central business areas or the town market. But many communities develop around several different kinds of nuclei (Harris and Ulman 1945). These may include the central business district, an industrial park, or a university. Once developed, a nucleus provides the focus for other types of development. Nuclei develop because

  1. Certain activities require specialized facilities. These are most easily provided at certain sites and create agglomeration economies.
  2. Certain kinds of units are interdependent. They need to locate near one another so that this interdependence will not interfere with operations.
  3. There are also economies of disagglomeration. Some units are completely incompatible. Thus, a retail district and a district composed of heavy industry would necessarily locate at some distance apart.
  4. High land costs attract certain kinds of units and repel others.

5. Political and social factors may dictate location of some units. A university may be located at a particular point because that is where an influential man wants it. Government activities may seek cohesion with other service activities or may be located by themselves.

In general, Von Thünen-type models are based on the concept that households tend to cluster about nuclei formed by other activity. This concept reveals lack of appreciation of the impact of modern transportation technology, notably the automobile. Development of shopping centers in American communities is largely oriented toward the existence of housing units. Thus, households in existence may themselves function as nuclei.

Location of Households
A great deal of time and effort have been expended in recent years in attempts to develop general principles that will satisfactorily explain why households locate where they do. In general, the models have been based on certain assumptions regarding the reaction of people, accessibility, space, distance, and transport costs. People may be assumed, for example, to be concerned with minimizing the cost of getting to the place of employment or of getting to a shopping area. The rents they are capable of paying are influenced by location of the residence with regard to the area where economic activity is carried on. In accordance with Von Thünen's thesis, rents (hence land values) tend to be higher the closer the site is to the community center. This implies that rents are actually negative transport costs. As Haig (1926, p. 422), one of the first space economists to give attention to households, expressed it:

> In choosing a residence purely as a consumption proposition one buys accessibility precisely as one buys clothes or food. He considers how much he wants the contacts furnished by the central location, weighing the "cost of friction" involved—the various possible combinations of site rent, time value and transport cost: he compares this want with his other desires and his resources and he fits it into his scale of consumption and buys.

Von Thünen model. Wingo (1961, pp. 63-68) has identified certain critical considerations in arriving at the amount, distribution, and value of land for residential purposes. He uses a Von Thünen format. Basic assumptions are

1. A population homogeneous with regard to income and tastes
2. Given location of employment centers
3. Given transportation technology
4. Known marginal value placed on leisure
5. Known marginal value placed on residential space by households

The Location Decision   141

    6. Constant prices, except those for residential space
    7. Price of land, zero at the community boundary, increasing with movement toward the center

He begins with the proposition that the relevant characteristics of the transportation system can be summed up in its cost characteristics. Monetary costs of transportation are defined as a function of distance traveled, terminal costs, and commuting time. Cost of transportation for a household at location i is given by X_i. The rent for a site $R = rq$, where r = location rent, and q = quantity of land. Costs of transportation and rent are linked. Regardless of location, each household spends a sum on rent equal to the cost of transportation to the community boundary, X_m (marginal location m); or rent on land is equivalent to cost of transportation saved by not incurring it. This can be expressed as

$$R_i + X_i = X_m \quad \text{or} \quad R_i = X_m - X_i \tag{5.3}$$

Position rent for land is equal to the annual savings in transportation costs compared to the highest cost in location use.

A diagrammatic solution. Assume that factors such as living space, physical and service amenities, location and prestige value are weighed by householders when they make a purchase. Assume also that the price of all other goods is given, household demand for space is uniform throughout the population, and space has diminishing utility for the household. In Fig. 5.3 position rent lines relating rental rates to size of plot are shown on a log chart as R_1 through R_{12} and a space demand curve (a, a) is plotted. Every household operates at some point on the aa curve (and every point

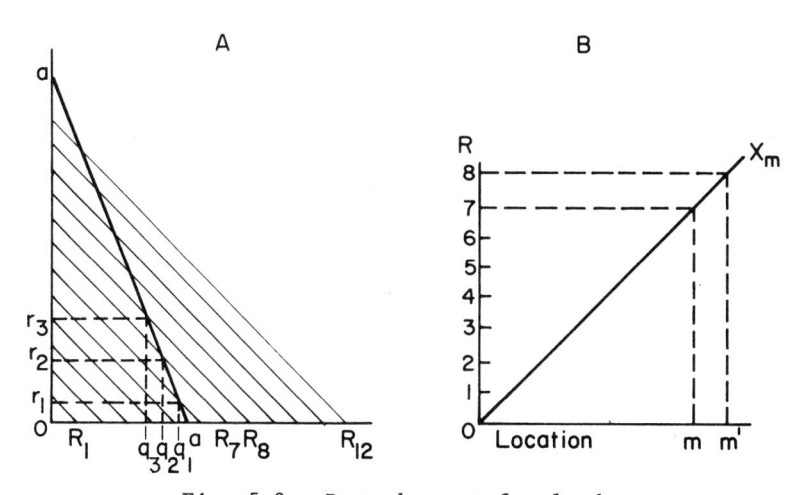

Fig. 5.3. Demand curve for land.

on aa lies on an R_i curve, since there are an infinite number of them).

Assume X_m constant for all users and let the community expand to margin m' ($m' > m$). This causes position rent to shift outward, so that the household enjoying position rent R_7 and lot size q_2 would shift to R_8 and cut back lot size to q_3. This is because of increased distance from the perimeter and a larger population. This means that the size of site occupied by the house is inversely related to the price of land. Let A and b be parameters related to the demand function for land, $b > 0$, and let P_i = price of land, then:

$$q_i = A^b/P_i \qquad (5.4)$$

At any given location in the community (5.3) will fix the money spent on position rent and (5.4) will determine the size of lot. Price of land emerges when the equations are solved simultaneously. This means that an equilibrium solution for each household is possible.

Now let t = the transport rate and d = distance, then $X_i = td_i$ and $X_m = td_m$. Equation (5.3) can now be rendered as (5.5).

$$p_i q_i + td_i = td_m \qquad (5.5)$$

Since X_m is zero at the community center and highest at the margin, it is a 45° line. Since rent is negative transport cost, it is highest at the center and goes to zero at the community boundary. Fixed position rents are paid by the household at each location; the rents depend upon distance from the community center (Fig. 5.4).

According to (5.4), demand curves will slope downward. Since we are assuming that households are homogeneous (have the same income and tastes), the demand curve will be the same for all house-

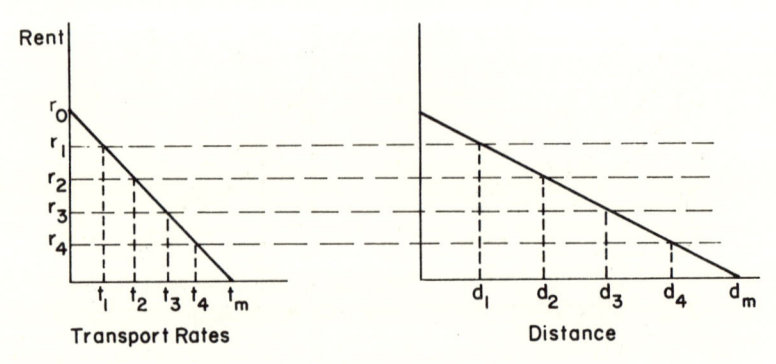

Fig. 5.4. Relationship of rent to cost of transportation.

The Location Decision

holds. The nearer the center of the community the higher will be the rent and the smaller the site. Given the household demand curve and the position rent to be paid in any concentric ring from the center (defined by $d_1, d_2, \ldots, d_m$), it should be possible to determine the price of land and the amount to be occupied by each household in that ring. Note that rents and transport rates move in opposite directions. At distance d_4, rent is r_4 and transport rate is t_4.

Equilibrium between demand for and supply of land is illustrated in Fig. 5.5. The supply of land within each concentric ring is fixed, hence the supply curves ($S_{d_1}, S_{d_2}, S_{d_3}, S_{d_4}$) are infinitely inelastic (vertical). Since the circumference of a ring increases with movement away from the center, if each ring is the same width, the aggregate amount of land contained in each one increases also. Thus we say $S_{d_4} > S_{d_3} > S_{d_2} > S_{d_1}$.

A market solution requires that the total supply of land within each ring must equal aggregate demand for land, within that ring, at the ruling price. Since the price of land must be consistent with individual equilibrium, the demand curve must intersect the supply curve where the position rent meets it. Households near the center of the community will pay relatively high rent and occupy relatively small sites. For total equilibrium to be achieved the households must distribute themselves over the community in such a way that the ruling land prices equate demand with supply in each ring. All equilibrium points (D_{d_1} to D_{d_4}) can then be joined to form a household demand spatial equilibrium schedule. An increase in the number of households will shift this curve to the left, since the supply of land is constant. This will cause households to pay higher rent and live on smaller parcels of land (or closer together).

A technological breakthrough lowering the cost and/or inconvenience of traveling or a rise in the income level may cause the

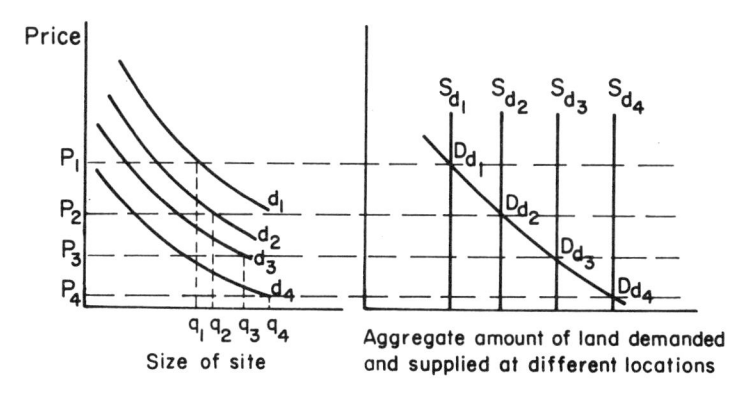

Fig. 5.5. Equilibrium between demand for and supply of land at various distances from the center.

community boundary to expand. This will make more land available and add supply curves. It will not necessarily lower the price of land, however, unless marginal transport costs become so low as to cause an across-the-board fall in spatial densities.

The solution to the model depends upon there being fixed budget constraints, which is realistic for short periods of time only. However, it might be approximated over time by drawing up demand functions for each of several income classes. This might help to explain such things as the tendency for site size and location distance from the center to increase with income. There are many things, of course, not allowed for in the model, such as competition for land in residential areas for nonresidential uses, or the fact that households reflect differences in taste. Nevertheless, it explains some of the regularities seen in the allocation of space among households and the structure of living densities and land values.

Yamada's model. Yamada (1972) notes that although most models dealing with residential location are concerned with the trade-off between accessibility and space, people have become interested in other factors as well, particularly leisure time and environmental quality. Yamada considers three possible trade-offs: (1) accessibility and space, (2) space and leisure, and (3) accessibility and environmental quality. He does this by introducing into the analysis a time element utilizing recently developed theories for the allocation of time, and an environmental element. He notes, for example, that distance from a central business district may have negative utility from an accessibility standpoint, but may have positive utility in terms of environmental quality.

A nonlinear programming model is used with both time and budget constraints. It is basically a Von Thünen concept, since it is assumed that a community located on a homogeneous plain has all its employment and services located in its central business district. It deals with a consumer who spends a certain proportion of available time traveling to and from the central business district. The consumer wants to maximize utility for residential location, subject to the two constraints, budget and time. Three kinds of costs are considered: transport cost (RD), time spent in travel, and negative utility of travel.

It is assumed that out-of-pocket money cost, t, is the linear and increasing function of radial distance from the central business district, (k), or $t = t(k)$, where $t' > 0$ and $t'' > 0$. Time spent in travel, C, is assumed to be a linear function of distance or $C = C(k)$, where $C < 0$, $C' < 0$, and $C'' = 0$. Note that time spent has negative value in the utility function. It is also assumed that the consumer has a fixed source of nonwage income, $\overline{y}$, and a wage income proportional to his or her working time, wW, where w is wage rate per unit of time and W is working time. Since working time is also an input in the utility function, and people are assumed to prefer leisure to work, it has negative value. Income, then, is defined as $y = \overline{y} - wW$, where $W < 0$. It is further assumed, in good Von Thünen fashion, that rent is a decreasing and

The Location Decision

convex function of distance from the central business district or $r = r(k)$, where $r' < 0$ and $r'' > 0$.

Since the consumer must pay for a quantity, q, of land at a rent $r(k)$, must also buy other commodities, z (a composite commodity), at a given price p, and must pay cost of transportation, $t(k)$, out of y, the consumer's budget function is

$$g_1(z, q, W, k) = \bar{y} - wW - pz - r(k)q - t(k) \geq 0$$

Two other constraint functions are also defined. One is a function on time expressed as

$$g_2(L, W, k) \equiv T + W + C(k) - L \geq 0$$

where T is total time available and L is leisure time. In other words, time spent at work and in commuting plus that spent on leisure activities cannot be more than the amount of time available. It is further assumed that the consumer must work at least $\bar{W}$ hours, which is fixed and standard. This gives us the other constraint function,

$$g_3(W) \equiv -W + \bar{W} \geq 0$$

which says that time taken from leisure for overtime work is greater than or equal to zero. Under these assumptions, then, the consumer's utility depends not only upon consumption of goods and land but upon the way time is allocated among leisure, work, and travel. It is also assumed that it is influenced by environmental quality.

Environmental impact is brought into the model by that assumption and further assumptions that environmental quality is a function of distance from the central business district and has positive value in the utility function. We have, therefore, $E = E(k)$ where E is environmental quality and $E' > 0$. Now the utility function is

$$u = u[z, q, L, W, C(k), E(k)] \tag{5.6}$$

All partial derivatives of u with respect to each element are positive and identified as u_z, u_q, u_L, u_W, u_C, and u_E. The utility function is assumed to be continuous, twice-differentiable, and strictly concave. The problem now becomes:

Maximize $u = u[z, q, L, W, C(k), E(k)]$

subject to $\bar{y} - wW - pz - r(k)q - t(k) \geq 0$

$T + W + C(k) - L \geq 0$

$-W + \bar{W} \geq 0$

$z \geq 0, \; q \geq 0, \; L \geq 0, \; k \geq 0$

Yamada suggests that this be solved be setting the constraints to zero thus making the formulas equalities and suitable for use of the Lagrangian. This also involves satisfying Kuhn-Tucker-Lagrange conditions for a maximum. A general conclusion can be drawn in this way that if travel time can be cut, the consumer can increase his or her satisfaction by enjoying more leisure with more land at a location farther from the central business district. Of course, if we relax the assumption concerning work having negative utility and make the model more realistic, this solution does not hold. People seem willing to put up with a certain amount of pollution in order to work.

Location of Business Firms

Richardson's locational equilibrium model. Richardson's locational equilibrium model is designed to show that a firm will locate at a point where the price of land is equal to the price the firm is prepared to pay to assure profits (1969, Chap. 6). The following assumptions apply to this model:

1. The community is completely centralized (no shopping centers)
2. The more central the location, the greater the access to consumers
3. The price of the firm's product is given (one may conclude at this point that sales volume and total revenue increase as the firm approaches the city core)
4. The firm is faced with a given structure of prices for land varying inversely with distance from the community center
5. The land is all of equal quality
6. The land is bought and sold in a perfectly competitive market
7. Firms aim at maximizing profits
8. No other factors affect the rent of land

The model. This model deals with bid price, or isoprofit curves. Let P = a price of land, d = a location, $\overline{X}$ = a constant level of profits, and bP = a bid price. The $bP = f(P, d, \overline{X})$ = the price of land bid by a firm at a location such that when the size of site is optimized the firm will achieve a constant level of profits.

The model has the following properties:

1. The bP function is single valued (there is only one P at each d).
2. There is no intersection of bP curves.
3. Lower bP curves represent higher profit levels and are preferred.
4. The normal slope of bP functions is downward, that is, the greater the distance from the center, the higher the operating cost, the lower the revenue, and the lower the rent. A set of

The Location Decision   147

bid price curves is thus analogous to a set of indifference
curves, under spaceless analysis, except that on an indifference
map the higher curves are preferred.

The bid price lines are labeled a', b', c', and d' in Fig.
5.6. These represent the preferences of the firm: $a' > b' > c' > d'$. So the firm would like to go as far as possible. But bidding for land produces a demand curve P_d that serves as a constraint line. The point D is the point of equilibrium, where profits will be maximized, setting location of the firm at d_e and rental at P_e.

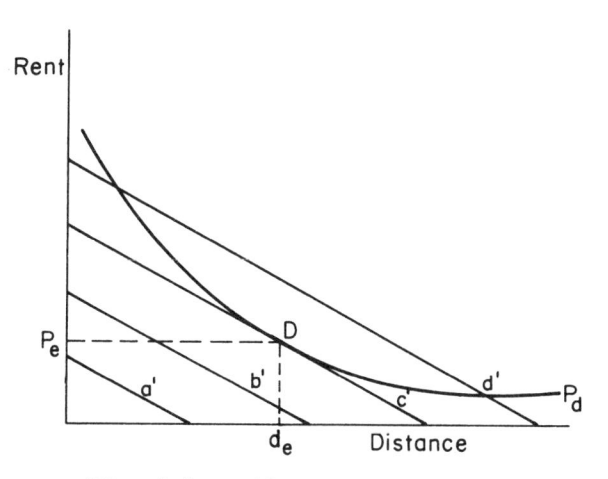

Fig. 5.6. Bid-price equilibrium.

The conclusion based on this analysis is that as a firm moves outward from the community center its revenue falls and its operating costs increase due to increased transport costs, but rent is lowered. At each location the rent differential is exactly sufficient to compensate for the change in operating costs and revenue, and thus a constant level of profits is attained and the firm is indifferent among locations. At each point between the center and the point where operating cost plus some minimum level of profits equals revenue, the firm will be willing to pay a certain land rental. A large number of such possible locations exist. The firm will locate at the point where the price it is prepared to pay will insure its profits at the proper level.

Reilly's law of retail gravitation. According to Reilly's law of retail gravitation, a town attracts retail trade from an individual customer in proportion to its size and in inverse proportion to the square of the distance separating the individual from the town center (1929). Thus, the boundary separating two communities could be defined, in terms of their attractions for shoppers, as the locus of points for which $P_x/d_{bx}^2 = P_y/d_{by}^2$ where P_x = population of town x, and d_{bx} = the distance of the center of x from a given point b on the boundary.

This turns out to be a special case of a more general model (Toyne 1974). Size is not necessarily an important factor by itself, rather it is associated with a number of others that make a particular point attractive to a customer. The frequency with which a customer will visit a given shopping center varies directly with its attractiveness and inversely with the distance to the center from the customer's home. Reilly's formula has the advantage that it can be readily utilized, whereas the more general model requires data development.

The formula for the general model is

$$F_{ij} = K(A_j^\alpha/d_{ij}^\beta)$$

where F_{ij} = expected frequency of interaction between customer i and destination j; A_j = attraction of destination j; d_{ij} = distance between i's home and j; K = a constant; α = a parameter suggesting agglomeration economies; and β = a parameter. The term A_j must be defined in some way (through surveys), and α and β must be estimated from survey data.

The Baumol-Ide model. The Baumol-Ide model does an even better theoretical job of explaining customer-store relationships than does the Reilly formula, but it is difficult to implement empirically (Baumol and Ide 1956). A consumer's demand function for shopping at a particular location is

$$F(ND) = WP(N) - V(C_dD + C_n\sqrt{N} + C_i)$$

where $F(ND)$ = net benefit realized by shopping at the location; N = number of items offered; D = distance between the customer's home and the shopping center; W and V = subjective weights assigned by the customer; $P(N)$ = a probability satisfaction function; C_d = transport costs (proportional to distance); $C_n\sqrt{N}$ = assumed cost of actually shopping; and C_i = opportunity cost of shopping elsewhere.

The implications of this model are that the minimum number of items required to induce a customer to shop at a shopping area increases with distance; the maximum shopping distance is where $F(ND) = 0$; and consumers discriminate among items according to their location. This means that a given shopping center may be optimal for a grocery but not a hardware store. This would depend upon weights supplied by the customer and may have no significance at all.

A General Conclusion

Attempts to explain location of household and other units

within a community in terms of the cost of friction of space give us some understanding of the general configuration of the community. But it must also be conceded that many other factors, some of which are impossible to measure, enter into the picture. In communities where the automobile is a big factor, patterns develop that are heavily influenced by time. Thus, shopping centers develop away from the community center because land is available for parking; thus customers save time and experience less inconvenience in looking for parking space. Once a person is in a car, he or she may visit several shopping centers or may restrict activities to one. There is no doubt that land used for a shopping center is more valuable than land used for residences. This is due to agglomeration factors but has little to do with location in reference to the community center.

SUMMARY

Location decisions involve investment, hence are long run in nature. This means that the decision involves the future and a degree of uncertainty. Uncertainty is defined by the amount and quality of information available to the decision maker. Success in utilization of available information is also partially influenced by ability of the analyst in making proper interpretations. Interpreting ability is based on information already held by the interpreter.

Seven general types of information are needed for location decisions. They may be identified by seven questions.

1. What alternatives are available?
2. What possible states of nature will have to be faced?
3. What factors will affect the states of nature?
4. What would be the consequences of each alternative for a given state of nature?
5. What is the probability of occurrence for each state of nature?
6. What strategies are available to the decision maker?
7. What choice criteria are to be used?

Location decisions are important in the founding, configuration, growth, and development of communities. Some of them will be made by firms, some by individuals, and some by public agencies. All of these are heavily influenced by the availability of information and skill in its interpretation.

REVIEW QUESTIONS

1. How does lack of information impinge on location decisions?
2. How do inaccuracies and distortion affect decision making?
3. Why are the right criteria important to the decision maker?
4. How might the tendency toward suboptimization impact on a location decision?

5. Discuss the role of sunk costs and joint costs in a location decision.
6. How can a decision maker, in an uncertain world, act to overcome uncertainty?
7. What is the basic hypothesis of spatial models concerned with community organization?
8. Discuss: concentric zone theory, sector theory, multiple nuclei.
9. Show how Wingo, using a Von Thünen approach, explains variation in rents (or cost of housing) in various parts of the community.
10. What did Yamada add to the explanation?
11. How does Richardson's model differ from those of Wingo and Yamada?
12. In discussing location of industrial and business units, how do the models of Reilly and Baumol-Ide differ in application?

REFERENCES

Alonso, W. 1964. *Location and land use*. Harvard Univ. Press.
Baumol, W. J., and E. A. Ide. 1956. Variety in retailing. *Management Science* 3:93-101.
Burgess, E. W. 1929. The growth of the city. In *The city*, ed. R. E. Park. Chicago: Univ. of Chicago Press.
Fales, R., and L. N. Moses. 1971. Land use theory and the spatial structure of the nineteenth century city. *Papers of the Regional Science Association* 28:49.
Haig, R. M. 1926. Toward an understanding of the metropolis. *Quarterly Journal of Economics* 40:421-23.
Harris, C. D., and E. L. Ulman. 1945. The nature of cities. *The Annals of Political and Social Science* 242:7-17.
Hirshleifer, J., and J. C. Riley. 1977. The analytics of uncertainty and information--an expository survey. *Journal of Economic Literature* 17:1375-1422.
Hoyt, H. 1939. *The structure and growth of residential neighborhoods in American cities*, U.S. Federal Housing Administration. Washington, D.C.: Government Printing Office.
Machlup, F. 1952. *The economics of sellers competition*. Baltimore: Johns Hopkins Press.
McKean, Roland. 1958. *Efficiency in government through systems analysis*. New York: Wiley.
Raiffa, H. 1970. *Decision analysis*. Reading, Mass.: Addison-Wesley.
Reilly, W. J. 1929. *Methods for the study of retail relationships*. University of Texas Bulletin 2944. Austin: Univ. of Texas.
Richardson, H. W. 1969. *Regional economics*. New York: Praeger.
Savage, L. J. 1962. Bayesian statistics. In *Recent developments in information and decision processes*, ed. R. E. Machol and P. Gray, pp. 162-67. New York: Macmillan.

Serck-Hannsen, J. 1970. *Optimal patterns of location.* New York: North Holland.
Thompson, J. H. 1961. *Methods of plant site selection available to small manufacturing firms.* Research Center, W. Va.: West Virginia Univ.
Toyne, P. 1974. *Organization location and behavior.* New York: Wiley.
Webber, M. 1972. *The impact of uncertainty on location.* Cambridge: M.I.T. Press.
Wingo. L., Jr. 1961. *Transportation and urban land.* Baltimore: Resources for the Future.
Yamada, H. 1972. On the theory of residential location accessibility, space, leisure and environmental quality. *Papers of the Regional Science Association* 29:125-235.

CHAPTER 6

The Community as a Supplier of Goods and Services

PRIVATE VS. COLLECTIVE GOODS

Goods and services can be supplied either through direct purchase by the household unit or through some sort of collective arrangement among households. There is a difference in the kinds of goods and services that can be provided in these ways; the first kind is called "private" and the second, "collective." The general nature of private goods is that their benefits flow to the individual household unit; that which is consumed by one unit cannot be consumed by another. Collective goods, however, can be consumed by more than one household. A swimming pool, for example, could be owned by one household making it a private good; but if owned by a neighborhood association, it becomes a collective good. The difference is that in the first case the consuming unit pays the full price and has exclusive use. In the second case each member of the association pays a lower price and has equal access.

Assume three households, each of which would like to have a swimming pool, with demand functions D_a, D_b, and D_c and supply function S (Fig. 6.1). A could afford to pay $27,000 for a size 4 pool; B could afford to pay $30,000 for a size 5; and C could afford $35,000 for a size 6. For $65,000 a large size 9, equipped with a diving board, can be had. This would amount to a payment of $21,677 each; or, if done proportionately, to demand. A's share would be $20,000, B's $24,000, and C's $27,000. By combining resources these households will have achieved access to a much larger and more satisfying facility for less money. These are restricted types of collective goods.

When collective goods are provided by an entire community, they are referred to as "public goods." In this case no one can claim an exclusive share, since access is free to everyone. For purely public goods, no one can be denied access for any reason. No attempt is made at pricing. All can enjoy them without subtracting from the use others make of them. Charging a fee for use of a public swimming pool amounts to exclusion. It is no longer a public

The Community as a Supplier   153

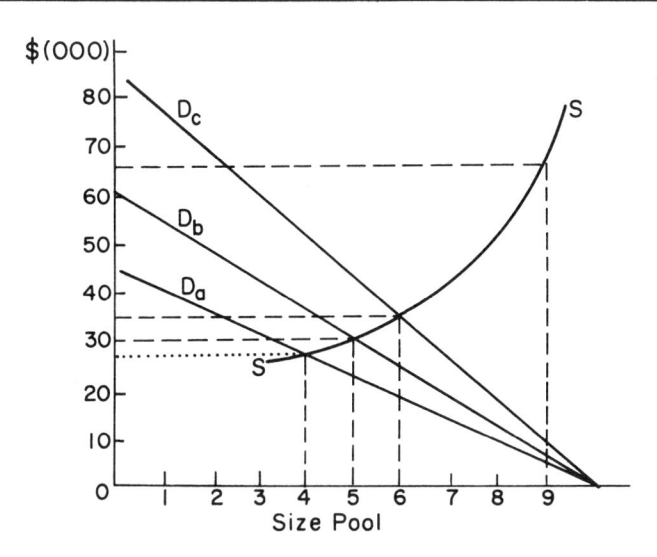

Fig. 6.1. Private vs. collective goods.

good. The same would have to be said if part of the public were excluded because of racial discrimination. Where the fees pay only part of the cost of operation or where full cost is paid from public funds for a restricted facility, it can be said to be "semipublic" in nature.

Communities may be involved in the distribution of restricted collective, semipublic, and public goods and services. Sometimes these are all categorized as social goods. Restricted collective goods are those that could be provided by the private sector, since full cost pricing is used, but are collective in the sense that more than one unit has access (such as a waste disposal system). Communities also engage in providing purely private goods (such as electricity and water) from which profits are often expected to go into the public treasury.

Community distribution systems are of two general kinds: nongovernmental and governmental. Nongovernmental systems are concerned largely with charity; they perform services and distribute contributions. These activities are collective in nature but are not public, since some parts of the public are excluded and tax funded support is not utilized. They are also peculiar in that the recipients are generally passive; they are selected by the donors. Another type of nongovernmental system dealing in collective goods is the swimming pool association spoken of previously, or a country club, or lodge of any type run by a nongovernmental body. Governmental distribution is more important, in most communities, than nongovernmental.

General Theory of Public Goods

In most societies, the market is relied upon for the distribution of private goods and services. Economists generally regard it as efficient and utilize it as a standard for comparison in analyzing the efficiency of the public sector. Efficiency of the market sector is related to the principle of rivalry and the principle of exclusion, that is, to the fact that goods and services sold can in some way be identified as a unit by the purchaser, and that exclusive use can be made of them.

Identification is not always easy. Contrast the purchase of a bag of potatoes with a ticket to Disneyland. In the one case, there is no trouble in identifying the purchase. In the second, the purchased item is the right to share experiences with several thousand other people, and it may not be evident just what that is in concrete terms, although benefits enjoyed may be considered personal.

There is no problem with identifying exclusion. The purchaser has equally exclusive use of the potatoes and whatever experiences the ticket allows. If either the potatoes or the ticket are lost or stolen, this right passes to someone else. Rivalry makes exclusion possible without loss of efficiency; it means that what is consumed by one unit cannot be consumed by another. In a well-functioning market, the buyer reveals preferences for particular goods or services by bidding. The seller responds to this signal by acceptance or rejection of the bid. On the basis of the number of these signals and their acceptability, the seller gauges the amount of goods and services to be offered in the market.

The principles of rivalry and exclusion are also utilized in classifying public goods.

Role of nonrival consumption. Certain types of goods and services are indivisible, that is, if one person consumes, the consumption of others is not affected. To some degree this is true in Disneyland and in other private and semipublic services, but there has to be a degree of identification of the service used in order to make it excludable and requiring a ticket. With purely public goods, this identification is not possible. Use of a public park, a drinking fountain, or even an art gallery may be classed as nonrival in consumption. This means that exclusion should not be attempted. Here the market cannot function because people will neither bid nor reveal their preferences. They receive the same benefits even though they pay nothing. The reason they pay nothing is that the general public has decided that these things should be available free.

Role of nonexcludability. The market fails as an efficient distributor where there is no possibility of exclusion or where only partial exclusion is deemed possible. A public street might be utilized more efficiently if some way could be found to charge for its use, but this is generally conceded to be impossible. Utilization of a bus system may be partially excludable if fees are set low, allowing low income individuals to have access, yet causing some payment for use of the service to be made. Nonexcludability causes market failure because people are not forced to reveal their preferences by bidding. There are, then, no clear signals to the seller, since people simply utilize what is available. The action function of the market is no longer operable.

Market analogy. Economists have long been concerned with the problem of efficiency in the public sector because it is difficult to determine what efficient use of resources consists of; and if known, what could be done to achieve it. Since the market is considered to be an effective allocator, they have tried to apply the same cost-benefit principles to the public sector.

The partial equilibrium approach illustrated in Fig. 6.2 is an example. At left is the usual type of demand and supply analysis. It has three households with demand curves D_a, D_b, and D_c based on given income distribution and prices for all other goods. The market demand curve is obtained by adding quantities demanded by each household at given prices. The supply curve is S, and E is the equilibrium point for the market at quantity OQ and price OP. Household A buys Q_a, household B buys Q_b, and household C buys Q_c. These three pay the same price, P.

Figure 6.2B shows the same pattern for public goods assuming price and quantity are determinable. The main difference is that the public demand curve is determined by vertical addition of the individual demand curves, since all three households receive the same amount. Price P is now the sum of prices paid by each. Household A pays T_a, household B pays T_b, and C pays T_c. So, $T_a + T_b + T_c = P$. They receive the same quantity but pay different prices in the form of taxes.

For the private purchasers, marginal benefit derived by each one equals the marginal cost, OP (QE). If output were less than OQ, each would be willing to pay more, since marginal benefit would exceed marginal cost. In this case the supply curve would shift to S'; and the new equilibrium price would be P'. On the other hand,

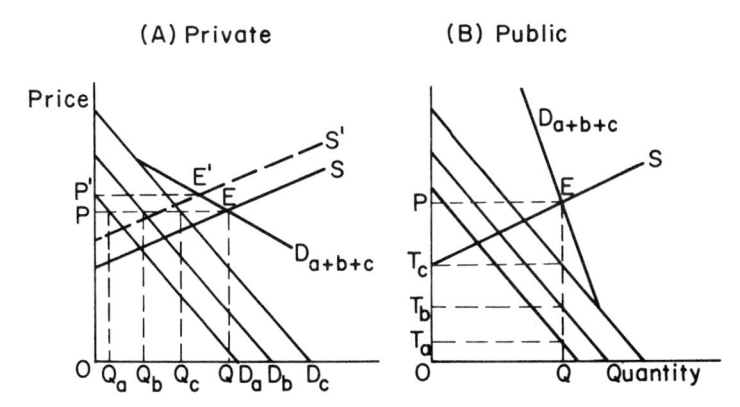

Fig. 6.2. Demand for private and public goods.

if output exceeded OQ, marginal cost would exceed marginal benefit so purchasers would pay less.

For the purchasers of public goods, point E reflects equality between the sum of marginal benefits and the marginal cost. For households the vertical distance under each demand curve indicates marginal benefit derived. Output OQ equates marginal cost and marginal benefit.

The important difference is that for public goods, the sum of the marginal benefits equals marginal cost, whereas for private goods, marginal benefits derived by each household equal marginal cost. Thus, for private goods, A, B, and C pay the same price but purchase different quantities and for public goods they pay different prices and purchase the same amount.

General equilibrium approach. The quantities of private and public goods produced, as well as their prices, are interdependent. That is, some private goods are used to produce public goods and vice versa. Therefore, a price change in one of these inputs will influence costs and price of the end product. To further complicate the process, when all people in a community are considered, utility functions come into conflict, and the welfare level of each one impinges upon the welfare level of all others. The result is a huge cross-impact matrix whose solution is highly complex and can take place only in the social process.

A collective view of the social process. Most economic theory is based on the assumption that consumption decisions are made by individuals. Preference maps drawn up to represent choices between varieties of private and/or public goods are mappings of individual indifference curves. As a matter of fact, more decisions are made on a collective than an individual basis. This does not rule out the fact that wants are experienced by individuals and that they have utility functions. What it does mean is that people, in making decisions, are heavily influenced by other people.

The household is the basic unit of a community. Most households consist of more than one person. Decisions made at that level are not likely to reflect the exact preference of any one household member. Rather, there is an attempt to maximize a collective utility function derived from the function of each member and itself a type of compromise. Once the compromise is made, it is reflected in the marketplace. One need only review ways in which decisions are made in one's own household--from purchase of types of breakfast cereal to choosing the family automobile--in order to understand this process.

In addition to the feelings an individual may have, for members of the household, there are likely to be utility functions that involve other people and things. These might include close relatives; members of a church, lodge, or ethnic group; a species of wildlife, portion of local geography, or environment in general; or all people of the community. When all the utility functions of members of a group are brought to bear on a matter of concern, a compromise utility function emerges to represent the preference of the group.

It often happens that the group preference function is at variance with preference of one or more of its members. As long as they acquiesce, their differences have no influence. If they do not acquiesce, conflict results. In this case they constitute a subgroup that is a pressure unit within the group. This unit will attempt to convince other members of the group that they should have a different group preference function. Where they succeed, a new and different function may emerge.

Every society allocates many of its resources in accordance with decisions determined or influenced by pressure groups. The major difference between a democracy and a dictatorship lies in the number of pressure groups allowed to operate and the range within which they can be influential. A pressure group can be said to be an articulate unit reflecting a composite of relatively homogeneous individual utility functions. The ease with which the group arrives at a consensus is a reflection of homogeneity among those functions. Where there are serious differences, subgroups develop to bring pressure on other members. In most groups the composite preference of the larger body results from conflict among subgroups.

Preference Revelation at the Community Level

For those goods and services provided by the community, as well as by the marketplace, efficient allocation is dependent upon the units revealing their preferences. Preferences can be revealed through voluntary contributions, payment of prices, and through the political process.

Voluntary contributions. If a person derives utility from others' consumption, he may find that he derives greater satisfaction from giving away some of his income than from adding to his ownership of goods and services. In some of these decisions, he may be acting as part of a group, in which case his giving is evidence of concurrence in the group preference. In other cases, he may follow his own preference, giving directly to another individual.

In this type of distribution, the utility function of the donor is of major importance. The donee must derive some satisfaction from being on the receiving end or the transaction cannot be consummated, but the initiative (except in cases of begging) is likely to come from the donor. Preference functions are rather obvious. For donor and donee welfare can be assumed to be maximized and allocation efficient.

Natural monopolies. Most goods and services sold by communities as private market goods and many of those sold as semipublic goods are in the category referred to as "natural monopoly." These are operations that, for efficiency reasons, are best allowed to monopolize. Most utilities come into this category.

There are two ways to handle natural monopoly: either make

the activity a public function, or assign it to a private company subject to regulation. As Mill stated it (1920, p. 143):

> When, therefore, a business of real public importance can only be carried on advantageously upon so large a scale as to render the liberty of competition almost illusory, it is an unthrifty dispensation of the public resources that several costly sets of arrangements should be kept up for the purpose of rendering to the community this one service. It is much better to treat it at once as a public function; and if it be not such as the government itself could beneficially undertake, it should be made over entire to the company or association which will perform it on the best terms for the public.

A natural adversary relationship exists when a natural monopoly in private hands is supervised by a regulatory agency. It is the business of the agency to represent the consumer and to make sure the monopoly provides efficient service at a reasonable cost. When the activity is publicly owned this relationship is lost. The regulated and the regulator become one. This, plus the concept of profit maximization, tend to make regulated agencies somewhat more efficient than publicly owned ones.

On what grounds, then, might a decision be made for public ownership? One argument often heard is that profits from a natural monopoly ought to go into the public treasury rather than pockets of stockholders. From an efficiency standpoint, this is no argument at all. In the operation of water and sewerage systems, the welfare consideration of public health is often given large weight. Where it is possible to obtain financing at lower cost by utilizing public bonding powers, this becomes an argument. The accompanying assumption is that equal efficiency will be attained.

Smith (1796, p. 300) observed there were some general criteria to determine what ventures are likely to be successful as government enterprises. They include a small capital account, operations that are routine in nature, and flow of revenue that is certain and steady. These guide communities away from anything very complicated or risky.

Whenever a community enters into a commercial operation it should operate as nearly like a privately owned one as possible. This involves charging all of the expenses that would be borne by private enterprise as costs against the operation, including an in lieu of tax payment equivalent to that which would be assessed. If this is not done, consumers of the service are being subsidized by the rest of the community. Even where all expenses are to be included, arguments will arise concerning equivalents. What amount of subsidy is received by issuing tax-exempt bonds and how should this be expensed?

Despite the problems involved, many public utilities whose services could be dispensed profitably by private enterprise are owned by communities. The only really good argument for this is that the collective utility function of the community could not be satisfied in any other way. If there is utility to be gained in having public ownership per se, then other measures of efficiency may not be appropriate.

Semipublic services. So far, natural monopolies have been discussed from the point of view of users paying full cost. One reason for public ownership may be a desire to subsidize users from the public treasury. Public transportation systems within communities are generally subsidized. For some reason an effective pressure group favoring such operations, and at low fares, develops very easily. Often the argument given is that of subsidizing those who cannot afford to own cars or take taxis.

The most common situation is that some users of public transportation have low incomes and some do not. Some low income people are heavy users, some light, and some nonusers. Any type of subsidization in kind has the major defect that is specific rather than general. A low income nonuser gets no subsidy at all. Communities wanting to subsidize for welfare purposes might find more effective ways than pricing commercial services below cost.

However, if the pressure group favoring such activity is able to convince the voting public, one must conclude that the collective utility function requires the subsidy to be paid. There is also the possibility that the public welfare may be maximized by having completely free transportation or free housing for the poor. These decisions might result in greater equity among eligible receivers.

On the other end of the spectrum, communities often institute user charges for what one would expect to be public services, thus converting them to semipublic by excluding those unable to pay. Charges for the use of swimming pools, playgrounds, zoos, and museums are some of these types of situations. Earmarking taxes collected from users for specific activities may be essentially the same thing as the institution of user charges. Streets and highways, for example, are often maintained with funds derived from taxes on gasoline. This is not as direct or as exclusive as charging tolls, but the general result is somewhat the same. Gasoline purchased also includes a ticket to use the streets. Riders of bicycles are subsidized by auto drivers under these circumstances.

Question of equity. Most decisions with regard to user charges for semipublic goods and services involve equity considerations. But subsidy always accrues benefits to users in proportion to their consumption of the service. Therefore, if redistribution of income is of major concern, the incidence of redistribution from a subsidy is not likely to be equitable. Further, since equalization of incomes is a broad social problem, it probably should be approached at higher governmental levels.

The question of equity should not enter into a decision to charge fees. Rather, the consideration should be the amount of value received by the public in general and by the user. Charging low fees to poor people in a community hospital has to be justified on the ground that their health is of interest to the community in general, not on the ground that it will help equalize incomes in the community.

Local efforts at equalization, if there are to be any, should be in the form of direct payments. Voluntary contributors will take care of some of this. If government is to get involved, care must be taken to make sure that those who are paying the taxes are receiving benefits at least equal to the cost of them. If benefits from seeing the poor taken care of are less than tax cost plus moving expenses, taxpayers may move away.

How to pay. Decisions concerning the amount of subsidy for semipublic goods are made in the political arena. What constitutes a "public good" varies among communities. It is generally felt by economists that efficiency of resource utilization rules out making charges for the use of indivisible resources (that is, those where use by one person does not interfere with use by others).

Using that guideline, user charges for parks, zoos, and museums are not economically justified. However, there may be extenuating circumstances. Where there is a queuing problem, user charges may be justified. For example, if the zoo were to fill to capacity from 10:00 A.M. to 4:00 P.M. every Saturday, a user charge for those hours would throw some of the users to other hours and other days when no charge would be made. Or if there is a huge traffic jam on a bridge every weekday from 7:00 to 9:00 A.M. and 5:00 to 7:00 P.M., tolls might be imposed for those hours to encourage travelers to use other bridges, or to vary hours of commuting. The alternative in these cases is to build too much capacity for ordinary use, thus wasting resources.

How much should be paid for police and fire protection? Economists would say that the marginal cost should equal the value of marginal benefit received by the general public from the protection. But, how can the general public determine marginal benefit for a public good or how is point E of Fig. 6.2B to be attained? This involves impact between needs for private goods and needs for public goods and is manifested in budget policy.

Budgeting

As indicated by Musgrave and Musgrave (1973, p. 64), budget policy must actually (1) operate within the context of a given state of money distribution; (2) call upon taxes to provide for public and semipublic goods, thereby allocating cost among taxpayers; and (3) provide a mechanism through which consumer preferences for public goods are revealed.

Samuelson model. Samuelson (1954) approached the budgeting problem by assuming the existence of an omniscient planner having at hand data concerning preference patterns, supplies of factors, and production functions. Assume two individuals, A and B, a private good, X, and a public good, Y. Further, assume a given distribution of income that does not change because of changes in the pro-

The Community as a Supplier   161

ductive process. The planner must allocate resources to X and Y in line with the known preferences of A and B. The instructions are to charge consumers for consumption of X and Y in accordance with a pricing rule such that the ratio of unit prices each consumer pays for X and Y equals the marginal rate of substitution in consumption between them.

The solution is shown in Fig. 6.3. Line CD is the production possibility line showing alternative mixes of X and Y that can be produced and are available to the community. Figs. 6.3B and 6.3C show the positions of A and B. Suppose income is divided between them so that A receives a share equal to OM/OC of the potential private good output and B receives ON/OC where $OM + ON = OC$; that is, the whole of private good output is divided between A and B.

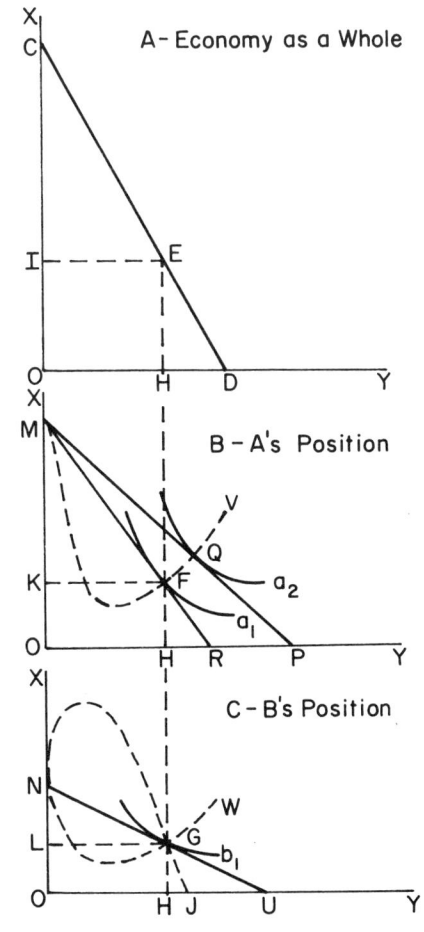

Fig. 6.3. Public and private goods with given distributions.

If one were to have A's indifference map and were to assume that price of X holds steady at M but the amount paid to obtain Y varies, a price-consumption line could be developed linking the points of tangency of the various budget constraint lines with indifference curves. In Fig. 6.3B this is illustrated by two indifference curves, a_1 and a_2, and two constraint lines, MR and MP. Line MV then would result if all indifference curves and all constraint lines were utilized. Given the price ratio OM/OP, for example, A's preferred position would be at Q where MP is tangent to the highest attainable indifference curve, a_2. Curve NW traces out a similar price-consumption line for B.

However, if the planner were to choose A's position first in every instance, and B's second, then the amount of X consumed by A would not be available for consumption by B. That is, at each point of tangency both A and B would consume the same amount of Y but the amount of X consumed by B would be that left after A's consumption was deducted from the total supply. Thus the price consumption curve for B, shown in Fig. 6.3C, would be the opposite of that for A or line NJ. Both NW and NJ intersect at G, the highest curve B could attain under the circumstances. This limits A to point F. Point E (Fig. 6.3A) indicates that the correct pricing and output solution divides total output between OI of X and OH of Y. Both consume the same amount of Y so it is not divided, but the amount of X is divided between OK for A and OL for B.

The essential characteristics of this solution are

1. Initial distribution of income is maintained
2. Ratio of the tax paid per unit of Y to the price per unit of X equals the marginal rate of substitution of Y for X for both A and B
3. Combined tax paid by A and B equals the total cost of Y

There are four important messages to be learned from this type of analysis. First, although taxpayers pay different amounts for public goods, they tend to consume the same amount of each. Second, there is competition for funds between private and public goods. Third, people are willing to pay taxes only as long as they feel the marginal utility received from public goods is at least as much as that received from private goods. And fourth, the budgeting process is the means by which preferences of members of the community are expressed.

The third conclusion might be interpreted to mean there would have to be direct consumption of the public good by that person. However, if we remember that people also have utility functions that reflect how they feel about other people's consuming, we see that marginal utility received from the public good does not have to include direct consumption. A childless person may be willing to be taxed for a public park to be used by neighborhood children because it contributes to peacefulness in the neighborhood or because happy children contribute to that person's utility function in general.

The Community as a Supplier

While this is a very simple model, it gives considerable insight into workings of the political process. The role of the omniscient planner is assumed by the people of the community. They know, in general, what their preferences are and express them in two ways: at the ballot box and through pressure groups. Of the two, pressure groups are often the most influential. Bond issue elections give a good clue to this, since they usually originate with a pressure group attempting to accomplish an objective. The outcome of the voting is also heavily influenced by pressure groups on both sides of the issue.

It is the job of a pressure group to sell its ideas to either the voters or their representatives. In a bond issue election, the sales pitch is to the voters directly. For most other issues persuasion is aimed at elected, or appointed, officials. Elected officials are likely to mirror the wants of a majority of the voting public (not necessarily those of the public in general) just before election. Between elections they have a great deal of leeway for decision making on their own.

Once a pressure group has obtained its objective, acquiescence on the part of the public is the same as agreement. This is true whether the public has perfect information or not. Those who do not like a given decision must either form as pressure groups against it or accept it. Very few issues are so plain to the public that a popular uprising occurs without some prodding from someone. The community utility function for any issue is a compromise and reflects sentiments of the most influential groups. Moral judgment is no more called for in this case than in that of inequity in market distribution. A primary attribute of good theory is that it explains the nature of the world, not that it passes judgment on it.

Community budget system. Budgeting is a means by which complex organizations can be guided to produce intended consequences. In a democracy it may also be a device for limiting the powers of government. Public budgeting systems are ways of making choices about means and ends. The two major questions are "to whom?" and "for what purpose?" (See Lee and Johnson 1973, Chap. 1.) The budgetary system can be likened to a cycle consisting of four phases: (1) preparation and submission, (2) approval, (3) execution, and (4) audit.

Preparation. Those responsible for preparation of the budget vary with communities. In some it is the mayor or the manager, in some it is department heads, and in others it is some combination of these. In all cases the guiding purposes should be clearly stated so the will of the people can be carried out with dispatch. The question of recipients is largely the responsibility of administrators.

Each administrator must determine what resources are needed to carry out the responsibilities given to him or her. It is also the administrator's responsibility to carry this message to superiors.

If too much is asked for and received, resources will likely be wasted. If too little is asked for and received, functioning may not be efficient. Usually an adversary-type relationship exists: it is best to ask for too much, so that when the budget is cut, there will be about the right amount. This fits in with the forces indicated previously.

The competition for funds between private and public goods usually results in a downward pressure on tax collections. The citizen's fondest dream is to get more public services with lower taxes. There is, therefore, a continuous public pressure on officials to cut budgets, while pressure to raise them comes from department heads saddled with public demand for more service.

If a community is large enough, it may have a budget office that acts as a buffer in this struggle and tries to obtain a proper balance between means and needs. At the same time, the budget office wants to submit budgets that will not be overruled and avoid situations where it has to cut back on agency requests. All of this requires considerable second-guessing, unless some basis exists for analysis. In all of this the budget is seldom considered as a whole. Rather attention is paid to budgeting for specific types of activities.

Approval. The approval phase is usually handled by the community's legislative body. Since it is that body's responsibility to match total means to total activities, it must pay attention to the overall budget. The administrators have provided a preference function; now it is up to the legislators to provide the constraint function. It is also in this phase that pressure groups again appear. No matter how successful a group may be in getting its desires incorporated into the community utility function, without proper budgeting, the desired results cannot be attained. If an increase in revenues is required, it may fall upon the pressure group to convince the public that revealed preference means being willing to pay.

The theory for the role played by pressure groups is found in Arrow's (1963, pp. 14-77) single peaked analysis of voting and public welfare. It is only important that the pressure group convince a majority of those making the decision that they should be of one mind. This applies to voting for a bond issue or special law as well as to decisions of a board.

Execution. Once a budget is approved, its execution is in the hands of administrators. Here pressure groups can have some influence, but usually their function is to see to it that the ends are accomplished for which they have pressured. Arbitrary budget cuts by top administrators can come in this phase and must be guarded against in the public interest.

It is in execution that accounting information is crucial. It reveals the transactions that occur as the budget is executed, thereby providing records to be used in holding persons and organizations responsible for the proper expenditure of public funds. It also has a future perspective in that it serves to stimulate research into the problem of adequacy of performance levels and plans.

Audit. Audits are useful for three major purposes: (1) to ensure compliance with stated objectives in budgeting, (2) to ensure honesty and prevent waste, and (3) to determine whether or not desired results have been achieved.

Budget as a source of program information. So far we have considered only that part of budgeting concerned with resources. In recent years considerable attention has been paid to budgets as sources of program information for evaluating what the local government does. The major problem has been to develop the kinds of information that are useful in analyzing programs.

The U.S. government approach has been to divide program structure into program categories, program subcategories, and program elements (Bureau of the Budget 1968). An illustration of how this might work out is taken from the Pennsylvania state programming structure (Mowitz 1970). It is as follows:

I. Category
   A. General Administration
      .
      .
      .
   B. Control and Reduction of Crime
     1. Subcategories
       a) Crime Prevention
         (1) Elements
           .
           .
       b) Criminal Law Enforcement
         (1) Elements
           .
           .
           .
       c) Reintegration of Adult Offenders
         (1) Elements
           (a) Maintenance of inmate security
           (b) Maintenance of inmates' physical-mental health
           (c) Counseling for personal and social problems
           (d) Education of inmates
            .
            .
           (k) Screening to determine risk

    This involves a great deal more than is customarily assigned to the budgeting process, such as development of information on a microscale to enable administrators to identify objectives, consider implications, determine possible pertinent costs, and analyze all possible alternatives. It is tied in with the realization that the general public very often has to form its utility functions without sufficient information concerning ramifications of particular projects. If public services are to be in accordance with the real wishes of members of the community, a great deal of emphasis upon developing and supplying adequate information is called for.

In this kind of budget system, emphasis must be placed upon measures of outcome, since the public and its employees, the administrators, should be highly concerned with results of activities. Bureaucracies are usually more concerned with carrying out activities rather than the results. Activity measures, such as number of patients treated or kilometers of road maintained, are fine for performance budgeting; but measures of impact are also needed. The efficient analysis of programs involves both types of measures. At this stage of development of the art, the measurement of impact is in need of attention. In the future, many communities will be faced with the need to inform on a much more useful basis than has been the case in the past. Pressure groups will be placed under greater scrutiny and their objectives will be weighed against actual accomplishment.

The development of program budgeting is a direct result of the desire to make comparisons of satisfactions derived from expenditures on private goods and expenditures on public goods. Some feel that the market guarantees efficient satisfaction of wants (that money will be spent wisely), but the political process does not. To the extent that taxpayers are kept in the dark with regard to program development, this feeling may be correct.

Multiyear planning. Lee and Johnson (1973) have observed that although few program budget systems are actually operational, those that are give some insights into possibilities. Multiyear plans developed around the components of program structure appear to offer good opportunities for linking goals, objectives, impacts, and outputs to resources. The plans indicate the accomplishments to be expected for a given commitment of resources. The major advantage is that they extend beyond the immediate budget year. This provides perspective of future directions. The plans usually consist of the current year and some specified number of years into the future. Each year the plan is revised to include an additional future year and drop the earliest one. Thus the multiyear plan of program budgeting moves until it comes to completion of a project if a completion date exists. An inherent problem in such planning is that unless some constraints are imposed, the resulting documents may make unrealistic economic and political demands on resources. Many communities have had experiences with projects that began small and grew like "Topsy." This becomes even more likely when plans run several years into the future without guidelines as to the amount of resources available for them.

With proper safeguards, this type of budgeting can be of help to community administrators. This is especially so because data requirements for analysis are spelled out in advance. Multiyear plans project both program and cost figures. Thus, agencies are immediately faced with the need for producing data that say more than that the program is progressing well.

One of the advantages to be gained from multiyear plans is better direction in capital budgeting. The year-to-year needs of the various programs include needs for housing, machinery, and other capital improvements. Sources of funding for capital need to be considered in terms of more than one year. Projections made, by source, can point out possible problems in advance. For example, some projects are begun with grants from higher levels of government; often these start at a high level and are then reduced automatically after a given number of years.

Where multiyear plans are to become bases for future decision making, the planning should be done in the office that prepares the budget, otherwise it is likely to be ignored. This structural linkage is important in gaining the compliance of other agencies with the system.

REVENUE SOURCES FOR COMMUNITIES

The ability of a community to furnish public and semipublic goods is directly related to its ability to generate tax revenues.

Property taxes

The property tax is generally considered to be the major source of local government income. Its origin lies with taxes on land. The theoretical basis for the land tax was developed by the Physiocrats who viewed agriculture as the only source of real income. Thus, they concluded that the only logical basis for taxation was land. David Ricardo added to this emphasis with his argument that land rentals required no effort on the part of landlords and should be taxed away.

Henry George accepted Ricardo's idea; but he went even further in his reasoning. The supply of land is fixed, therefore a tax on it cannot be shifted and cannot disturb the allocation of resources. The part of land that represents improvements to its original state should not be taxed. However, increased value of land due to a growing economy increases the value of pure rent and belongs to society. George's idea of taxing only land has been used by communities to encourage development and cut down on the amount of vacant land in the area. Further impact of his theory is seen in the new towns programs of certain countries where the developing corporation retains title to the land and uses the rental revenues for community improvements.

In most communities, taxes would be imposed on both land and improvements on land. In high technology societies, improvements are likely to be much more important than the basic characteristics of land. The property tax, therefore, impinges heavily on improvements. Where the tax is on business and industrial property, it amounts to taxing capital goods. But value of capital goods is directly related to the value of services it renders during its lifetime. Thus, in that case, such a tax amounts to taxing the income stream of the capital. This reduces the rate of return. However, companies utilize public goods and services for which they would have to pay anyway: it is cheaper to have public fire and police protection than to provide your own. Adequate evaluation requires consideration of benefits as well as costs. Labor pays property taxes on the property in which families live, whether they rent or own their own homes. Since the proportion of income spent on housing declines as incomes rise, property taxes tend to be somewhat regressive.

There is little evidence that property taxation has any significant effect on location of industry. Most studies of location decisions rate it low compared to other factors. Usually the most consideration is given to public goods and services supplied in relation to tax rates and assessment levels. Poor public performance coupled with high property taxes might prove to be discouraging.

Sales Taxes

Two major categories of sales tax are used. A general sales tax is imposed on the price of all commodities. An excise tax is specific to particular classes of commodities. If one visits a grocery store and pays 3 percent of the gross purchase as a tax, this is a general sales tax. If instead a tax is imposed only on the purchase of meat, dairy products, and fresh produce, with all other items tax exempt, an excise tax is indicated. Excise taxes tend to be added to the price of the merchandise, thus increasing marginal costs. General sales taxes tend to be assessed directly against the consumer. There is no way of determining directly their effect on price.

Sales taxes are easy to collect and tend to be fairly consistent in amount from year to year. This makes them popular. Since they are taxes on consumption, they are regressive with respect to income levels. General sales taxes are often assessed against final sales to the consumer, but they can be assessed at any stage of production. Taxes assessed at every stage where pricing is done are called "turnover" taxes. They encourage vertical integration among firms since the tax can be escaped by eliminating price transactions.

In the economic process there are many interdependencies. Some of the more important of these involve "intermediate products." These are final products of one firm that become inputs to others. For many products the number of stages where "intermediate products" are utilized becomes fairly large. At each of these stages, the producer has added a certain amount of value. That is, the products brought into the process as inputs have been changed and made more valuable through use of land, labor, capital, management, and governmental services to produce another product or service.

General sales taxes may be assessed on the value added at each stage. Such a "value added" tax does not encourage integration, since there is no way to escape the tax. An integrated firm merely increases the value added and pays the same tax as would be paid by several firms were they not integrated. In the United States, general sales taxes are usually assessed at the retail level directly against the consumer. In many other countries, including Great Britain and Canada, they are collected at the manufacturing level and passed on through increased prices. The consumer pays either way.

At the community level, an increase in the sales tax decreases the amount consumers have to spend and increases the amount to be spent by local government. The impact on the local economy depends upon purchase patterns of these two types of units. If the multiplier for households is larger than for government, the economy will suffer from the taxing policy. If it happens to be higher for government, there will be an increase in overall activity.

About the only way a consumer can escape a sales tax is to cut down on consumption. If it happens that a neighboring community has a lower tax, some escape can be found by buying there, but it is likely to be more than offset by transportation costs. So long as the tax is quite small in relation to price, consumers tend to react inelastically to a change, especially if the item being taxed is a necessity. Where a sales tax exempts necessities (such as food) and imposes heavily on those with elastic demand, its change in emphasis could cause a lowering of overall economic activity at the time it is imposed. This is because consumers would react to a price rise brought on by the tax by cutting purchases significantly. As indicated previously, taxation is more efficient and causes fewer economic problems if it is imposed on items for which demand is inelastic. This is why alcoholic beverages, tobacco, soft drinks, food, and drugs make good items for taxation.

Income Taxes

Use of the income tax as a source of revenue has often been considered a prerogative of higher governmental levels. In some states of the United States, municipalities are denied access to it. But it is used by many communities where this injunction does not apply.

The income tax is probably the most equitable tax possible, where it is used without too many loopholes. People pay in accordance with their ability. It is, therefore, considered to be progressive. Any tax reduces people's incomes. In general it is conceded that rich people tend to save more of their incomes than do poor people. Therefore, a progressive tax tends to reduce this source of leakage and increase multiplier effects in the community. A regressive tax reduces funds available for consumption.

An income tax can also be administered more fairly than other taxes. Since it is possible to make rather positive identification of the types of people being taxed, the tax can be adjusted to allow for disasters, large family units, and so on. A number of studies have indicated that people at higher income levels make more intensive use of public services than do those at lower levels. To the extent that is true, an income tax tends to equate marginal utility with marginal cost better than other taxes. It is, therefore, more efficient.

Payroll Taxes
If the community is not highly unionized, a payroll tax will fall on the wage earner thereby lowering his or her income. With heavy unionization it may be passed on through demands for higher wages. It does not matter whether it is collected from the employer or the employee, in either case. The imposition of such a tax will cut consumption by wage earners that will be offset by government spending.

Communities that are heavy labor importers often introduce such a tax on the grounds that these "foreign" workers are taking money out of town and are not supporting it. This is the same as imposing a tax on any other import. The community probably ends up paying it one way or another. If much labor is imported, it is because there is a local shortage, thus any tax will simply be passed back to the company through higher wage payments, thus increasing its costs.

Intergovernmental Transfers
Where benefits are strictly local, decisions should be local and the local area should impose its own taxes. Transfers from higher governmental echelons should be for local activities that have extensive spillover effects. Local people should not have to pay for benefits to other communities. Thus, there may be good reason for revenue sharing from higher levels with school districts, since education benefits everyone in the long run.

Sometimes communities become competitive over possible economic development. In spite of evidence to the contrary, they often feel that raising taxes will scare plants from settling in the community or drive their own plants away. This is an argument for state taxation and revenue sharing, since it puts all communities on the same basis.

This same sort of thinking applies when sales taxes are imposed. This time the fear is often real. People can evade a local sales tax by trading in another community. Whether they actually will do so or not depends upon how large the tax is in comparison to purchase prices of goods and whether or not the neighbor also has a tax, even though it may be a lower one. A tax covering an entire state or province and being shared with local governments on the basis of local collections avoids evasion. Where higher governments make grants from regular tax funds, they should be tied to certain activities that have substantial external benefits.

Debt Financing
Use of debt financing is especially attractive where extensive capital investments are necessary and financial reserves are low.

The Community as a Supplier

Usually this occurs in the face of growth. A number of arguments are made favoring use of debt, some of which are justified.

1. The argument is often made that the debt will be paid off with cheaper dollars than those borrowed. Several assumptions are made here. One is that inflation is more likely than not; another is that the lenders have not built an anticipation of inflationary trends into the interest rate.
2. Another argument is that since inflation is the common occurrence, construction today is apt to be cheaper than construction at some future time. This argument has to be analyzed in light of the assumptions indicated for the preceding argument. Construction tends to be a boom or bust industry. If it so happens that today the industry is in recession and has a lot of slack capacity, it may well be true that contractors will bid lower than at some time in the future when capacity is being utilized. On the other hand, if business is booming today, it may be a poor time for construction, regardless of general inflationary trends.
3. An argument making considerable sense is that the investment will be paid off by those who benefit. Since the citizens in a community change over time, those who vote a bond issue may not be the ones getting the most value from it.
4. One of the better arguments is based on need. If a facility is needed and resources are not available, the only alternative is debt.

A number of arguments are also made against use of debt.

1. Most community debt will be held by outsiders; payment of interest to them transfers resources out of a community. This is true, but it overlooks the inflow of investment funds that constitute a type of basic income from which there are multiplier effects. Further, it assumes the flow of services from the new facility are not worth more than the interest payments.
2. Governments and individuals alike should never go into debt, but should pay as they go. If this were true, the world would make little progress, since there would be few transfers from those with excess resources to those needing them. Debt financing for investment purposes allows a community to pay for facilities as it uses them, thus making it unnecessary to "pay before you go" as would be required if savings had to be acquired beforehand.
3. Constructing government buildings draws resources away from private construction and raises prices if done all at once; it should be spread out. This makes sense only if the industry is booming.
4. This generation should not make decisions that burden future generations. If this were true, there would be little progress anywhere. If the future generation is to get the benefit of use of the facilities (for which they will be paying), the decision has to be made by the present generation.

Debt financing should be looked at from the point of view of maximum welfare of all members of the community, present and future. Debt should be limited by the obvious ability of people to repay it. Ostentatiousness in the facilities should not be attempted unless there is a general consensus and willingness to sacrifice to support it. Communities who overborrow in relation to foreseeable means for repayment face the danger of having to default. It is rare that a community defaults completely; but facing difficulties in payment or having to defer can be a traumatic experience and can result in lowering of a community's credit rating. These facts do not justify avoiding debt financing under the right circumstances.

Any construction activity in a community is going to draw resources, no matter when it is done. When there is slack in building activity, public building can result in improved resource use. If the construction industry in the general vicinity is working at peak capacity, there is no slack and public building will compete with private building for resources. Here the utility functions of members of the community should come into play. If the public buildings are deemed by the people to be more important than the private ones, they should be built; but recognition should be given to the costs involved. The pressure group sponsoring the project should be forced to justify its program to the public.

SUMMARY

Goods and services can be supplied either directly to the household for its exclusive use or through some sort of collective arrangement. In general, private goods tend to be divisible ones and collective goods, indivisible. Restricted collective goods are owned and used by several households but are not available to the general public. When collective goods are provided without charge to the general public, they are called public goods. If user fees are charged but part of the cost is subsidized by the community, the goods are semipublic. Communities may be involved in distributing private, restricted collective (generally utility-type), semipublic, and public goods and services. The systems may be public or private. Private systems, including associations and charities, deal in restricted collective and semipublic goods and services. Public systems may deal in all types.

Private goods are said to have qualities of being rival (if one person consumes no one else can) and exclusive. Public goods are said to be nonrival and nonexclusive. Total demand curves for private goods slope downward and for public goods slope upward. Purchasers of private goods buy different quantities and pay the same (marginal cost) price. Purchasers of public goods buy the same quantity and pay different prices, the sum of which equals marginal cost. The important difference is that for public goods the sum of marginal benefits received by each household equals marginal costs.

Most decisions to purchase are made by groups, ranging from households to large pressure groups. They operate both in the market and in the public sphere. In the private sphere consumers reveal preferences by their demands in the market. In the public sphere they reveal preferences either through the ballot box or pressure groups. Pressure groups are the more important, since they operate at all times and are influential in the voting process.

When the governmental body of a community sells private goods, such as those supplied by natural monopolies, the natural adversary relationship between regulator and regulatee is absent, since they are the same agency. It is present when the utilities are provided by private industry. This plus the tendency toward profit maximization makes management more efficient in the privately owned utility. The publicly owned utility must operate as nearly as possible like a private company if resources are to be maximized under public ownership.

Semipublic services are involved too often in attempts to redistribute income, which is a very inequitable approach. If subsidies are to be provided for certain services, they should be in payment for utility received and paid for by those who actually are the recipients. The decision regarding the amount of subsidy for a semipublic good and the provision of a public good or service has to be made through the political process. Determination of marginal benefits and costs for public goods and services involves needs for private goods as well, since resources for both are limited; it is manifested therefore the budgeting process.

There is, therefore, competition between the two types of goods for the consumer's resources. People will pay taxes as long as they feel that the ratio of marginal utility to cost for public goods is at least equal to that for private goods. The community utility function for any issue is a compromise and reflects ideas of the most influential groups. The function is made manifest in the ways in which public funds are budgeted.

Budgeting is a means by which complex organizations can be guided to produce intended consequences. It may also be used as a device for measuring performance.

The budgeting cycle comes in four phases: (1) preparation by administrators who attempt to spread resources to do the jobs they feel the public wants done; (2) approval by the community's legislative body, which tries to match overall needs with means; (3) execution by the administrators who prepared the original budget; and (4) audit to determine compliance and conformance that is carried out by the legislature.

Budgets have been looked to in recent years as sources of information for cost-benefit analyses of programs. This has stemmed from the feeling that there should be some way to compare results in the public sphere on somewhat the same basis as in the private. Program budget systems are also useful in planning, although not many communities use them that way.

Communities have several sources of revenue. Property taxes are generally used in spite of numerous objections to them. They are related to the concept of land taxation that developed from the ideas of unearned increment. Sales taxes are the next most popular tax, although they tend to be regressive. Income taxes are often thought of as reserved for higher levels of government, but have a number of advantages over other taxes where local governments are allowed to use them. Payroll taxes are often imposed where a community imports considerable labor service from other communities; it adds to costs of local industry.

Communities often receive funds from higher governmental levels also. These transfers should be to pay for activities that have extensive spillover effects.

Use of debt financing is attractive, especially when extensive capital investments are needed. It should be used cautiously and with the maximum welfare of all members of the community in mind.

REVIEW QUESTIONS

1. Distinguish between private and collective goods.
2. When does a collective good become a public good?
3. How could a community-type distribution system be nongovernmental?
4. What is meant by the principle of rivalry?
5. What is meant by the principle of exclusion?
6. How are these principles used in classifying public goods?
7. What are the differences in price-quantity relationships that affect consumers of private goods versus consumers of public goods?
8. Why is it that consumption of private and public goods is too complex to be analyzed with partial equilibrium analysis?
9. What is meant by the idea of a collective utility function?
10. What are pressure groups and what roles do they play in determining collective utility functions?
11. What kind of a utility function does a person have who gives away part of his or her wealth?
12. What is a natural monopoly?
13. What are the two ways a community can handle natural monopolies and what are the advantages and disadvantages of each?
14. Is subsidization of semipublic goods, in order to redistribute wealth, a good economic decision?
15. When should user charges be utilized in paying for a semipublic good? When should they not be used?
16. What tool can be utilized by citizens to reveal preferences for public goods?
17. Explain the Samuelson model for the distribution of expenditures between private and public goods.
18. How does the general public express its preferences?
19. What questions should be answered by a budget system?
20. Why is there an adversary relationship between makers of budgets and administrators of programs?
21. What function does the legislative body of the community have in the budgeting process?

22. Why is accounting information crucial in the execution phase of budgeting?
23. What functions do audits play in the budgeting process?
24. What is meant by the term "program budgeting"?
25. How does program budgeting differ from ordinary budgeting?
26. What are the advantages and disadvantages of multiyear planning?
27. Discuss strengths and weaknesses of property taxes as sources of local government revenue.
28. Are there advantages to taxing land as opposed to taxing both land and improvements?
29. Do renters pay property taxes?
30. Distinguish between a general and an excise sales tax.
31. What are the advantages and disadvantages of sales taxes as sources of local revenue?
32. What are the advantages and disadvantages of income taxes as sources of local revenue?
33. Explain the economic impact of a payroll tax.
34. Under what circumstances should higher echelons of government pay for services performed at the local level?
35. When should a community borrow and for what purposes?

REFERENCES

Arrow, K. J. 1963. *Social choice and individual values*. New York: Wiley.
Bureau of the Budget. Executive Office of the President. 1968. *Planning-programming budgeting system*, Bulletin 68-69. Washington, D.C.: Government Printing Office.
Dalton, H. 1932. *The principles of public finance*. London: Routledge.
Hatry, H. P., and J. F. Cotton. 1967. *Program planning for state, county, city*. Washington, D.C.: George Washington Univ. Press.
Lee, R. D., Jr., and R. W. Johnson. 1973. *Public budgeting systems*. Baltimore: University Park Press.
Mill, J. S. 1920. *Principles of political economy*. London: Ashley.
Mowitz, R. J. 1970. *The design of Pennsylvania's planning, programming budgeting system*. Philadelphia: Commonwealth of Pennsylvania.
Musgrave, R. A., and P. G. Musgrave. 1973. *Public finance in theory and practice*. New York: McGraw-Hill.
Neenan, W. B. 1972. *Political economy of urban areas*. Chicago: Markham.
Peck, H. W. 1925. *Taxation and welfare*. New York: Macmillan.
Samuelson, P. A. 1954. The pure theory of public expenditures. *Review of Economics and Statistics* 36:387-89.
Smith, A. 1796. *The wealth of nations*. Philadelphia: T. Dobson.
Winfrey, J. C. 1973. *Public finance*. New York: Harper & Row.

CHAPTER 7

Economic Effects of Public Action

In its role as a supplier of goods and services, the community has fairly definite and identifiable effects on its citizenry. But there are many spillover effects from both this activity and other governmental activity that need to be identified as well, since they affect the utilization of resources. There are also spillover effects from private activity.

Spillover effects occur because activities engaged in by people have effects on other people. The result is that some people get hurt and some get helped through no action of their own. There are two serious issues involved here. One, the issue of equity, concerns who benefits and who pays for a particular benefit. The other concerns the fact that people receive spillovers whether they want them or not; thus, the revelation of preference may have nothing to do with the situation. This leads to distortion in resource allocation.

GOVERNMENTAL REACTION TO SPILLOVERS IN THE PRIVATE SECTOR

Market supply and demand curves reflect direct costs and prices; they leave out the indirect ones. Where there are spillover benefits, consumers are willing to pay more than the demand curves indicate. Where there are spillover costs the supply curve fails to reflect them.

In Fig. 7.1 the willingness to pay for the service offered is shown as DD, and the quantity that would be produced and taken is Q_1. But suppose the general public decrees that the community would be better off if more people had access to this service. In other words, there are spillover effects not taken into consideration by the market. When these are added, a new demand curve emerges ($\hat{D}\hat{D}$). This $X worth of the service is the amount that people who benefit from the spillover would be willing to spend to obtain the benefits. Thus, it is in the interest of society to have Q_2 produced and used. But this amount will not be produced unless

Economic Effects of Public Action 177

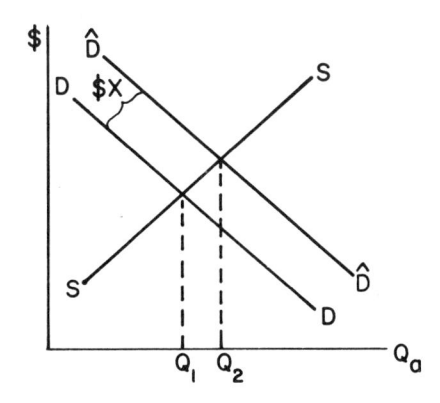

Fig. 7.1. Spillover benefits in a free market.

someone pays the higher price necessary to get the job done. Often this is accomplished by subsidy, as is the case with higher education where tuition pays only part of the cost. It could also be accomplished by having the public pay all of the cost.

Spillover costs also call for public action. Consider the case of the factory that pollutes the air. In effect the air pollution is a by-product of the production process, but since it has negative value to society, it must be treated as a cost. The supply curve captures all of the costs of production, but it does not include the pollution cost.

In Fig. 7.2, SS is the original supply curve, and $\hat{S}\hat{S}$ is the curve including pollution costs. The spillover cost is Y per unit of product. Any production above Q_2 involves greater marginal cost than marginal benefit to society. One way for society to take care of this situation is to force the firm to clean up its air, thus internalizing its costs and forcing it to a higher supply curve. Another is to impose a special charge to be used by local govern-

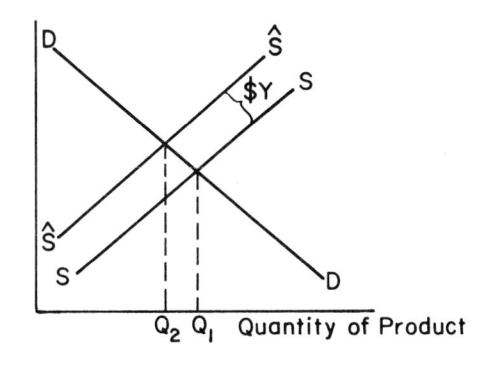

Fig. 7.2. Spillover costs in a free market.

ment in cleaning the air (assuming this were technically possible). Still another way is for society to assume the cost, either by putting up resources to clean the air or by living with polluted air. This approach allows industry to go on producing Q_1, whereas the above approaches would force it back to Q_2.

SPILLOVERS IN THE PUBLIC SECTOR
We noted in the last chapter that one of the reasons for public goods is that they violate the exclusion property and are nonrival. This means that they have a maximum amount of spillover. No one can be excluded once public goods are made available. We also noted that for semipublic goods the efficient approach to pricing is for the public to pay only for the spillover effects, forcing the recipients to pay for their own enjoyment. There are also spillovers related to revenue raising, revenue expenditure, and regulatory and criminal codes that have significant economic effects.

Taxation
The collection and expenditure of tax money has important impacts on resource allocation. When a citizen pays taxes, the money is not available for other uses, thus cutting opportunity for production of things needed by the household. The spending habits of government may be quite different from those of households. So, rather than being used to buy a new car, the money may be used to pay a garbage collector. The spillover effects would be that the local demand for automobiles may be reduced, whereas demand for things garbage collectors buy may be increased.

There are also spillover effects from taxation because some taxes are indirect; that is, it is possible for the person legally taxed to escape payment by passing the tax along to someone else. This kind of shift can often be accomplished if the firm taxed can include the tax in the price of its product. If the product is that purchased by a poor man, its real burden may be much greater than if purchased by a rich man. This factor is discussed under equity.

Income taxes. The income tax is a direct tax when applied against persons. It may not be direct if applied against a strong oligopolist that can either shift it to its workers through lower wages or to its customers through higher prices. Income taxes also have an important impact on dividend policy, investment policy, purchase patterns, and the profitability of the firm. For example, it is in the best interest of stockholders to have earnings held in the company for purposes of expansion, since capital gains tax rates are much lower than rates paid by most investors. This encourages in-house financing of investment. In consideration of alternative investments, a firm must consider after-tax earnings on the income flow.

Individuals in high income tax brackets often look to tax-exempt municipal bonds for investment. Money so invested provides a spillover to communities, since it provides a ready market for bonds at relatively low interest rates. Similarly, individuals and firms often use investment in farms and ranches as tax shelters, since relatively large expenses can be charged against them, thus providing a spillover to landowners.

The purchase and holding of inventory is influenced by its effect on the cost structure of the firm for income tax purposes. Various rapid depreciation allowances used in income taxation provide working capital. This is particularly important for young firms that have difficulty obtaining funds. Profitability of firms is generally assessed on an after-tax basis. Therefore, profit making objectives have to be expanded to allow for income taxes. For firms such as monopolistic competitors, which are unable to set prices on the basis of cost, income taxes can discourage investment by draining away funds that would otherwise be plowed back into the operations. Communities should be especially aware of this spillover effect.

Property taxes. Property taxes penalize property owners and cut down on the amount of money available for other things if there is no way to shift the tax to others. In the case of rental property, it is often possible to shift taxes to renters. This type of externality impinges largely upon laborers, since they tend to be renters.

Inheritance tax is a special form of property tax. In this case the public sector takes a certain proportion of the estate of a deceased person before it is bequeathed to the heirs. This is a direct tax with incidence on the heirs. Its difference from the usual form of property tax is due to its being levied only at the death of the property owner. The spillover effect is found in transfer of resources from the private to the public sector.

The concept of land as a base for taxation has been debated for many years. Recently there have been a number of shifts in the ways land is viewed. Environmentalism has directed our attention to land as a social resource rather than as a private property to be used according to the whims of the legal owners. Added to this, there has been a resurgence of the Henry George idea of the "unearned increment." It argues that increases in land values are often the result of social processes, and these values belong to the community. One result has been movement toward the land tax, which means only land would be taxed, and improvements on the land would not be. Spillovers claimed for this approach include less land speculation and more immediate use; better development of communities, since taxes are high on land in prime areas, but there is no tax on improvements; and better distribution of income. Those opposed maintain that a major part of the utility received from land is tied to flexibility in use, and the land tax forces people to develop improvements on land before they or the community are ready.

An alternative to the land tax is community ownership of land.

This approach appropriates all of the "unearned increment" for community projects. Leases are made on a long-term basis (ninety-nine years in some cases), and rentals are adjusted from time to time as land values change. Sometimes all of the land in a community is involved and sometimes only part of it. A number of examples exist in Europe and the South Pacific. Under the New Zealand land trust arrangement, for example, lands left undeveloped in a new community after a reasonable period are turned over to a nonprofit land trust. The trust administers it from then on, using the profits for community development projects. The English new towns, on the other hand, start with public ownership of all land within the town and the surrounding countryside. Rentals are used to provide all local services. The community corporation literally owns the community except for improvements on the land, which it strictly regulates.

Sales taxes. Sales taxes are indirect insofar as they can be passed on either by collection from the buyer or in the price of the commodity. Sales taxes that are not strictly ad valorem are often based on laws exempting goods having inelastic demand, such as food and drugs. This means that the taxes are imposed on goods with elastic demand. From the point of view of good taxing policy, exactly the opposite should be done. Goods with inelastic demand should be taxed in preference to those with elastic demand for two reasons, (1) revenue flow will be more even, and (2) taxation will not influence demand for the goods. Imposition of a sales tax on goods with elastic demand will then have the spillover effect of decreasing the total revenue of producers of the goods by more than the amount of the tax. It also means that less of these goods will be used by consumers than would be the case without the tax. This is an interference with efficiency of the market system. Reasons for these phenomena are illustrated in Fig. 7.3. In Fig. 7.3A the

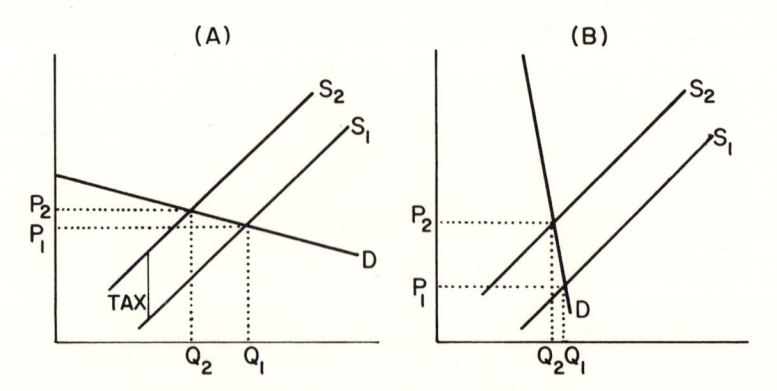

Fig. 7.3. Effect of a sales tax where demand is: (A) elastic (B) inelastic.

Economic Effects of Public Action 181

demand curve D is elastic, and a small change in the price causes a large change in the amount taken.

The supply curve of a seller is its marginal cost curve. Therefore, the imposition of a tax modifies the level of the curve. If the tax amounts to $1 per unit, this is the same as adding $1 to the marginal cost of producing and selling an additional unit of product. However, the seller would be unable to change the price sufficiently to pass the entire amount along, and some of it would have to be absorbed. Further, the quantity that would be sold would decline drastically, and this would reduce total revenues. Both the seller and the governmental unit would be the victims of this spillover.

In Fig. 7.3B demand is inelastic. A large price change would cause only a small change in quantity taken. Therefore, a tax could be easily passed on to the customer without causing a problem for either the seller or the governmental unit. The spillover effects of decisions to tax or not to tax goods with different elasticities should be quite apparent.

Equity. In the last chapter we discussed the use of a local subsidy for the purpose of affecting the equity of income distribution. Taxation is another tool utilized by communities for this purpose. It is much less selective than a subsidy, so probably preferable as a policy tool. A basic assumption made in this regard is that since government has to raise taxes, they should be raised in such a way as to disturb the welfare of society the least. This assumption also has a corollary that utility from private goods is more important in tax policy than utility derived from public goods. The entire emphasis is placed upon the amount of economic welfare lost when people give up some of their income to pay taxes.

The basic argument is dependent upon the concept of diminishing marginal utility. It is argued that as people's incomes rise, the utility of an additional unit of income increases at a decreasing rate, or, rich people can pay taxes easier than poor people. In marginal terms, marginal utility is declining as incomes rise. In Fig. 7.4 the same size tax is shown for both poor and rich people. That is, the difference between I_{r1} and I_{r2} (for rich people) and I_{p1} and I_{p2} (for poor people) is the amount of income lost to taxation. The loss in utility is shown on the y axis. If the assumptions on which the model is based are true, loss in utility by the rich is minuscule compared to loss by the poor (U_{r1} to U_{r2} compared to U_{p1} to U_{p2}). Thus, a taxing policy that hits higher income groups hardest is presumed to have a spillover in terms of lowering feasible loss of economic welfare. This is called progressive taxation.

Expenditures

In evaluating the effect of public expenditure on the community economy, the usual cost-benefit criterion should be used (that

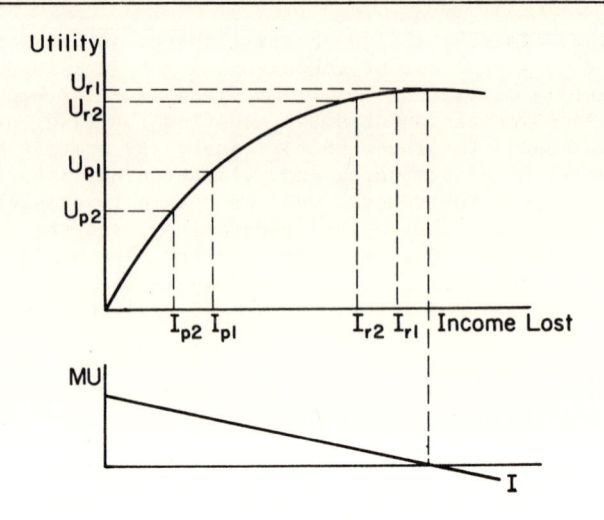

Fig. 7.4. Principle of diminishing marginal utility of income.

is, an expenditure is efficient if gains exceed costs). But among the gains and costs are many spillover effects that may be difficult to identify.

Payments for goods and services. In going about the ordinary business of carrying out mandates of local law, governments buy many goods and services in the local economy. The effect is much the same as if a local business were doing the buying. The local government buys with taxes that have been extracted from the economy and transforms its purchases into services utilized by local citizens. It often performs these functions because spillovers or market failures cause industry either to not produce or to produce in the wrong amounts.

Spillovers to individual members of society often result from these governmental activities. Thus, a quiet street may be widened to make it a feeder. The corner grocer, who developed to serve small purchase needs of the neighborhood, may find pedestrian traffic past his store has doubled. Whether this pleases or dismays the grocer depends upon the grocer's disposition toward expansion.

Suppose the community voted to use some of its resources to set up technical training for disadvantaged persons. One would expect a number of people to receive benefits. First, the people being trained would benefit; second, those who were concerned about disadvantaged persons would benefit. If the activity resulted in higher incomes for disadvantaged people, many other people would receive spillovers including the local merchants, the company hiring the workers, and even consumers of extra goods produced. These benefits are real but largely unmeasurable.

Transfer payments. Subsidies confer gains directly upon those receiving the subsidy. But as indicated with regard to public transportation in Chapter 6, subsidization may also have spillover effects. Suppose the subsidy were made to the local bus company in order to keep it afloat. The spillover effects might include lower fares to bus riders as a group. They might also include benefits to employers of maids who would have to provide transportation without the bus system. Subsidies paid directly to people may also create spillover benefits for the neighborhood grocer. They might, for example, make it possible for customers to pay their bills, thus cutting down on the volume of bad debt.

Summary for Public Costs and Benefits

So far in this chapter we have shown how public decision with regard to revenue collection and disbursement imposes costs and confers benefits on society. Many of these costs and benefits are of the external, or spillover, type and are difficult to identify specifically. This is why it is so difficult to make comparisons between the public and private sectors. Economists assume that the marketplace identifies and places values on goods and services that include spillover effects. This may or may not be true; there is no way to determine it. However, if people act as the models indicate they do, then spillover effects are evaluated along with direct effects when bidding is done.

In the public sector, on the other hand, there are no bidders; hence many costs and gains may fail to be accounted for because they are not perceived. Some may not be accounted for because no way can be found to give them a value. For example, how does one put a price on the effect of the income tax on the pricing policy of a firm? Or, how do we evaluate the fact that a given municipality was able to sell its sewer bonds at 4 percent? Economic analysis can, at best, cause debate to focus on evaluation issues, making sure that objectives of a given project are well stated, that cost estimates are realistic, and that allowances for benefits from externalities are neither too large nor too small for a realistic appraisal. The question that has to be answered is, "Do the gains to society exceed the costs?" If this cannot be answered affirmatively, the project should not be allowed. Unfortunately, many externalities have to be evaluated on the basis of judgment of the analyst.

In recent years vigorous attempts have been made to develop cost-benefit analysis techniques that will allow analysts to replace their own values with those expressed by citizens. Present value is a concept employed here. That is, given a choice between receiving a dollar today and a dollar a year from today, most people under most circumstances would choose to receive the dollar today because opportunities exist for earning interest on the dollar by allowing someone else to use it. If the price of using money owned by others is expressed as the amount paid for its use per year, then the price is called the annual rate of interest. If the annual rate of interest is 0.06 (6 percent), $1.00 can be rented out for a year by its owner who will receive $1.06 at the end of the year. Therefore, $1.00 received today is worth $1.06 to be received a year from today. The present value of $1.06 to be received a year from today is $1.00.

With these new techniques, the numerator of the cost-benefit ratio is defined as the present value of all economic benefits attributable to a proposed undertaking, as inferred from prices paid for like benefits in the private market. The denominator is the present value of the costs of undertaking and operating the project. So, B/C = present value of economic benefits/present value of economic costs. Where large capital investments are involved, the costs are broken into investment (those that have to do with getting the project set up), operation, maintenance, and repair.

For each of the major ways of disposing of government revenue payments for goods and services or transfer payments, benefit cost analysis can be brought to bear on the important question "Is society better off because of this expenditure or is it not?"

The principle of Maximum Social Gain can be stated: the public sector, in undertaking an activity, should choose that alternative for which the gains to society exceed the costs by the greatest amount and should refrain from any activity if its costs are not exceeded by gain (Fromm and Taubman 1973, p. 53).

In evaluating a specific proposal, more than just the costs and benefits of certain projects need to be examined. The first thing is to define what it is that the community wants to accomplish. This should be done in rather broad terms to facilitate the establishment of overall goals, and in more specific terms, to facilitate the establishment of specific goals aimed at accomplishment of the broad goals. A broad goal, for example, might be to improve the community as a place to live or to assure the smooth movement of traffic.

More specific objectives, or subgoals, would be aimed at the establishment of the best alternatives for accomplishing this. It is in the selection of alternatives that cost-benefit analysis can contribute most significantly. Both large and small ramifications of a project need to be considered. An alternative that costs more than is being lost by simply "living with" a problem, for example, is a poor choice.

Alternatives need to be examined, also, in terms of their various elements. If the major goal is to assure smooth movement of traffic, a subgoal might be to have an adequate bus service. But there are several ways bus service can be provided, thus there may be several alternatives for achieving the subgoal. Suppose one is to provide extended routing and maximum number of buses from 7:00 to 9:00 A.M. and 4:00 to 6:00 P.M., and a more limited routing and fewer buses the rest of the day. This will have certain capital and labor costs peculiar to it. Suppose a second alternative is to have a fairly extensive routing, but essentially the same number of buses all day. This will have a different set of costs and benefits.

Determining costs. Several classes of costs may be incurred in undertaking a project (Fromm and Taubman 1973). One set consists of those that are unique to the project itself. If it were not undertaken, these costs would not be incurred. As indicated with regard to choice of criteria, there are specific costs of a single project, and there are projects where the benefit can be attributed to more than one outcome, giving rise to joint costs.

Suppose solution to the traffic problem were to involve both a public bus system and the construction of feeder streets with express lanes for buses and traffic controls on other lanes. Certain aspects of street renovation would be specific to buses and others specific to automotive traffic. Other aspects would be joint between the two projects. The allocation of these joint costs should be to the overall goal to be achieved by combining these two methods of moving people. In short, the specific costs should not be greater than specific benefits, and likewise the overall cost should not exceed the overall benefits.

Another type of cost that must be considered is that which is incurred indirectly in carrying out a project. There may be opportunity costs to residents of a neighborhood from building a main feeder street through it. These are costs to society that should be considered, although they are not directly related to the project itself.

Analysts must also consider other types of opportunity cost. When idle resources are used to carry out a project, assuming there are no foreseeable uses for these resources within the project time period, the opportunity cost of using them may approach zero. But one must be careful about making assumptions about such costs. Quite frequently it is assumed that government owned factors are worth less than factor costs obtained in the marketplace. This could lead to projects that are unsound from a social standpoint. Other costs, of an indirect type, are negative spillovers from a given project. The best alternatives for solving one problem may create other problems. A well-known example of this is the straightening of stream beds that expedites flows of flood waters but ruins habitat for fish and wildlife.

Determining benefits. The problem of determining benefits involves not only the question of which benefits should be included but also how they are to be measured. It is easy to evaluate something that is bought in the market where a price is established. Where considerable externalities are involved, as often occurs, the measurement problem is of major importance. The same situation obtains when the main concern is the supplying of goods that are nonrival in consumption. Since use by one consumer does not interfere with use by another, there is no way to obtain a monetary value. We just have to assume that if people vote for something or support a decision by a legislative group to do something, the benefits are positive and probably greater than the costs. Actually the benefit side of the analysis collapses, hence measurement of costs becomes academic.

Where there are joint benefits from a project, we have a situation similar to that of joint costs. There are probably certain benefits that can be attributed to each part of the project separately and others that cannot be separated. Suppose a community lies near a major potential tourist attraction, but in order to make it useful, a surfaced highway, lodgings, and other amenities must be built. Once they are in place they can be used for other things. Suppose also that in order to provide for tourists, an electric generating plant must be built. By increasing capacity, the local community can be served as well. Costs and benefits for this portion of the tourism project can be assigned. But how would one determine benefits of the road as they accrue to the local populace? The road would also be of value in building and maintaining the power plant, but of what value?

Agglomeration effects from economic development activities are equally difficult to assess. Suppose new industries make it possible for existing industries to operate more efficiently. How might one assign these lower scale costs as benefits from industrialization? One way might be to try to estimate what it would cost to achieve the same end through other means. If agglomeration benefits derive from a better-trained labor force, one might estimate what it would cost to duplicate on-the-job training in a technical school.

Income redistribution. One of the most common mistakes made in the public sector is to include income redistribution effects in the calculation of benefits from projects. It is common, for example, to hold bus fares low, making subsidization necessary because low income people might be able to ride buses. As pointed out previously, people who ride the bus are not necessarily from low income groups. If redistribution of income is desirable, it is better to do it directly by a grant than to try to build it into projects that have little to do with charity.

National policies often reflect this type of muddied thinking. A defense related project, for example, may be assigned to an area with low information-base people where unemployment is high. The extra costs of the project incurred by doing this are considered to be more than offset by the creation of new jobs in the area. If the industry requires sophisticated techniques, the cheapest labor policy may be to attract skilled workers from other regions. Thus, aside from some possible linkage effects in the local economy, local people gain little from it. The whole process is one of draining resources from one area to another to do something that could have been done better in the first region. A direct subsidy to the local people in the subsidized region may have been much less expensive to the nation.

This does not mean that redistribution benefits should be ignored if they occur as spillovers from projects whose undertaking is decided by efficient criteria. If highly skilled labor were available in the region where the defense project was assigned, this might also change the analysis.

Criterion problem. As indicated with regard to location decisions, in choosing among alternatives, we must implicitly or explicitly adopt criteria, or tests of preference. One step in the process is to predict consequences of alternative projects. Another is to distinguish among preferred versus nonpreferred combinations of consequences.

Maximizing gain vs. minimizing cost. One of the least logical comparison criteria is to maximize gain while minimizing cost. Maximum gain is infinite, but minimum cost is zero. It would have to be a very unusual project that would be better than all others at both ends of the cost-benefit spectrum. For example, use of the criteria would rule out as preferred, a project that had very high benefits but whose costs were slightly above the rest of the alternatives.

Use of ratios. Another widely used criterion is the ranking of projects on the basis of gains to costs. If two different people are analyzing the same project, they will differ as to which effects are treated as costs and which as benefits. For example, widening of a city street to make it a major artery should lead to such clear benefits as lowering congestion and speeding up traffic flow, but it may also cause a lowering of maintenance costs for the existing roadway through economies of scale. These latter cost reductions can be interpreted as a benefit of the widening or as a reduction in cost. The resulting ratios will be quite different depending upon whether the value is added to the benefits or subtracted from the costs. This problem is especially bad when projects of various sizes are being compared. Suppose one project costs $100 with benefits of $1000, and another costs $10,000 and yields benefits of $30,000. It is not at all clear that a ratio of 10 to 1 is better than 3 to 1 in this instance.

Use of partial criteria. Sometimes only some of the consequences of alternative actions can be identified, and it is necessary to use "partial criteria." That is, ideally we should be able to choose a course of action that maximizes something, like the profits of a firm, the recreation opportunities of a community, or the housing facilities for the poor, subject to available resources. But often we do not know how to measure these objectives, so we pick some portion that we can measure, like number of people per room. This may ignore room sizes or other important factors. Thus, a weak partial criterion leads to poor decisions.

Wrong concepts of cost and benefit. Wrong concepts of cost or benefit may grow out of adoption of erroneous criteria. In a World War II study of ways to destroy enemy shipping, the criterion adopted was the ratio of enemy ships sunk (the benefit) to allied man-years of effort (the cost). In this study, man-years of effort included time spent in construction of vessels, production of equipment and spare parts, and training of personnel and their replacements. This is erroneous so far as it includes sunk costs. The sacrifice entailed by using equipment is its value in other operations not the cost of constructing it. Also, it is not necessary to sink ships to put them out of operation. Use of these criteria prejudiced the analysis against mine laying that would destroy shipping by disabling it.

Suboptimization. The suboptimization problem is as important in the public as in the private sphere. It is often very difficult for a community to have only one person or one committee look at all of its possible choices at the same time. Each decision impacts on others, and it becomes necessary to break decision making and analysis into pieces. The problem with this is that each piece will be examined by people with different viewpoints and different objectives. Even plausible criteria for solving problems at a lower level may not be in harmony with overall goals for the community.

There are also advantages to doing this type of analysis and decision making, since more detail can be considered. Further, there is less risk of tying all of the analysis to a single "bad criterion" that might be adopted at the higher level. In fact tying all analysis to a single "good" criterion might overlook important lower level impacts. Thus, suboptimizing may be the best choice, providing each analyst is aware of the relationship between the criteria being used at this level and those considered at the higher level.

Time. Another complication in the choice of appropriate criteria is time flow of benefits and costs. Most projects have long-term as well as short-term aspects. For example, investment costs may be incurred at one point in time, and maintenance costs may be incurred over years into the future beginning with some key year. Benefits will occur from completion into the future. Costs and benefits must be shown in terms of present values. Thus the cost would be

$$C = I + \sum_{t=1}^{n} MC/(1 + r)^t$$

where C = total cost of the project, I = investment cost, MC = maintenance cost, t = year, n = number of life years, and r = opportunity cost of capital.

Likewise, the benefit will be reduced also to present value by the same process, so

$$B = \sum_{t=1}^{n} YB/(1 + r)^t$$

where B = total benefit, and YB = yearly benefit. Calculation of the cost-benefit relationship (R) will then be $R = B/C$. If $R > 1$, the project is feasible. Alternatives could be compared by ranking R values, but a better method is to take the differences between B and C for all feasible projects. This would be an ideal criterion because it would allow maximization of net benefits to society.

Economics of Regulation
In addition to spillover effects resulting from public action to raise and expend revenues, there are numerous economic effects from public regulation of private activity that should be noted.

Public regulation of private morality. In every society there are laws regulating activities that are regarded by many of its members as purely private affairs. These include the performance of abortions, prostitution, gambling, and the use of various kinds of drugs such as alcohol, marijuana, and so on. Because of the ideological conflict, partakers of these goods and services seem willing to take risks in order to consume. Assuming that the utility function of a majority of the society favors some sort of control of these activities, what course of action would result in greatest social benefit? In short, which alternative gives the highest cost-benefit ratio?

One alternative is outright exclusion. There are a number of reasons that this is economically a poor decision. We must recognize that exclusion in the face of persistent demand does not work. The black market is the answer buyers and sellers give to that type of regulation; but the black market imposes costs on society. It results in a lowering of quality on the part of sellers, and it raises prices by imposing extra costs that must be met. The net result is that consumers receive lower value for a higher price.

The regulator might say, "Well, hallelujah! It serves the consumer of these things right!" But under the principle of maximum social gain, if penalizing consumers of these things are pluses, then the costs to society of increased crime due to black market activity must be counted also. Further, there is no way consumption of these items can be completely ignored on the plus side.

The other alternative would be regulation without exclusion. This alternative recognizes that minorities have rights as well as majorities.

Let us consider one of the oldest and most persistent services, prostitution. Prostitutes offer their customers a service that has two dimensions, quantity and quality. Quality is a function of (1) experience (information base), (2) physical makeup of the provider, and (3) investment in surroundings, appearance, and disease prevention. Quantity has its limitations due to physical limits, but it can be increased somewhat by lowering quality.

Assume that at the beginning of a period, prostitution in the community is legal and freely pursued. There is a competitive market on both sellers' and buyers' sides. The price (P_1) and quantity (Q_1) are determined by the equilibrium point (E) between supply and demand. Since all is on the up-and-up, houses of prostitution can advertise without risk; clients can compare prices and quality; information is relatively cheap to come by. Those houses not controlling venereal disease will lose their reputations and have to lower prices. Suppliers of the service can charge their opportunity cost with no risk factor added, since there are no threats of imprisonment or fines. Those demanding the service have no need to invest large amounts of time and other resources obtaining information to avoid risk of poor quality (venereal disease). (See Fig. 7.5.)

Now assume that the community decides to completely exclude prostitution. This causes the demand curve to shift somewhat, since there are some customers deterred by the thought of committing a criminal act. It is assumed that these outnumber those who are attracted because it is illegal. The new demand curve is D'. Cost of doing business has now increased for the suppliers. The supply curve shifts to S'. Since there are no legal houses of prostitution, the prostitutes have to take to the streets. They have to avoid detection or pay off the police. Quality of service declines, not only because of less attractive atmosphere, but also because of less attention to disease prevention and general physical deterioration. Since everything is underground, the flow of information to customers is restricted. Prices go up, and quantity offered and taken declines. As information about quality becomes more expensive, the wealthier clients have an advantage in seeking out healthy prostitutes. Venereal disease rates among the poor increase rapidly.

Suppose the community decides to leave sale of the service legal but to control it so that younger members of society cannot

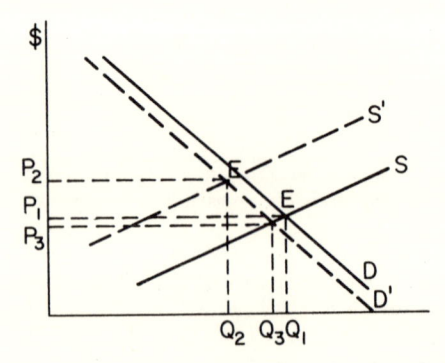

Fig. 7.5. Demand and supply of prostitution.

Economic Effects of Public Action   191

partake and so that mandatory disease control can be maintained.
Quality will stay approximately where it is; possibly some improvement will be noted. The supply curve will remain where it is, but
the demand curve will shift owing to exclusion of younger customers. The quantity offered and taken will decline slightly (Q_3),
and the price will also decline.

The same general type of analysis could be made for any of the
other "immoral" goods and services offered. An additional note
should be made of the fact that legal exclusion often invites a new
type of middleman, the crime syndicate, which takes over the job of
"protecting" the participants from the law in return for a large
share of the profits. This adds even more to the cost of doing
business and creates an additional burden to society. All in all,
if legislation in the morality area is to be attempted, control is
economically far superior to exclusion.

Economics of price controls. Another rather questionable area of
community intervention in the private sphere has to do with attempts to control prices: the price of gas, oil, water, electricity, housing, transport, or whatever is deemed by some pressure
group to be too high. A simple solution is offered: "set a lower
price and provide a system of enforcement that prevents chiselers
from getting away with illegal prices." This is another attempt to
redistribute income in the wrong way.

Suppose a community imposes controls on rentals. Further,
suppose the housing market is controlled by a monopolist with demand curve AR, average cost curve AC, and a marginal cost curve
(MC) that represent the supply curve for the industry (Fig. 7.6).
The price is reduced from P_1 (at which Q_1 of housing was rented) to
P_2. Instead of demand curve AR and marginal revenue curve MR, the
monopolist now faces a straight-line $AR = MR$ curve at $P_2 - \hat{P}_2$. He/
she could not afford to supply more than Q_2 of housing, since the

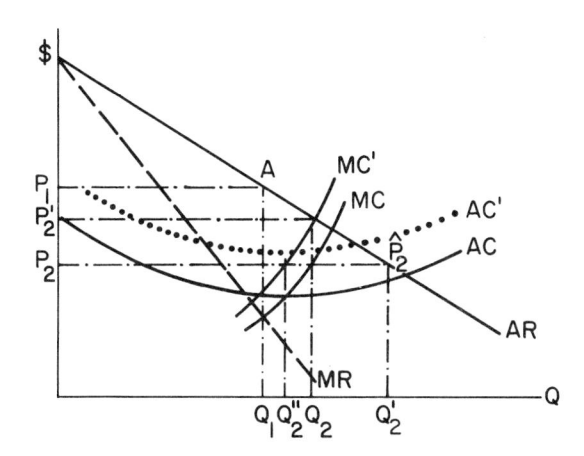

Fig. 7.6. Supply and demand for housing.

MC curve cuts the MR curve at that point, and he/she would lose heavily on the next unit supplied beyond Q_2. But at Q_2 people would have been willing to pay P_2', and for P_2 a supply of Q_2' units would be required to meet the demand. Thus, a large gap has been established between the supply of housing that could be made available and the amount needed to meet demand.

The supplier can set the terms with regard to meeting demand. He or she can accept bribes for preferred position on the waiting list. He or she can keep repairs to a bare minimum or below. Still he or she would not make as much money as before when charging P_1 and furnishing Q_1, even though more units are rented out. Whatever their condition may be, the landlord can continuously rent apartments, so why bother to clean them up between renters. Further, there is no incentive to build additional units. The result is a perennial shortage of housing.

Now suppose inflation occurs, and the cost curve shifts upward to AC'. There is now a new marginal cost curve as well. The landlord is losing money for each unit rented. In order to minimize losses he or she must cut the number of units back to Q_2. As renters move out, the landlord nails some of the units shut or abandons them. Demand is still at Q_2, and the situation for those without shelter grows more grim. Chances for black market operations increase.

If communities insist on controlling prices for any reason, there is one rule that could be followed to avoid the gap in supply and demand shown in Fig. 7.6. That is to price at the point where the marginal cost curve of the seller cuts the AR curve, as illustrated in Fig. 7.7. The price might be somewhat higher than regulators like, but the quantity offered will also be larger. Further supply and demand will be in balance. Instead of supplying Q_1 at price P_1, the supplier would provide Q_2 at price P_2. Once a price

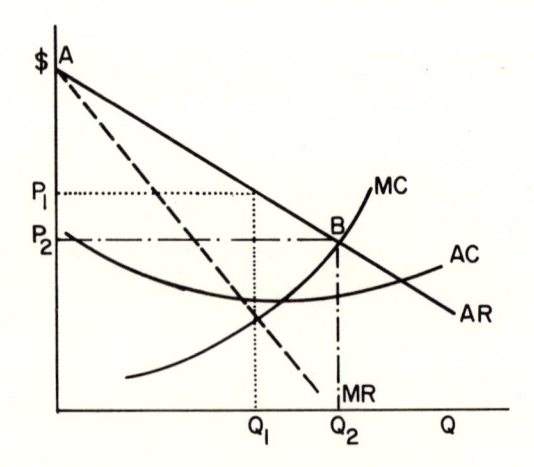

Fig. 7.7. Marginal cost pricing.

is fixed, the *AR* curve becomes horizontal at the price, and marginal revenue equals average revenue. Therefore, at point *B*, *MC* = *MR*, and an optimum is attained.

In the case of commodities such as electricity or natural gas, there are large variations in demand at different times of the day and different days of the year. If a single uniform rate is imposed, peak load users are subsidized by all other consumers. Costs of investing in and maintaining enough capacity to meet peak loads must be shouldered by all users. For these types of goods and services, the only sensible approach, where price control is deemed necessary, is peak load pricing. That is, at least two rates are used, a high rate for the peak periods and a lower one for all other times. This cuts demand during peak periods and shifts some of it to other hours. Skillful planning could eliminate brownouts and other periods of shortage such as water shortage, bus congestion, and so on. This problem is similar to the queuing problem discussed previously.

Economics of pollution control. The environment is a commonly held resource. That is, it is a valuable natural asset that cannot be reduced to private ownership. The mantle of air over our communities, the water courses, complex ecological systems, and large landscapes belong to everyone. This means that their services are available at zero price to the individual unit. There is a folk saying, "That which is everyone's is nobody's." The natural result is some type of abuse.

According to the materials balance principle of physics, the mass of inputs to production must balance with the mass of outputs. Thus, that which does not end up in a marketable product must yet be disposed of. Since leftovers have no price, disposal is done in the easiest and least costly way possible. At low levels of population and economic activity, the return of these "by-products" to the environment is harmless, since the environment is constructed to take care of a certain amount. When there is an overload, however, whether sewage from man or volcanic ash from nature, problems are created.

The environment as a receiver of waste has become a scarce resource. It is still regarded as costless to industries, local governments, and individuals. This is true even though others are finding they must pay to clean up certain segments before further use can be made of them. It is also true even though the bases of other industries are being destroyed. Since no one is responsible for the environment, everyone overuses it. As it becomes more and more degraded, the range of services it can perform for us gets narrower. At its limit a river may be useless as anything but an industrial sewer. Fear of fire may even keep barges away. These things indicate that there has been a fundamental failure in the market system.

Common ownership not only contributes to degradation of the environment, but also interferes with efforts to clean it up. There are no incentives for industries to develop the technologies necessary or to apply them, if known. The market system works quite well in stimulating exploitation of the environment but falls on its face where preservation is concerned. The result is that environment is mismanaged, overused, and degraded, with little attention paid to necessary technology and investment for its protection.

Compounding the problem is the fact that the control of pollution takes resources that could be used to produce other types of wealth. The other types can be identified in the marketplace and have prices placed upon them. To many people, the value of a clean environment is questionable, and environmentalists are viewed as kooks crying wolf. To these people, the choice between use of resources to build more automobiles versus pollution control is an easy one to make.

The environmentalist is a member of a pressure group and faces the same responsibilities as a member of any other such group. He/she must work to convince the people of the community they should have the same utility functions for clean air, clean water, plus a balanced ecology, as he/she does. Once the environmentalist has accomplished that task, he/she becomes responsible to society with regard to resources devoted to environmental purposes. In any community a decision has to be made. The question "How far can we go with pollution control?" is a matter of rational choice, requiring criteria for comparing and evaluating alternatives.

If the criterion chosen is the net amount of utility received by society from the productive process, then appraisal must be made of all facets of production. Assume a community has X resources to be used in production of G goods and services to serve the needs of households, government, and investment. Now assume that there is a by-product of P pollutants in the process. Assume that U represents utility attached to each facet of the process (that is, U_g is the utility attached to a unit of G and $-U_p$ to a unit of P). Pollution has negative utility value. Total welfare (TW) of society is enhanced by the productive process in accordance with (7.1), the balance equation.

$$TW = U_g G + (-U_p)P - X = U_g G - (U_p P + X) \qquad (7.1)$$

Now suppose it is decided to devote some of the resources to environmental control with E units produced. Set damages from pollution $D = P - E$, and let Y = resources required in pollution control. Goods and services are reduced by ΔG. The change in total welfare is related to the trade-off between ΔG and ΔD. Thus $\Delta TW = -U_g \Delta G - U_p \Delta D = -U_g \Delta Y - U_p \Delta D$, or an increase in welfare requires a decrease in treatment costs and a decrease in utility lost through pollution.

The relative values of the utility functions influences the outcome. Thus, if the populace has a higher utility for goods than for a clean environment, there will be a tendency to sacrifice less G and tolerate a higher D. On the other hand, if utility from G is lower than for D, a tendency will be noted toward greater sacrifice of G to obtain a large decline in D. If it is assumed that utility increases as G declines and decreases as D declines, then some balance will be found where $\Delta Y = -\Delta D$. This balance will be determined through support of antipollution laws at the local level (Freeman, Haveman, and Kneese 1973).

Economics of queuing. Many communities face queuing problems at public facilities. They range from the stacking of airplanes at the airport to traffic jams to lines at the drinking fountain in the park. Queuing costs money, but the impact varies with circumstances and individuals involved. For example, where an airliner is held up to allow small planes to land, the cost is very high; it includes fuel costs, time costs for crews, and the opportunity cost of the passengers on the plane. Offsetting that are the same costs for occupants of the small planes, but theirs are on a much lower level. Where cars are held up by traffic jams, motor fuel is wasted, time is wasted, automobile engines sustain extra wear, and people's nerves get frayed.

The problem with queuing is that it usually occurs at certain periods. The facilities are sufficient for ordinary use, but at certain times demand exceeds the supply. We have noted that utilities meet these problems with peak load pricing, a market-type solution. Those who wish to use a facility at a particular time when queuing is likely to occur are charged extra. This encourages many of them to shift to periods of lesser demand. Sometimes this type of solution is rather unpopular. If small planes were charged extra fees for landing at particular hours of the day, there undoubtedly would be some vigorous objections. For traffic jams, likewise, a toll system for certain hours is used. Tolls may be graduated downward with increased occupancy of cars. With one passenger the charge might be $1.00, for two $0.50, for three $0.25, and for four or more, nothing. This should encourage use of car pools. The alternative to queuing problems is to provide excessively large facilities requiring large investments. It is up to the community to decide.

SUMMARY

Spillover effects occur because activities engaged in by economic units affect the welfare of other units. They lead to serious misallocations of resources in many instances. Where spillovers indicate that larger quantities of a good should be produced than the private market is willing to supply, the public sector often moves in with subsidies. Since public goods violate the exclusion principle and are nonrival, they have a maximum amount of spillover. There are also spillover effects from other activities of government, such as the processes of raising revenue, expending money, regulating public activity, and enforcing the law.

Taxation takes money that could be used for other purposes. The incidence of taxation varies widely. Some taxes can be passed on to other people, and some cannot. There is always a problem of equity in taxation. It is generally contended that rich people suffer less loss of utility from paying taxes than do poor people. Taxes are called regressive if they impinge upon poor people and progressive if the rich have to pay. Income taxes are generally regarded as the most progressive, and sales taxes the least progressive. However, each type of tax has special spillover effects that should be noted by local officials.

In the expenditure of public funds, there are many possibilities for spillover. Where expenditures are made for goods and services to carry out public projects, spillovers occur both among those receiving the money and those affected by the projects themselves. Expenditures of transfer funds affect recipients directly, but have indirect effects on many others.

Spillover effects make analysis of benefits from public activity rather difficult. At best, economic analysis can cause debate to focus on objectives, cost estimates, and possible ways of identifying externalities. Numerous possible ways of accomplishing these objectives have been tried out in recent years. For all of them the important question is, "Is society better off because of this expenditure, or isn't it?" This is also expressed as the principle of maximum social gain.

In its activity of enforcing the law, local government creates many different types of spillover effects. For example, for public morality issues such as prostitution, gambling, abortions, and use of drugs such as alcohol, marijuana, heroin, and so on, it can be shown that regulation is economically far superior to abolition. If a community is going to get into the areas of price controls, the best approach is to price where the marginal cost and average revenue curves coincide. This will assure adequate supplies at a lower price than would otherwise be charged. Control of pollution involves giving up some resources, and the products that would result, in exchange for less pollution. Enhancement of social welfare depends heavily upon whether the people value goods more than lack of pollution. Where queuing is a local problem, a system of special charges for use of facilities during peak periods is the best solution.

REVIEW QUESTIONS

1. What is meant by a spillover effect?
2. How do spillover effects affect demand and supply curves?
3. Why do spillover costs call for public action?
4. Who should pay for spillover benefits?
5. Discuss some of the spillover effects of taxation.
6. Discuss some of the spillover effects of income taxes.
7. What spillover effects result from taxing inheritances?

8. What spillover effects are claimed for Henry George-type land taxation?
9. What is the spillover effect of imposing sales taxes on goods with elastic demand?
10. Why do spillover effects of taxation affect rich people differently than poor people?
11. Discuss some of the spillover effects that might result from local government carrying on its various activities.
12. What are the spillover effects of transfer payments?
13. What is the rationale behind cost-benefit ratios?
14. How do spillover effects affect such ratios?
15. In regulating private morality, why is outright exclusion usually an economically poor decision?
16. What are some economic advantages of regulation?
17. Would pure competition be preferred to either exclusion or regulation?
18. Discuss some of the economic effects of price controls.
19. What is marginal cost pricing and how might it be used by a community to control prices?
20. How should price controls be altered where there are peak use or other queuing problems?
21. Economists designate some goods as "free," meaning everyone can get them at zero cost. How does pollution affect the free character of the environment?
22. What is the natural result of people's having access to free goods?
23. How does common ownership interfere with efforts to clean the environment?
24. What trade-offs do communities find desirable as they approach environmental problems?
25. If net amount of utility received by society from the production process is the criterion chosen for comparing alternatives, what kind of model might the analyst use to assure that all facets of the production problem are covered?
26. What are the alternatives to user charges in solving queuing problems?

REFERENCES

Freeman, A. M. III, R. H. Haveman, and A. V. Kneese. 1973. *The economics of environmental policy*. New York: Wiley.
Fromm, G., and P. Taubman. 1973. *Public economic theory and policy*. New York: Macmillan.
Haveman, R. H. 1970. *The economics of the public sector*. New York: Wiley.
North, D. C., and R. L. Meller. 1973. *The economics of public issues*. New York: Harper & Row.

CHAPTER 8
Roles of People in Economic Activity

Needs of people provide the major reason for economic activity, and abilities of people provide the most important inputs into production. The characteristics of people are therefore of major interest in the study of any economy.

PEOPLE AS CONSUMERS
Aside from certain governmental activities, such as the military, most production is for the purpose of eventually producing commodities and services that directly satisfy human wants. In the process a great deal of productive capacity is devoted to the production of intermediate goods (goods that will be used as direct inputs to the production of other goods), and capital goods (durables that assist people in the productive function but are not used up immediately in the activity).

People as consumers dictate much of what will be produced (with considerable assistance from other people particularly those in influential positions in government and industry). In a perfectly competitive society, consumers would indeed be "kings." But in the real world of mixed capitalist and socialist societies, consumer sovereignty is somewhat a myth. In mixed capitalist societies, advertising is employed to build "utility" concepts in people's minds. In socialist and other totalitarian societies, consumers often take what is given to them by the bureaucracy. In all societies, there are "trend setters" who influence others' tastes.

Yet there is considerable power in consumer hands, usually buying power. Regardless of the way that utility functions are formed, people generally try to get the "most bang for their buck," or in economic terms, they try to equalize marginal utility per unit of money spent. This is known as the equimarginal principle. Symbolically it is shown as $MU_1/P_1 = MU_2/P_2 = \ldots = MU_n/P_n$, where MU represents marginal utility, P represents price, and n is number

Roles of People in Economic Activity   199

of goods. When a person is comparing two goods and reaches the
point where $MU_1/P_1 = MU_2/P_2$, he or she is said to be indifferent
between them. The amount of each one that will be acquired will
depend upon the budget available to be spent on them. Analysis can
be made by means of indifference curves.

These curves represent combinations of goods 1 and 2 for which
a person will be indifferent, or $MU_1/P_1 = MU_2/P_2$. The model is
drawn under a set of specific assumptions.

  1. Any point on a curve represents the same level of satisfaction as any other point.
  2. An indifference curve lying to the right of another represents a greater level of utility.
  3. A consumer has the ability to rank preferences via indifference curves, that is, he or she knows when he or she gets greater satisfaction.
  4. Indifference curves may not intersect.
  5. A figure showing all the indifference curves of an individual (the indifference map) represents that individual's utility function for the goods.

In Fig. 8.1 a set of indifference curves is shown with a budget
constraint line. Point A represents the optimum amount of goods
$X(X_1)$ and $Y(Y_1)$ that the consumer can purchase given the budget (I)
available and the relative prices of the goods.

When the price of one good changes, there are two effects:
income and substitution. The income effect comes about because a
price change means more or less money will be available to spend
on both products. The substitution effect means that price
changes, by themselves, cause changes in the combination of the
two goods that will be purchased. These two effects are illustrated in Fig. 8.2. Point A represents the optimum attained with
the same prices as in Fig. 8.1 with X_1 and Y_1 taken. The price of

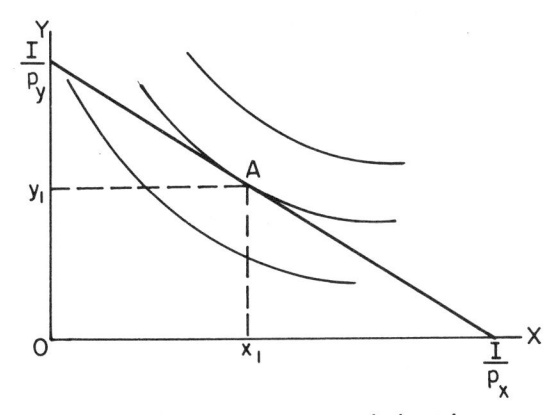

Fig. 8.1. Consumer optimization.

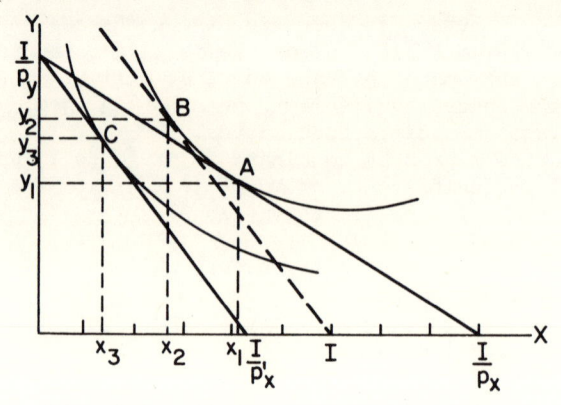

Fig. 8.2. Effect of a price change.

X rises to P_X'. This causes the budget line to shift left, since the budget (I) remains the same. A new optimum is now established at point C with X_3 and Y_3 taken. This change is in two parts, however. Suppose the consumer is granted just enough money to offset the income shift due to the price change. This gives him budget line I', which has the same slope as the new line established by the price change. Because of the slope difference from the original budget line, it is tangent to the original indifference curve at point B; the consumer has the same satisfaction as before, but the combination of X and Y has changed. The amount $Y_2 - Y_1$ of Y has been substituted for $X_1 - X_2$ of X. The income effect of the price change causes a further reduction in purchase of both goods, from Y_2 to Y_3 of Y and from X_2 to X_3 of X.

The rather large substitution effect suggests that this consumer reacted somewhat elastically to the price change. In other words, the price change caused the consumer to make a fairly large substitution of Y for X. This type of reaction is also a pertinent characteristic of consumer sovereignty. The more elastic the demand, the less control the seller has over the buyer.

Elasticity is defined as the slope of the demand function times the ratio between average price and average quantity for the part of the demand curve being considered. In order to discuss it, we must first derive the demand curve itself. This is done by extracting from Fig. 8.2 the quantity of X taken at the two prices P_X and P_X'. Let P_X = \$1.40, P_X' = \$2.91, X_1 = 4.1, X_3 = 1.3, and I = \$12.67. These data on prices and quantity can be transferred directly to the demand function shown in Fig. 8.3. The slope of the curve is $(4.1 - 1.3)/(1.40 - 2.91) = 2.8/-1.51 = -1.85$. Elasticity is $-1.85(2.16/2.7) = -1.48$, so demand is slightly elastic.

Consumers also react to prices of goods that have relationships with demand for other goods. These are known as cross elasticities. They are defined essentially the same as above, except that the comparison is between price of good X and quantity of good Y. Thus, the formula becomes $(\Delta Q_Y/\Delta P_X)(P_X/Q_Y) = \eta$, where Δ indi-

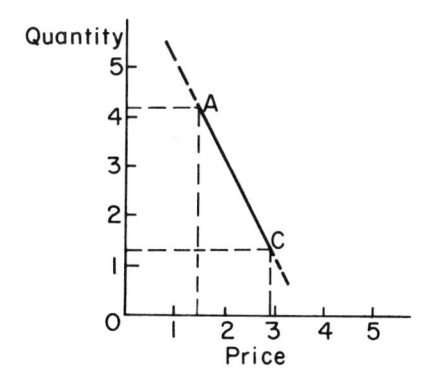

Fig. 8.3. Demand for good X.

cates change. In this case the elasticity value, η, can be either positive or negative. If it is positive, X and Y are substitutes for one another. If it is negative, they are complements. These differences are illustrated in Fig. 8.4. If cross elasticity is zero or nearly zero, we can say the goods are unrelated.

As people's incomes change, their reactions to certain goods change as well. Income elasticity of demand can be measured to determine the effect that a small change in income will have on consumption of particular goods. The curves that relate to income are called "Engel curves." Elasticity is defined as slope of the Engel curve times original income divided by original quantity, or = $(\Delta Q/\Delta I)(I/Q)$. Engel curves have a number of different shapes within any particular domain of interest.

These are illustrated in Fig. 8.5. The domain of interest is between $4000 and $30,000 income. Commodity A is a superior good in that as incomes rise, within the domain, the quantity taken increases, although at a decreasing rate. Commodity B is also a superior good, but the quantity taken increases at an increasing rate. This commodity is called a "preferred superior good" because

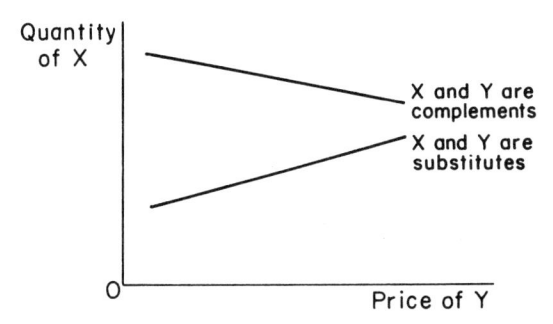

Fig. 8.4. Cross-elasticity of demand.

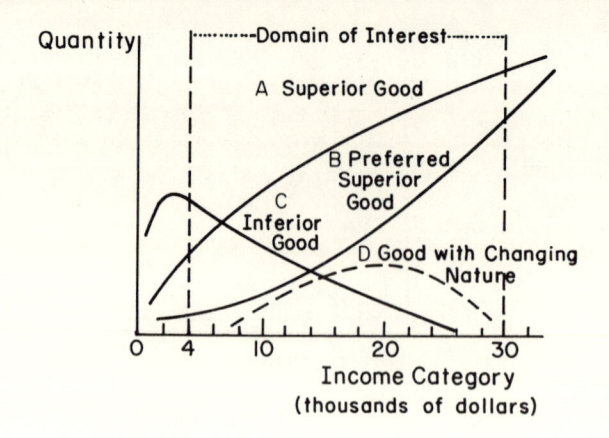

Fig. 8.5. Shapes of Engel curves.

its superiority increases with increasing income. Commodity B has higher income elasticity than does commodity A. Commodity C is inferior within the domain, in that as incomes rise the quantity taken declines (its income elasticity is negative). It may well have been superior at some lower level of income than is being considered. Commodity D is superior for incomes from $4000 to $20,000 but is inferior beyond $20,000. It is labeled a "good with a changing nature." These phenomena were discovered by Harmston and Hino in a study of demand for food products (1970).

Changes in income are often associated with changes in taste, hence attitudes toward individual goods. Other things, such as fads, also impact upon taste. Studied over time, significant changes can be seen in Engel curves for a particular good. Goods that were preferred superior at one time may change to superior; goods with a changing nature may become inferior, and superior goods may become goods with a changing nature. Some superior goods may also become preferred superior (Harmston and Hino 1970).

As tastes change, overall demand for products changes. This impacts on existing industries giving new life to some and signaling the death sentence for others. Thus, changes in consumption patterns of people are of great importance to communities whose industries produce consumption-type goods or produce inputs of importance to such goods.

One of the forces working to change consumption habits in Western-style economies is promotion, including advertising. We would expect a positive response of quantity to advertising expenditures. The extent of that response could be measured by multiplying the slope of the response line by the ratio between an original quantity consumed and an original advertising budget. This value we call advertising elasticity. Of all economic activities, promotion truly tends to create utility. If we say that utility exists in the mind of the consumer, then anything that provides additional information aimed at changing that utility is participating in the utility creating process. Thus, a testing laboratory report, such as those published by Consumer's Union, could also qualify. People's utility functions are influenced by a large number of variables, many of which are impossible to measure. We have touched on only a few of them here.

Lancaster Model

Lancaster (1966) has proposed a model that approaches the problem somewhat differently. Since in the traditional model discussed so far, analysis is based on an assumption of a "representative" consumer, we must assume that consumers are somewhat homogeneous in the way they look at individual goods. They can discern no differences in characteristics of a good, and the number of goods and characteristics of the goods are, therefore, equal.

Suppose, however, that each good has several characteristics. If the number of goods exceeds the number of characteristics, there cannot be a "representative" consumer because such a consumer would only buy until the desire for characteristics was satisfied. The fact that people buy all sorts of goods indicates they are not homogeneous in their attitudes toward individual goods.

Rather than a representative consumer, Lancaster (1971) uses a representative efficiency frontier. This frontier is developed from the concept of consumption technology. (Here technology is considered in terms of method instead of information.) The model used is based on the following assumptions:

1. There is a linear additive relationship between goods and characteristics.
2. All characteristics are quantitative and objectively measurable, that is, the statement "b_{ij} is the quantity of the ith characteristic possessed by a unit amount of the jth good" is universally understood and has empirical meaning.
3. If Z_i and X_j are quantities of the ith characteristic and jth good respectively, then
    a. (linearity) $Z_i = b_{ij} X_j$
    b. (additivity) $Z_i = b_{ij} X_j + b_{ik} X_k$, that is, given quantities of two goods X_j and X_k, the amount of the ith characteristic possessed by the collection (X_j, X_k) is the sum of the amounts possessed by each. Therefore in a system of r characteristics and n goods

$$Z_i = \sum_{j=1}^{n} b_{ij} X_j \quad (i = 1, 2, \ldots, r)$$

Assumption 3b can also be expressed in matrix terms as $Z = BX$, where Z = vector of characteristics, B = matrix of coefficients

(b_{ij}) relating goods and characteristics, and X = the vector of goods (X_j).

Consumption technology expresses the relationship between characteristics and goods, but the relationship between characteristics and people is expressed by preferences. Any particular bundle of goods will be preferred to another bundle if and only if the collection of characteristics in the first bundle is preferred to the collection of characteristics in the second.

Assumptions of preference include

1. Quasiordering over the set of all possible characteristics collections. Let P = preferred to, $\bar{P}$ = not preferred to, and I = indifferent between. Then
   a. If $Z^1 P Z^2$ and $Z^2 P Z^3$, then $Z^1 P Z^3$ (transitivity).
   b. For every pair of vectors Z^1, Z^2 either $Z^1 \bar{P} Z^2$ or $Z^2 P Z^1$ (completeness).
2. For any characteristics collection Z^*, the upper and lower preference sets $\{Z|Z^* \bar{P} Z\}$ and $\{Z|Z \bar{P} Z^*\}$ are closed (continuity).
3. For any two collections, Z^1, Z^2 should be such that $Z^1 I Z^2$, that is, any strong convex combination of Z^1 and Z^2 is preferred to either Z^1 or Z^2 (strict convexity).
4. For any collection Z^*, there is some collection Z such that $Z P Z^*$ (nonsatiation).
5. For any two collections Z^1 and Z^2 such that Z^1 has more of at least one characteristic and no less of any other than Z^2, we have $Z^1 P Z^2$ (all characteristics positively desired).
6. Given the opportunity to choose from some set Z of characteristics collections, the consumer will choose the collection that maximizes $U(Z)$ over Z.

The first three assumptions enable the summarization of consumers' preferences in terms of a utility function whose indifference curves are strictly convex to the origin. The next two assumptions, together with the first three, guarantee that consumer's preferences can be expressed as an ordinal utility function (neoclassical kind) with all first order partial derivatives positive.

The consumer's choice, given a budget constraint, can be formulated as the following optimization problem:

Maximize $U(Z)$
subject to $Z = BX$
$X \geq 0$
$PX \leq K$

The objective function being defined in characteristics space (C-space) and the feasible set being defined by constraints in the goods space (G-space), it becomes necessary to bring them into the same space. This is done by mapping one of them into the space of the other using the linking relationship $Z = BX$.

Now we have a choice. We can either express the utility function in terms of goods or the constraints in terms of characteristics. Since consumption technology gives characteristics in terms of goods, a most obvious choice is to map the utility function into goods space. Substitute $Z = BX$ in the utility function to obtain the consumer's optimizing problem in the form

Maximize $\mu(BX) = V(X)$
subject to $PX \leq k$
$X \geq 0$

Because the calculus cannot be used when the number of characteristics is less than the number of goods, nonlinear programming must be relied upon.

<u>Transformation between G-space and C-space.</u> General properties of mapping from a budget set in G-space to the feasible set in C-space can be illustrated by the following example. Let

$$B = \begin{bmatrix} 2 & 1.8 & 1 \\ 1 & 1.8 & 2 \end{bmatrix}, \quad P = [1, 1, 1], \quad K = 1$$

The budget set in G-space is the tetrahedron bounded by the coordinate planes and the budget plane $X_1 + X_3 + X_3 = 1$. (See Fig. 8.6A.) Its extreme points are

$$0 = \begin{bmatrix} 0 \\ 0 \\ 0 \end{bmatrix}, \quad X^1 = \begin{bmatrix} 1 \\ 0 \\ 0 \end{bmatrix}, \quad X^2 = \begin{bmatrix} 0 \\ 1 \\ 0 \end{bmatrix}, \quad X^3 = \begin{bmatrix} 0 \\ 0 \\ 1 \end{bmatrix}$$

Since $Z = BX$, we can express it as

$$\begin{bmatrix} Z_1 \\ Z_2 \end{bmatrix} = \begin{bmatrix} 2 & 1.8 & 1 \\ 1 & 1.8 & 2 \end{bmatrix} \begin{bmatrix} X^1 \\ X^2 \\ X^3 \end{bmatrix}$$

Hence, the transformation between G-space and C-space is determined by

$$Z_1 = 2X_1 + 1.8X_2 + X_3$$
$$Z_2 = X_1 + 1.8X_2 + 2X_3$$

and the images of 0, X^1, X^2, X^3 in C-space are

$$0 = \begin{bmatrix} 0 \\ 0 \end{bmatrix}, \quad Z^1 = \begin{bmatrix} 2 \\ 1 \end{bmatrix}, \quad Z^2 = \begin{bmatrix} 1.8 \\ 1.8 \end{bmatrix}, \quad Z^3 = \begin{bmatrix} 1 \\ 2 \end{bmatrix}$$

The set of convex combinations of 0, Z^1, Z^2, Z^3 is represented by area K shown in Fig. 8.6B. Points X^1, X^2, and X^3 are called extreme points of the budget set. Each of these maps into an extreme point of K, that is, Z^2 is an extreme point of K because it is the image of X^2, and no other extreme point maps into it. Based on optimizing theory, Lancaster shows that all possible optimum points lie on the outer boundary of K. Under an assumption of linearity, this boundary becomes a "representative efficiency frontier" that can, then, be used to examine consumer demand.

Lancaster's model is the basis for a great deal of theoretical inquiry, but it has not been effectively applied to actual problems. This is largely because qualities of goods, like utility, are psychological in nature. Psychologist Abraham Maslow (1954) has provided a conceptual framework that treats utility as a hierarchy of needs. It includes physiological needs (food, clothing, and shelter); safety needs (protection from risks beyond those of mere survival); need for belongingness and love (the need to be accepted by others); need for esteem and status (the need to be respected); and need for self-realization (the need to understand one's role in the world). These needs are the framework for assessment of qualities in various kinds of goods. Food, for instance, could have qualities that satisfy several of these needs including nutrition, background for social intercourse, and gourmet qualities that provide status.

The importance of people as consumers to the community economic system lies in the market they create for locally produced goods and services. It was noted previously that local economies exist

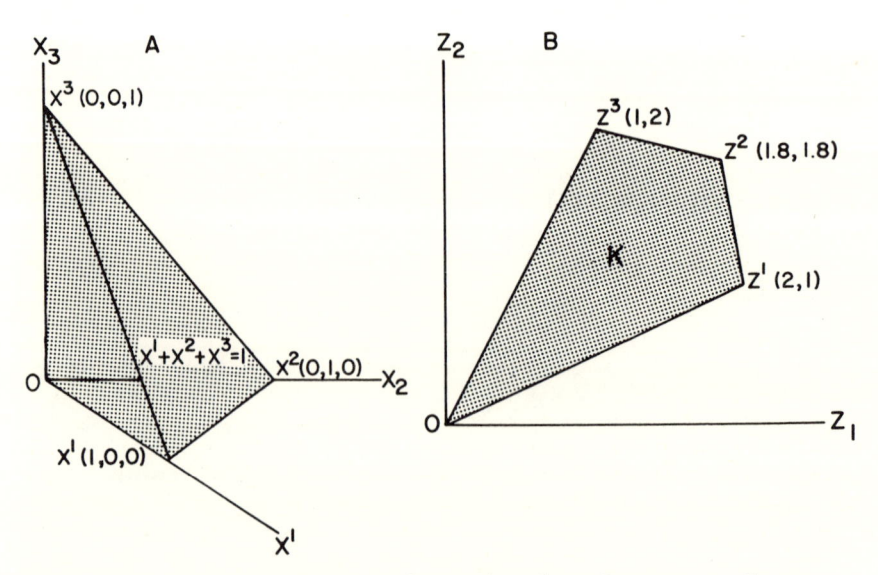

Fig. 8.6. An illustration of mapping from G-space to C-space.

because of specialization and trade. The relationships among buyers and sellers who are residents of the community give us multipliers. Relationships established with residents of other communities give us exogenous demand and back flows of basic income. Any factors that affect consumption are, therefore, of prime importance to community decision makers.

PEOPLE AS CONSUMERS AND PRODUCERS

The distinction between the act of consuming and that of producing is not a pure one. Where a person derives pleasure from work, we say he or she receives "psychic income." This is one way of saying he or she receives utility from the act of production. Other less esoteric acts are also combinations of consumption and production. The act of driving an automobile is the production of a service. If it is done in the family auto, it is also an act of consumption. If it is done in a taxicab, it is strictly production with the product sold to someone else.

An individual complemented by certain nonhuman resources is really a multistage, multiproduct production unit. He or she is multistage in that certain acts go through several phases and multiproduct in that, as Lancaster (1971, p. 133) has pointed out, "the simplest consumption activity will be characterized by joint outputs." Lee (1980) has shown that consumption is closely aligned with production, so that the previous statement can be applied to an action that is at once consumption and production.

As an example, we can take a person eating a meal. This person is utilizing certain capital durables, including tools, to convey certain commodities to his or her mouth where the process of mastication takes place and the intermediate product is conveyed by swallowing to the stomach for digestion. These types of action are duplicated in many industrial plants. But the meal may be both a final consumption good satisfying the need for satisfaction (utility) and an input to further activity. The latter will often be a service for which the person is paid a wage or salary.

The food is a commodity input that is consumed in the activity. Again Lancaster (1971) has noted that consumption is an activity with its level related to goods consumed in that activity. So, one says the activity may consist of eating a big meal or a snack. The energy developed by one will be greater than the other.

Human-nonhuman Unit

An individual, in carrying out his or her activity function, utilizes a number of resources. Some are drawn from himself or herself while others are nonhuman in nature, including land and durable capital. As indicated previously, the human-nonhuman production unit utilizes flows of commodities that are consumed in the activity. For example, a person plus an automobile that the person can drive constitutes a human-nonhuman productive unit. In its activity it consumes gasoline, tires, and oil. In addition there is wear and tear on both the human and nonhuman parts. This is generally thought of, in the case of capital goods, in terms of their supplying streams of services until they are eventually consumed. Land, of course, does not depreciate.

The automotive unit produces a transportation service that may be consumed by the driver, his family, friends, or in the case of a taxi driver, his fares. A person eating a meal uses capital consisting of a table, chair, dishes, and implements and consumes food and drink that satisfies taste and other aspects of the utility function and at the same time provides energy for further activity.

Human resources can be broadly classified into the physical and the mental. Nonhuman resources are those that complement the human but cannot be identified as part of its physical or mental components. Artificial limbs, pacemakers, artificial kidneys, and other orthopedic supplies are part of the human resource, although in many ways they resemble parts of capital items.

We can say that both human and nonhuman segments of the productive unit contain parts that are endowed and parts that are acquired. Endowed portions of the human resource are those acquired through heredity plus physical traits common to everyone. Endowed portions of nonhuman resources are those received by the person involved without effort on his or her part, such as the natural environment. Acquired portions of human resources are largely related to ingestion of information, although certain physical parts and health can be acquired as well. Financial, land, and capital resources are usually acquired. Further discussion of the productive unit as such will be found in Chapter 9.

Home Production Activity

People seldom operate by themselves. The basic social unit for consumption, production, and consumption-production is the home. Traditional models in economics characterize the household as the consuming unit of the economic system receiving final goods and selling labor services to the "productive" parts of the world. Householders are considered to have only two alternatives, work (meaning outside employment) and leisure (Leftwich 1973, pp. 16-17). It was noted in Chapters 1 through 3, however, that the household is considered one of the major productive units in a community economy with the alternative of producing for its own needs.

Buetler and Owen (1980) have shown that the household, like the individual, can be viewed on a continuum from production through consumption. They classify productive activity into two categories: (1) market production that is either performed outside the household for pay or profit or performed in the household with the product to be sold in the market, and (2) home production, performed in the household for use in the household. Home production is then subclassified into separable and inseparable categories. Separable production is performed by hired employees of the household, thus it is not consumed by the producer. Inseparable production is performed by household members and is consumed by household members or given directly to others without pay.

It can be said that inseparable production is aimed directly at consumption. If a member of the household is the consumer, it is called intrahome consumption. If someone outside the household is the consumer, it is called extrahome consumption. Inseparable production is never exchanged, hence it has only use value.

Theoretical model. The Buetler-Owen home productivity model assumes that the family or household is the basic decision-making unit. Its problem, then, is to choose among competing ends in order to maximize a family (or composite) utility function, subject to certain resource constraints. The utility function is arrived at within the household and represents a compromise among the individual utility functions of the members. Individual utility functions are based on Maslow's hierarchy of needs (physiological, safety, love and belongingness, esteem, and self-actualization). Hence, the family utility function has the same basis, and is a function of basic human needs of all its members.

Lancaster's concept of characteristics is also a part of the model, since characteristics are considered the basic components, or arguments, in the household utility function. All potential combinations of characteristics are ordered from most to least desired, a preference ordering. These preferences are based on basic needs; thus, characteristics of goods that satisfy the utility function are those that meet basic human needs.

Development of these characteristics comes about as the result of production activities aimed at satisfying specific needs. Thus, they have utility to those whose needs are to be satisfied. The preference ordering must necessarily, then, be over the characteristics of the goods.

Production activities. Production units consisting of human and nonhuman resources utilize commodity inputs to create activities. Modification of the Buetler-Owen theory is made here for our own purposes. A given household may contain one or more of these production units. The human resource part is a resource produced and/or controlled by the household. The nonhuman resources and commodities used in activity generation may or may not be produced in the household and may or may not be controlled there.

Household owned resources utilized outside the household for market oriented activities are likely to be controlled outside the household. Those producing within the household for exchange outside it are subject to some outside influences (such as market forces), although most control is within the household. The household receives income in exchange for the goods produced by these market oriented activities that may be used to buy inputs to further family production and consumption.

Resources employed directly in household production activities can be hired in the market place and/or owned by household members. In either case, control is vested in the household. The objective is consumption either by household members or someone designated by them (as in the case of charity). The first is referred to as intrahousehold consumption and the second as interhousehold consumption. Production by hired workers is called separable household production, since the producers are not the consumers. Since nearly every activity performed for direct household consumption could be done by a hired employee, the latter designation has little operational significance. Control and use are the more important criteria. We assume that household production by hired employees cannot be obtained directly in the marketplace. In essence what we have is the matter of comparative advantage. The household supplies a worker to the market whose earnings in that capacity exceed what could be earned by working at home. Hence, he or she finds it advantageous to hire someone to perform his or her share of the home production function.

Role of the household in production. The household is an economic unit similar to all other units. It produces some things it uses itself, and it exports some things to pay for imports. In technically advanced countries, most households export the services of human beings and import commodities and services of other human beings. In underdeveloped countries, a very large proportion of commodities used may be the products of household production. In either case the human resource is the most important product of the household.

Nature of Human Resources
The term "human resource" refers to the bundle of skills and abilities a person utilizes in producing activities. It is significantly determined by natural ability (that is, genetic endowment, general health, and physique) and information base. Natural ability is partially endowed and partially acquired. It can be divided into the physical and the mental. Some societies utilize more of the physical powers, and others use more of the mental ones.

Role of information. There are three major categories of information that impact on economic activity. Intelligence information provides the basis for decision making. The extent of uncertainty faced by a decision maker is inversely related to the quantity and quality of intelligence available. Attitudinal information is basic to the acceptance, processing, and screening of other information. Skill-type information is basic to the development of expertise.
All human beings start building their information bases at birth. Information that will affect the attitudes of people is absorbed from their environment, including the homes in which they are reared, the community in which they live, and the people with whom they come in contact. This basic information is used to screen additional information as it is received. Education provides information that also provides prerequisite information for understanding and absorbing still more information. We stop building our base when our brain ceases to function adequately. By the

time we are teenagers our screening devices are in place, our attitudes toward society, learning, work, and certain types of information are fairly well set.

Skill-type information is basic to productivity. We can identify five subtypes in which people tend to specialize, when they specialize at all: scientific, technological, operational, maintenance, and coordinational.

Scientific information acquaints us with the nature of the world. The degree to which a society possesses or has access to it determines the society's potential for sophistication. The hunter at Catal who developed a superior arrowhead had to know something of the nature of the stone he was using. The group that sends a man to the moon has to know a great deal about the nature of the universe, computers, solar energy, rockets, and so on.

Technological information allows one to use scientific information effectively. We use our knowledge of the nature of things to change the state of things; but a good technologist has to have certain characteristics that enable him or her to sense where a change can be made in a product. Since practically all new products are redesigns of old ones, this is an important addition to the information base. Only rarely is a good scientist also a good technologist. The scientist is concerned with adding to basic knowledge. The technologist is concerned with designing something that will fulfill certain needs better than the existing products. All that is embodied in a new piece of capital is a better design. Technology exists in the information base of the designer. When we transfer a new machine to an underdeveloped country, we are not transferring technology; we are transferring the fruits of technology. To transfer technology means to transfer the ability to create new products that will meet needs better than old ones.

Operational information allows one to use the capital products produced by the technologist. A good bulldozer or carryall operator does not have to know anything about designing the machine. He or she does have to know how to get maximum production from it. As machines become more sophisticated, the information level of the operator has to rise with them. Sometimes good operators can make suggestions for better design of a machine. This does not necessarily make them technologists, although it might if carried far enough.

Maintenance information allows one to keep machines and other capital operating at peak efficiency. Sometimes a good operator is also a good mechanic. But most often these are separate specialties. As capital gains in the information level of its design, the job of the maintenance man becomes more difficult and requires that his information level rise. Lack of good maintenance expertise can be disasterous to any operation. But the maintenance of a shovel and a wheelbarrow is quite different from the maintenance of a 100 m^3 electric shovel.

Coordinational information is necessary in order to bring together the various factors of production in an efficient manner.

Economists have sporadically recognized this function, which is often called "management." It is sometimes separated from "labor," which lumps all other skills into one category.

Attitudes. Attitudes affect people's abilities to ingest other kinds of information and to do certain things well. Information supplied by an individual's family, community, religious, and social environment, for example, will affect attitude toward learning in general, toward achievement, toward certain kinds of jobs, and so on. The structure of the society in which a person lives is both a result of and contribution to attitudinal factors. For example, in many parts of the world vertical family relationships have developed as a way of averting risk. In turn, the extended family cuts down need for saving, discourages risk taking, and discourages achievement. Information supplied to the individual by this system says that it does not pay to earn more money because it all goes into a common pot and the hard worker is no better off than the slacker.

Such a structure works against economic change by limiting both supply of and demand for money to be used in purchase of capital goods. In addition, mobility of the individual is limited both in space and in the economic sphere. If by some quirk of fate there should be a particularly energetic individual who breaks out of the mold and becomes an entrepreneur, the extended family will tend to burden him or her with the necessity of providing jobs for relatives. Other types of family relationships can also affect growth. Landes (1949) has noted that in many French enterprises there is a reluctance to grow beyond abilities of family members to handle the situation. Primogeniture in some societies results in aggressive attitudes on the part of younger family members. Equal inheritance in others results in plots too small for effective agriculture.

Another effect of attitudinal information is development of the concept of class structure. This concept limits social mobility and interferes with efficient use of resources. Structures based on bloodlines or race are especially pernicious, since they contribute to the information base the knowledge that struggle against the system leads only to frustration. Innovation needed for reasonable growth can only come with hope of financial and social reward. This hope must be built into the information base of everyone in the society. Grayson has noted the peculiar attribute of America that it is middle-class minded (1955, p. 97). Millionaires go to work just like everyone else. Middle-class people are not afraid to get their hands dirty. There are social rewards for hard work.

The association of landholdings with class has been the mark of many societies and seems inevitably to lead to economic problems. Mosk (1951) noted that in Latin America, the development of large landholdings by European conquerers was accompanied by right of peonage over the natives. Thus, the class structure consisted of those who owned land and those who did not, with considerable racial overtones. Those Negro slaves and natives who became landholders were made "honorary whitemen" through a "blood purification" ceremony. A factor of major importance to further development was the flow of information into bases of the landowners to the effect that investment should be limited to landholdings. This limited capital accumulation that could have provided growth and jobs for the peons.

Class based on racial, tribal, religious, geographic, and other factors is basic to concepts of discrimination that cause so many problems in the development and use of human resources. It is especially pernicious in its effects on attitudes of those against whom the discrimination is aimed. Even when the tide turns, as is currently the case with the American blacks, its effect lingers on. Many of the basic conflicts within and among societies result from this tendency of people to array themselves in classes based on these factors. Conflicts of the Mideast, Ireland, Cyprus, and Africa are examples.

Religions and other similar philosophies not only provide bases for class structure, but they also contribute a large amount of attitude-forming information. Creation of a positive (Puritan) or negative (fatalistic) work ethic has long been regarded as in this realm. Religious views also create attitudes toward the assimilation of information that affect ability to function economically.

The Puritan ethic, derived from Puritan injunctions to work, save, and achieve spiritual satisfaction through material reward, has been credited with enhancing growth in America. It has also had a negative effect. The converse of the philosophy is that those who do not work, save, and receive material reward must be sinners. Therefore, the poor are poor because they deserve to be that way. This is the "flawed character" explanation for poverty that is basic to much discrimination against minorities.

Religions stressing asceticism, abstinence, and cultivation of the spirit tend to load the information base with negative attitudes toward work and achievement. Denominations that stress the importance of learning load the base with positive concepts toward the assimilation of information. The Church of Jesus Christ of Latter Day Saints emphasizes the importance of knowledge to salvation. Conversely, those that stress nonlearning or learning in limited subject areas, create negative attitudes toward assimilation of information.

Geographic proximity makes people alike. A Roman Catholic in North America is likely to reflect basic philosophies that are more nearly comparable to a Congregationalist neighbor than to a fellow Catholic in Argentina. Various communities may have Christians, Jews, and Moslems among their inhabitants. If they are located far enough apart, the differences in attitudes among the communities will be greater than differences within them. Every person tends to modify his or her philosophy by accepting some of the beliefs of frequent contacts.

Regional differences in attitudes make a great deal of difference in rapidity and sustenance of economic development. The contrast between the open-minded Japanese and many other Orientals cannot escape our attention. People residing in an isolated region often resist change because it is threatening to them. They know the local pecking order, the ideas that are socially acceptable, the situations to avoid, and so on. Anything that tends to upset this makes them very uneasy.

Attitudes are basic to productivity, ability to change, and even availability. Economists have been somewhat reluctant to consider attitude and economic phenomenon. Marshall (1961, p. 87) called Senior's statement concerning "desire for distinction" a half-truth. Economic man is defined as selfish, rational, knowledgeable, and unchanging; an obvious attempt to apply *ceteris paribus* to attitude. Yet, in some areas attitudinal factors are discussed at length.

Utility functions have been explored in considerable depth, including the concept of revealed preference but excluding other attitudinal factors, such as negative and composite utility. (Lee and Wallace [1975] encountered this phenomenon in studying demands for health facilities.) Composite utility functions have been acknowledged casually by many writers and are important in looking at distribution of collective goods. The effect of risk aversion on managerial decisions has been explored at great length. The backward bending supply curve of labor--often considered an economic oddity--is logical if viewed as the product of an information base containing the message that $X is sufficient for the moment and tomorrow will take care of itself.

Skills. The following kinds of information, scientific, technological, operational, maintenance, and coordinational are basic to the formation of skills.

1. Knowledge of the nature of things is basic to all information and all economic activity whether one operates in an unsophisticated or sophisticated society. The computer specialist designing new software must know something of the nature of computers and information flows.
2. Technological information allows one to use scientific information effectively; we use our knowledge of the nature of things to change the state of things. A person may be an excellent scientist without being able to apply the knowledge; but one cannot be a good technologist without some scientific knowledge, although technologists are not, generally, scientists.
3. Operational information allows one to use and maintain the products of technology.
4. Maintenance skills allow one to keep capital goods producing.
5. Coordinational information is necessary in order to bring together the various factors of production in an efficient manner. Coordinators need not be as proficient as scientists, technolo-

gists, or operators in order to be efficient managers, although some expertise in these areas can be advantageous at times.

Societies exist, however, that are strong in technology, operations, and maintenance but weak in management. Lokanathan has indicated, for example, that in the Punjab, the artisan class of Sikhs, the Ramagariahs, possess ingenuity and technical skill (1965, pp. 176-178). They are able to adapt foreign machinery found in large factories to their smaller operations, making them prosperous in the field of light engineering. But they have been unsuccessful in moving from small undertakings to medium level enterprises because they lack coordinational skills.

Many analysts are confused on this point. Svenillson (1965, p. 406) equates "know-how" with "technical knowledge" and states, "It is . . . the availability of industrial know how that determines efficiency in building, organizing, and running industries." It is important to point out that one's information base may be high in knowledge allowing efficiency in technical processes and low in knowledge concerning building, organizing, and running industries.

Intelligence. Intelligence is information concerning the operation of an economy or a portion thereof. It covers such areas as markets, operations, and finances. Intelligence information tends to be somewhat momentary. It may or may not have lasting value.

Flows vs. stocks. Information flows have been treated extensively in economic literature in recent years. Stigler's 1961 article contained an admonition to economists to pay more attention to the importance of information flows. Since then, Stigler (1974), Nelson (1970, 1974), and Rothschild (1964) have written about product markets; Gould (1970), Stigler (1961), and Telser (1964) have written on market information in general; Arrow (1970), Demsetz (1969), Gould (1974), and Hirshliefer (1971) have published ideas on innovation; and Alchian (1970), Gronau (1971), McCall (1970), Stigler (1962), and Whipple (1973) have written about labor markets. Theil's book was published in 1967 and is on the subject of information flow generally. Arrow (1969, 1970, 1971) has treated the problem of information development under free enterprise and (1962) has made the major contribution to substitution of information for labor. Kornai (1971) has concerned himself with flows of intelligence used by coordinators, particularly the hierarchical structure through which they occur.

In capital theory a distinction is drawn between flows of capital and stocks into which the flows accumulate. Essentially the same concept must be used to explain the relationship between flows of information and the information base. The learning process is essentially stock building: information is stored for purposes of retrieval when needed. There are other ways that information can be stored, such as on tapes and in books. But it does not contribute to the human resource until it is stored in the brain. All information entering the information base must flow from somewhere. So flows are not limited to intelligence information. The reason for interest shown in that type of information seems to be the prime role played by it in decision making under uncertainty. The impact of information on production has been acknowledged many times, but little has been done with it.

For purposes of analysis, skill development can be considered somewhat a long run phenomenon. It has been of more interest to educators than to economic analysts. Attitudinal development has been of interest to other social scientists, psychologists, sociologists, and cultural anthropologists. Economists should be interested in anything that influences production. Particularly, we should be interested in the development of human resources. The human-nonhuman unit and role of information in creating change is considered further in Chapter 9.

COMPOSITION OF POPULATION

The characteristics and traits of the people who make up a community can be observed at some moment in time, and this information can then be used in analysis of the community itself. Composition of the population dictates major changes that may be imminent. People are the consumers of goods, the users of land, and the most important factors in production. But the ways in which they perform in these roles differ as age, sex, racial and ethnic, and socioeconomic compositions differ.

Significance of Age

A population with a preponderance of young people will differ from one with a preponderance of older members in such areas as productive capacity, needs and problems, outlook, and mode of life. If the age distributions are extreme (that is, children versus retirees), the economies will have in common a majority of consumers and scarcity of workers. A community made up of young families needs schools, churches, pediatricians, baby-sitters, playgrounds, and access to good jobs for parents. A community of old people needs churches, geriatricians, nursing homes, drugstores, and mortuaries. In either case, service and trade industries are likely to dominate economic activity.

The work force of a community consists of people between the ages of fourteen and sixty-five. However, Hicks (1973) has observed that at a low level of technology almost the whole population is engaged in producing goods and services. Perhaps work force should be defined in terms of effectiveness, then age would be unimportant in the definition.

Significance of Sexual Distribution

As with differences in age, sexual variations influence many aspects of human behavior. Physiological capacity, attitude, participation in the labor force, tendency to join social organizations, and occupational preferences sometimes differ between males and females. Since women have lower death rates than men, and since only women bear children, the levels of mortality and fertility are directly related to the proportion of women in the population.

There is sexual selectivity in migration. In some cases men move more easily than do women. In others women are the more mobile. The deciding factor seems to be the kinds of jobs available in the target area. Men tend to move toward mining, forestry, fishery, farming, and some types of manufacturing activity. Women tend to move when the opportunities are in office work, services, and types of manufacturing. Where the distribution between the sexes becomes out of balance, many social problems tend to surface. Prostitution increases when there is a preponderance of males. A preponderance of females is often accompanied by higher rates of illegitimacy. In either case, family stability is threatened.

Family stability is important for the mental health of the children especially where there are no other social ties, such as an extended family, to compensate. Children who grow up with security are able to handle change much more satisfactorily than those who do not. Everyone needs a secure base from which to face life.

Marriage also seems to have a stabilizing influence on adults. Marital status has long been known to be related to the incidence of crime, suicide, mental illness, and automobile accidents. Marital status also determines where one lives, works, plays, and the kinds of social organizations one belongs to. Further, residential mobility is higher among single persons than married ones.

Significance of Racial and Ethnic Differences

As with age and sex, racial and ethnic composition of a population often has significance for a great many aspects of human social life. In communities where there are no racial differences, ethnic differences tend to be exaggerated. For example, in many African communities, people from different tribes find themselves in conflict. If there are no significant physical differences, religion will often be substituted, as is the case in Irish communities. Race and ethnic characteristics are often determinants of place of residence, schools attended, job skills acquired, kinds of jobs held, and amount of wages earned. The paths used in migration are also strongly influenced by these characteristics.

Inequalities related to racial and ethnic groups and their effect on nutritional standards affect intelligence and mortality. Thus, discrimination tends to be self-fulfilling in that by labeling a group inferior they actually become so. Breaking this vicious cycle is an extremely difficult task, since productivity is heavily influenced by an information base that is partially related to ability. Discrimination also leads to deviant behavior that reinforces prejudice. The poverty problem faced by many communities, particularly the segregated ones, such as enclaves, ghettos, and reservations, is directly related to discrimination. As will be shown when we discuss these areas, the cycle caused by discrimination is directly responsible for most of the serious situations found there.

Socioeconomic Characteristics
　　Socioeconomic characteristics are directly related to the factors discussed to this point in the chapter. Yet, they have their own impact as well and need to be considered.

Education. The information bases of members of a labor force are related to the general education they have received as well as special training and experience. In an industrial society, educational status of the population is an indication of the extent to which highly trained technicians are being provided to carry on complex tasks. The educational level of a community determines, to a large degree, consumer buying habits; attitudes and opinions on social, economic, and political subjects; and ability to vote and otherwise participate in political life. Hence, the efficiency with which the community furnishes goods and services on a public basis is influenced by education. Pressure groups are apt to be more objective, and people are less apt to acquiesce in things they do not like, where the people are educated.

Income. In general, people get paid according to their abilities, hence money income is a good index of economic well-being. The trend of per capita income is a good indication of the trend in standard of living. Differences in family incomes can be utilized as indicators of differences in housing, nutrition, use of leisure time, health, and even family size and living arrangements. Poverty levels are often designated in terms of income.

Characteristics of the labor force. The ability of a society to be productive depends very largely upon characteristics of the segment of its population of working age that participates. As indicated previously, in communities within underdeveloped areas, most of the population may be engaged in work in order to stay alive. The higher the information level of a society, the less apt this is to be true.
　　In technical societies, a large proportion of a person's time until the age of sixteen or more is taken in education. This loss of productive time is made up very rapidly through increased productivity. Size and distribution of the labor force, technical abilities, and other characteristics reveal how a community is organized to earn a living, its potential for industrial growth, and the general well-being of its members. Industrial location specialists place a great deal of emphasis on the gathering of information concerning the labor force, when selecting sites.
　　Size of a labor force depends not only upon population of the proper age, but also upon participation rates. In some societies, women do not work outside the home. This was generally true in the United States until World War II when they took defense jobs.

Since that time, they have been entering the labor market in ever-increasing numbers.

Occupational structure of a labor force is a reflection of the industry of the community or of nearby communities that import labor services. In a technical society, one of the major problems lies in a constantly changing structure of occupations. Obsolescence in skills accompanies obsolescence in equipment. This requires continuous training and retraining of labor force participants. Educational facilities have to be adapted to this situation. In less developed areas, occupations are relatively stable. But as a community begins to change, changes in occupations occur. For example, the introduction of scooters as transportation requires the training of scooter mechanics.

Migration and Population Shifts

It is common to refer to migration as "voting with the feet." This is an apt way of putting it, since it implies voting for or against something. People who move think things are not desirable where they are and/or that they will be better off somewhere else. It also implies permanence in movement as well as distance. The things being voted for or against are usually economic in nature. That is, a better-paying job, access to better services, a cheaper place to live, or even just a vague notion of "seeking one's fortune" are the types of objectives that motivate people to move. This does not rule out the fact that people move for other reasons as well.

Following the lead of Todaro (1969, p. 139), we can conclude that most decisions to migrate are functions of two major variables: (1) the income differential and (2) the probability of obtaining a job in the new area. For any one migrant these values are seldom "givens"; rather he or she arrives at them after sifting through information supplied from various sources. Only in those areas where there is conscious effort to supply people with job information can decisions be made on the basis of anything but expectations carrying a fairly high margin of error. This may partially explain the continued movement in underdeveloped regions of the world from rural communities to urban slums where prospects for jobs are often very low.

What, then, causes similar movement in the developed regions as well? To the two variables listed, one must add other amenities available in cities in a nation such as the United States. These include higher welfare payments, availability of better health services, educational opportunities, and even opportunities for income from illicit activities. One must also consider the push many rural residents receive due to automation of the agricultural industry. If there are no jobs available, the prospects of even part-time work in an urban community may be highly appealing, considering the other advantages involved.

Community-to-community migration. More movement of people occurs among rural communities located close to one another than from rural communities to cities. One reason for this is that information concerning opportunities is likely to be better. Another is that family and other social ties do not have to be broken completely. Still another is that many moves come after an extended period of commuting. Yet another is the high cost of moving over long distances.

In the urban area, community-to-community movement is often done in the process of upgrading housing. It may or may not be associated with greater economic opportunity. As was indicated in a previous chapter, costs (in money or time) of commuting to an existing job may well figure in movement to communities nearer places of employment. But this may not be an overriding consideration for persons in upper income levels. They may even move further away to live in communities of higher quality.

In the cities of advanced nations, it is common to see a wave effect. As occupants of older bedroom communities move into newer ones, their places are taken by migrants from inner-city communities. Eventually the inner city is left with dilapidated housing and too few tenants to make it worthwhile for landlords to keep up the property. Thus, many inner-city communities develop into ghost towns, where buildings are vandalized and ransacked. This presents an opportunity for renewal and the attraction of a new wave of migrants who enjoy central city life if they can have proper police protection and other amenities.

Characteristics of migrants. Migrants tend to be people who can make social adjustments easier than others can. They are willing to strain or even break close social ties by interposing distance. Still they try to minimize uncertainty as much as they can, and will often follow relatives, friends, and others from a home area who had moved previously. This is particularly true when movement is made over a very long distance or to completely foreign areas.

Mobility of people changes with various stages of life. Young families tend to be more mobile than older families. Individuals are more mobile than families. In an advanced society, young people who have just finished school or other training tend to move very readily. As they establish families and begin to put down roots in new communities, buying homes, finding friends and social organizations, their mobility diminishes. It becomes slowest in middle age, and picks up again at retirement. In underdeveloped areas, the young adults are also mobile, but the older people are not. They need the security of the family and home community.

Migrants tend to be the more intelligent, better-trained, younger, and more aggressive members of a society. These are the very people needed by a community to keep it growing and developing. An originating community will find its problems compounded by loss of its best human resources. A destination will be reinforced by gaining their services.

An interesting feature of migration paths is that they often work in both directions. People reared in a particular community have sociocultural ties that will often pull them back if the new

Roles of People in Economic Activity 221

community is not to their liking or if opportunities for comparable real income (considering both earnings and cost of living) become available "back home." Of course there is usually a time limit on this situation for any one migrant or migrant family. A person who has been away thirty years may have little attachment left to the original home.

SUMMARY

In terms of economic activity, people operate in two ways that are somewhat interrelated. They are the ultimate consumers of goods and services, and they are the major contributors to production.

As consumers, they are influenced by many things, including suggestions of other people, tastes, advertising, prices, and income. Economic theory suggests that logical people will try to get equal value for each dollar spent. This provides the basis for analysis of the impact of price change on quantity taken. The overall impact results from both the income and substitution effects of price changes. The extent of substitution depends upon price elasticity of demand or the way people react to a price change for a given good. The income effect is caused by the impact of price changes on the amount of money people have to spend.

People's incomes also change for other reasons. The way people react toward goods as incomes change is measured by Engel curves. These reactions impact heavily on industries producing the goods, hence upon communities in which the goods are produced.

Lancaster has proposed a model that says goods have characteristics and consumers react to these characteristics. A good may have several characteristics. A consumer's choice, given a budget constraint, can be formulated as an optimization problem in which characteristics are associated in the same space with the goods. Maslow's work contributes the concept of utility as a hierarchy of needs.

The distinction between consumption and production is somewhat obscured by the fact that some commodities and services consumed are inputs to the furnishing of productive human services, but others are strictly consumer goods. Thus, a person consumes for both purposes. Oftentimes the same commodities serve both objectives.

Use of the household in a community model must take into consideration this attribute of the individual. It must also consider the fact that the household in which the person lives serves both as a producer of goods and services and as a consumer of inputs. Further, some household products are sold to other units in the economy. Thus, the linkages of human beings to other economic units within the community are very complex. Most models make no attempt to break these down, largely because the collection of data concerning them is very difficult. Yet the impact is important and must be recognized.

A community's greatest asset is its people, and a people's greatest asset is ability to utilize information. Attitude is an important adjunct to knowledge in the information base, and attitude is largely the product of environment.

Family relationships determine one's ability to react to other people, the way one interprets the world at large, and one's propensity to take risks and to accumulate wealth. Class relationships along with racial, religious, and cultural factors often determine the extent to which one has opportunity and will be rewarded for innovative activity. These factors, in turn, help shape attitudes. Religions and other philosophies often determine the way we look at hard work, saving, investing, and the accumulation of wealth. They can encourage or they can inhibit these characteristics generally associated with productivity. Cultural differences make it hard for people to understand one another. It is very difficult to graft institutions from one culture onto another; yet this is often attempted in economic development work.

The characteristics of a community are largely determined by the physical and socioeconomic characteristics of its inhabitants. These include age, sex, race and ethnic composition, education, income, and other characteristics of the population.

The future of a community is heavily influenced by the mobility of people. Immigrants tend to strengthen and out-migrants to weaken. In general, it can be said that the propensity of a person to migrate depends upon real income differentials between the home community and other communities of which he or she has knowledge, the chances he or she thinks there are of obtaining the kind of job desired, direct costs of movement, age, his or her information base, attachment to the home community, marital status and family responsibilities, intercommunity differentials in supply and quality of social services, and his or her general health, ability, and aggressiveness.

REVIEW QUESTIONS

1. Why are the characteristics of people important in studies of economies?
2. Is it true that consumers "dictate" the production of final or consumer goods?
3. What is the relationship between the equimarginal principle and indifference curves?
4. What is meant by the term "consumer optimization"?
5. Do price changes directly affect people's choices among goods?
6. What is meant by the income effect of a price change?
7. How does Lancaster's model differ from the usual neoclassical model?
8. What do Maslow's categories of need add to the theory?
9. Why would one refer to a human being as a multistage, multiproduct production unit?
10. What does a production unit (as defined in the text) consist of, and how is it related to commodity flows?
11. What is the relationship between consumption and production so far as an individual is concerned?

12. Why would we consider a household or home as a basic economic unit?
13. What two major economic activities are provided by the household?
14. What types of information tend to impact on economic activity, and what role does each play?
15. Define human resource.
16. What are the seven categories of information contained in the human information base?
17. What effects do attitudes have on the building of information bases?
18. How does structure of a society affect the information base and vice versa?
19. How does this work to inhibit or encourage growth?
20. What is the general effect of class structure on attitudes of people?
21. How can religions affect
    a. the ingestion of information?
    b. attitudes toward achievement?
    c. discrimination against minorities?
22. What effect does geography have on attitudes?
23. What types of attitudinal information have been analyzed as economic phenomena?
24. How do *each* of the following information types affect skills: scientific, technological, operational, coordinational, maintenance, intelligence?
25. What is the relationship between flows and stocks of information?
26. How does age composition of a population affect economic activity in a community?
27. How do migration patterns differ when the migrants are predominantly male? Female?
28. How can ethnic differences affect economic activity?
29. What kind of vicious circle does discrimination determine?
30. How does education level in a community affect economic and social attributes?
31. How does information level of the general population relate to growth and development of a community?
32. How does rural-to-urban migration in underdeveloped nations differ from that in developed nations?
33. What is the most common pattern of intraurban migration?
34. Are migrants different from nonmigrants?

REFERENCES

Alchian, A. A. 1970. Information costs, pricing, and resource unemployment. In *Micro economic foundations of employment and inflation theory*, ed. E. Phelps. New York: Norton.

Arrow, K. J. 1962. The economic implications of learning by doing. *Review of Economic Studies* 29:155-73.

———. 1969. Classification notes on the production and trans-

mission of technological knowledge. *American Economic Review, Papers, and Proceedings* 59:29-35.
———. 1970. Economic welfare and the allocation of resources for invention. In *Essays in the theory of risk bearing*. Chicago: Markham.
———. 1971. Political and economic evaluation of social effects and externalities. In *Frontiers of quantitative economics*, ed. M. D. Intriligator. New York: North Holland.
Blaug, M. 1976. The empirical status of human capital theory: A slightly jaundiced survey. *Journal of Economic Literature* 14:827-55.
Buetler, I. F., and A. J. Owen. 1980. A home production activity model. *Home Economics Research Journal* 8:16-26.
Demsetz, H. 1969. Information and efficiency: Another viewpoint. *Journal of Law and Economics* 12:1-22.
Gould, J. P. 1970. Diffusion processes and optimal advertising policy. In *Microeconomic foundations of employment and inflation theory*, ed. E. Phelps. New York: Norton.
———. 1974. Risk, stochastic preference and the value of information. *Journal of Economic Theory* 8:64-84.
Grayson, H. 1955. *The crisis of the middle class*. New York: Rinehart.
Gronau, R. 1971. Information and frictional unemployment. *American Economic Review* 61:290-301.
Harmston, F. K., and H. Hino. 1970. An intertemporal analysis of the demand for food products. *American Journal of Agricultural Economics* 52:381-86.
Hicks, W. 1973. Interrelations between population, employment and economic development: A bibliography. *Workshop Report No. 2*. Washington, D.C.: Agricultural Development Council.
Hirshleifer, J. 1971. The private and social value of information and the reward to inventive activity. *American Economic Review* 62:561-74.
Kornai, J. 1971. *Anti-equilibrium*. New York: North Holland.
Kuznets, S. 1955. Toward a theory of economic growth. In *National policy for economic welfare at home and abroad*, ed. R. LeKachman. Garden City, N.Y.: Doubleday.
Lancaster, K. 1966. A new approach to consumer theory. *Journal of Political Economy* 74:132-57.
———. 1971. *Consumer demand: A new approach*. New York: Columbia University Press.
Landes, D. S. 1949. French entrepreneurship and industrial growth in the nineteenth century. *Journal of Economic History* 9:45-61.
Lee, M. L. 1980. *Consumption sets and the theory of consumer behavior*. Working Paper, Univ. of Missouri at Columbia.
Lee, M. L., and R. Wallace. 1975. Modification in economic behavior. Paper presented at Southern Economic Association meeting, Atlanta.
Leftwich, R. H. 1973. *The price system and resource allocation*. Hinsdale, Ill.: Dryden Press.

Lokanathan, P. S. 1965. Entrepreneurship: Supply of entrepreneurs and technologists with special reference to India. In *Economic development with special reference to East Asia, Proceedings International Economics Association*, ed. K. Birrell. New York: Macmillan.

McCall, J. J. 1970. Economics of information and job search. *Quarterly Journal of Economics* 84:113-26.

Marshall, A. 1961. *Principles of economics*. New York: Macmillan.

Maslow, A. H. 1954. *Motivation and personality*. New York: Harper & Row.

Mosk, S. A. 1951. Latin America versus the United States. *American Economic Review, Papers and Proceedings* 41:367-83.

Nelson, P. 1970. Information and consumer behavior. *Journal of Political Economy* 78:311-29.

———. 1974. Advertising as information. *Journal of Political Economy* 82:729-54.

Rothschild, M. 1964. Models of market organization with imperfect information. *Journal of Political Economy* 72:44-60.

Stigler, G. J. 1961. The economics of information. *Journal of Political Economy* 69:213-25.

———. 1962. Information in the labor market. *Journal of Political Economy* 70:99-105.

———. 1974. A theory of oligopoly. *Journal of Political Economy* 82:44-60.

Svenillson, I. 1965. Technical assistance, the transfer of industrial knowhow to non-industrialized countries. In *Economic development with special reference to East Asia*, ed. K. Birrell. New York: Macmillan.

Telser, L. 1964. Advertising and competition. *Journal of Political Economy* 72:537-62.

Thiel, H. 1967. *Economics and information theory*. Chicago: Rand McNally.

Todaro, M. P. 1969. A model of labor migration and unemployment in less developed countries. *The American Economic Review* 59:138-48.

Whipple, D. 1973. A generalized theory of job search. *Journal of Political Economy* 81:1170-88.

CHAPTER 9

Change as an Economic Phenomenon

It has been said that there is no such thing as "status quo." Constant change is the general order of things. As inviting as the concept of no change may be to some people, there is no way to avoid it. At the community level, this means that as long as people live at a level above bare subsistence, the community itself will change over time. Communities are continually being born, developing, or dying.

Economic reasons for change are not always easy to understand. The production process is one vehicle of change. Money plays a significant role in resource allocation and reallocation. The structure of industrial firms influences change. Scale effects and economies of size play a role. Diversification among product lines may cause basic changes to come about. Even the decision-making processes within firms, labor organizations, governments, and other social agencies are generators of change that impact on communities.

ROLE OF PRODUCTION

The productive process plays several roles in change. Some are related to relationships among basic factors. Others are related to the input structures of industries and their backward and forward linkages. Still others are related to types of industries in an area and shifts in input linkages among them.

Production can be defined as the process by which people, aided by capital, energy, and land, transform raw materials and intermediate commodities and services into economic goods. Economic goods include tangibles (commodities) that can be stored and intangibles (services) that cannot. Final goods are the ultimate objective of the process, since they are the ones consumed by people. Intermediate goods make up the bulk of economic transactions and are produced goods used up directly in production. Most of them become physically a part of the new product, but some, such as lubricating oils and services, become a part only in an indirect way.

Human resources play the major role in production, as they do in consumption. A detailed discussion of the concept was given in Chapter 8. At this point, we define human resources again as the physical and mental capacities of people and the information bases they have developed. The latter serve to provide them with attitudes and skills that are applicable in production. Human resources are often called human capital, since part of the process of information base development and of health and nutrition improvement involves an investment of resources.

There is a tendency to include, in the classification of capital, producers' durables (fixed capital) and stocks of raw materials, semifinished and finished goods that become part of new products (circulating capital). The problem with this is that fixed capital produces a string of services over time, while "circulating capital" is the product of most sectors in an economy and the major portion of inputs in the intersectoral model. In order to express production in terms that can be related to the input-output structure of a community, "circulating capital" is considered as material inputs to production paid for by exchanges among industrial sectors. Fixed capital is paid for as payments to the household.

The same situation applies to land. Water, air, forests, and minerals are defined as land but are often used as direct inputs to production. Land rent paid to the household does not include payment for these inputs. Rather, it covers land in its supportive role as bases for buildings, roadways, railways, airways, waterways and ports, power lines, pipelines and as the vehicle to convey nutrients to crops, forests, and pasture.

We separate energy from other intermediate goods because it plays a distinct role. Energy is defined as the work that a physical system is capable of doing in changing from its actual state to a specified reference state (*American heritage* 1971). The physical system, be it animal or machine, converts inputs, such as food, coal, and natural gas, into a power that can be used to accomplish work. In some cases, the power is produced simultaneously with the work; in others, such as the production of electricity, the power is produced separately, and the work is done by machines capable of converting power into work.

Energy makes production possible. Human energy is necessary under all circumstances, but it can come in two basic forms: muscle power and brain power. We can also get muscle power from animals; their possibilities for brain power are limited. Emphasis on muscle power typifies low information base economies, whereas emphasis on brain power typifies high information base systems. The latter tend to be more productive than the former.

Production Function

The quantity of goods produced is a function of the services of people, capital, and land plus energy, materials, and intermediate goods. Materials and intermediate goods include all commodity flows used up in production. The first are raw materials provided by the land, and the second are produced materials (semifinished goods) that include metals, lubricating oils, plastics, manufactured parts, and so on. Thus, we can express it as $Q = f(P, K, L, E, M, G)$, where P = people, K = capital, L = land, E = energy, M = materials, and G = intermediate goods. Production can be increased by increasing either the quantity or quality of the productive factors and other inputs or by increasing quantity and quality at the same time.

Quality is a function of information level. The particular role played by a person depends upon the kind of information possessed. A scientist does research to try to determine the nature of the world. A technologist trys to use scientific knowledge to affect the part of the world represented by capital, intermediate goods, and consumption products. The operational part of the economic world is inhabited by those who use tools, machines, and facilities. The maintenance portion keeps these in good repair. Coordinators organize the activities of others and direct the production process. In so doing they utilize intelligence-type information to examine markets, plan for future production, and examine current activities. Education, training, and experience are utilized to increase the information level, hence productivity of these people.

The information level of capital is determined by the technologists who design it. This is a continuous process. New and more productive capital is continually evolving from old varieties. The evolution can proceed no faster than the information level, including imaginative ability, of the designers will allow. There is considerable interplay between ideas for new capital, for new intermediate goods, and for new consumer products. Thus, the revolution in electronics has produced many products for intermediate use, consumption, and production; and many different industries have resulted. Stereophonic sound gave rise to a large recording industry that in turn encouraged certain types of plastic production. Linkages in a high information world are necessarily complex.

In order to get a better understanding of the relationship of the variables involved in production, it is often good to consider how it was done in simpler times. Particularly as we consider the impact of the productive process and the effect of change on a community, let us again consider the situation at Catal.

A simple economy. We have noted that Catal developed because certain people became knowledgeable about certain things. They were located in the general area of a natural resource; but, as Zimmerman (1964, p. 8) has pointed out, a material becomes a resource only after someone finds out how to use it. The information base of the people enabled them not only to utilize obsidian in making products, but also to recognize their economic advantage and to exploit it. Arrow (1962) refers to the process of learning by doing. This was the only way the people at Catal had of obtaining information. Their first problem was to learn how to make superior obsidian points, then they had to learn that it was more advantageous to produce points and trade them for tigers than it was to hunt tigers.

As people learn, their capabilities expand, but some people learn more readily than others. Compared to the surrounding area, the level of technology in Catal was high. But the information base has to be broader than that portion manifested by technology. Scientific knowledge was necessary in order to develop the technology. The ability to knap obsidian points superior to those produced by anyone else lay in some knowledge of the characteristics of obsidian. This enabled them to select that material with best knapping qualities. The ability to weave fine cloth had its base in some knowledge of the characteristics of wool, hair, and looming. The ability to develop a drilling tool for beads lay in some knowledge of the characteristics of stone and the process of drilling. Some knowledge of social structure was necessary to enable them to organize a community and to take advantage of specialization.

Production at Catal involved people using tools and buildings (capital), soil and surface (land), exertion (energy), obsidian, stones, wood, copper, bone, hides, hair, and wool (materials), and government and other services (intermediate goods). In carrying out these processes, they used operational, maintenance, and coordinational skills.

Thus, we see that information played a very important role, although it was at a very low level compared to the situation faced by producers in a technical society. It was not greatly different, however, from the level used by most producers in the world today. The general types of information needed have not varied in 10,000 years.

Matching information bases. The productivity of a particular piece of producer's capital is dependent upon the technological skill of the designer, the operational skills of those who produce and operate it, maintenance skills of those who keep it operating, and coordinational skills of management, as well as the level of sophistication of the capital and materials being used in its production. Thus, in both production of new capital and in its operation, the information level of the people involved is all important. For maximum production from any human-nonhuman production unit, the abilities of the people and the technology of the nonhuman factors have to be in equilibrium. This concept can be explained by use of conventional neoclassical production theory, placing some limitations on use of the models.

Neoclassical production theory. There are two broad classes of production functions in neoclassical theory: fixed and variable proportions. A fixed proportions function exists if the technique of production requires a unique combination of inputs. Conversely, a variable proportions function exists if the technique does not require a unique combination of inputs. The first fits situations where inputs cannot be substituted for one another; the second fits situations where substitution among inputs is possible.

A fixed proportions function is homogeneous of degree one if the technically determined input-output ratio is independent of scale for each input. (That is, no scale economies are possible.) Where the input-output ratio is not independent of scale, but the input ratios are constant, the production function is merely homogeneous. Scale economies and diseconomies are possible in the latter case. Inputs in fixed proportions functions are limitational (Ferguson 1969) in the sense that an increase in one of them, usage of the others remaining constant, will not expand output.

There are no limitational inputs in variable proportions production functions, since an increase in an input is both a necessary and a sufficient condition for an increase in output. Ferguson defined this condition as "limitative," since it is responsible for that portion of the isoquant beyond which any other input becomes superfluous. The economic region, then, is defined as that area within which all inputs are limitative. In this region all inputs are also substitutes.

In dealing with equilibrium in the human-nonhuman unit, we will utilize a fixed proportions function. We will define inputs as capital (surrogate for nonhuman resources) and labor. In so doing we will use both the conventional definition of labor (L) in which the information level does not change and Allen's (1968) efficiency unit $\overline{L} = \alpha L$, where α is the information level of the labor force. A similar set of definitions will be given to capital.

First we consider the case where conventional definitions are used. If a firm has only one available technique of production, the ratio of inputs is constant, since there is no other technical relation among inputs. In (9.1) let X_1 = capital (K) and X_2 = labor (L):

$$Q = \min(X_1/\gamma_1, X_2/\gamma_2) \qquad (9.1)$$

where Q is physical output, the γ_i are variables that are functions of Q and that always change proportionately; and the X_i are the physical quantities of inputs. We fix materials, intermediate goods, and energy for this analysis.

At any point on the ray defined by the relationship (9.1),

$$X_1/\gamma_1 = X_2/\gamma_2 \qquad (9.2)$$

$$X_1/X_2 = \gamma_1/\gamma_2 \qquad (9.3)$$

These are the only technical conditions governing input relationships. (See Fig. 9.1.)

Assume maximum available quantities of X_1 and X_2 are $\overline{X}_1$ and $\overline{X}_2$, each of which defines a one-dimensional hyperplane. Then $O\overline{X}_1$

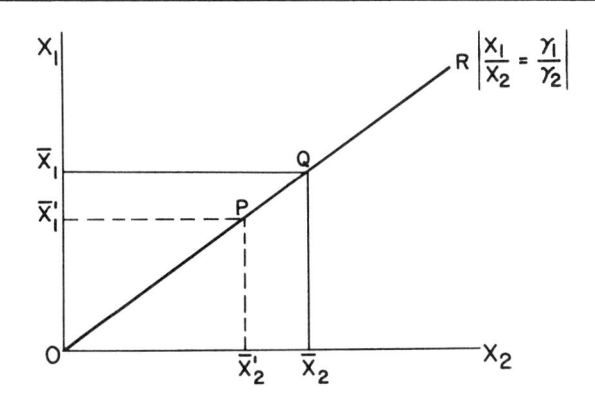

Fig. 9.1. A fixed coefficient production function.

and $Q\bar{X}_2$ define a hyperbox that imposes n contraints on output ($n = 2$). A one-dimensional hyperplane that uses all of the inputs is defined by R. It could use less than the total supply of any one; whether it does or not depends upon the technical relationship given by (9.3).

The situation depicted in Fig. 9.1 is clearly limitational. That is, Q is the greatest amount that can be produced with input of $\bar{X}_1$ and $\bar{X}_2$. An expansion in X_1 without a comparable expansion in X_2 would not lead to an expansion in output; hence this is a necessary but not a sufficient condition for expansion. On the other hand, a contraction in X_1 to $\bar{X}_1'$ would lead to a contraction in production to point P; hence such a reduction is both a necessary and a sufficient condition for a decrease in output.

Achieving an equilibrium in the human-nonhuman relationship. It should be obvious at this point that this conventional look at a fixed proportions function carries the implied assumption that information is constant. All change in production occurs because there is change in hours of labor and of capital usage. We now turn the tables and assume the number of capital and labor hours to be constant. All change in production is assumed to take place because there is a change in information.

In Fig. 9.2 we have a situation similar to that in Fig. 9.1 except that T is amount of technology and S is amount of skill. In short, we are dealing with $\bar{L} = \alpha(t)L$ and $\bar{K} = \beta(t)K$, where L and K are fixed. Represented by α is a skill level and by β is a level of technology. The ratio β/α is constant everywhere along the ray R and is equal to the amount of technology represented in design of the capital divided by the amount of skill possessed by the labor force. In this case because of our assumption of equilibrium, $\hat{R}$ is a 45° line. That is, everywhere on this line the levels of technology and skill are matched.

If the community is initially at point C producing Q_1 of product, an increase in the skill level of the labor force to S_2,

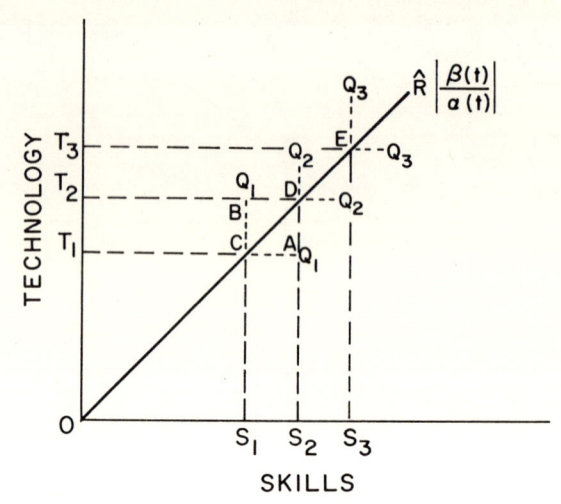

Fig. 9.2. Information equilibrium between capital and labor.

without a concurrent increase in capital technology, would not increase production. Rather, the increased labor skills become redundant, bringing the relationship to point A on the same isoquant as point C. Conversely, an increase in technology to T_2 without an increase in skill level would determine point B with the same result. In order to achieve movement up the ray to point D, at which equilibrium will again be established on the higher isoquant Q_2, technology would need to rise to T_2 and skill level to S_2. Likewise, movement to point E requires T_3 of technology and S_3 of skill to produce Q_3. This matching of information levels is important to communities in nations at all levels of sophistication.

In underdeveloped nations, it is very often true that even the low information base of the work force is higher than the technology of capital available to them. This has led to the argument of appropriate technology, the idea of furnishing technology that can be handled by the work force without extensive retraining. An example would be to furnish a plow with a metal share and superior design to a farmer who has been using a wooden plow.

In developed nations, there are segments of the labor force who become obsolete because the only technology available is above their skill levels. This problem is especially important in communities where these unemployed persons live. There have been cases where local efforts to increase economic activity have attracted certain industries that have had no discernable impact on the local labor force because they have found it more efficient to import labor at the proper skill level. This has surprised local leaders who thought they were working to improve the lot of the indigenous worker.

Thus, we see that problems of achieving the proper balance are to be found in all parts of the world. This occurs because the problem of poverty is found everywhere and is intimately connected to productive capabilities of people. The problems of a labor force in an American urban ghetto are not basically different from problems of a labor force in a community in an underdeveloped country.

The information level necessary for the design of a machine has been called the technology of the machine. This is basic to the concept that technology is somehow "embodied" in the machine. Whether or not this is true, it can generally be said that the more sophisticated machines have the greatest productive potential. It is only a potential until persons whose information bases are high enough are assigned to run and maintain the machine. This matching of information levels becomes even more important as technical sophistication increases, but is important at all levels.

The preceding discussion suggests that capital and labor are complementary. This is contrary to the conventional wisdom that maintains they are substitutes. The basic assumption behind the substitutability hypothesis is that capital and labor are homogeneous; thus, they do the same tasks. The fact is that both capital and labor are heterogeneous. Not only is it impossible for a piece of capital by itself to replace a person, but also people tend to be different, and differences in design make machines of the same genre different.

This will be demonstrated with the very simple task of building a road. The model utilized here has three basic assumptions: (1) capital and labor are basically heterogeneous, (2) for any given level of sophistication, production units are homogeneous, and (3) there are constraints such that factors must be combined in strict proportions (Eckaus 1955).

The task to be faced is that of producing a roadway by moving dirt from the side of the right-of-way to form a borrow pit, and placing it on the roadbed in the proper manner. We assume this is to be done in an underdeveloped area, where such a road would be considered adequate.

The situation illustrated in Fig. 9.3 is one of extreme lack

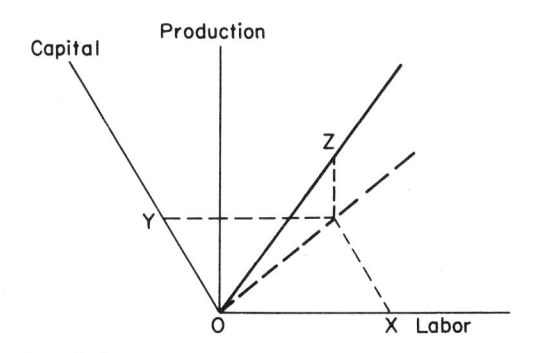

Fig. 9.3. Unsophisticated production set.

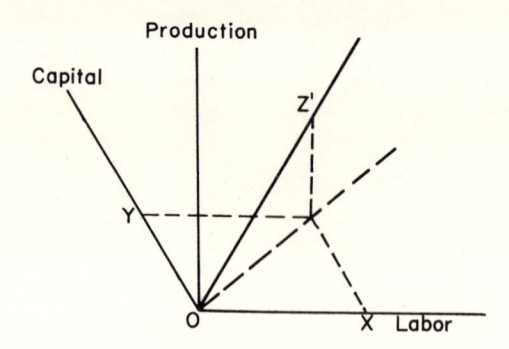

Fig. 9.4. Substitution of wheelbarrows for baskets and pushing workers for carrying workers.

of sophistication. There are X workers with Y baskets and shovels to move the dirt. Within a given time period t, they can build Z kilometers of roadway. All materials are supplied by the land, and all energy is supplied by the workers.

Let us suppose that due to a grant from an aid program, the project is supplied with wheelbarrows to replace the baskets. Now the sophistication level has changed; we have a different kind of capital. But do we also have a different kind of worker? (See Fig. 9.4.) One cannot argue that it requires exactly the same level of ability to push a wheelbarrow as to carry a basket. First a different set of muscles is involved, second a different set of skills is required. There must be some investment in training. If the local culture is such that women carry burdens in baskets and only men push wheelbarrows, the sex of the work force may change also.

The increased productivity of the new unit means that X workers and Y barrows and shovels now product Z' roadway within time period t; $Z' > Z$. A deepening in the human-nonhuman resources has resulted, and gross product has increased. All materials are supplied by the land, and all energy is supplied by the workers.

Let us move now to a time when the workers have gained a considerably higher information base and the investment situation has improved. In Fig. 9.5 the situation utilizing machines is illustrated. Now the energy source shifts. Workers are no longer the sole source, a major contribution comes from a material that is an intermediate good.

There are other major changes in the two production processes. Assuming the same number of workers overall, some of them would now be required to maintain the machines, and some would be required to obtain needed supplies. Only Y' machines would be required; $Y' < Y$. Production would rise dramatically to Z'' for period t. Again, the substitution is between overall production units, not between capital and labor. In the one case a unit might be defined as three persons, two wheelbarrows, and a shovel and, in the other, three persons and a machine. These units are hardly comparable in

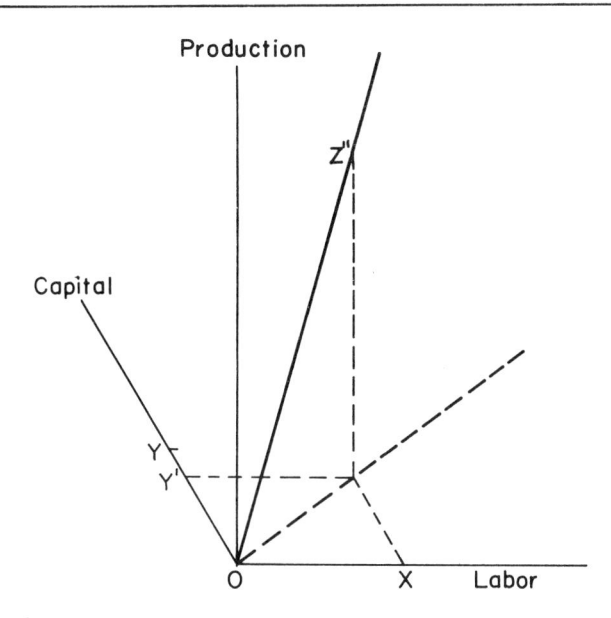

Fig. 9.5. Substitution of machines and trained operators for pushers, wheelbarrows, and shovels.

terms of sophistication, yet they produce the same product.

In making this analysis, we are also overlooking the increased social capital and other institutions of a more advanced economic system that are required to produce with the latter units. Education and training of operators, mechanics, and administrative personnel requires extensive investment. Technology of the machines requires more sophisticated production processes also. In turn, this requires greater sophistication of production labor and capital. Efficiency of distribution systems also has to be at a high level.

Figures 9.3, 9.4, and 9.5 represent three production sets from a production space that is defined by products and processes. There are numerous production sets within this space, each defined by three things: the level of technical information used in designing the capital, the skill level of the labor force, and the resultant production level. Decision makers choose among them on the basis of economic objectives.

A production space is depicted in Fig. 9.6 for production units at four information levels (processes) and three levels of production, a total of twelve production sets. Rays R_1, R_2, and R_3 represent different production processes or proportionate relationships between number of units utilized and the amount of information input involved.

Decision makers have a choice among processes for any given level of production (Q_1, Q_2, or Q_3). Set B identifies the utilization of process 1 to produce at level Q_2. This process operates on

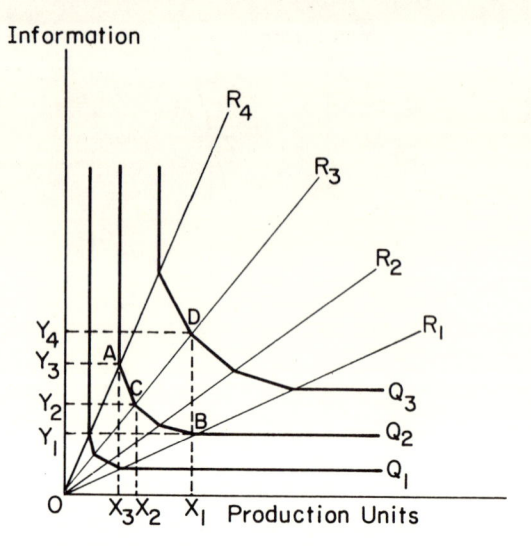

Fig. 9.6. Production space.

a low information level requiring only Y_1 of information to form X_1 production units. Movement to a higher ray or process involves abandonment of lower information base people and capital and substitution of more information into the design of capital and skill levels of the people. Better-designed capital and better-trained people would make up the new units. Choice of production set A would mean production of the same Q_2 units of product but with only X_3 production units operating at the higher information level of Y_3.

Thus, we see that the introduction of more sophisticated capital and better-trained people will cause abandonment of lower information capital and people. The capital becomes obsolete, but the people are capable of rejuvenation, providing their information base is sufficient to absorb and utilize new information, and they have access to training.

If the objective is to produce Q_2 of product, only part of the labor force can be trained at the new level. Since people are heterogeneous, it is likely that the more capable ones will be hired and trained. Thus, $OX_1 - OX_2$ workers will be unemployed. The number of units employed would be slightly higher at point C, defining a set based on X_2 units, Q_2 production, and a Y_2 information level. The Y_2/X_2 proportion information level defines process R_3 that also has potential for utilization of the entire labor force, provided markets can be found for the production of Q_3 units. This would involve selection of production set D. Much more information would be required to train additional workers and to provide intelligence information and coordinational skills necessary to produce and market products at this higher production level; thus, Y_4 information level is required.

Very often the introduction of sophisticated capital into a community having a very low information base labor force (many may be actually or functionally illiterate) will necessitate the importation of skilled labor. This throws old capital and labor out of work and explains a phenomenon noted repeatedly in underdeveloped areas of the world. Usually the new methods are introduced to produce for an old market. One argument is that products are better and cheaper. There is considerable doubt about quality necessarily being better. The cheaper part depends upon relative wage levels, capital costs, and the existence of equilibrium between human and nonhuman resources within the production unit. One thing is certain: this procedure tends to lower standards of living for the lower skilled people.

If the policy objective in a community is to improve employment opportunities for an existing labor force, decision makers need to ascertain the level of trainability of the workers. Trainability involves attitude, literacy, experience, previous training, and native ability. Often good progress can be made by providing technical schools and by selecting industries willing to train workers to the needed skill levels. Where there are workers with low levels of trainability, emphasis should be placed on attracting or developing industries whose technical level is the best the local people can handle. In some cases, people working in existing industries are underemployed because they are capable of handling a higher level of nonhuman resources than they are being provided.

A community in any society needs to consider these facts in embarking upon economic development programs. Since this process usually involves trying to attract capital, the skill level of the local labor force needs to be considered. Some communities sponsor local technical colleges to train workers in order to attract certain types of industries. Where the basic information level of workers is such that people are readily trainable, industries may also be willing to train workers. Often the companies selecting rural communities will have low information processes precisely because the available labor force is unskilled. Urban communities are usually less fortunate in this process because agglomeration diseconomies cause cost structures of the firms to be high in such environments.

Use of Resources for Expansion

A society influences current and future production by the use of its resources. As indicated previously, when there is an imbalance between human and nonhuman resources, there will be either underemployment or unemployment, depending upon the extent of the imbalance. In the above illustration, selection of process R_4 means that a high information capital plus skillful people can produce the amount needed with less units. The unemployment results from substitution among processes. In this section, we speak about a lack of balance within units.

If all resources are used efficiently, the economy will operate on its production possibility frontier. Such a frontier is

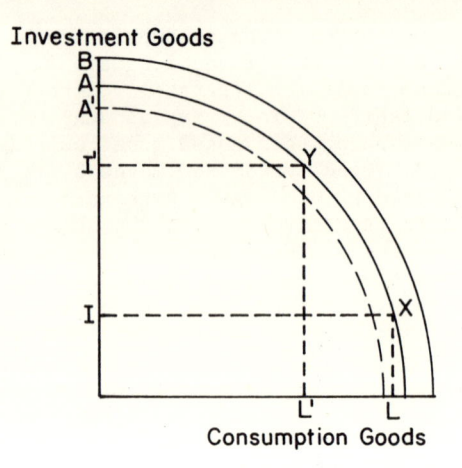

Fig. 9.7. Production possibility frontiers.

shown in Fig. 9.7. Here the choice is between goods for consumption and goods for investment. In the latter category are goods used in human resource development and maintenance, such as educational and health services. The category also includes resources used to design and produce capital goods and to improve upon the land.

Frontier A represents a true frontier as of a given time period, and A' represents a situation where there are underemployed resources. The latter is not a true frontier, since by definition that implies the most efficient combination possible given the information available. Surface A' results when human-nonhuman resources are not in equilibrium. For example, the labor force may be perfectly capable of moving dirt with wheelbarrows but is only provided baskets. A similar situation could occur if human resources capable of using bulldozers were provided only wheelbarrows and shovels. Unemployment occurs when human resources are provided no nonhuman resources at all or vice versa. This could also make achievement of frontier A impossible.

Change that results in either underemployment or unemployment of resources is detrimental to the local economy. Thus, a national recession, resulting in a lowering of demand for local products, could throw local resources into unemployment and impact negatively on the economy via the multiplier effect explained in Chapter 3. The same result might occur if a local plant becomes obsolete, and the firm decides to move the operation to an up-to-date plant in another community.

<u>Shift of the frontier.</u> In order to achieve frontier B (Fig. 9.7), a society must add productive power. This can be done by either widening or deepening the productive units. Widening consists of producing more workers at the same skill level and more capital at the same technical level as that already existing. There is no in-

crease in efficiency of the production unit, but since there are more of them, more goods are produced. Deepening means to produce both workers and capital with greater production capability. There is an increase in efficiency or more production per unit. Frontier B could be accomplished, theoretically, with no increase in numbers of units if they could be converted to the higher information level. However, that is not the way it is usually done. Deepening usually occurs with new units. In this case, B could be reached with less of them than would be the case with widening. The new units would add to those available for production as well as being more productive than the old.

The possibility of shifting from A to B depends, to a considerable degree, upon the choices made between production of investment and consumption goods. If production is at point X, for example, emphasis is upon production of consumption goods (C), and enough investment goods (I) may not be forthcoming to accomplish the needed shift. On the other hand, production at Y will produce I' of investment goods, which may result in hardship on consumers and inefficient use of investment.

One way to accomplish the shift from A to B is to concentrate production of investment goods so as to get an optimum combination of deepening and widening of productive units. In a society where information develops very rapidly, for example, an area that curtails development of and opportunity for technological talent could rapidly fall behind.

Even small communities often find that major opportunities for growth come from the minds of local inventors and other technology oriented people. One common mistake is to discourage or fail to encourage these people. Often technologists lack coordinational skills, hampering them in producing and marketing the products and services they develop. There are numerous success stories (success defined in growth terms) where communities have provided support for technologists with good ideas, resulting in the development of new industries. Support often includes providing people having necessary coordinational and operational skills.

Rationing of resources between investment for widening and investment for deepening also involves a possibility frontier. Assume that resources can be used interchangeably to produce either existing capital or better-designed models; education facilities and other training can be used to produce either operators for existing or better-trained operators for the better-designed capital; and technology research can be included as an input to deepening of production unit resources.

Production at point X of Fig. 9.8 would give emphasis to the design and production of more productive capital and the intensive training of human resources. Production at Y would mean emphasis on existing programs to produce more workers with the same skills and capital with the same capacity as that currently being used. Productivity of each productive unit produced at X would be higher, hence fewer would need to be added to reach possibility frontier B (Fig. 9.7). Assuming that use of the investment budget at point Y would bring the economy to the B frontier, use of it at X would

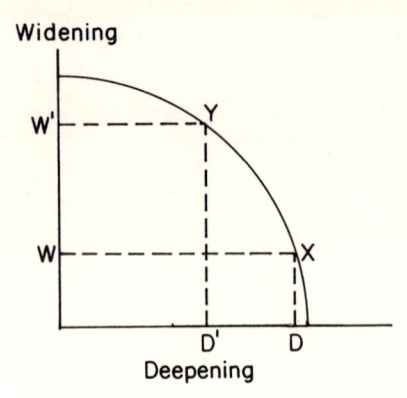

Fig. 9.8. Production possibility frontier for production units.

bring the economy to a frontier somewhat beyond B, providing there was a proper balancing between the human and nonhuman components.

Problem of obsolescence. When a sophisticated machine is replaced by one even more sophisticated, it is said to be obsolete. The people associated with it also become obsolete unless retrained at a higher level. In those nations participating in the highly automated segment of the world, the problem of obsolescence is of major importance. Machines designed for twenty years of service may be replaced in ten. The information base for design of the new machine may be so much higher than the old as to make the latter's continued use impossible. When this happens the operator and maintenance man also become obsolete. Society is then faced with the need to retrain people to catch up with the information base of the new machines.

Obsolescence is less of a problem in those parts of the world just entering the industrial era. What may be obsolete to one company or one part of the world may be a new technology to another. For example, larger airlines that find it necessary to acquire larger and more sophisticated planes in order to service long flights, often sell their "obsolete" equipment to smaller lines serving shorter flight schedules. Eventually these items become obsolete to the new owners as well. The same situation can be seen with regard to underdeveloped nations. It may make more sense to encourage them to start with equipment they can understand than to try to introduce them to the latest thing.

One problem of advanced nations is their tendency to expect everyone to have the same general sophistication they have. Much frustration and waste of resources could be avoided if in aid programs, technological offerings were tailored to the information levels of the people to be helped.

Role of supportive capital. People and machines must have places to work. Design of a building can contribute materially to productivity. Proper heating, cooling, and lighting; the right combinations of colors; proper layout for materials and product flows --they all contribute. It is poor management to place sophisticated people and machines in a building so poorly designed as to inhibit material flows, produce uncomfortable working conditions, or create problems in disposal of waste. A fast locomotive cannot perform on an ill-designed and/or poorly maintained roadbed or track. A washboard road can increase maintenance needs of trucks. Eroded land loses its ability to produce crops. The sophistication level of supportive capital must match that of people and machines to which it lends support.

For a community interested in development, it is important that local building codes encourage efficient building construction, that local utilities be made available in efficient ways, and that streets and rail sidings are adequate for the jobs they will be expected to do. Where a community is constructing facilities for lease to potential industry, it has even greater control over supportive capital. Mistakes can be made, however, and are often difficult to remedy. Good planning can pay off handsomely.

Land as a factor. The concept of land held by classical economists was related to its original and indestructible qualities-- generally thought to be fertility. Today's concept includes earth, sky, minerals, topography, climate, water availability, location, and esoteric properties. But in considering land as a productive factor, there must be a separation of some of the qualities.

Land holding up a building or a roadbed or serving a farmer may be playing a purely supportive role. In this case, the major difference between it and supportive capital is that the latter is used up eventually. Land does not need to be depreciated. (Erosion is poor management, not depreciation.) A particular piece of land may become obsolete for certain uses, however. Minerals (and in many cases air and water) are material inputs, hence are not in the supportive classification. Topography, climate, location, and esoteric properties are site values that contribute to production in several different ways. Topography, for example, is important in making land useful in its supportive role.

The geography of a community is important in growth and development. Physical qualities of soil are important to some industries, such as agriculture. Topography can be an asset or a liability, depending upon its effect on construction, access, scenery, and so on. Community planning should be done in such a way as to accent the asset values and compensate for the liabilities of topography. Climate is also important in many ways. Costs of heating and cooling are important to many industries. Tropical heat is generally considered to be a deterrent, as is arctic cold. Where labor migration is important to a development program, climate can play a decisive role.

Location of the community with regard to markets, raw materials, producers of intermediate goods, labor supplies, and other important factors were discussed in Chapters 4 and 5. It was pointed out there that where there are geographic liabilities, other important factors have to offset them to make a location attractive.

Roles of material and energy inputs. In addition to raw materials obtained from the land, there are many types of material inputs ranging from natural inputs, such as trees and fish, to semiprocessed inputs of all kinds. Farm products, primary metals, fiberglass, and plastics represent one type. Semifinished goods, such as parts for machines, represent another. Thus, each business, industrial, and governmental unit has ties to other units from which it receives inputs of goods that have been partially or wholly processed. A major part of economic activity is concerned with production and marketing of these intermediate goods.

Many of these goods have substitution and complementary relationships that make it possible for decision makers to choose among them according to physical requirements and relative costs. Thus, a producer of fiberglass boats may have product designs calling for use of plastics for various parts of the boat. If prices for plastic are relatively low, the producer might choose a design utilizing a maximum of plastic. If they are relatively high, the producer may choose to use a minimum of plastic and may choose the design that will accomplish this. If physical specifications require fiberglass for the hull, plastics are limited as substitutes to other portions of the boat.

Let us analyze the production function depicted in Fig. 9.9. The decision maker has four possible processes involving the use of fiberglass and plastic. To produce twenty boats, he or she may choose a combination of F_1 fiberglass and E_1 plastic, or F_2 fiber-

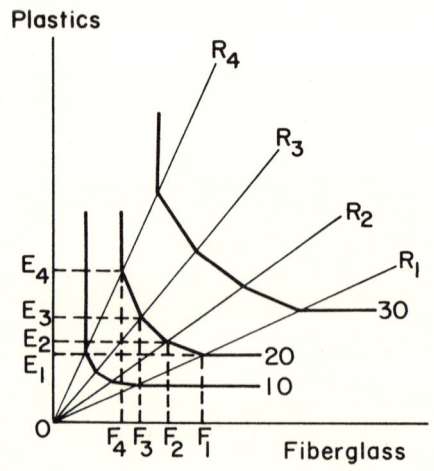

Fig. 9.9. Production function for boats utilizing fiberglass and plastics.

Change as an Economic Phenomenon

glass and E_2 plastic, or F_3 fiberglass and E_3 plastic, or F_4 fiberglass and E_4 plastic.

Production with process R_1 may be visualized as an all-fiberglass boat with plastic seats and trim. Production process R_2 would add a plastic dashboard and added plastic trim in substitute for fiberglass. Production process R_3 would substitute a plastic deck for the fiberglass one. And production process R_4 would require the upper part of the hull to be made of plastic as well. Thus, the decision maker can choose among the four combinations to get the cheapest, the one with most market appeal, or the one with greatest durability, depending upon the objectives.

Changes in input relationships are common, particularly when one material is a substitute for another. These substitutions may be short term or long term. When furnaces have the proper design, there can be substitutions among coal, oil, and natural gas to meet temporary shortages or price fluctuations. Where rather complete retooling and redesign are necessary, substitution of a material, such as aluminum, for steel, or fiberglass for aluminum may be considered rather permanent.

The effects of these changes on a community will depend upon the backward linkages existent in the local economy. Suppose, for example, that in a given community there is an aluminum plant and a manufacturer of aluminum boats. A shift to the use of fiberglass in the boats may require that the major input for boats be imported. This would also force the aluminum plant to look for new customers, which may lead to increased export of aluminum to other communities. The economic structure of the community would change, leading to smaller multiplier effects.

Technology may cause change by changing the basic input requirements; that is, a way may be devised to make aluminum stronger so sheets can be thinner and less is required to make a boat. Technology also influences through development of new products. The change may be generic (television vs. radio), or specific (transistors vs. tubes). These types of change also impact on linkages by changing sources.

Sources of energy also change and can have major impacts on local development possibilities. For example, the building of a natural gas line into a community can make it attractive to industry. Technology can be expected to contribute greatly in this field in future years by making it possible to use solar and other possible sources of energy more efficiently. The process of obtaining energy from the sun may someday result in the location of communities in space that will export electricity and other products to earth.

<u>Possible impact of shortages</u>. Shortages are possible among all factors of production, including information. The energy situation has dramatized the way that shortage of one set of inputs can affect the utilization of others. Energy is particularly acute in a sophisticated society, since so much of the work is done through machines, and since so much energy is needed for heating, cooling,

and lighting. A shortage of an input may also be a reflection of shortage of information. When the iron ore was exhausted in the Mesabi Range, it was necessary to turn to other sources. The taconite left there was of no value. However, once information was developed to make utilization of the taconite possible, iron ore began flowing from the Mesabi again.

Shortages of information are not due to its being used up, but to its not yet being used extensively enough. In sophisticated societies, the growth of information is expected to continue. And, in line with Zimmerman's observation, that which is not useful today will become useful tomorrow simply because we find out how to use it. As indicated in the United States energy study (Campbell 1964, p. 59):

> The structure of energy sources, uses, and transformations is extremely involved. A whole complex of competing methods of using existing stocks of resources can satisfy our energy demands, although at anytime, with a given technology, only some will be used, more costly methods being rejected in favor of cheaper ones. . . . A wider range of processes must be considered, for what is inefficient today may be efficient tomorrow. . . .

Bottlenecks are well known in industry. Given time they can be worked out and new input relationships established. But while they are in effect, the lack of one input may dictate uses to be made of others. This comes as a result of complex linkages.

Services as inputs. We have noted the fact that certain factors produce streams of services. These are not the only services used in production. There are also service inputs resulting from linkages, particularly at the local level. One unit has as its product services that are inputs to another unit. Thus, a producer of business services would have as its customer a producer of textiles that would sell its product outside the community. The business services firm would own machines, hire people, have inputs of paper and possibly repair services to its machines. These service inputs are more complex than those coming from a single factor.

Such inputs can be compared to semifinished products, since they are often dependent upon other industries for their markets. They are also like lubricants and other materials that are consumed in production without physically becoming part of the end product. Where the end product is a service, no inputs may become physically part of it. This type of transformation is strictly ethereal.

One must consider that the end service is a bundle of the services of all inputs to it. This is one way of looking at transformation. A step further would be to consider all products as bundles of services. This certainly applies to durables utilized by consumers over time. It is a bit harder to apply in the case of some nondurables, such as food, unless one considers the energy provided by food as a type of service.

Change as an Economic Phenomenon   245

An example. Production becomes a function of the services of various inputs by which they are transformed into some output. Let us consider the case of an oil refinery. The structure is a mass of pipes, distilleries, cracking units, and storage tanks. The cracking units and distilleries are similar to machines, since they are the means by which energy is applied to the process. There are also buildings housing the offices and the computers that control the operation. This is a sophisticated factory, and the information level of those who work here is high.

The crude oil enters the distilleries and cracking units from storage tanks via pipes. A wide variety of products is possible by separating groups of hydrocarbons through heating (distillation). The gases that boil at the lowest temperature are given off first, and these are used as fuel for the plant. As the temperature of the petroleum is raised, hydrocarbons with 5 and 6 carbon atoms are given off, and these are used as solvents for rubber and varnish.

The next group, material that boils between 85° and 200° Celsius, is used as gasoline. Material that boils between 200° and 300° Celsius is kerosene. The residue can be of either of two types, depending upon the type of oil used. Some oils contain paraffin that becomes either an input to other industry or is packaged as a consumer good. Other oils leave a thick, black pitch called asphalt, which is used in paving.

The amount of gasoline to be recovered from distillation is limited. By using the cracking process, which amounts to breaking down the crude oil with intense heat, three times as much gasoline can be recovered. Thus, the plant has two processes, and the combination depends upon the volume of various products desired. This information is developed by management and conveyed to the computer operators. The computer makes the decision as to how much oil is to go where, and what temperatures are to be used.

In addition to its major input of crude oil, this plant purchases electricity, business services, repair services for office machinery, office supplies, government services, and other goods and services. Although the chemist would say the products of the plant contain only ingredients that were in the oil, the economist would say they also include these other services plus the services of labor and management. The process could not go on without them, therefore they become part of the product. This is what is meant by transformation in the broadest sense.

Role of price changes. Changes that occur in prices of factors have a number of different roles to play in change that affects communities. To illustrate some of these let us imagine a company producing one product with linear production function $Q_Y = 5X$, where Y = the product, and X = hours of operation. Suppose further that the firm faces a linear demand curve designated by $P = 20.5 - 0.010Y$. Nonhuman resources (such as machines, support capital, and land) that are used by the workers are sufficient for an aggregate of 160 hours of operation per day, with cost of maintenance and repair of $640.00 or $4.00 per hour. Raw material per unit of Y product is worth $1600 or $10.00 per hour and labor costs $8.50 per hour. Thus, the firm has constant marginal cost of $22.50 per operation hour.

So, Q_Y = 5(160) = 800 units of Y. The price received is P = 20.5 - 0.01(800) = $12.50. Total revenue, $TR = PQ = 20.5Q - 0.01Q^2$ = $16,400 - $6400 = $10,000; (dTR/dQ) = marginal revenue, MR = 20.5 - 0.20Q = 20.5 - 16 = $4.50. Marginal revenue product is equal to marginal physical product times marginal revenue, or $MRP = MPP_X \cdot MR_Y$ = 5 × $4.50 = $22.50. Thus, the firm has marginal cost of operation exactly equal to marginal revenue product. This is the most it can afford to pay per operation hour.

Now, suppose the labor union has considerable strength and is able to coerce the company into adding wages and perquisites equal to an additional $2.00 per hour. The marginal cost is now $24.50 or $2.00 above the marginal return. Since the firm cannot operate very long with that type of cost situation, management must look to its options. One option would be to close down and move to an area with lower wage rates. This is feasible only if labor of proper skill levels could be obtained and if the labor savings were sufficient to offset shutdown, moving, and other costs that would be incurred. Firms do make these decisions, however, and communities lose industries because of them. Other communities gain industry in the same process.

Another option the firm might consider would be to shift the marginal revenue product by either increasing marginal physical product or marginal revenue or both. There are problems attendant to this procedure. Firms often compensate for excessive labor cost settlements by investing in capital and training to take them to a next higher process ray. But this often means cutting back on process hours, hence the laying off of workers, since they can now produce the same amount in less time.

If the demand curve cannot be moved, keeping the same number of workers employed could lead to overproduction and attendant marketing problems. As an example, suppose the second ray would increase the function to $Q_Y = 6X$, then 160 processing hours would produce 960 units. Using the previous demand function, MR = 20.5 - 0.02(960) = 20.5 - 19.2 = $1.30, $1.30 × 6 = $7.80. The company is in worse shape than it was before. Holding to the old isoquant, $6X$ = 800, and X = 133 1/3 hours. This would keep the old MR of $4.50, 6 × $4.50 - $27.00, which allows $2.50 for added costs of maintenance and repair of the more sophisticated new machinery and other nonhuman resources. But it would mean fewer work hours.

Not only will increases in labor costs affect the firm, but changes in raw material costs (because of price or transport cost increases) could have the same general effect. Firms are not always in a position to shift the MRP curve. Alert labor leaders will recognize the limits beyond which they cannot go without losing jobs for their workers.

But unions also have a positive impact on a community by assuring that workers receive a fair wage. This increases spendable income and, thus, the local market for all goods. As plants are updated to higher information levels, local workers gain in skill; productivity of the production unit increases. Since the marginal physical product per operation hour increases, the amount that can be paid each factor increases as well. Unions have the job of assuring that workers get their fair share.

If productivity does not increase, the only way the firm can shift the *MRP* curve is to raise prices. It can do this only insofar as it has a fairly inelastic demand curve and the power to cause it to shift to the right. Monopoly or oligopoly power leads to administered prices, a fairly common occurrence in the advanced economies of the world. But there are limitations even there; if prices are increased too much, people will find substitutes.

Both firms and unions have a common interest in maintaining increased productivity as information level increases make it possible. If they do not do this, their plants will eventually become obsolete. This means that skills of the work force will be obsolete along with productive potential of the capital. Obsolete plants lead to failures and plant closings.

ROLE OF MONEY IN CHANGE

Money has purposely been left out of the discussion to this point, since it is not involved directly in the productive process. As we have seen, a viable and productive community could exist in the distant past without it. It is doubtful that viable communities can exist in the present world without money. A common medium of exchange is necessary for a price system, and price systems play significant roles in change. They are also important in allocating resources to the productive process in order for people, as consumers, to gain maximum satisfaction.

Money has a price system of its own. Interest is the price one pays for the use of money. The use of money gives one power to command resources. For this reason, availability of money is important in production and in change as well. An input does not have to be physically scarce to disrupt a productive process. Lack of money to buy it will do just as well. Financing is a key factor in all aspects of production and consumption.

Money has another interesting characteristic. It is easily conveyed and easily stored. Hence, it tends to be accumulated by certain segments of society. In democracies, certain people and institutions gain control. In dictatorships, the government tends to control the supply. This piling up of the power to command resources conveys great power over the productive process to certain segments of society. This power can be used to satisfy or to thwart the wishes of society as a whole. It is employed in determining whether or not a given development will take place. In community development, one of the major activities is called "attracting capital." What is really meant is "attracting money." The investment part comes after the power is obtained to attract necessary resources.

STRUCTURE OF INDUSTRY

One often hears the remark that American technology is dynamic because large corporations have much money to spend on research and development. Scherer (1970, p. 348) quotes National Science Foundation data to show that in 1966, research and development outlays amounted to $22.2 billion, and 70 percent of research was performed by private industry. But only 33 percent was actually funded by private industry. The federal government performed 15 percent in its own laboratories, paid for 37 percent performed by private industry, and at least partially supported the 12 percent performed at universities and the 3 percent performed in nonprofit institutions. Jewkes, Sawyers, and Stillerman (1959, pp. 71-85) examined 61 important inventions and found that industrial research laboratories were the sources of less than a third of them. Other studies have found similar information. New products and processes seem to be the work of independent inventors, academicians, and small firms.

As Scherer (1970) points out, the initial work on an invention requires very little in terms of resources. It is at the development stage that the real need appears. The research and development departments of large corporations are particularly well equipped to take an idea that has merit and bring it through the costly development process and onto the market. Still, a large proportion of development work seems to be done by medium-sized and small firms. His general conclusion is that the process of invention, running from original ideas through development to promotion and marketing, requires firms of all sizes, each with its own special advantages and disadvantages. There seems to be no particular advantage to bigness, so far as technological development is concerned.

A corollary to the idea that big firms with lots of money help bring about technological change is the idea that a monopolistic market structure favors innovation. Scherer's general conclusion on this point is that a little bit of monopoly power may be helpful, but a high concentration is apt to actually retard progress by restricting the number of independent sources of initiative and dampening small firms' incentives to try to gain market position. We have noted that even if pure competition were highly desirable, it is possible only in a spaceless world. This may not be a bad situation for technological change so long as restriction of markets falls considerably short of monopoly.

ECONOMIES OF SIZE

Aside from the impact of structure on technology, size itself may influence. For example, it may be that a large firm is more mobile and can move to take advantage of possible situations; or it may be that a larger factory can exploit a new product more easily than a small one; or that a new process can more easily be adapted.

The management of an individual firm has an incentive to expand as long as expansion will provide a way for utilizing its resources more efficiently. Each manager must face the question, "Is there a best size for the operation?" Penrose (1959) has indicated that the attainment of such an "equilibrium position" is precluded by three significant obstacles.

1. Resources are indivisible, which means that some combination must be made of them in such a way as to make most efficient use of all of them. There may not be a combination that does not call for a very large and varied output. At least there may be no way to combine all of the inputs in terms of the smallest units in which they can be acquired, since each may be capable of rendering different amounts and kinds of services.
2. Heterogeneity in the services available from the resources with which the firm works permits the same resources to be used for many different purposes and in many different ways. Possibilities change with changes in information. Both an automatic increase in knowledge and an incentive to search for new knowledge are built into the firm. Services that resources will yield depend upon the abilities of the people using them. Capabilities of people are often shaped by the resources they work with.
3. Expansion spawns expansion, and new productive services are continually growing from the old ones.

The role of specialization must also be considered. As a firm grows, it develops new ways to take advantage of specialization, and this creates new needs for specialization that in turn may create a need for greater size. Thus a "vicious circle" is created in which size leads to specialization and specialization to greater size. Since expansion of firms is based on opportunities to utilize resources more efficiently, there may be no absolute limit to the size of a firm.

Economies of size make it possible for a large firm not only to produce and sell goods and services more efficiently than smaller firms but also to introduce larger quantities of new products more efficiently. These economies can be technological in the sense of actual production, or they may be managerial. Managerial economies arise when purchases, sales, and financial transactions can be made on a large scale.

In an expanding economy, a large proportion of the growth of existing firms will be related to increased demand for their existing products. It is less risky and cheaper to expand in this fashion. Where new products are introduced, there may be no existing utility functions for them. In that case demand must be created by promotion. Thus, by advertising and promotion, firms are actually capable of producing utility, and this requires resources. Large firms can pay for promotion because of their control of money.

Economies of size may be experienced in the expansion process as well as in operations. Under given circumstances, a firm may be able to put additional output on the market cheaper than any other firm, large or small. These economies of growth are related to the collection of productive resources owned by the firm. Such economies can only be attained when the firm expands. Once it has expanded, they disappear. Economies of growth will remain as economies of size only if the firm is forced to reorganize its activities to take advantage of them. Thus, it may have to acquire blocks of other resources in order to take full advantage of existing ones. These other resources would then create opportunities for further expansion.

DIVERSIFICATION

Many successful and highly efficient firms are highly diversified. This seems to contradict the commonly accepted premise that integration is likely to be "inefficient." In times of change, it may well be that ability to diversify gives a firm important advantages in choosing alternatives for investment. There are a number of ways that firms can diversify. One way is diversification within the same general area of specialization; the production of more products based on the same technology and sold in the firm's existing markets. Another is to go into completely new markets with completely new products but using the same production base. Yet another is to expand in the existing market with new products based on a different technology. Variation on that is to expand into new market areas with these products.

Very few firms diversify into fields completely foreign to their previous experience. There is enough uncertainty in business without inviting trouble. In addition to lack of experience, there is a likelihood of getting committed beyond the possible monetary resources the firm can command. In order to maintain a market position, a firm must be willing and able to devote sufficient resources and to keep investing in that area. Otherwise it will have to withdraw from the field.

Diversification is a way of assisting change, but it has its limitations. The more monetary resources a firm can command, the greater its chances of making a success out of a new line of products. Even there, the information base of management is important. Where firms acquire industries with which their management is not entirely familiar, acquisition of the acquired firm's management is often an important factor in successful operation.

ROLE OF THE FIRM IN CHANGE

It is said that change begets change. Every so often an innovation is introduced that causes a maximum amount of change to be born. One of these was the corporate entity. It is the corporate structure, making the firm essentially immortal, that allows it to command the resources making change possible in the economic sense. In speaking of the firm, therefore, corporate structure will be assumed.

A firm may consist of one or many productive units. A productive unit is a larger scale unit than a production unit, previously defined in terms of human-nonhuman resources. A productive unit may be thought of as a single plant. However, there may be more than one productive unit housed in one building. A unit that produces more than one product with essentially the same technology is one unit. If more than one product is produced with two different technologies, two productive units are present. The firm usually introduces change through these productive units.

As was indicated previously, production is the process of combining and coordinating materials and services in the creation of other valuable goods and/or services. It is the transformation of input flows into output flows. The coordinators of this process are the managers. Managers at the unit level are concerned with specific operations. These are the people who interact within most community economies. Managers at the firm level, when the firm consists of more than one unit, are concerned with broader phases of coordination. Their decisions affect the communities within which the firm's units are located or may become located, but the decision process may completely lack consideration of local values or local impacts. Thus, a decision to drop a particular product line in favor of a new one will likely be made in terms of information concerning technologies and markets on a wide geographic basis. Since multiunit firms are coming to dominate production in much of the world, they are very important to those concerned with the impact of change on communities.

Decision Making at the Firm Level

The primary economic function of a firm is to make use of resources for the purpose of supplying goods and services to whatever markets it happens to be serving in accordance with plans developed and put into effect within the firm. Thus, the essential difference between economic activity inside and outside the firm is that the former is organized administratively, but the latter is not.

The larger the firm, relative to its market areas and other firms in its industry, the more its activities are determined from within and the less from without. The strength of a firm lies in both its ability to command resources (the amount of money at its disposal) and its ability to influence its markets. In its role as an autonomous administrative planning unit, management of the firm is guided by policies that are framed in the light of their effect on the whole enterprise. Short run problems arising within any one productive unit must be dealt with in accordance with procedures that make the decisions stay within the bounds of overall policy. Policy, like plant structure, is changed only in the long run. These facts are not always understood in communities.

Long run decisions are generally concerned with making changes that will enhance the firm's chances of making money. It is to management's advantage to have as much control over resources as possible, hence the tendency is to retain earnings. Thus, growth and profits become twin goals in the selection of investment programs. The ability of a firm to move toward these goals is dependent upon management's imagination and vision. There are no stereotypes. Efficiency minded management is concerned with improving quality of products, getting a larger share of the market, reducing costs, better ways of handling things, and so on. Empire builders are interested in growth. Very seldom does a firm have both types in key positions.

Innovation and imagination are in many ways the antithesis of efficiency. Yet, they are the avenues through which change is most likely to come. Managers have to act on the basis of expectations, and expectations differ, depending upon the disposition of managers to take chances in the hope of gain. The implementation of change is often tied to a manager's willingness to commit effort and resources to speculative activity. Once a decision to change has been made, the major limitation may again be managerial in nature. Having an innovative head does not guarantee that the firm will be able to develop management teams able to to work together effectively as it expands. Lack of managerial resources can be worse than lack of money.

On the other hand, having an efficiency expert for a top executive with innovative second and/or third echelons may lead to the formation of competitive firms. Middle management people may think they see opportunity passing the parent company by. Sometimes a company's research and development unit will develop a new product that management does not care to exploit. It can either sit on it or license it out to someone, often one or a group of its more aggressive employees, who start a new firm. Thus, there are several ways in which a firm can contribute to change. The main problem faced by those who strike out on their own is that they lack the financial resources of the larger firm. An aggressive big firm can effect change more quickly than a smaller one.

Firm and Community

There are many different types of firm-community relationships. In some the community is heavily dependent upon the firm; in others the firm may be heavily dependent upon the community. There are numerous combinations between. In the first case (the company town), decisions by management of the firm are extremely important to the community. But these decisions may be made without consideration of welfare of the community, because, as we have noted, the decisions consider the welfare of the whole enterprise. These sorts of conflicts are difficult to alleviate. The best long run solution for any community is diversification.

To be dependent upon one firm is to be dependent upon the factors that affect its welfare. Change may come in the form of a new product that may or may not be produced in the same areas as the old. Plants become obsolete, and newer technologies of new plants may create an entirely different set of locational factors. Management may not always be efficient; the firm may lose its markets and go bankrupt or be acquired by another firm.

Where the firm is heavily dependent upon the community, it is relatively small. It may sell only to the local market. Or it may be heavily dependent on the peculiar technical skills of the people. Change within the community or change in outside markets can easily upset this type of relationship. Further, if the firm turns out to be dynamic, it may outgrow its dependence on the community. Again diversification among industries may be important to community economic health.

GOVERNMENTS AND CHANGE

Governments tend to resemble large firms in their activities. They tend to make decisions on a group basis and to be more influenced by their own administrative organizations than activity outside. The social goals of a nation tend to be set by governments based on the influence of pressure groups. As was noted previously, pressure groups have the most influence in democracies and the least in dictatorships. Thus, a dictatorship may determine that its goal is to build up armaments, when its people would prefer more bread. Yet, even a strong dictatorship cannot exist with active resistance from a majority of its citizens.

Like a large corporation, once a government sets goals, it can often bring large amounts of resources to their attainment. These resources are often used for research and development, since many goals are capable of giving a normative nature to change. The Soviet Union and the United States decided to give priority to exploration of space. Each diverted resources in its own way to the problem, and both were successful. There are spin-offs from normative research that can be useful in other lines of endeavor. For instance, war tends to hasten technical change.

Governments also influence change through powers of taxation and expenditure. Tariffs may be used to shield a new industry until it can get on its feet. Subsidies may be used for the same general purpose. Taxes may be used to inhibit growth of a particular industry. Subsidies may be used to encourage development of a particular activity without thought being given to the information base, and this can result in a disaster or a continual drain on the economy. Often governments of underdeveloped nations regard certain industries from the point of view of prestige rather than economics. Thus, one may insist on having a flag airline; another, a steel mill, and so on. Perhaps in all cases, what is really needed is to improve productivity of farmers to bring the people above subsistence level. Resources drained from the economy for these purposes may hold down needed community development and may actually interfere with needed change.

Governments also have other powers that may influence community development. Laws may be specifically designed to encourage development of new communities with or without subsidy. Laws may require government approval for location of industry. Governments may nationalize existing industries, thus directly influencing change. Governments may be the sole owners of industries, in which case they act as firms in the economic sphere. Governments may set out to change whole regions, thus having an impact on all communities within those regions. The Foss developments in southern France and TVA in America are excellent examples of this.

Perhaps one of the more important areas of governmental impact, from the community standpoint, is the influence on the overall economy. This includes control of the money supply and fiscal activity in democracies. In dictatorships, the discouragement of innovation may be of major importance. Governments also interact internationally, and the results often change the economics of communities. International aid programs have potential in this direction. International agreements on use of the seas could have more impact in the future than lack of such agreements have had in the past.

OTHER SOCIAL SYSTEMS AND CHANGE

The effect of governments on change is apt to be rather direct. However, there are many other social systems that influence communities in subtle ways, and their overall impact is as great if not greater than government's. We have noted previously that attitudes are important in change. Attitudes are heavily influenced by philosophies. Some philosophies, such as the Protestant ethic, have a positive influence on change. Other philosophies of the fatalistic type tend to inhibit change.

Some social philosophies are based on religious concepts, and others seem to have grown in place. Thus, philosophies that place one class of people above another can be very inhibiting by keeping capable people out of decision-making positions. A philosophy that says people of a particular color, race, religion, and so forth are not allowed to operate in given areas of endeavor, or conversely, one that says only people of a given configuration, area of birth, or whatever are allowed to operate, is inimical to change also. Any philosophy that interferes with efficient allocation of resources and the free play of innovative forces has the effect of slowing change and slowing community growth.

DUAL ECONOMY

Economic change in rural areas of underdeveloped nations is often inhibited by their dependence upon stagnant agricultural industries for their basic income. The concept of dualism was introduced by Sandee (1960) with a model of the India economy that treats agriculture separately from the rest of the economy. A dual society, by his definition, is one that is basically agrarian but is trying to move toward industrialization. Its problem is how to actually accomplish the move when its agriculture is producing just slightly more than is needed for subsistence.

Sandee's model has several important aspects to it. One of these is an illustration of the use of taxation to obtain capital. Since it is very difficult for people who do not have a big surplus to save, and since development of capital is important in getting other industries under way, taxation is used as a way of forcing austerity on the people in order to promote growth. This model imposes most taxes on the urban sector, since that is the area considered to have the nearest thing to a surplus.

A number of other people have utilized the dual concept, since it allows one to simplify matters by keeping the dominant industry, agriculture, separate from the industries considered important for growth. Fei and Ranis (1969, pp. 129-64) have gone even further. They see dualism as an actual characteristic of an economy at one period in its development. Thus, they identify four types of economic systems that occur in historical sequence: (1) the agrarian society, (2) the open agrarian society, (3) the dualistic society, and (4) the industrially mature society.

The agrarian society is self-sufficient. It does not engage in trade to any extent. Thus, values of specialization are not present. Every farmer produces most of the things a family would need. This was typical of frontier farming in the United States, and it is probably typical of much of the underdeveloped world today.

An open agrarian society has begun to specialize. A Prairie farmer finds he can produce wheat more advantageously than anything else, so he trades wheat with someone whose advantage lies in raising cattle. Intracommunity trade leads to intercommunity trade, which leads to interregional trade. But this society is still strictly agrarian. Greater efficiencies from specialization and trade have not freed it very much.

However, these very efficiencies lay the basis for accumulation of capital that is necessary in entering a dual world where industries other than agriculture can be encouraged. In the view of Fei and Ranis, most of the underdeveloped world is in the position of trying to move from an open agrarian to a dualistic economy. It is being frustrated by "inability to shake off the endemic structural characteristics of agrarianism."

In attempting to explain the causes of agrarian stagnation, Fei and Ranis adopt the concepts of Physiocrats who regarded agriculture as the only really productive industry, the product of which was used to finance "sterile" classes of economic activity. To this is added the causal explanation of the classicists. Thus, the economics used to explain phenomena in preindustrial society is used.

Fei and Ranis use two models. Fig. 9.10 represents the flows of food from the agricultural sector and services from the other sectors. The Q units of food produced by agriculture are split with H of them consumed by the farmers and R by workers in the service sector. The T units of services are also split with C units going to sustain cultural, religious, and military activities and A units flowing back to agriculture.

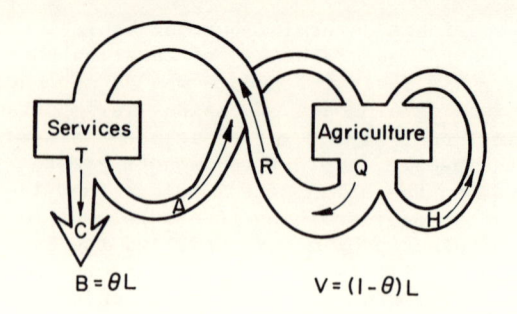

Fig. 9.10. Flows of food and services.

The contribution of classicists was to point out the important role played by human resources. Let L be the total labor force and θ be the proportion employed in service industries. Then there are θL workers in service and $(1 - \theta)L$ workers in agriculture. Now, if we accept the premise that food will be distributed in the same proportion as workers, we have

$$\theta = R/Q \quad \text{or} \quad R = \theta Q \tag{9.4}$$

We now recognize R represents a surplus product of agriculture that can be traded for services. Therefore, its existence is necessary for a service sector to exist. From (9.4) we see the proportion of the labor force that can be used to produce services is dependent upon the proportion of agricultural production available to feed it.

Now, by using the surplus labor ratio θ and farmers' productivity $P = Q/[(1 - \theta)L]$, the basic relationships between production and consumption can be determined. From (9.4) we have

$$Q = R/\theta \tag{9.5a}$$

and from the definitions of P and C,

$$P = [R/\theta]/[L(1 - \theta)] = R/[\theta L(1 - \theta)] \tag{9.5b}$$

$$C = [R/\theta]/L = R/(\theta L) = P(1 - \theta) \tag{9.5c}$$

Then $C/P = (1 - \theta)$, so the fraction of the labor force used in agriculture must equal the proportion of its product used for consumption.

Now we can utilize the second illustration (Fig. 9.11) to summarize these relationships. In Fig. 9.11A, θ is measured on the x axis and P and C on the y axis. The distance $o \to m$ represents the amount of labor used in nonagricultural pursuits, and $m \to \theta_o$ is the amount used in agriculture ($o \to \theta_o = 1$). Representing consumption of nonagricultural products is $c_o \to q_o$, and $q_o \to c$ represents con-

Change as an Economic Phenomenon   257

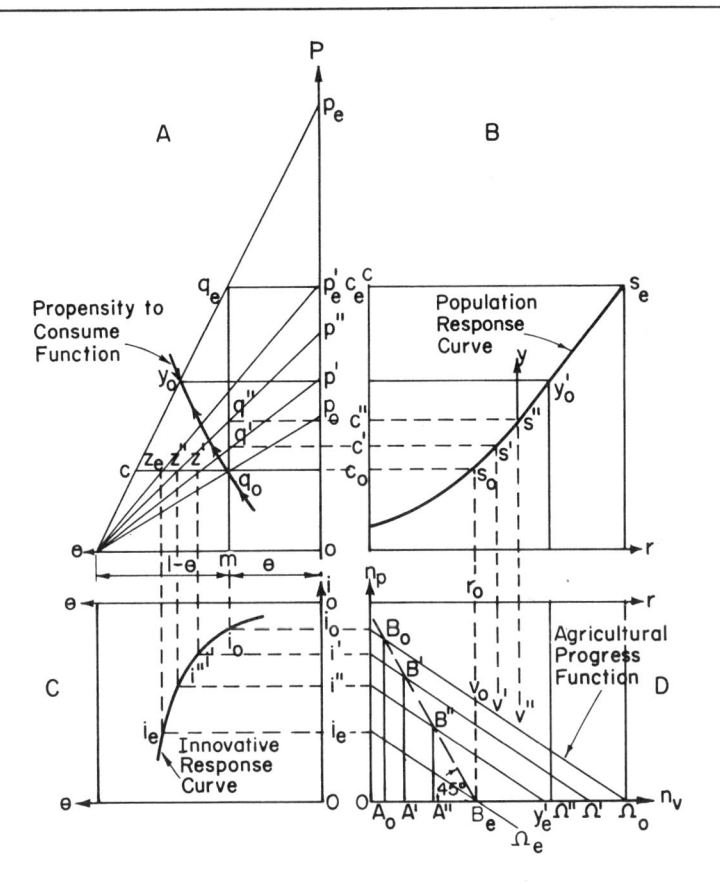

Fig. 9.11. Impact of agricultural production on use of labor.

sumption of agricultural products. But the distance $c_o \to q_o = \theta$ and, by (9.5), $c_o/p_o = (1 - \theta)$.

This means that if production of agricultural products increases (for whatever reason) from p_o to p' to p'' to p_e, the value of θ must increase as well, assuming consumption remains constant. But consumption will increase from q_o to q' to q'' to q_e so long as θ remains constant. Thus, high agricultural productivity will lead to either a larger proportion of labor force allocated to the service sector or a higher standard of living.

Now, agrarian stagnation may be defined in terms of long run stability of θ, p, and c. The authors use a Cobb-Douglas production function, in which land is assumed fixed, to relate rate of technological change in agriculture to the growth rate of agricultural labor force, $n_v = \eta(1 - \theta)L = (dv/dt)/v$, as follows:

$$Q = c^{it}v^{\alpha} \qquad (9.6a)$$

$$\eta_p = i - (1-\alpha)\eta_v \quad \text{(negatively sloped straight line in Fig. 9.11D)} \quad (9.6b)$$

$$P \equiv Q/v \quad (9.6c)$$

The $\eta_p(\Omega)$ curve represents the struggle between innovation that causes production to rise and the law of diminishing returns causing it not to rise so fast. The vertical intercept i represents innovational intensity, for any given value of which the rate of increase in agricultural productivity declines with increases in growth rate of the agricultural labor force. Defining $V = i/(1-d)$, point V_e on the horizontal axis of Fig. 9.11D is a point of long run stagnation, since at this point $\eta_p = 0$ or innovation is just being offset by diminishing returns.

If we look at progress function Ω_e and the relationship to the population response curve in Fig. 9.11B, we see the result of an initial productivity gain in agriculture in cases where the increase goes to increase consumption by the population. Note that the loci of the population response curve are defined by the points of equilibrium between average productivity of farmers and a static labor force ratio. (The authors call this a Jorgenson-Classical thesis of stagnation [Jorgenson 1961].)

This curve is postulated by

$$r + \phi(C) = \eta_L \quad (9.7)$$

This means that growth of the labor force (population) is controlled in some way by consumption standard C. In other words, if every time there is an increase in agricultural production it goes to feed the population (none of it being available for investment), this consumption adjustment mechanism will cause stagnation.

Figures 9.11A and 9.11B then are tied together by the fact that the propensity to consume is defined by the population response to an increase in production. Starting with the initial values of p_0, c_0, and q_0 in Fig. 9.11A, determine s_0 in Fig. 9.11B. With constant θ (no relative reallocation of labor), $\eta_v = r$. That is, $\eta_v = \eta(1-\theta)L = \eta(1-\theta) = \eta_L$, but if $\theta = 1$, $\eta_v = 0 + \eta_L$. This enables one to identify (via r_0) v_0 on the agricultural progress function in Fig. 9.11D. This point occurs on a positive portion of Ω_0. Since η_p is positive at that point, productivity of farmers will increase to p' in the next period. Population response will then cause consumption rate to increase to c', which defines s', hence depresses the rate of increase of p further to v'. But v' is still positive, so the productivity (P) of farmers will increase to p. These rounds will continue until the equilibrium points q_e, c_e, s_e, and p'_e are reached.

Thus, according to the Jorgenson-Classical analysis, long run stability of the rate of production increase per agricultural worker (p_e) is due to control of the population growth rate by the consumption standard in such a way as to suppress or encourage labor productivity gains when consumption and productivity levels are either too high or too low. This same mechanism is responsible for stability in the rate of consumption by consumption units supported by the entire labor force (c_e) and surplus labor ratio (θ_o) as well as population response to increased production (r).

The authors also present an alternative thesis. If the increased agricultural surplus is "used" to get a labor reallocation adjustment, stagnation will also result. For this thesis, innovative intensity (i) is inversely related to the surplus labor ratio θ_o. So, $i = f(\theta_o)$ where $f'(\theta_o) < 0$. In other words, an increase in innovation in agriculture requires more people to create the capital to make the innovation work. This means that the only way a surplus can be made available to nonagricultural production is for innovation to decrease.

This adjustment mechanism is shown in the relationships among Figs. 9.11A, 9.11B, and 9.11D. We begin with an initial position i_o on the innovation response curve for which the agricultural progress function Ω_o in Fig. 9.11D is defined at i_o, and production is defined at q_o in Fig. 9.11A.

Note that a movement to i' involves a decrease in both i and the agricultural progress function (η_o). But these are related to the fact that θ is no longer constant, hence the rate of increase in the total force (r) and the agricultural force (η_v) are not the same, but $\eta_v = r - \eta_p$. [Note that $\eta_p + \eta(1 - \theta) = 0$ when C is constant.] This latter relationship is shown along the 45° line from B_e to B_o. Since $0 - A_o$ measures η_v on the horizontal axis, the only point where $\eta_v = r - \eta_p$ is at point A_o, which means that B_o is uniquely determined. Since η_p is positive at this point, production of agricultural products will increase in the next period (Fig. 9.11A). Assuming C remains constant, the value of θ will increase by the value from q_o to z'.

This means that innovation intensity must decrease to i', producing a new agricultural progress function Ω'. In this fashion the rate of increase in agricultural production is continually decreased until a long run equilibrium position is attained at B_e.

By synthesizing the two approaches (one calling for stagnation at the higher product p_e and the other at the consumption point c_o), it is possible to get a solution that fits the real world, since any increase in agricultural production will be used partially to increase consumption and partially to induce greater labor allocation to the nonagricultural sector. This has been designated as the propensity to consume function shown in Fig. 9.11A.

When labor productivity increases, the increased consumption standard (C) will induce an additional population increase, and the increased labor allocation θ will reduce innovative intensity. Both forces, then, put a brake on expansion in agricultural productivity. The long-term equilibrium position will occur at some point between those previously indicated, say y_o to y_o'.

This analysis seems quite complex, yet it is a simplification of a very complex situation. It explains why communities dependent upon agriculture in underdeveloped areas face an extremely difficult growth problem.

Policies controlling either population growth or the consumption function itself would amount to intervention in an interrelated situation that would make it possible to avoid reaching a stagnation point.

SUMMARY

Economic change in any community is heavily influenced by the information base of the inhabitants plus that of people living in the region of which it is a part. Information manifests itself in many different ways. All of the factors that enter into the productive process are heavily influenced by it.

Production is a process by which inputs are transformed into outputs. It is accomplished by combining and coordinating factor services and materials in accordance with certain technologically determined processes. The coordination is done by management.

The technology is developed by people on the basis of scientific knowledge. All of the factors and materials are influenced by information. There must be a balancing of the levels of workers with plants, animals, machines, and all other capital with which they interact. In addition, the information base of management must be in harmony with these factors in order to do an effective job of coordinating. The more sophisticated the level of the productive process the more conducive it is to change.

Money is necessary to orderly change, since it represents control over resources. It is also necessary to market development and orderly allocation of resources to productive processes. Those who control money have the ability to inhibit as well as encourage change.

A perfectly competitive market is not necessary for orderly economic change, but a monopolistic market is not desirable either. Larger firms have control over resources that enable them to make and adjust to change more rapidly than smaller firms. But the information base of management has a great deal to do with the directions that change is allowed to take.

Governments can affect change in many ways. Taxation can be used to encourage or to discourage it. Subsidy can be used to affect its direction. Decree can also be used as an important influence.

Other social systems have more subtle but equally powerful influences. Economic change in rural areas of underdeveloped nations is often inhibited by their dependence upon stagnant agricultural industries for basic income. It is often necessary to initiate policies controlling either population growth or the consumption function itself in order to avoid an extremely difficult growth problem.

REVIEW QUESTIONS

1. Under what conditions would you expect a community to be able to stay as it is?
2. Distinguish between goods and services. Is it of any importance to make this distinction?
3. What functions do land, water, and air perform?
4. What do we mean by "partially finished goods"?
5. What two functions do producers' capital perform?
6. What is the role of human beings in production?
7. What are the two ways production can be increased?
8. What information was required for the people at Catal to develop their relatively simple economy?
9. Why is it important that level of sophistication of capital and human resources match?
10. What is the difference between looking at capital and human resources as substitutes and as complements?
11. How could obsolescence in an advanced society be a boon to less-advanced societies?
12. How does the modern day concept of land differ from that of the classical economists?
13. What is the difference between the influence of material inputs and the influence of producer's durables on location of a plant?
14. How could substitution among material inputs influence the economic structure of a community?
15. What impact does an energy shortage have on community growth?
16. What is the difference between service flows from capital and those purchased in the market from their producers?
17. How do services enter into an end product?
18. Why is money important to a modern community?
19. What is the price of money?
20. How does money contribute to limited control of resources?
21. How does money influence community development?
22. Do large corporations with large research and development departments develop the new products and processes in American society?
23. What roles do size of firm and monopoly power play in the development process?
24. Is there, in general, a best size for a firm?
25. What advantages do large firms have in the introduction of new products?
26. How do economies of growth and economies of size interact?
27. Are diversified firms necessarily inefficient?
28. Why do firms tend to diversify in the same general area of their original operation?
29. What role does the information base of management play in diversification?
30. What is the importance of corporate structure in bringing about economic change?

31. What role does the productive unit play in change?
32. How do management decisions in multiunit firms affect communities?
33. What is the difference between economic activity occurring within a firm and outside activity affecting the firm?
34. How is this related to the firm's strength?
35. What roles do innovation and imagination play in implementing change?
36. What roles do managerial resources have?
37. What is the major drawback to a situation where a community is heavily dependent upon a firm?
38. Why is diversification always a good idea?
39. How do governments resemble large corporations in their abilities to affect change?
40. How can powers of taxation be used to influence change?
41. How are subsidies used to influence change?
42. What are some other government regulations that influence change at the community level?
43. How do international programs influence communities?
44. What are the endemic structural characteristics of agrarianism that Fei and Ranis say are frustrating movement of the underdeveloped world from agrarian to dual economy?
45. What is a dual economy?
46. Show how changes in consumer propensities can stymie growth of nonagrarian industry even though agricultural production increases.

REFERENCES

Abramowitz, M. 1956. Resource and output trends in the United States. *American Economic Review* 46:5-23.
Allen, R. G. D. 1968. *Macro-economic theory*. New York: Macmillan.
American heritage dictionary of the English language. 1971. Boston: Houghton Mifflin.
Arrow, K. J. 1962. The economic implications of learning by doing. *Review of Economic Studies* 29:155-73.
Cambel, A. B., ed. 1964. *Energy R & D and national progress*. Washington, D.C.: Government Printing Office.
Denison, E. F. 1962. *The sources of economic growth in the United States and the alternatives before us*. New York: Committee for Economic Development.
―――. 1967. *Why growth rates differ*. Washington, D.C.: Brookings.
Eckaus, R. S. 1955. The factor proportions problem in under-developed areas. *American Economic Review* 45:539-65.
Fabricant, S. 1954. *Economic progress and economic change*. New York: National Bureau of Economic Research.

Fei, J. C. H., and G. Ranis. 1969. Agriculture in the open economy. In *The role of agriculture in economic development*, ed. E. Thorbecke. New York: Columbia Univ. Press.

Ferguson, C. E. 1969. *The neoclassical theory of production and distribution*. New York: Cambridge Univ. Press.

Galbraith, J. K. 1967. *The new industrial state*. New American Library.

Jewkes, J., D. Sawers, and R. Stillerman. 1959. *The sources of invention*. New York: St. Martin's Press.

Jorgenson, D. W. 1961. The development of a dual economy. *Economic Journal* 71:309-34.

Kendrick, J. 1961. *Productivity trends in the United States*. New York: National Bureau of Economic Research.

Mansfield, E. 1968. *The economics of technological change*. New York: Norton.

Nelson, R. R., M. J. Peck, and E. D. Kalachek. 1967. *Technology, economic growth and public policy*. Washington, D.C.: Brookings.

Penrose, E. T. 1959. *The theory of growth of the firm*. New York: Wiley.

Sandee, J. 1960. *A demonstration planning model for India*. Calcutta: University of Calcutta.

Scherer, F. M. 1970. *Industrial market structure and economic performance*. Chicago: Rand McNally.

Schmookler, J. 1952. The changing efficiency of the American economy, 1869-1938. *Review of Economics and Statistics* 34: 214-31.

Schumpeter, J. A. 1939. *The theory of economic development*. Trans. R. Opie. Cambridge, Mass.: Harvard Univ. Press.

Schultz, T. W. 1971. *Investment in human capital: The role of education and of research*. New York: Free Press.

Solow, R. M. 1957. Technical change and the aggregate production function. *Review of Economics and Statistics* 37:312-20.

Tobin, J. 1967. Comment: On developments in production theory. In *The theory and empirical analysis of production*, ed. M. Brown. New York: National Bureau of Economic Research.

Zimmerman, E. W. 1964. *Introduction to world resources*. Ed. H. L. Hunker. New York: Harper and Row.

CHAPTER 10

Community Dynamics: Growth, Decline, Stagnation

Unless the inhabitants of a community are at subsistence level with no hope of changing their situations, their community is going to change over time. This means it will either grow or stagnate and decline. In this chapter, we shall be dealing with the phenomenon of dynamics for all communities except enclaves. These will be dealt with in Chapter 11.

ROLE OF INNOVATIVE PEOPLE

It has been noted in preceding chapters that people are a community's major asset. From a growth standpoint, they may also be its greatest liability. A great deal depends upon how innovative people are. Innovation manifests itself in the ability to bring about change of the proper sort. Jacobs (1969), for example, has emphasized ability to "add new work to old," or in other words, to continually improve products. Any community that produces the same commodity or service from year to year will eventually get into trouble because other communities will take its markets with improved products.

There are numerous theories concerning the events that bring innovative people together to spark development of a community. Adna Weber (1899) postulated that continued growth is dependent upon ability to specialize. The interdependence of communities, making possible specialization and trade, allows innovation to flourish. Communities become known for their expertise in certain crafts, services, manufactured goods, and so on as people add new work to old.

Some communities also develop skills in improving upon products from other communities. Thus, one often hears of import replacement as an ingredient for growth. It is most effective if the replacement is an improvement over the product being replaced. By the policy of import replacement, the community increases its linkages; it does not reduce its volume of imports but changes the

items being imported. Thus, it creates demand for products of other communities and encourages creativity.
   Cooley (1894) found that innovation was related to transportation conformation. It was his hypothesis that innovative people are drawn to breaks in the transportation system where transfers from one type of carrier to another are made. Actually, this would be more related to founding of communities than continued growth. However, as transportation technology improves, there are bound to be spillovers in areas where it is a big economic factor, such as in coastal towns, at intersections of major highways, and railroad terminals.
   Innovation plays an important role between a community center and its hinterlands. New ideas tend to be accepted more readily in town than in rural areas, particularly in underdeveloped parts of the world. In the United States, differences between rural and town people are rapidly disappearing. However, there are still major differences between residents of urban and rural communities everywhere in the world. Jacobs (1969) has noted that urban communities tend to add to the opportunities of their rural counterparts by creating new demands for rural goods and by furnishing technologies necessary to fulfill these demands. On the other hand, they reduce opportunities by replacing products produced in rural areas by those produced in urban ones.
   While these observations are true to a degree, one finds a great deal of innovation in rural communities as well. The ability of such communities to grow is not entirely dependent on spillover from urban regions. However, innovative people in rural communities are more likely to be stifled by lack of recognition and support. It appears that "oddballs" are more readily accepted where there are larger concentrations of people. But this does not rule out real possibilities of growth in rural communities based on ideas developed by their own residents.
   Innovation can take many forms; it is not confined to production of new products. The ability of a community to make itself attractive to site location specialists from larger centers may itself be a form of innovation. Not all industrial development programs are alike. Some communities are continually passed by in the site location race. Others have phenomenal success in snaring new plants. Generally, such successes can be attributed to novel ideas and hard work of only a few people.

Efficiency vs. Innovation

   Adam Smith is credited with the idea of division of labor (specialization) as a basic economic principle leading to efficiency. He failed to recognize, however, that there is a basic difference between efficiency that creates wealth and innovation that creates growth. Schumpeter is credited with having recognized the difference. Specialization makes work efficient; it does not create conditions for growth. To a considerable degree, there is an adversary relationship between efficiency and innovation. Inno-

vators tend to be inefficient in the usual sense. In development
work, chances of success are enhanced if there is duplication of
effort. Different people bring different preconceptions and insights to the work and enhance chances of breakthroughs. Eminence,
reputation, or past success of any individual may not be reliable
indicators of future success. For every success, there are likely
to be a lot of failures.

Efficient people feel ill at ease with innovators. This probably accounts for the use of research and development departments
of large corporations to develop products dreamed up by individuals
and people from small companies. This type of activity has a product that can be measured by management. It also probably accounts
for unwillingness of community leaders, who are usually managers of
some type, to give support to the tinkerers and other innovative
types in the community. A common "horror" story in economic development work is of the inventor of a viable idea who is ridiculed in
his hometown and is unable to get financial support. Some of these
people are forced to sell their patents or move to other, usually
larger, communities. Probably a large proportion of those who do
get local support get it from close friends and/or relatives. Occasionally, however, there are leaders who recognize the value of
innovation and who seek out innovators for purposes of community
growth. These leaders are usually innovative people themselves.

One area that community leaders overlook quite often is the
possible spillover effect from the research and development efforts
of large corporations. As was observed in Chapter 9, when a company is operating efficiently, it is disruptive to introduce new
lines of products. It is not uncommon, therefore, for a company to
"sit" on a new idea purchased from some inventor or developed by
one of its own staff. Joan Robinson (1962) has observed that a viable economy must always have room in its interstices for innovative small operators who can develop ideas or products that larger
companies have trouble fitting into their overall operations. Such
small operators are often former employees of a company who either
buy a patent from it or simply develop ideas from their corporate
experience that they use in successful enterprises. Such break-
aways may not be good for the parent company, but they are good for
the community.

Discontinuities

For many reasons, community economies often become proficient
in production, but they fail to introduce new products and services. An important cause of this lies in the nature of economic
units. Once such a unit becomes established, it becomes efficient
by doing things in a repetitious manner. It may even be expanding
its regular line of products into new markets, thus creating an il-
lusion of success that masks the fact that the community may be approaching a point of discontinuity. Such a point occurs when suddenly there is no more expansion after a period of growth. This
can be a dangerous point because it can lead to stagnation. If
there is to be effective action with regard to community develop-

ment, catching the economy at a point of discontinuity and starting renewed activity is a good use of resources.

ROLE OF MONEY IN COMMUNITY GROWTH
There must be balancing of innovation with control of resources to bring ideas to fruition. Entrepreneurship is a rare combination of ability to raise funds, willingness to take risks with new ideas, and managerial ability.

Community Bankers
Local bankers are key persons in community development, particularly in rural communities. Willingness to move in the financial area can often spell doom or success to all types of expansion and growth. There are many ways that this can be done. Since good banking requires one to avoid taking unnecessary risks with other people's money, there are often projects whose success would help community growth, but whose riskiness is above allowable limits for bank financing. But bankers can often be key people in bringing venture capital to bear on these projects. A venture capital corporation can be formed to take on risky projects with the idea it is being done for community development purposes. In some cases, government programs, such as SBA guaranteed loans, can be used to help carry part of the burden.

Overconservatism and unwillingness to get involved in community growth on the part of bankers can at worst be devastating and at best be inhibiting. Some bankers exceed the bounds of even a prudent person in making or refusing to make loans. Some bankers refuse to make loans in areas with which they are not entirely familiar. A good community banker will continually look for ways to assist new industries, regardless of his or her past experience. There are many ways to find out about new industries, and bankers are in business to perform a service. They have an obligation to the community to learn all of the angles necessary to have money available when it is needed.

Often the needs for money exceed local resources. Links established by bankers with banks and other financial institutions in other communities are often important in furnishing capital. Bankers should also be aware of governmental programs that can be of assistance, and they should recommend them when it is in the best interest of their customers.

Small firms that have been expanding fairly rapidly can develop discontinuities also. These usually occur after a long period of struggle when the firm is suddenly faced with a takeoff in demand for its products. At that point, a large infusion of capital is needed for expansion, and the company has used up all its ready sources. A good banker will recognize a discontinuity and will help the client work out ways of getting past it. The fact is that good bankers are not in great supply. Failure to obtain money at this juncture makes the firm ripe for takeover by a larger firm. Or if this does not happen, a long period of struggle lies ahead, sometimes leading to bankruptcy.

Use of Community Credit

In many areas, laws allow communities to issue general obligation bonds for the purpose of purchasing land and constructing buildings for lease to industry; this is often really a lease-purchase arrangement. From the point of view of industry, there are several advantages: (1) it solves a big money problem; (2) it gets the money at a relatively low rate of interest; (3) it has certain tax advantages, since the rental becomes a cost rather than an investment; and (4) it has the same effect as additional leverage without the disadvantages.

There are some advantages from a community standpoint as well: (1) it entices industries that might go elsewhere; (2) where the rental includes an allowance in lieu of taxes (which it should), the tax base is actually expanded; (3) this is one way a community might assist a local firm at a discontinuity in its growth pattern; (4) it gets the community involved in planning its own destiny; (5) a community-owned development should be easy to control from an environmental point of view. There are also drawbacks for society as a whole: (1) certain firms obtain financing at rates below the market in which others have to operate; (2) plants are often enticed to move from one community to another thus robbing Peter for Paul's enhancement.

Subsidies

New firms moving to a community are often subsidized, for example, by the extension of tax breaks. In general, this is a poor practice. It tends to attract marginal firms. Viable companies are more interested in other things than in being subsidized. If a company cannot pay its way, it should be suspect. This argument does not rule out the possibility that a local person with a viable idea might not be fruitfully subsidized in formative years. The infant industry idea does have merit in some cases.

Capital Development in Underdeveloped Areas

The classical idea that investment must come from savings and that savings result from deferred consumption is a useful concept in underdeveloped areas. This implies the economy can be developed to a point where the people are above the subsistence level. Once products can be sold for money, the possibility of savings develops. At this point, it is imperative for community growth that financial institutions be established. Much capital can be forthcoming from the use of underutilized labor, such as in construction of buildings. But the purchases of better machines and tools requires money.

The "know-how" to develop a financial infrastructure is often lacking in these types of communities. Some success has been reported in the establishment of credit union-type arrangements. Production credit associations are also possibilities, since government money can be introduced through them. Growth beyond a very primitive level requires ability to command resources. Lack of a good financial structure can be detrimental to community development.

PROBLEMS INHERENT IN GROWTH

Oftentimes we approach community growth as though it were all sweet and no bitter. There are numerous problems communities must contend with as they grow.

Indivisibilities

One problem stems from the fact that growth often occurs in lumps. That is, a new firm moving to a community does not grow gradually; it comes all at once. If the situation is such that it hires a majority of its labor force from unemployed or underemployed local workers, it may place no additional burdens on amenities, such as schools, sewers, water supplies, housing, and streets. But if it moves its labor force in, the sudden influx may place extreme burdens upon local facilities.

Pollution

Growth often means a lowering of environmental standards. New wastes must be taken care of in some way. Additional autos, homes, and factories increase pollution of the air. Noise levels increase with increased size. More people mean more congestion in the use of roads, swimming pools, theaters, parks, and other public places.

Governmental Complexity

It is easier to get things done in a small community where everyone knows everyone else than in a larger one. One of the problems of growth is that demand for public and semipublic goods tends to grow; this increases the number of people needed to operate local government. Whereas before needs could be ascertained through a sort of general consensus, it now requires the formation of pressure groups to get things done. Or, if pressure groups were used before, more of them are required because there are more issues to be decided.

Waste of Resources

As communities grow in our present world, they tend to be highly inefficient in the use of resources. There are not enough resources in the world to allow everyone to live as people in middle-sized American communities live. In the past, the argument has been that the price system will take care of it. The problem has been that the productivity of most people has been so low they have not had high enough incomes to demand the amenities people in advanced societies take for granted. Further, until recent years, communications have been so inefficient that they have not known about them.

In the present-day world, people are aware of the fruits of higher information levels and are demanding some of them. If their productivity begins to rise, the pressure of demand on resources will rise also. Prices will go up, but since resources are extremely scarce, the price level will freeze out the aspiring nations. This can lead to civil strife of extreme proportions. The only feasible solution is for the people in advanced societies to put their resources to work finding more efficient ways to do things under all circumstances. But most important, the communities of the future should be designed for more efficiency than has been the case in the past.

BUILDING OF NEW COMMUNITIES

In the past, community growth seems to have been explainable in terms of epigenesis; a process of gradual diversification and differentiation has been involved. A young community started with a meager economy based on its exports. Often it would import a large share of its materials, semifinished goods, and consumption goods. It grew because its people either serviced each other with existing products or saw chances in import replacement. As local industries developed, to supply either the local consumer or existing export industries, they became potential exporters themselves. As trade increased among the local units, the multiplier effect of export trade increased. Thus the community grew from within and without. Such growth was by no means limited to commodities. Services were exports, the major difference being that people usually came to the provider of the service, whereas the commodity could be transported over space.

Planned Communities

Most of the planned communities to date are based on Ebeneezer Howard's garden cities concept. The basic idea was to give people a house and a garden. Some of the modern adaptations have incorporated the idea of making all centers within walking or bicycling distance. This has involved some rather intricate handling of roads and overpasses to avoid crossings. It has also meant increase in density. Instead of eight houses per acre, there are twelve--and more apartment complexes are built into the plans.

From an economic standpoint, an interesting adaptation of Henry George's single tax philosophy was used. In England and other parts of the world as well, the new towns are owned by corporations, the original stock of which may be subscribed by the government. The corporation purchases the land on which the town is to be built plus all of the surrounding territory, giving the finished town a "greenbelt" several miles wide. The land is held and put out on ninety-nine year leases with rentals subject to periodic renegotiation. No building is allowed in the greenbelt, which is available for farming. The corporation also has complete control of the type of building within the town. This arrangement appropriates the increased land rental (that George argued was due to society) for the community, since the corporation is the community's governing body as well. Investment in and operation of the public sector is thus connected to land values.

In some instances, the corporation also builds industrial and commercial buildings in order to control the architecture. Industrial areas are screened from residential by bands of trees that serve to cut air and noise pollution. Major highway arteries are also banded by trees. These towns try to accommodate to the automobile with underground parking in shopping areas. But their pedestrian focus is also aimed at curbing auto use as much as possible.

There are several questionable features about the garden city concept. One is the necessity for a rather dictatorial attitude on the part of government with regard to the location of industry. In recent years, towns have been located 100 km or so from the nearest large city with the idea of self-containment. This has meant the furnishing of jobs for inhabitants at the time they move to the town. In order to do that, it is necessary to know just what industries are going to locate there. Another questionable feature is the limit on growth. While the towns tend not to reach the maximum size for a rather long time (many midland towns are designed for 100,000 people), eventually they will be bumping against the ceiling. What happens then? Are they to be allowed to stagnate? Innovative people are not apt to stay where expansion is impossible. A still further question concerns the idea of low density housing. This type of housing is a heavy radiator of energy; and one of the serious problems for the future of the human race is our waste of energy coupled with the rate at which we are sending heat into the atmosphere.

Planned communities for the future. The new form of community development will have to be concerned with conservation of resources. Our present wasteful ways may someday make the world uninhabitable for our species. On the other hand, if we can design communities that will allow us to maximize the use of resources, we may be able to avoid a crisis. We have the physical knowledge to do this, but do we have the social knowledge to make the necessary adjustments?

We can learn a great deal about methods of survival on this planet from sustained life systems designed for astronauts. Hydroponics, for example, is an efficient way to grow plants in which soil is not needed. Thus, the utilization of acres of land for growing is not necessary. It can be done inside a building. Further, much of the chemical fertilizer needed can be obtained by recycling sewerage. The information base necessary for development of an efficient community lacks input from the social scientists. The biological and physical scientists are way ahead of us.

Changes are occurring, in the advanced nations of the world, that are indicative of life-styles of the future. Television and computers are being used to create new and efficient communications systems. These are being supplemented by instantaneous reproduction systems. The idea of instantaneous transmittal of a letter is no longer a dream. Checkless banking is getting nearer with the development of devices that allow the use of finger and voice prints for identification purposes. This will eventually lead to a cashless society as well. The home of the future may also double as the place of work. We may put parents back in the household because they do not have to leave it every day. With plants being operated by computers and more and more people getting involved in special personal and other services, more work can be done from the home.

If conservation of energy dictates that homes be closer together, perhaps in the form of town houses, or condominiums, many recreation facilities can be shared and made part of the home complex. This combination of residence, work, and recreation in one area will change life-styles quite drastically. These are, of course, only some of the new concepts that will affect the planning of future communities. People need to understand that lifestyles are changing and to have opportunities for input to influence these changes.

It is necessary that economics change also to give us a better understanding of resource use and distribution in the postindustrial world. Our current concepts will not do. For one thing, we have largely ignored the role of information, although it is the most important single factor in the changing role of people in the world. The role of government in affecting change is not well understood. Public finance studies have not yet come to grips with efficiency problems in public resource use. Too many of our models still begin with assumptions of perfect competition, constant technology, a homogeneous labor force, and a spaceless world. If theory is to tell us the nature of the world, these unwordly assumptions must go.

The communities of the future will continue to exist with oligopolistic market structures, continually changing technology, and wide diversifications in ability and information bases; there is little to indicate that space will be any less important. Further, these are the very factors that will make the difference between viable communities and those headed for trouble.

Knowledge is basic to good planning. Perhaps the efficiency of the development corporation has been sufficiently demonstrated in the British experiment, as Osborn (1969) contends. If so, its managers will need guidance to make sure that world resource needs are taken into consideration, along with local economic, topographical, and social considerations. And people in general will have to be educated to understand why communities cannot sprawl about the countryside, and why it is necessary that their ideas of a good place to live become part of the input to the planning process.

Necessary links among communities will be important in the future as in the past. Planning will have to take into account possible differences in product and service mixes among the communities within a region, a hemisphere, and the world at large. These intricacies along with endogenous linkages will have to be examined by computer simulation as part of the planning process. Social scientists will also be faced with the need to introduce planned communities into the underdeveloped areas with all of the cultural problems this will entail. This is the only possible way that aspirations can be met and the problems of population control can be solved. The alternative is massive starvation, social unrest, and possible complete annihilation.

Role of planning in community development. The planning unit of a community is the key to orderly growth. A good one will prepare to meet all of the requirements of the population now and in the future. It must look at water supply, waste handling, traffic patterns, recreation, service needs, and all other factors that will affect or be affected by growth. The master plan should be continually under review.

Planning and zoning should go together, but zoning should never be allowed to be more than a tool in implementing planning policy. Spot zoning, which is allowed to occur far too often, can make good planning almost impossible. It would be better to have no planning at all, hence no zoning, than to allow zoning appeals boards to change zoning at will.

There should be a zoning appeal apparatus, but it should be hedged about with restrictions. A zoning change should almost never be made to accommodate an individual. Yet, most of them seem to be made just for that purpose. If the situation in a particular area has changed so that a zoning change will more adequately serve the public or if there is a real problem involved in compliance with existing zoning regulations, the zoning board should become an advocate for change before the planning commission. The situations where individuals have legitimate appeals for zoning ease are few and far between.

If the planning function is being adequately handled, most of the problems relating to overutilization of public facilities can be anticipated and avoided. Good planning can be used, along with debt financing, to adequately handle planned growth.

Planning and promotion. Too often the functions of planning and promotion are separated. Industrial development corporations, for example, often control industrial parks that may or may not conform to the overall master plan for land use. By making themselves adjuncts to the planning process, they can influence the proper kinds of growth in areas where industrial uses of land make the most sense. Promotion and planning should also pay attention to growth in service industries. Health services and wholesaling are important export industries in many communities.

Shotgun propaganda approaches to development are generally undesirable. Information should be used to pinpoint desirable types of development. Every community should have up-to-date files of information about all of its resources, human, natural, public, and so on. It should be capable of putting together a special compilation to meet the needs of specific prospects, particularly prime prospects.

A firm is a prime prospect if it fits into the overall plan for growth in the community, which means that it fulfills specific needs; and the community assets fulfill the needs of the company.

Impact of exogenous decision makers on community planning. Communities everywhere are heavily influenced in planning for growth by events and decisions made outside their borders. Colm and Geiger (1967) point out that regardless of the form the economic system may take, there is some combination of public planning and private decision making involved in the changes that occur. Where the planning is done at a national or regional level and the private decision makers have considerable resources at their command, their activities are likely to impinge heavily on communities trying to plan for growth.

Communities in less developed areas. In less developed countries, these decisions may be "life or death" affairs. Communities in countries of Latin America, Asia, and Africa face a number of common difficulties. In general, the infrastructure of most parts of a country is inadequate to sustain much growth. Transportation is inhibited by lack of roads, railroads, ports, airports, and water transport; communication is usually very primitive. Power lines and other sources of energy may be nonexistent at worst and unable to meet demands at best. Because there is inadequate tax base, social capital such as schools, health facilities, and shelter tend to be lacking also. Thus, communities have no base from which to begin growth. To make matters worse, investment capital is seldom available, and information bases of local residents contain little that would make them good operators, maintainers, technicians, or coordinators. Low information base economic activity is all that is possible. In these circumstances national governments have assumed most of the planning functions, and local communities have little control over their destinies.

Colm and Geiger (1967, p. 6) have identified three types of functions these governments must assume in trying to bring about development. The first is national development planning, consisting of defining goals, finding money and skills, and identifying specific projects that are likely to make the most contribution to the goals. Most countries try to do this in some systematic way, although the degree of sophistication varies considerably.

The second is to develop and manage the public sector. This consists of the usual functions of protection from external and internal enemies, and the undertaking of investments so large and pervasive in importance to the whole economy that only the government is in a position to handle them. These include such things as basic infrastructure and social overhead capital. In many cases, riskiness of initial business ventures discourages private capital investment, which means that government ownership of many of the new economic activities is necessary. In socialist countries, this approach will be used deliberately, since private investment is frowned upon.

The third function is to stimulate, guide, and assist private initiative and activities so that they also contribute to achievement of national development goals. Governments seem always to be faced by the fact that no matter how much the rulers would like to replace all significant private economic activities by public ones, there are certain segments that are best served by individuals, given proper incentives. Most less developed countries find that the market mechanism is a less wasteful way of making many kinds of economic decisions and getting many tasks accomplished than a system of centralized direction to production, investment, and consumption. Attraction of investment from outside the country is dependent upon a certain amount of freedom of action. Many countries depend upon this type of development to gain experience in areas that build up technical, operational, and coordinational skills in the local population. This occurs only if local people are lured into responsible jobs.

Other possible benefits are derived from linkages between foreign enterprises and local suppliers of inputs. These arise partly because of markets and partly because of financial and technical assistance that may be supplied to get local suppliers started. With good local earnings opportunities, foreign capital can be manipulated to gain considerable advantage to a local economy, if the government is sufficiently aware of the possibilities and sufficiently insistent upon realizing them. The advantages of this to local communities is obvious. In fact, certain communities may get greater gains by cultivating politicians than in any other way. Where a natural resource is involved, of course, most of the potential benefits will be available near the material source.

Communities in more developed areas. Many countries in more developed portions of the world do a lot of planning at the national level. This can vary from guidance-type planning to complete control over movement of money, people, and capital resources. Thus, communities have to adjust their own planning to the situation facing them. For some, no local planning will be allowed. But most communities have areas in which they can plan and attempt to implement their plans. The problem may be to find those particular areas in which they can make economic contributions without coming into direct conflict with national or regional goals.

Economies are always complex. This means that national planning cannot possibly be detailed enough to take into consideration all of the economic activities needed to make things go. There are always opportunities, therefore, for good operators to fill needs. Local communities can do a great deal to encourage this type of entrepreneurship. Communities are often as skeptical of these business innovators as of the strictly technological kind. Yet, they may be the keys to growth for many areas.

GROWTH VS. NO GROWTH CONTROVERSY

No growth advocates argue that the disadvantages of growth outweigh the advantages. The assumption is that a static situation is possible. But there is no such thing as a status quo, except for people living at an absolute subsistence level. One simply cannot preserve communities that have any possibilities for change without some kind of outside subsidization. Thus, a village might be maintained as a historical site by federal subsidy.

In order to approach the idea of no growth, it is necessary to look at the two basic ways that communities change, either by growth or decline. There can be an increase or decrease of bodies and/or an increase or decrease in real income. The importance of either is related to the amount of slack in the local economy. A reduction in income will create slack by causing people and other resources to be underutilized. An increase in income will utilize slack already existing in the economy. If there is slack in an economy, it is counterproductive to try to increase the population. Thus, under those circumstances no growth (narrowly defined) may make sense. But if there is no slack, a no growth approach means people must be satisfied with the income level as it exists, which is, at best, a short run idea. As indicated previously, where there is stagnation, eventually there is decline.

Often advocates of no growth cite limited resources as their major argument. Resources have always been limited. This is why the science of economics was developed. People must learn to optimize, which means getting the greatest good for society from the limited resources available. In a society with constantly increasing population pressure, this probably means recycling wastes along with more efficient use of everything.

According to the physical law of conservation of mass, the weight of materials used must equal that recycled and wasted. It is the wasted part that causes pollution problems and limits growth possibilities. There are additional limitations in biological processes, such as the amount of energy it is possible to obtain from mineral resources, the current flow of energy from the sun, and the mass of people who can exist on the earth. Thus, we do have some actual limits to overall growth. Kenneth Boulding has observed that anyone who believes exponential growth can go on forever in a finite world is either a madman or an economist. At present, the world is still below the asymptote by a considerable amount, and community growth is still possible in this context. There are advantages to slow growth. The proper infrastructure can be provided, and strains on community resources can be avoided. This type of development fits well with the planning process, as it should.

DIFFERENCES IN COMMUNITIES IN URBAN AND RURAL REGIONS

The most significant difference between communities in rural and urban regions is the distance from another community. This, of course, makes all the difference in the world, because it determines the amount of interaction, hence, degree of specialization, that each community can develop. One of the most significant features of urban regions is the development of labor service exporting and importing communities. To a degree (and excluding involuntary enclaves), people can choose which parts of the region they wish to live in because commuting costs are not large. Thus, two workers in an office in the central business district may live in suburbs several miles apart. The traffic pattern for a shift change in a large industrial area will reveal many divergent streams as workers aim for their home communities. These communities are likely to have separate corporate structures from the ones in which the work is done. Many urban regions will have more than one industrial area. Workers have opportunities to change jobs not only among plants in one community but among communities as well.

The same pattern exists for spending as for earning. The home community will have one or more shopping areas, but choice is not limited to these areas. Literally any community in the region is available, including such labor importing communities as the central business district where some of the larger retail and service operations in the region may be located. Cooperation among communities interested in promoting growth is likely to be much closer in an urban than a rural region. People are much more aware of their interdependence. Agglomeration economies and diseconomies are much more important. Distance is less of a factor.

The automobile and the jet plane impinge heavily on urban regions. The airport forms the nucleus for an important community. Highways provide impetus to growth for certain communities and decline for others. Parking problems plague the older communities and provide opportunities for the new ones. They also change emphasis on business types. Downtown areas are entertainment centers in many cities, since parking is less of a problem at night. This also encourages the growth of stadiums and convention centers. Since plants are no longer dependent on rail transport, they tend to locate in communities on the city's periphery where they can also take advantage of assembly line production requiring large horizontal work areas. On the other hand, better communication occurs in the central business district, so central office functions tend to locate there.

The automobile has also had an important impact on rural communities. In agricultural areas, it has made many small communities obsolete. It is no longer necessary for farmers to be near a town, rather it is more important for them to have access to larger community centers where they can get more services. Many small towns in advanced nations are consequently disappearing. The location of a superhighway can also have a heavy impact. For towns located nearby, it tends to draw them toward it. For those further away, it tends to reduce their importance. Many rural communities have airports, but commercial service is not nearly so important as it is to urban areas. However, privately owned planes are likely to be more important as people try to overcome the friction of distance.

Rural communities develop economic ties, but they are more likely to be in terms of exchange of products. Some intercommunity commuting occurs if towns are less than 80 km apart. There is more of a sense of rivalry than is found in urban areas. Agglomeration economies and diseconomies are less important, and distance is more important. Where an urban area's problems may stem from too rapid in-migration, a rural area is likely to suffer from out-migration.

Rural communities tend to provide jobs for their inhabitants. Therefore, there is usually very little cooperation within a rural region in economic development work. Attempts to develop regional economic development activities are not likely to be very successful. Most regionally oriented activities tend to be imposed from state, provincial, or national governments.

More effort has to be expended on trying to attract money to the community than is the case in urban regions. Innovation in development activities is, thus, much more important. Since potential investors are less likely to have information about the community, development of adequate information to fit their needs is very important. Rural communities are also more likely to gain from use of such things as industrial bond issues to build buildings.

SUMMARY

Change is inevitable in most situations. Whether or not it results in stagnation and decline or in growth depends largely upon the ingenuity of the people involved. Growth comes from adding new products except for certain short run situations. New products come from the activities of innovative people. There is some disagreement about what brings innovative people together in a particular place. Generally, urban communities have more innovators than rural ones. This may be partially due to greater chance for exchange of ideas and to greater toleration for "oddballs."

Innovation and specialization are basically different concepts. Innovators tend to be inefficient and specialists to be efficient. Innovation is basic to growth, and specialization is basic to production. Community growth depends upon its innovators. Communities that do not introduce new commodities and services into their product lines will eventually reach a point of discontinuity. At this point, the actions they take (or fail to take) will determine whether they stagnate and decline or continue to grow.

The bankers of a community can be key people in attracting money. This applies both to money they make available as loans and to sources of equity funds. Communities can also help by using general obligation bonds. But use of subsidies to attract industry is not usually a good idea. In underdeveloped areas, lack of suitable financial institutions is often a major handicap to growth.

Problems as well as benefits can arise from community growth. Growth can be "lumpy," in which case strains may be put on local facilities. Pollution problems may develop. Government can become more complex. Resources may be wasted. Prices may rise as a result of pressure on these resources.

In recent years, a number of attempts have been made to build communities "from the ground up." A number of innovative ideas have been used in doing this. Garden communities in England have been developed by corporations that own all the land in and immediately surrounding the town. These are pedestrian oriented communities. Their major problem is that they utilize too much land and probably radiate too much energy into the atmosphere. They also grow because industries are assigned to them and limits are placed on community growth.

For the future, more attention will have to be paid to efficient use of resources. Communities will be built to accommodate people with new life-styles influenced by high technology. More attention will also have to be paid to the development of adequate linkages among communities. Planning and development should be complementary activities. This means that the promotion entity and the planning entity in a community should work as partners.

Every community is heavily influenced by activities at higher governmental levels. Some communities can only act as they are allowed by activities or lack of activity on the part of higher echelons. In underdeveloped countries, community growth is particularly vulnerable to this situation. In more developed areas, such activities may or may not make a large difference dependent on the political philosophy in the country.

The growth vs. no growth controversy is not presently a concern for most communities. However, it must be anticipated. The world is not infinite in its resources, and no growth advocates point this out rather forcefully. The solutions are not in the realm of community economics, however.

Growth and development take place differently in communities in rural and urban regions. This is largely due to the impact of distance or the lack of it. Urban communities have certain spillovers and interdependencies that rural communities do not have.

REVIEW QUESTIONS

1. Why is it important to consider dynamic aspects of community economics?
2. What is meant by "innovation"?
3. Discuss two theories concerning events that bring innovative people together.
4. Contrast innovation in rural and urban regions.
5. How are efficiency and innovation related?
6. What is a discontinuity in a community? In a company?
7. How does money supplement innovation?
8. What roles should bankers play in community development?
9. Should communities use their own credit to entice industry?
10. Should they give subsidies?
11. What are some of the problems involved in proper use of money in underdeveloped areas?
12. Discuss four problems inherent in growth. Can you think of others?

13. What is meant by saying growth in the past is explainable in terms of epigenesis?
14. Discuss some of the main features you would expect to see in a planned community.
15. Why will planning new communities in the future be quite different from planning of the past?
16. What roles do you see social scientists playing in future planning of new communities?
17. Why should planning and development go together?
18. How do outside decision makers impinge upon community planning?
19. What three functions might a government in an underdeveloped country assume in order to bring about development?
20. Can communities in underdeveloped countries actually do anything to speed their development?
21. How can foreign investors in a country contribute to development of the country?
22. Do governments in developed areas limit activities of communities? Explain.
23. Do no growth adherents have a viable argument?
24. Can there be continued economic growth in a community?
25. What are the two ways communities can grow?
26. Outline the major differences between urban and rural communities.

REFERENCES

Brush, J. E., and H. E. Bracey. 1955. Rural service centers in southwestern Wisconsin and southern England. *Geographical Review* 45:559-69.
Colm, G., and T. Geiger. 1967. Public planning and private decision making in economic and social development. In *The challenge of economic development*, ed. R. J. Ward. Hawthorne, N.Y.: Aldine.
Cooley, C. 1894. *The theory of transportation.* New York: American Economic Association.
Jacobs, J. 1969. *The economy of cities.* New York: Random House.
Jones, E. 1966. *Towns and cities.* New York: Oxford Univ. Press.
London, the Greater Council. 1965. *The planning of a new town.* Working paper.
Osborn, F. J. 1969. *Green-belt cities.* New York: Schocken Books.
Osborn, F. J., and A. Whittick. 1963. *The new towns.* New York: McGraw-Hill.
Robinson, J. 1962. *Essays in the theory of economic growth.* New York: St. Martin's Press.
Rodwin, L. 1956. *The British new towns policy.* Cambridge, Mass.: Harvard Univ. Press.
Thomas, D. 1970. *London's green belt.* London: Faber and Faber.
Weber, A. 1899. *The growth of cities in the nineteenth century.* New York: Macmillan.

CHAPTER 11

Economics of Involuntarily Formed Enclaves

Enclaves develop in human society for two reasons. First, the power elite may discriminate against those of a different tribe, race, class, religion, or language and force them into specific areas. Second, people having these or other differences (such as great wealth) find life easier or more satisfactory in the company of those with whom they have a common background.

In general, people entering enclaves for the second reason are also capable of leaving when it is in their interest to do so. Those who enter enclaves because of discrimination do not have the same freedom, and this gives their communities distinct characteristics that are of interest to us. Such enclaves are largely exporters of unskilled (low information base) labor services. The flow of basic income has very little multiplier effect, in many instances, because linkages within the enclave tend to be weak. In consequence, incomes tend to be low. The major problem is poverty.

SOME ECONOMICS OF DISCRIMINATION

If an employer has two potential employees of equal quality, one having and the other not having acceptable social or physical conformation, and if the first is employed at $3.60 an hour when the second would have been willing to work for $2.60 an hour, it can be said that the employer is discriminating and also is placing a value of $1.00 per hour on his or her willingness to discriminate. In other words, the "privilege" of discriminating is worth $1.00 an hour to the employer.

According to Arrow (1973) discrimination means that some economic agent has a positive valuation for one person and a negative valuation for a second for which said agent has both the willingness and opportunity to pay. The above employer is willing to reduce profits in order to eliminate employment of "undesirable" workers in the enterprise. Another type of payment might be made by workers who may be willing to work for lower wages if there are no "undesirables" in the firm.

Employer Discrimination

Case of perfect information. If an employer has perfect information about the abilities of workers, discrimination implies a reflection of taste, that is, a willful selection of one person over another of equal ability. Here one assumes some costless method of determining differences, such as color of skin, facial features, sex, proclaimed religious preferences, mode of dress, or possession of a high school diploma. One also assumes that mixtures of workers do not affect efficiency of an operation from a technical standpoint.

Assume two differentiated groups of workers, A and B, having the same supply function, where each worker is a perfect substitute for each other worker, or where $MP_a = MP_b$. If labor markets are competitive and there is no discrimination, $MP_a/W_a = MP_b/W_b$. But, if there is discrimination, the equilibrium conditions indicated do not hold; there is a smaller demand for the workers discriminated against, and the cost of producing output is greater than would otherwise be the case (Becker 1971, pp. 41-42). Refer to Fig. 11.1. Let XX be a production isoquant and WW be the relevant price line if there is no discrimination. The coordinates of point E at which wage WW is paid are A_1 of A and B_1 of B employed and the mininum cost is OW for the production of X units.

Discrimination against B decreases demand for those workers to B_2, and increases demand for A workers to A_2. The money cost of producing X units now increases to OW' with $\hat{W}\hat{W}$ the new budget constraint line. Where there are not equal numbers supplied in the two populations, the results are essentially the same but a little harder to illustrate.

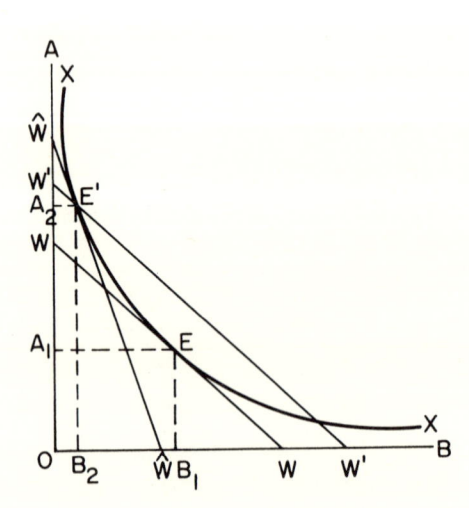

Fig. 11.1. Effect of discrimination (case of perfect information).

Case of imperfect information. Where employers do not have perfect information (a much more realistic assumption), discrimination may be thought of as a distortion of perception, rather than taste (Arrow 1973, pp. 23-31). That is, if they perceive that the B workers have lower productivity than the A ($MP_B < MP_A$), they will hire them only if they will work for less. This does not imply that discrimination due to taste may not also exist with imperfect information. This will be investigated later. First, we investigate the situation where effects of preconceptions are the same as those of tastes.

We observe there are costs attached to hiring and firing people. That is, there are administrative costs of bringing a person onto the payroll or removing a person from it, and there are training costs of new personnel and loss of experience when people are fired. Thus, if because of preconceptions an employer hires all A workers, there would be some major costs involved in firing some A workers in order to hire B workers, should the employer discover his or her preconceptions to be wrong.

Second, we observe that for any particular worker, there are costs involved in determining true productivity. That is, the costs indicated above have to be incurred in order to find out if the preconceptions are right or wrong. For any one employer, this may not be true, providing someone else has taken the step and can provide the proper information. In any case, the information is not free to society. Third, we assume that neither labor force is homogeneous and that the employer has some preconceived idea of the distribution of productivity within each of the two categories, with probabilities P_A and P_B for skilled workers.

Assume there are two kinds of jobs to be filled; all workers can do one, but only skilled workers can do the other. Assume no personnel cost for filling unskilled positions but such cost for filling skilled positions. If a worker hired for a skilled job turns out actually to be skilled, the employer can keep him or her (since no other employer knows this). If the worker turns out to be unskilled, a hiring cost will have been incurred that will lower profits.

Assume marginal productivity of all skilled workers is the same. Let r be the return per skilled worker needed to cover personnel costs. If an A worker is hired, a wage W_A must be paid, and net gain to the employer is $MP_S - W_A$. Expected returns on the hiring of an A worker as skilled, then, is $E(\pi) = (MP_S - W_A)P_A - (1 - P_A)r$. Similarly for a B worker, $E(\pi) = (MP_S - W_B)P_B - (1 - P_B)r$. If the employer is a perfect guesser, all of the workers hired for skilled positions will be skilled ($P_A - P_B = 1.00$), and $1 - P_A = 1 - P_B = 0$. Let $q = P_B/P_A$; then

$$W_A = qW_B + (1 - q)MP_S \tag{11.1}$$

So, for any situation where $P_A > P_B$ and $q < 1$, W_A will be somewhere between W_B and MP_S. The probability of hiring for a skilled job a

B worker who turns out to be unskilled is higher than for an A worker, so it will be necessary for $W_B < W_A$ in order to recoup personnel costs. The employer will adjust wages offered B workers according to his or her perception of the amount of such costs that need to be obtained. If a union contract, a law, or some other rigidity makes it impossible to offer lower wages to B workers, the employer may simply refuse to hire such workers.

Over time an objective employer would be able to determine if perceptive probabilities equate with reality. If the employer then refuses to change his or her perceptive probabilities (assuming they are lower than reality), he or she will demonstrate discrimination based on taste. The wage offered for B workers will be lower than is necessary to recoup personnel costs.

Investment in human resources. Assuming that the individuals in both groups have the same basic abilities, differences will be due to investment in education, training, and cultural changes necessary to produce favorable attitudes toward high productivity, punctuality, acceptance of orders, and so on. However, discrimination is insidious in that it creates discouragement, low standards of living, poor health, and low education levels. Thus, we have Myrdal's (1962, p. 75) theory of the vicious circle. The perception of inferiority becomes the reality. And the reality makes cultural change exceedingly difficult.

The importance of attitudes in ingesting other information has been demonstrated by Sowell (1970, p. 283) in the case of Dunbar High School in Washington, D.C. During the period 1870 to 1955, this all-black school, which was housed in a substandard physical plant, sent three-fourths of its graduates to college. During one five-year period (1918 to 1923), fourteen degrees were earned at Harvard and Amherst. Dunbar students had parents with steady but not lucrative jobs. They had good, stable family relationships. The parents were willing to sacrifice to educate their children, and the children were taught to value education. Owing to discrimination against blacks in university faculties, Dunbar was able to obtain highly qualified teachers. The first black general, cabinet member, senator (after Reconstruction days), and federal judge, along with the discoverer of blood plasma, were Dunbar alumni. During World War II, Dunbar graduates constituted a large percentage of high ranking black army officers.

Sowell points out that the school was financially poor, its classes large, its buildings poorly maintained and overcrowded. The thing it had in its favor was that "it inspired students with confidence that they could do anything in spite of anything." This is quite a contrast with the usual educational situation in enclaves. It depended upon the happy combination of dedicated teachers and training in the home that stressed the value of education.

Bloom (1964, p. 60) has shown that most of the variance in intellectual achievement of adults can be accounted for by the time a child reaches five. Jarrett (1968, p. 25) concludes that the child conditioned by its society to think of itself as inferior and a nonlearner acts in an inferior way and becomes a nonlearner. Enclave children tend to be immobilized by views of their abilities held by parents, peers, and teachers. They develop a sense of indifference toward learning and helplessness before society.

Sowell (1970, p. 221) emphasized the importance of the family in terms of family size, parental attitudes toward learning, self-discipline, and respect for teachers. Enclave children tend to be born into homes financially, educationally, and psychologically unable to prepare them for school. Both children and parents need to understand that a good education is worthwhile but requires hard work; and that failures can be overcome by repeated effort.

Arrow (1973, p. 27) points out that success breeds success; the proportion of any group qualifying as skilled is an increasing function of the gain from qualifying. In other words, the human resource is not developed in a perfectly competitive market. Assuming again that there is no basic intrinsic difference between workers in groups A and B, we expect the supply schedules to be the same.

Let W_u be the wage and MP_u the marginal product for unskilled workers, and let $V_A = W_A - W_u$ be the gain for a worker from group A qualifying as skilled. Then postulate an increasing function $S(V)$, such that (11.2) $P_A = S(V_A)$. Let $MP_u = W_u$ and $r = (MP_S - W_B)P_B$. We note that MP_S and MP_u are determined by the supplies of skilled and unskilled labor that are, in turn, determined by P_A and P_B. Now if a system consisting of equations

$$P_A = S(V_A), \quad P_B = S(V_B) \tag{11.2}$$

$$MP_u = W_u \tag{11.3}$$

$$r = (MP_S - W_B)P_B, \quad r = (MP_S - W_A)P_A \tag{11.4}$$

is established, it will be a system in the unknowns, W_A, W_B, W_u, P_A, and P_B. From symmetric formulation of the system, it can be seen that there can be a symmetric, nondiscriminatory equilibrium where $P_A = P_B$ and $W_A = W_B$. But can there also be discriminatory equilibria? And is the symmetric equilibrium stable? Arrow (1973, p. 28) shows that discriminatory equilibria do exist and that stability of the symmetric equilibrium depends on the parameters of the problem. Assume the B labor force is small compared to A so that their responses have little effect on MP_S and MP_u, hence on W_A, W_u, and the proportion of A workers qualifying as skilled. From (11.1), (11.2), and (11.4) and the definition of V_B, the equilibirum for the B labor force is

$$P_B = S[MP_S - MP_u - (r/P_B)] = S_B(P_B) \tag{11.5}$$

That is, as P_B tends to zero the wage differential between skill levels (V_B) decreases or tends to $-\infty$,

$$V_B = MP_S - MP_u - (r/P_B)$$

and

$$W_B = MP_S - [(MP_S - W_A)P_A]/P_B = MP_S - (r/P_B)$$

At equilibrium, then,

$$P_B = S(W_B - MP_u) = W_B - W_u = V_B$$

There may be more than one solution of this. An equilibrium is attained at $P_B = 0$. Since there are only a small number of B workers, the effect on MP_S and MP_u is negligible and can be ignored, thus the right side of (11.5) is dependent largely on P_B. Both sides are graphed in Fig. 11.2. Where employers have high perceptions of B workers qualifying for skilled jobs ($P_B \to 1$) S_B, the proportion actually qualifying will lie below it (point P^1). Where they have low perceptions ($P_B \to 0$), the differential between skill levels becomes very small.

Equation (11.5) is satisfied at both P^1 and P^2, where the S curve intersects the 45° line. Now, Fig. 11.2 could be interpreted as a diagram for analyzing the propensities of A workers as well. Thus, if $P^1 = P_A$ and $P^2 = P_B$, this would be compatible with equilibrium conditions. We see, then, that discrimination due to differing performance is possible, even though the basic assumptions concerning probabilities are symmetrical with respect to the identifying feature of the B workers.

The question now arises, "Are these equilibria stable?" If the effects of the B workers on the labor force are not negligible, they may be unstable. Assume that if the desired supply of skilled workers exceeds the actual, there will be an automatic increase in the number of qualified skilled workers, or

$$\frac{dP_B}{dt} = K[S(V_B) - P_B] \tag{11.6}$$

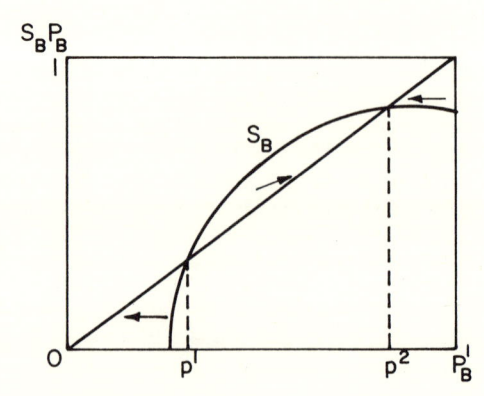

Fig. 11.2. Relationship of actual vs. perceived proportion B workers qualified as skilled.

which is the same as saying that the movements of P_B are those indicated by the arrows in Fig. 11.1. In perceived probability of qualification of B workers over time, the change is some function of the difference between the proportion of those who actually qualify and the perceived proportion of the moment.

Using the dynamic assumption (11.6) together with the same assumption for P_A, we can now assume that the effects of reactions of B workers on the whole labor market are substantial. Let W_S be the common value of W_A and W_B at the nondiscriminatory equilibrium, and let P be the common value of P_A and P_B. Then $V = W_S - W_u$ is the common value of V_A and V_B. Let E represent the elasticity of $S(V)$ with respect to V. From (11.4) the definition of r, we have

$$MP_S - W_S = r/P \qquad (11.7)$$

at the symmetric equilibrium, or the excess of marginal product over wages. So, the condition for stability is

$$E(MP_S - W_S)/(W_S - W_u) < 1 \qquad (11.8)$$

The higher the value of elasticity of the supply schedule for qualified labor, and the greater the differential between marginal product and wages of skilled workers, the more likely the system is unstable. But the larger the wage gap between unskilled and skilled workers the more stable the system.

As Reder points out (1973, pp. 34-35) the preceding analysis ignores response of labor supply to the wage differential. Following the same assumptions of homogeneity in productive capacity and identity of supply schedules, we can examine situations where (1) there is no taste for discrimination, and all workers are paid the same and are equally productive, and (2) the same quantity of A and B labor is supplied as above, but no employer will hire B labor unless W_B is less than W_A by at least some amount u.

The first situation is in a position of static equilibrium if L_A and L_B are both supplied and demanded. The second situation is much more complex. Here L_A is both supplied and demanded at wage W_A, but L_B is supplied at wage W_B but is demanded only at wage $W_B - u$. This means that L_B can be an equilibrium quantity only if B workers have zero wage elasticity in the interval from $W_B - u$ to W_B. If the supply elasticity is positive, the quantity of B labor offered at the equilibrium point would be less than L_B, hence the equilibrium wage would be above $W_B - u$ but less than W_B. The effect of labor market discrimination against a particular group of workers will be understated, if the reduction in quantity of labor supplied is ignored and wage elasticity is not zero.

Another factor of importance is the incidence of unemployment. Assume three options in the use of time: (1) paid employment, (2) unemployment, and (3) nonmarket activity. Unemployment can be equated with job search; and if it is assumed that the opportunity cost of an unemployed worker is zero, it cannot exist with market equilibrium. However, if this is not true, there may exist a market equilibrium (with unemployment). This is important, because it may suggest continued unemployment in certain sectors of the labor market.

Davis (1973, p. 8) has suggested a model of this general type. In this case the opportunity cost of job search is the amount to be earned in a service-type job. The objective is to obtain a job in manufacturing that pays higher wages.

His argument is based on the low information base of the ghetto worker; the oligopolistic nature of the market; and the fact that manufacturing, which he considers the only viable employer, is continually increasing the sophistication of its capital and cutting down on the number of employees. This situation leads naturally to high unemployment and low income in the ghetto, since the only jobs the workers can possibly find would be low paying service-type that are not especially abundant.

On the supply side, Davis argues that net investment made for the training of blacks is significantly less than for whites (both in schools and on the job). Thus, white educational levels rise along with incomes. But, for blacks, lifetime earnings reach a peak with educational levels somewhere between the ninth and twelfth grades. They then fall until the end of college and rise again for those finishing graduate school. This implies that the supply schedule for the individual black is infinitely elastic at some low rate. This maximizes the investment in education.

Given these circumstances, it is profitable for both the employer and black worker to perpetuate low wages and poverty. The situation is shown in Fig. 11.3. The real wage rate (W) is shown on the y-axis and the number of unskilled black workers (L) on the x-axis. The point E represents an initial "equilibrium." (This is not an equilibrium in the usual sense, since supply is perpetually above demand. This concept is best interpreted as a starting point.) The equilibrium is between demand for ghetto labor and a supply curve that has become horizontal at some wage (W_m) that has been set by interplay between the companies and the unions. Thus, it is not a competitive wage.

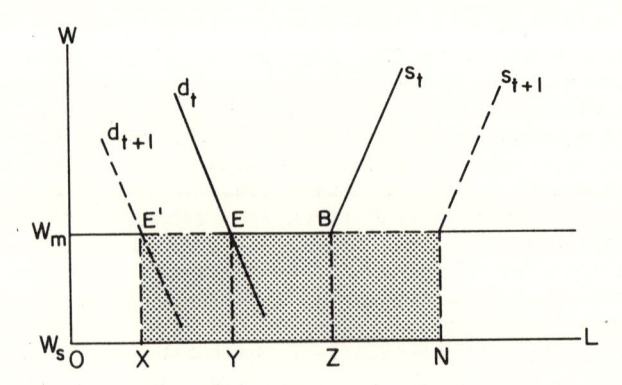

Fig. 11.3. Annual losses in real income (ghetto workers).

At this initial point there is a surplus $Y - Z$ of labor that would work at real wage W_m. Now two events transpire to aggravate the situation. The supply at $t + 1$ (because of increased in-migration and population growth) shifts to the right (to ON). Demand shifts to the left (to OX) owing to greater automation. The new hiring point is E'. The amount of surplus labor has increased by three times.

The shaded portion represents loss of income as workers are forced to seek service work at the lower wage W_S. Rising productivity results in increased wages for skilled workers rather than a lowering of prices, because of the oligopolistic nature of both the employers and the suppliers of union labor. Unskilled workers become obsolete and are laid off. Their incomes plummet in the face of a rising price level. Of course, there are other factors affecting prices, which Davis ignores; one of these is the increased level of transfer payments of which welfare and unemployment compensation are components.

The above phenomena are obvious in other types of enclaves as well. Spanish-speaking communities and Indian reservations in North America, tribal enclaves in South Africa, and colored enclaves in Europe have essentially the same types of situations.

INVOLUNTARY ENCLAVE AS A COMMUNITY ECONOMIC SYSTEM

In addition to high unemployment and low incomes, people in enclaves have to face a situation of very little economic activity within the community. Generally speaking, capital is lacking in enclaves. Businesses of any consequence are likely to be owned by outsiders, usually members of the predominant society in the area. Any locally owned businesses are limited in size and usually family operated. In neither case is it likely that very strong linkages will be established with other businesses in the community. Supplies will be purchased outside the enclave, and hired labor often will be imported as well. Consequently, multiplier effects of inflows of basic income will be small. As an economic entity, the community is weak.

The charge is often made that prices charged within the enclaves tend to be higher than for similar goods outside. This is hard to prove, since kinds of goods purchased by enclave residents are quite different from purchases outside. However, there are several good economic reasons why it may be true. Extension of credit is costly because losses are high. This limits volume sales. Insurance rates are high because buildings are not maintained as they should be and amenities, such as fire hydrants and police protection, are inferior. Losses to pilferage tend to be high. In addition, there is a certain amount of spatial monopoly. Residents tend to shop within the enclave, which allows sellers to raise prices in face of inelastic demand.

Housing in an enclave tends to be substandard. Where there are landlords, this may be due to overcrowding. "Slumlords" charge relatively high rents to assure that they get back their investment before things collapse and because they are in monopoly-type situations. High cost of investment, high cost of upkeep (including cost of possible abandonment), generally high taxes, and very high risk factors also contribute. Where housing is privately owned, it tends to be of cheap construction--often of earth or other easily formed materials. This type of housing has few amenities. Lack of capital is glaring as well as lack of means for maintenance.

This type of community is also a very inefficient supplier of public goods. It seldom has control over its public areas. A basic adversary relationship exists between its residents and residents of other areas who generally have control of government services. Local pressure groups can only make themselves heard by taking radical measures that have very short-term effects. Revelation of preferences for public goods is greatly hindered.

In summary, the enclave is a community whose major source of basic income is sales of low information base labor services, supplemented by such transfer payments as the outside world chooses to send there. This basic income is either spent outside or, more likely, spent inside the enclave but with merchants whose own ties to the community are weak. Hence, money flows out of the enclave almost as fast as it flows in. Prices may be high because cost of doing business is high and sellers of goods and services (including landlords) tend to have some spatial monopoly power. The economy is generally stagnant or declining and the situation tends to get worse over time, since each situation is interwoven with each other one.

SOLUTIONS

The problems are quite easy to determine, but the possible solutions are not. They are tied closely to productivity of human resources. People are productive in accordance with the abilities they bring to the productive process and the opportunities they have to use those abilities. Abilities and opportunities are in some ways separable items and in other ways inseparable. They are separable to the degree that opportunity is completely exogenous to the situation, and they are inseparable to the degree that it is endogenous. This brings us to two basic arguments with regard to the causes of poverty.

The first argument, which Schiller (1973, p. 40) calls "restricted opportunity," states that poor people are unproductive because they do not have adequate access to good schools, good jobs, and governmental protection, subsidies, and service. These are constraints imposed by society, and no amount of individual effort will enable them to escape. An implication of this, also, is that provision of improved opportunities will assure that less people will be poor. The second argument he calls "flawed character." This argument is derived directly from the Protestant ethic. By stressing the spiritual values of work, saving, and achieving, it also stressed the relationship of vice to laziness, nonsaving, and nonachieving. This led to the conclusion that misery and vice go together, hence poverty is the result of individual defects in aspiration and ability.

Sowell (1970, p. 220) argues that it is a little of each. He disposes of the low ability argument by showing that no one has been able to definitely prove anything about it. In short, there are so many flaws in research done on ability differences among races, ethnic groups, and others that nothing definitive can be said about any of it. One thing that seems to hold possibilities is the use of some type of remedial learning to try to instill in young people some of the necessary attitudes toward learning, work, and other attributes that make productivity possible. This may rescue some of the abler persons in the enclaves, providing it is done by people who understand the culture they are trying to change.

Perhaps of more importance would be a program to change attitudes of parents. Bruner et al. (1969) point out that "certain, possibly critical, emotional, linguistic, and cognitive patterns associated with social background are already present by the age of three." Hess and Shipman (1968) list three interconnected influences on children associated with poverty.

1. The missing of opportunity and encouragement of goal seeking and problem solving plus the absence of the feeling of power to change things with realistic expectation of reward for effort
2. Lack of linguistic skills so that language can be used as an instrument of thought, social control, interaction of planning and so on, which encourages development into a productive adult
3. The weak pattern of reciprocity; parents expect too little of their children, and this is supplemented by attitudes of teachers and peers

This situation is emphasized when one compares enclaves containing Chinese or Jewish people with those containing black, Spanish-speaking, and native-American residents. In the one case, there is a spirit of achievement. Children are exposed to managerial skills and attitudes because businesses in these enclaves are owned by the people who live there. In the second case, the businesses are owned by outsiders and the children, not having been exposed to these things, very seldom think in terms of becoming business people. However, blacks who moved into the ghetto from the West Indies became successful business people in the 1920s and 1930s because they came from a society in which success in business among blacks was a common thing.

The obstacles to be overcome in an enclave can be formidable. So long as the population has a low information base, it is vulnerable. In a technical society, its abilities rapidly become obsolete. Additional problems stem from low savings (most of which are invested outside), hence lack of access to money; power to command resources is weak. A further complication is found in lack of leadership and innovation. A member of a traditional enclave society is uncreative because the world is seen as arbitrary and not subject to analysis and control. Since nothing can be perceived to be done about it, the reaction is to passively accept things as they are.

Hagen (1962) defines a traditional society as consisting of an elite class, some trader-financiers, and the simple folk. This is essentially the same as the society to be found in an enclave. Change is difficult in this kind of society. The small business person has difficulty getting money because he or she is considered a "poor risk." The elite classes are not usually interested in industry. This leaves all change to someone from outside.

But every such society has a few creative individuals. These people have a different perception of things. They tend to antici-success whenever they try something. The achievement of one success tends to reinforce the feeling for the next try. But there are enough failures that success does not become a foregone conclusion, and they feel an urge to continually try new things and assure themselves.

What happens to creative individuals in enclaves? They become hemmed in by social pressures against innovation. In order to express themselves, they may turn to crime, since it gives them a challenge and a reward for using their wits against society. They may simply find some way to escape. Or they may try to bring powerful forces to bear against the inertia of their society. This often takes the form of violence. Violence aimed at concrete goals and accompanied by good leadership might accomplish good at times. But in the case of ghetto riots of recent years, ghetto residents were the ones victimized, in part because both goals and leadership were lacking.

Does this mean that the problems of enclaves are hopeless? This would be true only if they are societies that cannot turn out capable and dedicated leaders. Geertz (1963, p. 145) maintains that entrepreneurship and effective social leadership are possible developments from a wide range of cultures. However, he does make six suggestive generalizations:

1. Innovative economic leadership occurs in fairly well-defined and homogeneous groups
2. The innovative group crystallizes out of a traditional group that has had a long history of contact outside its own community
3. The larger group, out of which the innovators emerge, has to be experiencing a fairly radical change in its relationship with the wider society of which it is a part
4. On the ideological level, the innovative group conceives of itself as a main vehicle of religious and moral excellence within a generally wayward, unenlightened, or heedless community
5. The major innovational problems faced are organizational rather than technical
6. The function of the innovator in a transitional but "pretakeoff" society is to adapt established means to novel ends.

What this means for the enclave community is that leadership is likely to develop from the portion of the community that has had a fruitful relationship with the outside community. These leaders will be idealistic and bent on change. They will also be highly concerned about forcing recognition of excellence from a reluctant white society. They will accomplish change by working with established enclave organizations and adapting them to change in novel ways.

SUMMARY

People are forced into enclaves against their will whenever the power elite is capable of bringing social or other pressure against them. Usually these people have low information bases, hence have difficulty performing at skilled or semiskilled levels. Enclaves are also weak economic systems with very little multiplier effect from incoming money flow.

Discrimination plays a prominent role in creating the problems as well as the existence of enclaves. It operates both at the employer and employee level. Some employers are willing to sacrifice profits in order to avoid employing "undesirables." Some employees will work for lower wages when they do not have to work with "undesirables." Where an employer has perfect information about the abilities of workers, discrimination is completely willfull. But where such information is not perfect, discrimination may result from a distorted perception of the actual abilities.

Discrimination is insidious in its influence on attitudes, health, and educational opportunities. In particular, the influence on attitude is important, since it gives the one discriminated against a perception of inferiority that then becomes reality. It influences ability to learn, aggressiveness in pursuing goals, and willingness to try to change the environment. Attitudes of parents, peers, and teachers are also important. It has been shown that if parents have a positive attitude toward learning, their children will also, and discipline will not be a problem. If teachers also have positive attitudes toward abilities of their students, they will do a better job of teaching. Enclave children tend to be immobilized by views of their abilities held by parents, peers, and teachers. Another effect of discrimination is that it creates situations (particularly in a technically advanced, oligopolistically oriented market) where it pays employers to cut down on employment and wage rates for low information base workers and it pays workers to stop their education at some low level.

As indicated previously, enclaves are not very strong as economic systems. Much of the economic activity is carried on by firms owned by nonresidents; these often use imported workers and have very few linkages of any kind within the area. Poverty tends to make people poor risks for credit, hence locally owned businesses tend to be small and family operated. Costs are usually high, and this leads to cutting of services and raising of prices where there is sufficient monopoly power to do so. Enclaves also are very inefficient suppliers of public goods. Local people generally have very little control over this situation. These economies are usually approaching stagnation or declining and the situation gets worse over time.

REVIEW QUESTIONS

1. Why do people enter enclaves?
2. How can we determine whether or not an employer is discriminating in employment practice?
3. If an employer has perfect information about the abilities of workers, what effect will discrimination have on the equilibrium between marginal product and wages?
4. If an employer does not have perfect information, what situations might lead to discrimination in hiring?
5. How does discrimination affect investment in human resources?
6. Discuss Arrow's proof of the existence of discriminatory equilibria.
7. How does he support the idea that such equilibria are stable?
8. How does Reder modify Arrow's analysis by introducing the supply side?
9. Discuss the possibility of equilibrium with unemployment, and show how it can exist in an enclave.
10. Is there any way workers caught in the above situation can extricate themselves?
11. Why is economic activity so low in an enclave?
12. What impact does this have on inhabitants?
13. Why do prices and rents tend to be high in enclaves?
14. Are there solutions to enclave problems?

REFERENCES

Arrow, K. 1973. The theory of discrimination. In *Discrimination in labor markets*, ed. O. Ashenfelter and A. Rees. Princeton, N.J.: Princeton Univ. Press.
Batchelder, A. B. 1966. Determinants of productive intelligence. *The economics of poverty*. New York: Wiley.
Becker, G. S. 1971. *The economics of discrimination*. Chicago: Univ. of Chicago Press.
Bloom, B. S. 1964. *Stability and change in human characteristics*. New York: Wiley.
Bruner, J. S., et al. 1969. *Studies in the growth of manual intelligence in infancy*. New York: Society for Research in Child Development.
Coles, F. A. 1974. The economics of minorities. *Review of Black Political Economy* 4:47-58.

Davis, F. G. 1973. *The economics of black community development.* Chicago: Markham.
Foley, E. P. 1968. *The achieving ghetto.* Washington, D.C.: Washington National Press.
Fusfeld, D. R. 1970. The economy of the urban ghetto. In *Financing the metropolis: Urban affairs annual review*, ed. J. P. Crecine and L. H. Masotti. Vol. 4. Beverly Hills, Calif.: Sage.
Geertz, C. 1963. *Peddlers and princes: Social development and economic change in two Indonesian towns.* Chicago: Chicago Univ. Press.
Hagen, E. E. 1962. *The theory of social change: How economic growth begins.* New York: Wiley.
Hess, R. D., and V. Shipman. 1968. Maternal influences upon early learning: The cognitive environments of urban pre-school children. In *Early education, current theory research and action*, Conference on Pre-school Education. Hawthorne, N.Y.: Aldine.
Jarrett, J. S. 1968. The meanings of equality. In *Pygmalion in the classroom: Teacher expectation and pupil's intellectual development*, ed. R. Rosenthal and L. Jacobson. New York: Holt, Rinehart & Winston.
Lowe, J. R. 1967. *Cities in a race with time.* New York: Vintage.
McMurrin, S. M., ed. 1971. *The conditions for educational equality.* New York: Committee for Economic Development.
Myrdal, G. 1962. *An American dilemma.* New York: Harper & Row.
Reder, M. W. 1973. Comment. In *Discrimination in labor markets*, ed. O. Ashenfelter and A. Rees. Princeton, N.J.: Princeton Univ. Press.
Schiller, B. R. 1973. *The economics of poverty and discrimination.* Englewood Cliffs, N.J.: Prentice-Hall.
Sowell, T. 1970. *Black education, myths and tragedies.* New York: David McKay.
Vatter, H. G., and T. Palm, eds. 1972. *The economics of black America.* New York: Harcourt Brace Jovanovich.

CHAPTER 12
Methodologies Useful in Community Analysis

In this chapter some of the methods utilized by analysts in appraising community economies will be discussed. Serious students will want to refer to the various references given, as well as look elsewhere for good models. This area is continually changing, yet there are a number of models that analysts find useful in one situation after another. Most of these will be introduced.

Analysts are particularly interested in the general economic structure within the community and relationships to other communities. Specifically, local linkages and interaction among units within the community are important, as are interactions between units of two communities. They are also interested in trends in population, including characteristics, such as income, age distribution, and changes in employment. In addition, every analysis tries to define the states of nature faced by the community, such as weather, natural resources, topography, and geography, and tries to ascertain how they influence economic activity.

COMMUNITY STRUCTURE
Economic Base Concept

Some of the more useful models for looking at community economic structure utilize the concept of an economic base. According to Sirkin (1959) economic base analysis is drawn from the idea that the economic product of an area can be divided into two parts: (1) output and productive services sold outside the area, and (2) output absorbed internally. If internal absorption bears some known relation to the amount sold outside the area (the economic base), then forecasts of total economic activity can be derived from forecasts of the economic base.

Community multiplier. The measure used to connect the two parts of the economic product is the multiplier. Fouraker (1955) defined a regional (community) multiplier as the relationship between a change in investment and the resulting change in gross regional (community) product. This is an extension of Machlup's international trade multiplier (1939). The connection between that idea and the economic base depends upon acceptance of the idea that increased production for export is a direct result of investment. This idea ignores any possibility of slack in the local economy that would allow additional production for export without investment, and it ignores the impact of change in the information base leading to greater production without additional capital.

But these assumptions do not rule out multipliers resulting from changed relationships. Thus, models can be changed to allow measurement of changes in production no matter what the reason. The message to be gained from Machlup's model is that multiplier theory is based on an elastic supply of credit. This means that there is a direct multiplier effect from increased production not only in the community where it occurs but in those communities receiving the extra product. Thus, there are positive benefits from trade to all participants. These increases are fairly continuous; but in order to measure them, it is necessary to stop the action at certain intervals. Thus, a given multiplier measures the situation as of a particular moment in time.

Economic base model. The economic base model is a rather simple one that attempts to (1) identify basic export activities, (2) determine the expected change in these activities, and (3) measure the impact of these changes upon nonbasic activities of the community. The original approach using this model assigned whole industry sectors to either export or nonbasic categories. Agriculture, mining, and manufacturing were considered to be basic (export) industries. Retail and wholesale trade, communication, transportation, utilities, services, and local government were treated as nonbasic.

In recent years, a somewhat more sophisticated approach has been used. Recognition is given to the fact that almost all activities in a community produce for both the local and the export market. Allocation is usually made between the two by means of location quotients. For any one sector, the proportion of world, national, or regional production accounted for within the community is divided by the proportion of personal income. Which of the larger units to relate to, depends upon the situation. The unit should be large enough to give a realistic ratio. In the United States, for example, the relationship is usually to the nation. If the quotient happened to be 1.5, the analyst would assume that 50/150, or one-third of the output of that sector would be exported; the rest would be consumed locally.

Location quotients tend to show inputs to exporting industries as exports; that is, if a community produces beer, it may also produce beer cans. Although the cans are really sold locally, the quotient would count them as exported. To this degree it overestimates. However, it also underestimates for those industries where some of the products are imported, since the quotient tends to estimate net above consumption. Tiebout (1962) suggested a more accurate but more costly method: sample the firms in the community to determine actual shipments of goods and services out of the community. Where the multipliers are based on employment, ratios are calculated between the proportion of the labor force employed by the industry nationally and locally. The idea is that exporters tend to have a larger proportion of workers employed than does the nation.

In order to determine change in exports from the community, it is necessary to study three things: overall demand for the products of each sector, estimation of probability of new plants locating or old plants leaving the community, and evaluation of the competitive position of the local industry (that is, is its cost structure average, below average, above average?). Once these estimates are prepared, the possible impact on the community must be estimated. The multiplier can be fairly simple. If employment is used and one-third are employed in export industries, then two nonbasic jobs should develop for each new basic one. If money values are used, a multiplier base on one-third exports would estimate two nonbasic sales for each basic one.

Note that only one multiplier is developed by this method, since it is necessary to aggregate in order to identify basic and nonbasic relationships. Such a multiplier leaves a great deal of the local interaction out of the analysis. It is not possible to identify the industries in which the greatest impact is being experienced. This type of analysis also ignores the fact that growth can take place by strengthening linkages, thus increasing multiplier effects. This type of growth is often referred to as "import substitution." Inputs that had been imported are now produced locally.

Input-output model. The input-output model, used to develop the community multiplier, belongs to the broad spectrum of economic base. It provides information on the structure of the local economy and, in that sense, is a picture of an economy as of a moment in time. It is unique in this ability. An apt analogy is that a given model is similar to the frame of a motion picture. Where models are constructed several years apart, it is possible to spot the impact of change by comparing them; this is similar to the action seen by comparing motion picture frames in a movie projector.

Input-output models require considerable resources and expertise to construct. Harmston and Lund's *Application of an Input-Output Framework to a Community Economic System* (1967) gives complete directions. Even with this help, the analyst needs to have some background in mathematics and regional economics. Nevertheless, there are large numbers of small region and community models being developed. University of Washington at Seattle and University of West Virginia at Morgantown publish directories of these models at irregular intervals. The United Nations, Department of Economic and Social Affairs, also compiles bibliographies of regional and community input-output models. Any references for these sources would be out-of-date, so the best strategy for anyone interested in them would be to contact the agency and ask for the latest compilation.

Input-output models are especially useful in guiding economic development policy, since they place at the analyst's fingertips information on current industry mix, linkages among industries within the economy, and linkages with industries in other communities. The possible impact of a new industry on various parts of a local economy is very useful information. For example, the amount of local tax increase resulting from introduction of a new industry is only partially that paid by the industry itself. The new money introduced into the economy, through linkages with other industries, will also generate tax revenue. The same can be said of personal income; payrolls of the new industry are only part of the picture.

It is not necessary to have a sector in the model for the new industry. All that is needed is a vector of possible local expenditures by that industry that can then be multiplied against the local multiplier matrix. As an illustration, let us suppose a given local economy has five economic sectors, and suppose, also, that it has attracted a new industry that expects to buy something from each local sector. Assume also that the values shown in Table 12.1 are those of the community.

Total expenditure by the new industry is $720,000, which is the total of values in the expenditure vector in Table 12.1; and total impact on the economy is $2,345,650, which is the total of values in the direct and indirect impact vector. If we add the multipliers across columns in the multiplier matrix, we obtain the total impact per dollar expended in each sector. In this case it is 3.36 for sector one, 2.53 for sector two, 3.39 for sector three, 3.28 for sector four, and 3.28 for sector five. These are quite large multipliers that signify quite intensive linkage among industries in the community. Also, total impact of local expenditure can be obtained directly (i.e., $2,345,650/$720,000 = 3.26). These multipliers include the direct effect, so to obtain indirect effects, we must subtract 1; the latter effects in total are 2.26 per dollar spent by the new industry.

TABLE 12.1. Impact of a new industry upon the community ($1000s)

Expenditures of new industry

$$\begin{matrix} 1 & 2 & 3 & 4 & 5 \\ [60, & 35, & 50, & 75, & 500] \end{matrix}$$

Multiplier matrix

$$\begin{matrix} & 1 & 2 & 3 & 4 & 5 \\ 1 & 1.34 & 0.23 & 0.36 & 0.57 & 0.86 \\ 2 & 0.12 & 1.08 & 0.25 & 0.34 & 0.74 \\ 3 & 0.34 & 0.36 & 1.28 & 0.42 & 0.99 \\ 4 & 0.18 & 0.43 & 0.48 & 1.21 & 0.98 \\ 5 & 0.21 & 0.42 & 0.32 & 0.46 & 1.87 \end{matrix}$$

=

Direct and indirect impact

$$\begin{matrix} 1 & 2 & 3 & 4 & 5 \\ 80.4 & 13.8 & 21.6 & 34.2 & 51.6 \\ 4.2 & 37.8 & 8.75 & 11.9 & 25.9 \\ 17.0 & 18.0 & 64.0 & 21.0 & 49.5 \\ 13.5 & 32.25 & 36.0 & 90.75 & 73.5 \\ 105.0 & 210.0 & 160.0 & 230.0 & 935.0 \end{matrix}$$

Total impact on

$$\begin{matrix} 1 & 2 & 3 & 4 & 5 \end{matrix}$$
= [220.10, 311.85, 290.35, 387.85, 1,135.50]

We note that in the work values used to obtain the vector of direct and indirect effects (which appear in matrix form in Table 12.1), we can ascertain the impact of expenditure by the new industry upon every sector of the economy. For example, the $60,000 spent for goods produced in sector one results in an additional increase in demand for intermediate goods of $20,400 making a total impact on sector one of $80,400. For sector two, $13,800 of new business was generated. For sector three, the impact amounted to $21,600, and so on. This type of information is important to business people in each sector.

Total impact on each sector of the expenditure of $720,000 is shown in the direct and indirect effect vector. This amounts to $220,100 for sector one, $311,850 for sector two, and so on. This information is also useful for planning.

The same approach as that used above can be used to measure the impact on a community of the loss of an industry. The only difference is that the expenditure vector would contain information on money that would have been expended, had the industry remained; and the direct and indirect effects on each sector and the whole community will represent overall money lost. This method is also useful for measuring the impact of tourism (Harmston 1979), the impact of retired people, and the impact of the expansion of an existing industry.

Intercommunity tables. Input-output tables are also useful where strong ties exist with other communities. For example, suppose your community supplies an important input to an industry in another community, and plans are being made for expansion of the latter industry. Having an intercommunity model would enable you to determine the overall effect on your community. Of course, where there are several links among industries in neighboring communities, the impact will be greater than where links are weak.

Intercommunity models have the same functional format as community models but are laid out somewhat differently. Table 12.2 illustrates a very simple model. Each community has only three sectors and each sector is linked to all others. Exports and imports represent links these two communities have with the rest of the world.

The superscripts in Table 12.2 indicate trading relationships between communities, and the subscripts indicate trading relationships among sectors. Thus, X^{AA}_{11} is the amount sold within community A by sector one to itself; X^{AB}_{11} is the amount sold by sector one in community A to sector one in community B; X^{BA}_{21} is the amount sold by sector two in community B to sector one in community A. Again the multiplier table will ignore the rest of the world and will reflect the impact of industries in both communities. This is illustrated in Table 12.3.

The superscripts in Table 12.3 represent intercommunity impacts, and the subscripts represent intersectoral impacts. Thus, M^{AA}_{11} is the multiplier effect upon production in that sector of a

TABLE 12.2. Layout of an intercommunity model

		Sectors in A			Sectors in B			Exports rest of world	Total product
		1	2	3	1	2	3		
A	1	X_{11}^{AA}	X_{12}^{AA}	X_{13}^{AA}	X_{11}^{AB}	X_{21}^{AB}	X_{31}^{AB}	E_1^A	Y_1^A
	2	X_{21}^{AA}	X_{22}^{AA}	X_{23}^{AA}	X_{12}^{AB}	X_{22}^{AB}	X_{32}^{AB}	E_2^A	Y_2^A
	3	X_{31}^{AA}	X_{32}^{AA}	X_{33}^{AA}	X_{13}^{AB}	X_{23}^{AB}	X_{33}^{AB}	E_3^A	Y_3^A
B	1	X_{11}^{BA}	X_{12}^{BA}	X_{13}^{BA}	X_{11}^{BB}	X_{12}^{BB}	X_{13}^{BB}	E_1^B	Y_1^B
	2	X_{21}^{BA}	X_{22}^{BA}	X_{23}^{BA}	X_{21}^{BB}	X_{22}^{BB}	X_{23}^{BB}	E_2^B	Y_2^B
	3	X_{31}^{BA}	X_{32}^{BA}	X_{33}^{BA}	X_{31}^{BB}	X_{32}^{BB}	X_{33}^{BB}	E_3^B	Y_3^B
Imports rest of world		I_1^A	I_2^A	I_3^A	I_1^B	I_2^B	I_3^B	Trade	
Total product		Y_1^A	Y_2^A	Y_3^A	Y_1^B	Y_2^B	Y_3^B		

TABLE 12.3. Intercommunity multipliers

Impacting community and sector		A			Sub-total	B			Sub-total	Total
		1	2	3		1	2	3		
A	1	M_{11}^{AA}	M_{12}^{AA}	M_{13}^{AA}	M_1^{AA}	M_{11}^{AB}	M_{12}^{AB}	M_{13}^{AB}	M_1^{AB}	M_1^A
	2	M_{21}^{AA}	M_{22}^{AA}	M_{23}^{AA}	M_2^{AA}	M_{21}^{AB}	M_{22}^{AB}	M_{23}^{AB}	M_2^{AB}	M_2^A
	3	M_{31}^{AA}	M_{32}^{AA}	M_{33}^{AA}	M_3^{AA}	M_{31}^{AB}	M_{32}^{AB}	M_{33}^{AB}	M_3^{AB}	M_3^A
B	1	M_{11}^{BA}	M_{12}^{BA}	M_{13}^{BA}	M_1^{BA}	M_{11}^{BB}	M_{12}^{BB}	M_{13}^{BB}	M_1^{BB}	M_1^B
	2	M_{21}^{BA}	M_{22}^{BA}	M_{23}^{BA}	M_2^{BA}	M_{21}^{BB}	M_{22}^{BB}	M_{23}^{BB}	M_2^{BB}	M_2^B
	3	M_{31}^{BA}	M_{32}^{BA}	M_{33}^{BA}	M_3^{BA}	M_{31}^{BB}	M_{32}^{BB}	M_{33}^{BB}	M_3^{BB}	M_3^B

one-unit change in exports from sector one of community A to the rest of the world; M_{12}^{AB} is the impact of a unit change in the same exports upon production in sector two of community B; M_1^A is the overall multiplier effect upon production in both communities of a one-unit change in exports to the rest of the world; M_{21}^{BA} is the impact of a one-unit change in exports from sector two in community B to the rest of the world upon production in sector one of community A; M_{32}^{BB} is the impact of a one-unit change in exports from sector three in community B upon production in sector two of community B; M_3^B is the total impact of a one-unit change in exports from sector three of community B upon both communities. The total impact on each sector could be obtained by adding those multipliers pertaining to the community; thus, $M_{11}^{AA} + M_{12}^{AA} + M_{13}^{AA} = M_1^{AA}$ or the total impact of a one-dollar increase in export to the rest of the world by sector one of community A upon community A.

If the area of immediate interest is community A, and a new development is taking place in community B that will lead to additional world exports, the table segment of interest is summed in M_i^{BA}. That is, it is of interest to know what effect the new development will have on A. Note that in these tables, the intercommunity relationships are treated separately from relationships with all other communities in the world.

Linear Programming

A recurrent problem faced by communities is one of identifying specific industries that can operate profitably in the local economy. A community has certain resources that are assets in growth and development. At the same time, it faces scarcities in certain resources that act to constrain it. A related problem is that of diversification in order to avoid getting too tied in to the problems of any one industry.

The basic problem, then, becomes how to make the best use of the resources available. Linear programming was designed specifically for such problems. A community has an objective of maximizing local income that can be expressed as a linear function, subject to certain constraints expressed as linear inequalities. These constraints could be natural resources, access to markets, limited transportation facilities, skill levels of the labor force, capital limitations, and so on.

Suppose the above community has a set of water, land, and labor constraints. It is looking at two industries. Industry A requires more water than industry B. Industry B requires more labor than industry A. Industry A requires more land than industry B. Let X_1 be the activity level of industry A and X_2 the activity level of industry B. The level of income resulting from these activities is Z.

Each activity has a set of data indicating the amount of input from each resource required for it to generate $1 of new local personal income. This can be expressed in the following matrix notation:

$$\begin{bmatrix} a_{11} & a_{12} \\ a_{21} & a_{22} \\ a_{31} & a_{32} \end{bmatrix}$$

We say that the community wishes to maximize $Z = X_1 + X_2$ subject to

$$a_{11}X_1 + a_{12}X_2 \leq R_1$$
$$a_{21}X_1 + a_{22}X_2 \leq R_2$$
$$a_{31}X_1 + a_{32}X_2 \leq R_3$$

(12.1)

where R stands for a resource; i.e., R_1 = water, R_2 = land, and R_3 = labor.

We now provide the necessary information: R_1 = 6000 acre-feet of water, R_2 = 1400 acres of land, and R_3 = 4500 hours of labor. The values of the A matrix are as follows:

Resources	A	B
Water	0.8	0.5
Land	0.2	0.1
Labor	0.5	0.7

A graphic solution is shown in Fig. 12.1. The community would gain an optimal $8 million in income by attracting enough of industry A to produce $6 million and enough of industry B to produce $2 million. Land and labor turn out to be the most constraining factors in this case.

Of course, real problems are not solved with graphics but by a form of mathematical manipulation or iteration. However, there will always be a corner solution to a linear programming problem as shown in Fig. 12.1. The procedure used is called the simplex method, and it can be used with any number of industries and resources. In this method, slack variables are introduced that have values from 0 to the upper limit on the resource. When all of a resource is being used, the slack variable for that resource has 0 value. Thus, in the above problem, there would be X_3 that disposes of water, X_4 that disposes of land, and X_5 that disposes of labor. The constraint formulas would be

$$a_{11}X_1 + a_{12}X_2 + a_{13}X_3 + a_{14}X_4 + a_{15}X_5 = R_1$$
$$a_{21}X_1 + a_{22}X_2 + a_{23}X_3 + a_{24}X_4 + a_{25}X_5 = R_2$$
$$a_{31}X_1 + a_{32}X_2 + a_{33}X_3 + a_{34}X_4 + a_{35}X_5 = R_3 \quad (12.2)$$

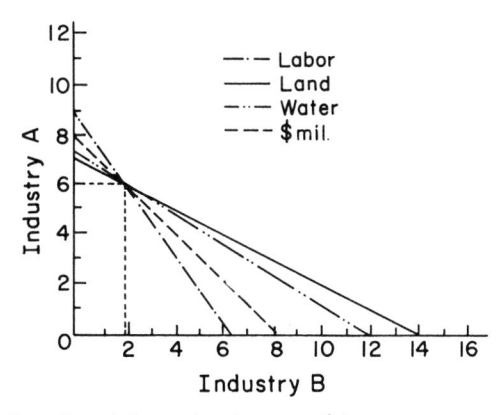

Fig. 12.1. Graphic solution to linear program.

Coefficients a_{13}, a_{24}, and a_{35} have value 1; but a_{14}, a_{15}, a_{23}, a_{25}, a_{33}, and a_{34} have value 0, since they apply to resources not required. The matrix would appear as follows:

$$\begin{bmatrix} 0.8 & 0.5 & 1.0 & 0 & 0 \\ 0.2 & 0.1 & 0 & 1.0 & 0 \\ 0.5 & 0.7 & 0 & 0 & 1.0 \end{bmatrix}$$

The method for solving this is explained in any good book on linear programming; and there are also computer programs that can be used.

The dual. The dual of a linear programming problem is generally a minimization problem. This can be solved by first solving the maximization problem. Of course, the dual of a minimization problem would be a maximization problem. The problem faced previously called for solution by maximization. Its dual would yield prices for water, land, and labor that would minimize costs. These are called shadow prices. If local prices were higher than the shadow price, the society would not be willing to pay it.

In setting up the dual for solution, values appearing in matrix columns would appear in the rows. Thus, the constraint would appear as

$$a_{11}P_1 + a_{21}P_2 + a_{31}P_3 \geq C_1$$
$$a_{12}P_1 + a_{22}P_2 + a_{32}P_3 \geq C_2 \tag{12.3}$$

where C_1 and C_2 are costs per unit for firm A and firm B, respectively. Values from the preceding matrix give us

$$0.8P_1 + 0.2P_2 + 0.5P_3 \geq \$1$$
$$0.5P_1 + 0.1P_2 + 0.7P_3 \geq \$1 \tag{12.4}$$

Since we are talking about $1 of personal income generation, we set the C values at $1. Since water is not a constraint at the margin, the shadow price $P_1 = 0$. (See Fig. 12.1.) Decisions have to be made in terms of the constraining resources, land, and labor.

Gravity Models
    Physicists have a model that describes the gravitational force, F, that each mass (M_J or M_K) exerts on the other. It is

$$F = G(M_J M_K/d^2) \tag{12.5}$$

where G is a parameter and d is distance. This is the prototype of gravity potential and spatial interaction models used in the social sciences, where the region is conceived of as a mass. According to

Bramhall (1960, p. 494), this mass is structured by certain principles that constrain and initiate action among individuals making up the mass.

For example, let us assume a metropolitan region, with population P, that consists of a number of different communities. Through origin and destination studies, the number of trips taken among the various communities in the region can be estimated with confidence. Let this number be T. Now assume that the population is homogeneous with regard to income, tastes, age distribution, occupational structures, and other socioeconomic factors.

Suppose it is desired to determine the number of trips originating in community i and terminating in community j. Assume no cost involved in travel (the friction of distance = 0). The representative individual in the region could be expected to travel to j in the proportion P_j/P; and since the population is homogeneous, an individual in i would take the average number of trips or T/P. Designate this ratio as $G = T/P$. Then the number of trips a resident of i will take to j is $G(P_j/P)$, and the number of all individuals in i that will take trips to j will be $P_i[G(P_j/P)]$ or $T_{ij} = G(P_i P_j/P)$.

Isard (1975, p. 43) has shown that there are a number of factors that influence interactions among communities, such as income, age distribution, and all of the other factors held steady in the above model. These can be entered into the model by a weighting procedure giving us the general model (12.6)

$$I_{ij} = G[(W_i P_i)(W_j P_j)/d_{ij}^b] \qquad (12.6)$$

where I is interaction between communities i and j; W_i and W_j are weights; P_i and P_j are populations; d_{ij} is distance between i and j; b and G are parameters; and $G = T/(Pd_{ij}^b)$ by definition.

For example, assume a two-community region with d_{ij} = 100 km, P_i = 50,000, P_j = 20,000, P = 70,000, W_i = $8000 per capita income, and W_j = $10,000 per capita income. By means of an origin-destination study, it is determined that there are 2000 trips made between these communities every day. We define G = 2000/70,000 × 100 = 2.86, and b = 1. Then there are I_{ij} = 2.86[(8 × 50)(10 × 20)/100] = 228,800/100 = 2288 interactions between i and j on an average day.

Weights can be derived from many sources depending upon the problem needing solution. Composite indices may be used as weights where several variables are felt to be important. Likewise, distance may be measured on the basis of geography, culture, religion, race, or whatever else may tend to keep people apart. For example, Isard (1975, p. 43) cites a study made by the Netherlands Institute of Economics. This was an analysis of the interaction between

French-speaking and Flemish-speaking areas of Belgium. Telephone calls were observed between same-language areas at different geographic distances from one another, and it was found that distance could be predicted reliably by

$$I_{jk} = GP_j P_k / d_{jk} \qquad (12.7)$$

But when researchers examined data for calls originating in one language area and terminating in another, they found it necessary to use

$$I_{jk} = GP_j P_k / (2.8 d_{jk}) \qquad (12.8)$$

In other words, language differences increased effective distance by a factor of 2.8 times the geographic distance.

We can conclude that gravity models are quite versatile in helping the analyst to gain an insight into community-to-community interaction, no matter what may be influencing it.

Measures of Specialization

We have noted several times that the basic economic reason for the formation of communities is opportunity for specialization and trade. In order to analyze a community in this regard, it is necessary to determine a measure or "coefficient of specialization." Usually this is done by comparing employment or value added in certain "basic" industries of the community with some standard, such as a region or nation. It can also be done by using a certain time period in the community's own growth as the standard. As an example, the analyst may be interested in knowing how the community compares in employment in manufacturing with the immediate region. Calculation procedure is illustrated in Table 12.4.

TABLE 12.4. Calculation of a coefficient of specialization

All manufacturing	Percentage of total employment in all manufacturing Community	Region	Difference v. community and region Greater	Lesser
Food and kindred products	8.7	5.7	3.0	
Textile mill products	2.1	3.9		-1.8
Apparel	2.0	3.1		-1.1
Lumber and wood products	15.6	6.9	8.7	
Furniture and fixtures	8.3	1.1	7.2	
Paper and allied products	9.8	5.7	4.1	
Printing and publishing	5.0	5.6		-0.6
Chemicals and allied products	1.2	4.9		-3.7
Petroleum and coal products	0.0	0.3		-0.3
Rubber and plastics	1.5	4.2		-2.7
Leather and leather products	2.5	3.6		-1.1
Stone, clay and glass products	10.6	2.3	8.3	
Primary metal industries	0.5	4.4		-3.9
Fabricated metal products	7.5	7.2	0.3	
Machinery, except electrical	7.0	13.0		-6.0
Electrical equipment and supplies	8.2	12.6		-4.4
Transportation equipment	5.6	9.2		-3.6
All other	3.9	6.3		-2.4
Total	100.0	100.0	31.6	-31.6

The coefficient of specialization for the community is 31.6. Its manufacturing is much more specialized than is that of the region. From the table, areas of specialization are easily spotted, as are areas where other communities in the region are more specialized than this one.

Trade Area Boundaries
There are a number of ways to delineate a community's trading area. One way is to get origin and destination data from travelers. Highway planning agencies often collect this type of information; they ask for purpose of the trip, point of origin, and destination. Providing surveys have been conducted on all major routes about the community, it should be possible to sort out those people whose purpose was to trade. As one moves to survey points away from the community center, it should be possible to spot the points of indifference between it and other communities.

Another approach is to use Reilly's law of retail gravitation. This involves merely knowing the population of competing communities and the distance between them. Thus, for communities A and B located 30 km apart, assume the population of A is twice that of B. Then the square of the distance from A to the point of indifference should be twice the square of the distance from B to that point. In this case, the distance from A would be about 17.5 km and from B would be 12.5 km.

The analyst should recognize that these trade area boundaries only apply in a general way. When specific goods are considered, the hierarchical relationships intervene. That is, the more specialized the good or service, the larger the market required in order to offer it at all. Thus, for these goods, larger market areas (in terms of population) are required than for the more staple commodities and services.

POPULATION PROJECTIONS
Since human resources constitute the most important assets of a community and since people impinge upon the economy in so many different ways, the analyst finds very useful the data relating to numbers of people. One of the first tasks of a population projection is to review trends and try to get a fix on the future.

Many different techniques are utilized. In general, they are classified as either direct or indirect. Direct methods are extrapolations from past trends. Indirect methods try to explain population growth in terms of various causative factors, some of which are economic, others social and still others political in nature. Ansley Coale (1972), Nathan Keyfitz (1968), and S. Park (1970) discuss more sophisticated techniques than the ones included here.

Projection by extrapolation
Graphics. The graphic method is one of the simplist. It consists of plotting numbers against time for such years as information is

available, determining a trend line either by sight or least squares methods, and projecting the trend into the future. Where curves appear to be linear, plain coordinate (Cartesian) scales are used. Where curvilinear relationships seem to be present, plotting on semilogarithmic paper will convert to a straight-line relationship and will assist in projecting.

Graphic extrapolation necessarily assumes that relationships existing in past years, particularly those of the immediate past, will continue into the future. This assumption is valid only so long as there are no "turning points" or fluctuations that do not fit past trends.

Functional relationships. When the lines to be used for extrapolation are defined in mathematical terms, they can be expressed in terms of some law of growth that defines population as a function of time. Future changes are then expected to follow the same relationship. The major advantage over graphic methods is that the relationships may now be subjected to statistical tests. Another advantage is that refinements and modifications can be introduced. These are usually based on certain developments, such as changes in the birthrate, that can be anticipated in future years.

Polynomials are usually used for short-term projection. A polynomial is a sum of two or more algebraic terms, each of which consists of a constant multiplied by one or more variables raised to some nonnegative integral power. The first degree polynomial is a very simple function.

Define P as population and θ as number of years past some base year t. Then $P_{t+\theta} = P_t + f(\theta)$ where f reflects all the determining factors in population change. The first degree polynomial (straight line) takes the form (12.9).

$$P_{t+\theta} = a + b\theta \qquad (12.9)$$

Since a is the intercept, it represents the population as of the base year. The b represents the slope of the line drawn as the nearest explanation of past population trends.

If it is found that trends do not fit a straight line, it is necessary to use higher degree polynomials. These may be fitted by least squares also. For example, the parabola (second degree polynomial) requires three constants, $P_{t+\theta} = a + b\theta + c\theta^2$. If c is positive, the line is concave from above. If it is negative, the curve is convex from above. In either case, the rate of population change is smooth and continuous; but a concave curve implies growth size increments, whereas a convex curve implies decreasing growth.

The major objection to many of these curves is that when projections are to be made a considerable distance into the future, they continue toward infinity. Since all growth functions tend to have asymptotes, polynomials are useful for only a few years.

Possibly a little more accurate short-term projection can be made with an exponential curve. Exponential curves are of the form $P_{t+\theta} = ab^\theta$. Again a and b are constants. Data are also fitted to these curves by means of least squares. Malthus's famous theory of population growth used the equation $P_{t+\theta} = ae^{r\theta}$, where r was an assumed annual rate of change. One of the best-known of these curves was first developed to figure compound interest. When used to estimate population, it takes into account the fact that populations also compound themselves. This curve is of the form $P_{t+\theta} = P_t(1 + r)^\theta$ and is a straight line when plotted on semi-log paper. This curve also allows growth to go toward infinity.

By modifying the exponential, it is possible to introduce an asymptote, hence obtain a constant percentage decrease in absolute growth increments. For example, let k be an asymptote, $a < b < 1$, and $a < 0$. Then the curve $P_{t+\theta} = k + ab^\theta$ will limit growth, since it must approach zero as a limit at some value of θ.

The Gompertz curve describes a series in which growth increments of the logarithms are declining by a constant percent. It differs from the modified exponential in that it is asymptotic at both ends (S shaped in plain coordinates). This means that growth starts with small increments; in the next stage, they are increasing in size; and in the last period, they are decreasing.

Analysts find that most growth situations have this configuration, hence S-shaped curves are often referred to as growth curves. The Gompertz is considered to be especially realistic for a limited area, such as a community. Often population change will follow this pattern up to a certain level. It will stay at that general level for some time, then begin another growth curve.

These types of curves are especially useful to analysts, since they avoid the defects of polynomials and exponentials in forecasting impossible growth situations. The mathematical formula for the Gompertz is

$$\log P_{t+\theta} = \log k + (\log a)b^\theta \qquad (12.10)$$

where k represents the upper limit. The lower limit is 0.

The logistic curve is widely used in population research. It represents an even further modification of the exponential. It has the general mathematical form of $P_{t+\theta} = k/1 + e^{a+b\theta}$ and is usually fitted through three points, equidistant in time, selected from past history. The selection does not need to be random in any sense. Logistic curves are also S shaped. The major weakness is their dependence on the past for their general determinants. One application is to forecast a base population with a logistic curve and then add forecasts based on various scenarios of possible economic growth from which employment projections can be made and converted to population estimates.

Comparative methods. The comparative method was developed out of frustration concerning demographic information. The basic idea is that if the community being analyzed has social, political, and economic characteristics similar to another community or larger area at some time in its past, then one would expect it to develop in somewhat the same way. Thus, the forecast for community A is established by actual experience in community B.

A refinement of the comparative approach is to establish ratios that are then projected as functions of current and past ratios. The general mathematical form is

$$P_{t+\theta}/\hat{P}_{t+\theta} = f(P_t/\hat{P}_t, P_{t-1}/\hat{P}_{t-1}, \ldots, P_{t-n}/\hat{P}_{t-n}) \quad (12.11)$$

where P is population of the other area used for comparison, and $\hat{P}$ is population of the community of interest. Where forecasts of population of the pattern area (which may be the region in which the community exists) are available, these are utilized. If they do not exist, the forecaster will have to make these forecasts as well.

A modification of this method is to assume that there are relationships between the growth of population and some component of it or that of some other area. Employment is often used as an internal element, although the analyst may find some other measure more appropriate. Electrical meters and telephones are used, although there are serious problems in trying to obtain proper ratios. Employment at the national, state, provincial, or regional level may be utilized as an outside element, as may population growth in general or in particular, such as age groupings, race, and sex ratios.

Statistical techniques. Population growth for a given community may also be forecasted by use of regression and correlation or covariance analysis. A large number of causative relationships may exist in a community, including employment, investment, changes in exports, changes in birthrates and death rates, and migration patterns. If these relationships can be assumed to be approximately linear, the mathematical form is

$$P_{t+\theta} = a + b_1 x_1 + b_2 x_2 +, \ldots, + b_n x_n \quad (12.12)$$

where a, b are constant coefficients and x represents an independent variable.

If the relationships are nonlinear, a general form of the equation is

$$P_{t+\theta} = a + f_1(x_1) + f_2(x_2) +, \ldots, + f_n(x_n) \quad (12.13)$$

Where it is desirable to look at the impact of one factor separate from the rest, partial correlation techniques may be used. In order to use this approach, it is necessary to assume no change in causal relationships for future time periods. This may not be true, but it is a problem with all extrapolations. Further, it is necessary to assume that all deviations of the dependent variable from the regression line will be normally distributed with constant variance. In fact, this may not be true; observations used to establish the relationship may not be independent.

Of probably greater significance is the fact that it is not necessary to have a strong causal relationship to get a strong statistical indication. Actually, the causal relationship may be with other variables that are not even in the analysis if those variables are related to the dependent and independent ones in such a way as to bring about a statistically significant link. Analysts have to use considerable discernment in choosing variables for analysis.

Nonstatistical approaches. A number of fairly unsophisticated techniques are used in population forecasting. Generally, these involve the summing of changes in the major elements that influence growth, such as births, deaths, migration, and annexation or abandonment of territory. These are usually referred to as component methods.

In the age-cohort survival approach, differences in birthrates and death rates for various age, sex, and often, racial groups are considered. First, the natural increase of population is projected. This is done by first projecting birthrates for women in each age-group within the childbearing age category. Second, the numbers of women expected in each age-group is determined, which leads to an estimate of the number of live births. Third, numbers of surviving infants are calculated from infant mortality tables. (This gives the number reaching age one.) Other mortality tables are then used to estimate age-groups in future years.

This method ignores migration, which is all right so long as inflows and outflows of migrants are reasonably balanced within age-groupings. But large errors are possible when migration is an important factor in population change.

Where migration is important, it can be incorporated by adding births and in-migration to get an inflow component and deaths plus out-migration to get the outflow. In general the relationship is of the form

$$P_{t+\theta} = P_t + (aP_t + x) - (bP_t + y) \qquad (12.14)$$

where a is the birthrate during the period θ, b is the death rate during the period θ, x is in-migration during the period θ, and y is the out-migration during the period θ.

Actually, this becomes a system, since the forecast for each year becomes the basis for forecasting births and deaths in future years. In- and out-migration have to be forecasted based on factors determined by the analyst to influence such movement. The usefulness of the method is based, to a large degree, upon accuracy of forecasts of migration as well as birthrates and death rates.

Employment

Estimates of future employment are necessarily tied closely to population changes. First, the analyst must determine size of the potential labor force. This is done by utilizing estimates of population for the proper age-groups by sex. Next participation rates must be estimated for each of these groups. The result is a projection of labor force available to work. The next important factor is proportion of unemployment expected at each time period.

This is a tricky component to estimate. It involves trying to anticipate such things as cyclical and other shifts in the local economy, and the impact of new technology.

Since cycles in a community are closely related to cycles in larger economies, the analyst usually begins by looking at the larger area. However, there are peculiarities in each community, due to its industrial mix, that must be taken into account. This means the analyst must look most intensely at trends in the industries having the greatest effect on employment in the community. Beyond that, linkages of these industries to other units in the economy are important. This can be approached easily, if there is an input-output model available.

Income

Changes in income in a community may or may not be related to changes in employment. The U.S. Census delineates eight possible components of personal income, including:

1. Wages and salaries
2. Net farm self-employment income
3. Net nonfarm self-employment income
4. Interest, dividends, and other business income
5. Transfer payments (including retirement, unemployment insurance, gifts, and public assistance)
6. Nonmoney income "in kind"
7. Capital gains
8. Withdrawal of savings, insurance benefits, loans, and tax refunds

Only the first four are directly related to economic factors that lend themselves to forecasting. The rest are based on policy decisions or are types about which information is often difficult to obtain.

Methodologies for estimating both personal income and gross community product were discussed in the first part of this chapter. None of them includes all eight of these components as income. It is a prerogative of the analyst to determine what he or she wishes to include in personal income estimates.

SUMMARY

This chapter discusses methodologies commonly utilized in analyzing the economics of communities. It particularly emphasizes methods useful in analyzing economic structure (such as economic base and input-output models and measures of specialization), ways of determining trade area boundaries, and models for estimating population, employment, and income.

REVIEW QUESTIONS

1. What is the basic idea behind the "economic base" concept?
2. How does it tie into the multiplier concept?

3. What important ideas did Machlup contribute concerning the multiplier?
4. What is an economic base model?
5. Discuss two ways of defining basic and nonbasic activities.
6. What is a "location quotient"?
7. How is an economic base multiplier calculated?
8. What are some weaknesses and strengths of the economic base model?
9. How does the input-output model relate to the economic base concept?
10. What is the difference between an input-output model with technical and with local linkage coefficients?
11. How would one develop estimates of gross/product from a transactions table?
12. Differentiate between types of information to be gained by studying rows versus columns of a transactions matrix.
13. What is to be learned from input ratios? Output ratios?
14. Suppose that for the community described by the multipliers in Table 12.1 a new industry with the following local expenditure pattern was imminent: sector one, $100,000; sector two, $5000; sector three, $10,000; sector four, $100,000; sector five, $500,000. Ignoring any input from construction of a new plant, figure the probable impact of this industry on the community economy.
15. Why would analysts want to find substitutes for input-output models?
16. How would you go about finding out how specialized a given community is?
17. What are two ways of determining trade area boundaries? Can you think of any others?
18. Analyze the various methods of making population projections discussed in the text, taking into account both strengths and weaknesses.
19. Estimates and forecasts of employment and income are tied closely to estimates and forecasts of population. Why is this true? What special information do you need about population in order to use it for this purpose?

REFERENCES

American Society of Planning Officials. 1950. Population forecasting. *Planning Advisory Service Report 17*. New York: American Society of Planning Officials.

Bogue, I. J. 1950. A technique for making extensive population estimates. *Journal of the American Statistical Association* 45:149-63.

Bourque, P. J., and M. Cox. 1970. *An inventory of regional input-output studies in the United States*. Seattle: Univ. of Washington, Graduate School of Business, Occasional Paper 22.

Bramhall, D. F. 1960. Gravity potential and spatial interaction

models. In *Methods of regional analysis*, ed. W. Isard. Cambridge, Mass.: M. I. T. Press.
Braschler, C. H. 1972. A comparison of least squares multipliers with other methods. *Journal of Regional Science* 12:457-68.
Coale, A. J. 1972. *The growth and structure of human populations: A mathematical investigation*. Princeton, N.J.: Princeton Univ. Press.
Doeksen, G. A., and D. F. Schriner. 1974. *Interindustry models for rural development research*. Oklahoma State Univ., Agricultural Experiment Station Bulletin T-139.
Fouraker, L. E. 1955. A note on regional multipliers. *Papers and proceedings of the Regional Science Association*. 1:H-1 to H-*. Philadelphia: Regional Science Assoc.
Harmston, F. K. 1979. A case study of secondary impacts comparing through and vacationing travelers. *Journal of Travel Research* 19:18-20.
Harmston, F. K., and R. E. Lund. 1967. *Application of an input-output framework to a community economic system*. Columbia: Univ. of Missouri Press.
Isard, W. 1975. *Introduction to regional science*. Englewood Cliffs, N.J.: Prentice-Hall.
Keyfitz, N. 1968. *Introduction to the mathematics of population*. Reading, Mass.: Addison-Wesley.
Machlup, F. 1939. Period analysis and multiplier theory. *Quarterly Journal of Economics* 54:1-27.
Park, S. 1970. Least squares estimates of the regional employment multiplier. *Journal of Regional Science* 10:365-74.
Rogers, A. 1975. *Introduction of multiregional mathematical demography*. New York: Wiley.
Schmitt, R. C. 1954. An application of multiple correlation to population forecasting. *Land Economics* 30:277-78.
Seigel, J. S. 1953. Forecasting the population of small areas. *Land Economics* 29:72-88.
Sirkin, G. 1959. The theory of the economic base. *Review of Economics and Statistics* 41:426-29.
Smith, T. L., and P. E. Zapf, Jr. 1976. *Demography*. Sherman Oaks, Calif.: Alfred.
Snow, E. C. 1941. The application of the method of multiple correlation to the estimation of post-censal populations. *Journal of the Royal Statistical Society* 74:1-17.
Spiegelman, M. 1968. *Introduction to demography*. Cambridge, Mass.: Harvard Univ. Press.
Tiebout, C. M. 1962. *The community economic base study*. Committee for Economic Development, Supplementary Paper 16.
Department of Economic and Social Affairs. 1964. *Input-output bibliography, 1960-1963*. New York: United Nations.
Bureau of Census. *Current population reports, population estimates*. Service P-25, various years. Washington, D.C.: Government Printing Office.
Wolfe, M. 1955. The concept of economic sectors. *The Quarterly Journal of Economics* 69:402-20.

CHAPTER 13
Problems and Opportunities

The field of community economics has not been extensively examined despite the efforts of a few inspired individuals who recognize that most economic activity--most human interaction of every sort--occurs within some sort of community structure. The previous chapters have documented much of the information available. But there are many problems that need to be addressed, both in terms of understanding community economics and getting a grip on factors that will affect the future of communities. As usual, problems also present opportunities--for better research, more useful data, better contributions to public decision making and to growth and development of communities.

In this chapter we will look at problems and opportunities in terms of the units that form the basis for community development and growth as well as the macromilieu within which decisions are made.

THE HOUSEHOLD
Communities develop because people find that at some geographic point, they have common economic interests. These interests draw them together and cause them to develop economic units that have strong links to one another. Households, which are the most basic as well as most numerous of these units, will be considered first.

Economics has had little to say about the role of households. The first conference of any significance to address the subject of "the new home economics" was organized by T. W. Scultze in 1973. Becker's book *A Treatise on the Family*, was published in 1981 and provides the most theoretical approach attempted thus far. In order to understand community economics, it is very important that the role of the household be understood.

What Households Do
Households provide human services of many kinds. Some are

aimed at understanding the nature of the world and are provided by
people called scientists. Some are aimed at applying scientific
principles in the development of new products for consumption and
investment and are provided by people called technologists. Some
are aimed at the making and distribution of goods and are provided
by people called laborers.

Laborers vary in skill level from highly sophisticated professionals, through skilled operators of capital equipment, to very
low or unskilled workers. They provide most of the human service
contribution of the household.

The work of laborers is coordinated by managers who also coordinate the interface between human and nonhuman resources in general. Sometimes the coordinating function is subsumed into an entrepreneurial function that involves innovation, part of which is a
technological function. This serves to illustrate that under some
circumstances, the same person may provide more than one type of
service.

Each community has its own unique combination of households
whose members have the abilities delineated above. The character
of the community is heavily influenced by this mix. Generally
speaking, communities with the fewest problems are those whose
households operate at the highest levels of information. Communities with the most problems have high concentrations of people
with low skill levels.

Households as productive units. Households also operate as productive units, hiring labor at times, and producing goods and services
that may be consumed internally or traded to other households and
economic units. Thus, they operate similarly to the other economic
units in the community. The other units also produce some goods
and services that are used within the firm and for which there is
no market price. These are used as inputs to production, and the
resulting product is sold in the marketplace.

Some of the goods and services consumed in the household,
whether produced there or purchased from outside sources, are also
inputs to the production of human services. The problem with the
household is that it is the consumer of final products as well. If
the value of gross national product (GNP) were calculated accurately, it would identify the value of final products consumed by the
household.

Final products can either be investment or consumption goods.
Households make investments in terms of capital goods, land, or human resources. Thus, a given household may own a home and the land
upon which it is situated, have some rental property and/or some
stock in a corporation, and have a savings account. It may also be
paying for education of its members and for health services to keep
them productive.

The home produces a string of services consumed over time by
the family unit. The rental property produces a similar string of
services that are sold to final consumers. The stocks represent
ownership of capital goods of various kinds. The savings account

also represents, to some degree, the ownership of capital and land. The healthy, educated people are human resources.

In addition to the house, households may own other consumer durables, such as automobiles, furniture, appliances, and lawnmowers that represent investments in consumer goods. However, these consumer goods can also produce trade goods. For example, a household member may use the lawnmower to mow other people's lawns for pay. Household commuters may haul other commuters in the family automobile for a fee. The family may take in boarders.

In less developed countries, the household may produce a very large proportion of goods and services consumed by members of the unit. In communities occupied by these families, trading relationships will be quite minimal.

Problems Due to Lack of Understanding

It is difficult to make comparisons among communities of the world because of differences in household participation. It is also difficult because of a paucity of information concerning households. We do not have good theoretical models of household activity, hence our community models are lacking an important ingredient.

In setting up intersectoral models to picture the internal economic workings of the community and to identify multiplier effects, we tend to treat investment in capital goods as an exogenous inflow of funds. But investment in consumer goods, with the possible exception of houses, is generally treated inside the model as though the goods were consumed in the year of purchase. Investment in human "capital" is usually handled the same way. For example, expenditures for education and health services are considered to be 100 percent consumption.

Microeconomics, in general, tends to treat the household as made up of consumers of final products. The whole field of consumer demand is based on the idea of individual utility functions. Although the household is also viewed as the owner of resources, input into these resources, from consumption of such things as food, has been ignored. Not even Becker (1981) treats this aspect of family life.

Lack of good information has led model builders to make rather arbitrary decisions with regard to the role of the household. Since there are no good statistical techniques for separating goods that are inputs from those that are final consumption goods, models tend to treat households in the community as though all goods and services purchased and consumed were inputs to the production of human services. Goods and services produced within the households are ignored completely. Those entering the market are often treated as links to other microunits, when information is available concerning them.

The discipline of home economics, which antedates economics in general, would naturally be looked to as a source of information concerning the household. Ben-Porath (1982) who is himself somewhat of a pioneer in this area, has given us a fine review of Becker's work along with contributions of others. He hails Becker as the "uncontested intellectual leader of what has become known as the 'new household (or home) economics.'" The books is a "treatment of (a) the allocation of roles and resources and distribution of income within families; (b) the formulation, dissolution, growth, and structure of families; and (c) the implications of these analyses for inequality and social mobility" (pp. 52-53). All of these subjects are important to the understanding of communities, but they represent only a beginning. As Hannan (1982) has pointed out, the methods of collection and analysis of data on households has outrun the theory. Although Becker has pulled together much existing theory, it has its weaknesses; and further, it tends to focus exclusively on within-household relationships.

These relationships are important, but households interact strongly with other units, and the impact of within-household decisions on the community in general needs exploration. Further, institutions probably impact heavily on intrafamily decision making. All of these phenomena need study.

Role of Information

In addition to problems created by lack of information about households, there are problems because of lack of understanding of the role information plays in the activities of human beings. The ability of the human brain to ingest, analyze, and use information is basic to all human progress. The strength of households is dependent upon the strength of its members and the strength of the members depends upon information possessed and used by them.

Communities are only as strong as the households within them. Conventional production theory treats human resources as though all productive change depends upon the physical presence or absence of workers. When a shift is made to a more sophisticated production method, it is said to be a move toward capital intensity. In recent years, it has become common to infer that this includes both physical and human capital; but if any information change is involved, it is called technology. The latter has become a catchall word for all information change, rather than the very precise meaning other scientists and engineers tend to give it. Actually, technology is a specialized branch of information.

The result of all this manipulation is that the models treat labor in terms of quantity, but never in terms of quality. In fact, quality is also somewhat ignored in the case of capital, since the models generally handle both labor and capital in physical terms. Technology is added as an afterthought.

The fact that all analysts will admit, when cornered, is that technological developments result in better designed capital and that the productivity of this capital depends upon the skills of those operating and maintaining it. Overall, the interface between capital and labor is enhanced by coordinational skills of management.

When a new, more productive, human-nonhuman unit is substituted for a lower information unit, both the old capital and the old labor become obsolete. Those workers who fail to be retrained and employed in the higher level jobs, for whatever reason, remain unemployed. The old capital can be junked, but the old workers are still a part of the community work force. Their problem becomes the community's problem.

Unemployment is always a serious community problem. But this kind of unemployment is more insidious than that which develops because of a recession or other economic aberration, because it is not solved when the problem that caused it goes away. New economic theory is needed to guide decision making with regard to human obsolescence. It appears most logical that the theory must be based on a better understanding of the way information changes impact on productive activity.

Those engaged in community development must be especially aware of the need for equilibrium between the technological level of capital and the skill level of labor. If the objective is to create jobs for people with low skill levels, the wooing of high technology industry may contribute nothing to a solution. On the other hand, where workers are skilled or capable of becoming skilled, the introduction of low technology industry may waste human resources.

In many communities of developed and underdeveloped parts of the world, people of relatively low skill level are capable of handling more sophisticated capital than they have available to them. The furnishing of an "appropriate technology" under these circumstances becomes a major challenge.

Role of Population Shifts

In general, people migrate to improve their situations. Such improvement may include higher pay, but it does not have to. Many other factors cause people to move. Some of these are: safety, lower living costs, less congestion, access to more services, nearness to relatives, better government, or better recreational opportunities. Often, just the perception that things will get better faster in the new place causes a move.

According to the United Nations' report on world population (1977), "ever since the last century, the percentages of urban population in total population have been rising in a progression that started in a few countries then spread to some others and by now (1973) has come to embrace the whole world; the eventual outcome of this revolution in human settlement patterns is not yet within sight. As a combined consequence of accelerated general growth, and rising urbanization levels, the urban population itself is now growing with exceptional speed" [about 4 percent per annum]. The report goes on to point out that in the more developed parts of the world, the urbanization trend has extended over a much longer period than in undeveloped areas and is now beginning to recede. In the underdeveloped areas, the trend toward urbanization started rather precipitously in the 1950s and is still under way.

The use of the terms "urban" and "rural" with regard to migration simply specifies that people move from communities where interaction with other communities is less intense to those where it is more intense. Ostensibly, the more intense environment creates greater opportunities for attaining whatever the migrant is seeking.

Urban regions are made up of a number of diverse kinds of communities. Some are highly affluent, some are holes of poverty, and others are in between. New migrants are most likely to end up in the poor communities, unless they bring with them skills, and/or contacts to help them move in more affluent circles. Without extensive cooperation from the more affluent communities, the rapidly expanding poorer ones can create many environmental and social problems for the urban region. In order to avoid those problems, the urban region must provide jobs at least as fast as the population expands and preferably at a faster pace to keep up with people's aspirations. Further, the jobs need to be matched (on an informational level) with the possible skill levels of the unemployed and underemployed population, many of whom will be in-migrants.

Job opportunities. One of the advantages that urban communities have over rural ones is the multiplicty of job opportunities. Sometimes analysts take this quite literally and view the entire region as a single, large labor market. But, in fact, it may be made up of a number of small markets, owing to transportation costs. For people with very low wage rates, commuting costs can create major constraints.

Often, subsidized bus systems are used to move people from low skill level labor-exporting communities to areas where jobs are available. This works best when jobs are located together so that a large number of people can be unloaded at one terminal spot without causing problems in getting to the proper place of employment. Even with subsidies, commuting costs can be a burden, if the distance from home to work is very far.

But the problem of matching the labor-exporting community with the labor-importing one is minor compared to the problem of moving resources into production, so as to provide the necessary jobs. In underdeveloped parts of the world, a shortage of investment funds is a perennial problem. A shortage of entrepreneurial talent may be equally as great a barrier. Where there are potential entrepreneurs, a shortage of information concerning opportunities may inhibit growth. Lack of an adequate social infrastructure in terms of roads, railroads, and efficient postal and telephone services can also inhibit economic expansion. Good industrial sites need these plus others such as good drainage, sewerage, water, electricity, gas, rail sidings, and adequate safety.

In developed countries, there is often a movement to influence industrial movement to low skill, labor-export communities, such as the urban ghetto, by means of subsidies. But location of industries of any size in a city that was not designed to accommodate trucks, where land costs are high and land area is limited, where government services, such as fire and police, are inadequate, where sewer and water systems are old or obsolete; and where agglomeration economies from the existence of other industries in proximity are missing, would require subsidies far beyond the aspirations of even the most liberal legislator.

There is the added factor that the kinds of routine jobs that can be done by low skilled labor can be done better by robots.

There are, of course, low skill jobs in the service industries, but service industries are heavily market oriented and tend to be close to the people who use the service. The market for services in a ghetto is a limited one, at best.

The ultimate salvation for the urban migrant must be in training for higher skill levels and the provision of jobs at those levels. Education and training are of little value, unless jobs are available. In underdeveloped areas, this must be preceded by an appropriate technology approach to jobs, matching new jobs to existing skill levels. Raising the skill levels of large groups of people is a long-term affair, requiring extensive resources.

In the developed part of the world, education and training must get underway immediately. The alternative is the presence of a large number of obsolete human resources having no role to play in the economic system. Despite our tendency to downplay the value of work and emphasize the value of leisure, there is a great deal of value in having a meaningful role to play in society.

Government as employer. It is often suggested that the government should step in and provide jobs if the private sector cannot do so. There is a major difference between a "make work" job and one that provides a needed service. The challenge to government, therefore, is to provide meaningful work that produces a needed good or service to persons who may be left behind by a rapidly expanding information explosion. This applies also to developing countries who aspire to the latest technology in capital, which requires the highest skill level in labor. In a region with low information base people, this approach means widespread unemployment, even though the GNP may be growing. As an employer of last resort, government has a tremendously important challenge.

Rural in-migration. In some developed countries, there has been a reversal of the trend to move from rural to urban areas. The reasons for this have not always been apparent. A study of migrants to nonmetropolitan high growth areas in the midwestern United States reveals that the migrants were motivated by a wide variety of social and environmental considerations, of which employment was a minor issue (Whiting 1980, p. 21). Eighty percent of those sampled moved near (67 percent) or into (33 percent) towns with less than 5000 population. About 60 percent of the total were moving from central city communities of urban regions rather than suburbs. Many of them were originally from rural communities, however. The sample also suggested that the in-migrants were younger than the indigent population of the receiving communities.

This type of in-migration creates many new opportunities for growth and development in the receiving communities. In-migrants bring with them training and talents, a certain amount of funds, new ideas for economic activity, and so on. Their impact is usually quite evident in new construction and the provision of new goods and services in the community.

Retiree migration. While evidence suggests that most urban-to-rural migrants are not retirees, there is also evidence of some movement of retirees to rural areas. Retirees who move also have a number of different types of motivation. Some are returning to the place they grew up. Others are seeking a quiet place to retire, or one with the right kinds of recreation opportunities, or one where they will feel safe or where there are other retirees.

They bring to the community some skills and resources. But mostly they bring an influx of new funds. In-migrants in general tend to be more affluent than those who do not move. Retirement pay is a flow of basic income to the community. Research indicates that the multiplier effect of retiree expenditures compares quite favorably with that of expenditures in a rural community by farmers and other operators of export businesses (Harmston 1981).

Role of Population Growth

The world population doubled, from 2 billion to 4 billion, between 1945 and 1980, a span of 35 years. It is expected to double again by the early years of the twenty-first century. The reasons are that mortality is declining; fertility rates are high; marriage age in many countries is low; populations are young; and the number of women in or approaching the childbearing age is growing rapidly (World Bank 1981, p. 102).

A United Nations' report notes that despite the much more rapid growth in urban populations in the less developed regions of the world, the population gain in the rural areas between 1970 and 1975 was even larger (1977, p. 112). As a point of interest, the latter were growing at a speed as high as that of urban areas in the developed world (1.7 percent per year). In developed areas, rural population was declining by 1.0 percent per year prior to recent developments.

A comparison has been made of birthrates and death rates for industrial countries, middle income (developing) countries, and two regions of low income countries. In low income countries, crude birthrates fell from 45 to 37 per thousand between 1960 and 1979, and death rates fell from 24 to 15 per thousand. Over the same period, in middle income countries, birthrates fell from 41 to 34 per thousand, and death rates from 15 to 10 per thousand. Thus, in the former, birthrates were down 18 percent but death rates declined by 38 percent; and in the latter, birthrates dropped 17 percent and death rates dropped 33 percent. In the industrial countries, the birthrate change is slowing and the death rate change is rising. Death rate declines in the underdeveloped world are also slowing down. In many places most of the decline came as a result of campaigns against diseases, such as malaria and cholera. Further declines will have to be achieved by improvements in such areas as nutrition, sanitation, water supplies, and health services in general.

The World Bank (1981, p. 108) concludes that poverty and population growth are interrelated. That is, poverty can be attacked by attacking its concomitants (such as poor health, lack of education, and lack of equal status for women), which in turn will contribute to economic growth. On the other hand, economic growth, accompanied by family planning services, helps slow down population growth.

Growing populations provide both opportunities and problems. A community can develop without population expansion by increasing production and income per family. It can also develop by expanding to serve a market made larger by population growth. Population growth without expanded production means lower per capita income and probably some increase in unemployment and underemployment. If there is to be control of population growth, it has to be initiated at the national level; there is little the community can do. It must, however, live with the consequences, one way or the other.

INFORMATION REVOLUTION

The developed world has been engulfed in an information revolution since the 1940s. New information has been attained in the sciences, applications of scientific knowledge to the development of new products has expanded, and the computerization of nearly every facet of our lives has made gathering, processing, and use of information unbelievably swift and accurate. Nearly every scientific field has been significantly affected by the information developed and the efficiency by which it can now be handled.

A myriad of new products has appeared for our use. Many others are just beginning to appear. Futurist oriented persons who work with scenarios present many different options for the household and communities of the future. Generally speaking, it is expected that new efficiencies in communications will make it possible to perform many work tasks from our homes. This will change quite drastically the function of the household and its linkages to other economic units.

New Uses for Space

One of the most significant outcomes of the information revolution has been our exploration and utilization of space. With the space shuttle now a proven possibility, the probability is high of establishing economic units in space to take advantage of its unique attributes. Space communities within the foreseeable future are not only possible but highly likely. These communities will need to be very carefully planned because they will be carrying the attributes of earth (such as gravity, horizons, plants, animals, air, and water) into a completely foreign environment.

The economics of a space community will be no different from the economics of an earth community. The community will specialize in certain goods, for which it will have comparative advantages, and will trade them with other communities on earth, the moon, or whatever else trade ties may be established. Within the community, there will be very heavy trade interrelationships as people produce and distribute goods to satisfy needs of the local market. Prices will perform their usual roles of allocating resources and facilitating trade.

ENERGY

One of the probable exports from space communities to earth

will be solar energy, in the form of electricity or some other form. As an outcome of the information revolution there will likely be many other energy sources in the future. It is very likely that one day we will hail OPEC countries as our benefactors for making us see our existence in a world of abundant, artificially cheap energy as precarious and rather stupid. Addressing our energy needs has always been an inevitable necessity.

There are two ways we can approach the energy crisis. The first and easiest is conservation. This approach could affect communities by making them more compact, since energy conservation would argue that we need to be closer together. We would have town houses rather than single family dwellings. Our business districts would all be within huge shopping malls. Some planners would enclose the whole community under one roof.

The other alternative is to find better sources of energy. If, for example, the problem of electricity storage can be solved, it may be more efficient for us to be spread out. Each house could have its battery of solar cells and generate its own energy. Whichever way it goes, we can be sure that energy will have long run impacts on community structure.

In the short run, we have to live with expensive energy. This has led to the growth and development of energy resource producing communities. Oil towns and coal towns have had a new surge of activity. Many new communities have been established to exploit newly discovered or developed deposits. This will probably continue for some time. These new communities are built around operations utilizing the newest capital designs and highest skills of operation, maintenance, and coordination.

NEW PRODUCTS

The information revolution guarantees there will be many new products in the future. New products impact on communities in several ways. For one, they present new opportunities for growth. For another, they cause obsolescence and sudden changes in factory location. Those concerned with having a viable community economy must be alert to new developments that could affect it. Complacency, in a rapidly changing world, can be deadly.

The economic units that make up an economy are owned and operated by people. Some of them live in the community and own community oriented assets. Some of them do not live in the community, and their assets are company oriented; decisions regarding their use are aimed at maximizing the welfare of the company. The local economy may figure only peripherally in the making of a decision.

New products come from fertile minds of technologically trained and oriented individuals. All of them live in one community or another. A very large proportion of products are produced originally in the hometown of the inventor. New services also originate in individual minds, and represent opportunities for growth and development. Health services is one example of a rapidly growing industry. In addition, existing goods and services can form the basis for local growth where someone sees an opportunity opening up.

Not all opportunities are related to the private sector. Government installations are also growth components. In a dymanic world, the functions and location of government units also change.

SUMMARY

Communities develop because people see certain advantages to living close together. Thus, the basic unit of a community is the household and the local economy is heavily influenced by decisions made within households. To understand community economics, we need better understanding of the household and its role in the economy.

The most important single attribute of human beings is ability to utilize information. Thus, understanding the role information plays in economic life is crucial to understanding the effective use of resources. The information revolution is upon us, and as economists, we have yet to develop a useful set of theories to explain the nature of the world it is producing.

In addition to these attributes of persons and households, population shifts and population growth are important in the economics of communities. Death rates are declining but still lie somewhat below birthrates everywhere in the world. In the past, high death rates have served to keep population in check. They no longer perform that function. If we are going to change the control mechanism, we need to do something with the growth mechanism.

REFERENCES

Becker, G. S. 1981. *A treatise on the family*. Cambridge, Mass.: Harvard Univ. Press.

Ben-Porath, Y. 1982. Economics and the family-match or mismatch? A review of Becker's "A treatise on the family." *Journal of Economic Literature* 20:52-64.

Hannan, M. T. 1982. Families, markets and social structures: An essay on Becker's "A treatise on the family." *Journal of Economic Literature* 20:65-72.

Harmston, F. K. 1981. A study of the economic relationships of retired people and a small community. *Regional Science Perspectives* 11:42-56.

U.N. Department of Economic and Social Affairs. 1977. *World population prospects as assessed in 1973*. New York: United Nations.

Whiting, L. R., ed. 1980. *Rebirth of rural America: Rural migration in the midwest*. Ames, Iowa: North Central Regional Center for Rural Development.

World Bank. 1981. *World development report 1981*. New York: Oxford Univ. Press.

INDEX

Activity measures, 166. *See also* Program budgeting
Administration principle, 93. *See also* Separation principle
Advertising, 198; elasticity of, 202; and utility, 202
Age-cohort survival methods, 311
Agglomeration: diseconomies of, 7, 113, 117; economies of, 7, 85-86, 113-16; and Lösch, 92; and pollution, 12; and Weber, 75. *See also* Internal economies of scale; Transfer economies
Attitude, 210, 212-14. *See also* Regional differences; Social structure
Automobiles, impact of, 277

Bankers, and economic growth, 267
Basic income, 6, 49; and exports, 45; turnover of, 36. *See also* Exogenous relationships
Barter, 23
Baumol-Ide model, 148
Benefit-cost analysis. *See* Benefit determination; Cost determination; Criterion problem

Benefit determination, 185-86
Beutler-Owen model, 209-10
Birthrates, 322
Budget: community system of, 163-65; constraints of, 199; as information source, 165
Budgeting: policy of, 160; and Samuelson model, 160-61. *See also* Program budgeting
Business firms: location of, 146, 148. *See also* Baumol-Ide model; Reilly's law of retail gravitation; Richardson's equilibrium model

Capital: circulating, 226; effects of, 234; fixed, 226; goods, 198; investment of, 32; supportive, 240; and underdeveloped areas, 268
Catal Mound, 23, 24
Central business district, 9
Central place theory, 76
Change: concept of, 226; and diversification, 250; and dual economy, 254-60; and economies of size, 248; and firms, 251; and governments, 253; and industrial structure, 248; and money, 247; and production, 226; and social systems, 254

Collective: decision-making, 156; and utility function, 156
Common economic interest, 4
Community: bankers, 267; budget, 163; Catal Mound, 24; commercial ventures, 158; cooperation, 18, 277; credit, 268; definition of, 4: differences, 276; interdependence, 6, 264; location of, 75, 85; matrix of, 47, 49; multiplier, 5, 36, 47, 62, 296, 298; open economy model, 44; planning of, 17; rural, 6, 276; urban, 9, 276; structure of, 296. See also Money, circulation; Multipliers
Community economies: and labor cost, 246; and price changes, 245; and substitutions, 243
Community model: and change, 62; and exports, 48; and investment, 48; and leakage, 47; and price changes, 62; stability of, 62; uses of, 63
Community planning, 273-76. See also Planned communities
Comparative methods, 309
Competition: among communities, 7, 276
Complementarity: of capital and labor, 233; of materials and energy, 242
Concentric zone theory, 137-38
Cost determination, 185
Costs and benefits, 13, 183-84. See also Benefit cost analysis; Marginal costs and benefits
Counterflows, 23
Crime, 9-11
Criteria, 13, 134, 158
Criterion problem, 187-88

Death rates, 322
Debt financing, 171
Demand: elasticity of, 94; and freight rates, 97; and product differentiation, 96; and taste changes, 203

Descarte's ovals, 103
Demand cone, 88-89
Demand curve, 146
Development: and capital, 241; and diversification, 250; and dual economy, 254; and firms, 251; and investment, 238-39; and land, 241; and material and energy, 242; and obsolescence, 240; and price changes, 245; and resources, 237; and social systems, 254. See also Government action
Discontinuities: in communities, 266; in small firms, 267
Discrimination: economics of, 281-89; employer, 282-89; and human resources, 284; solutions to, 290
Distribution, 27-28. See Marketing
Diversification, 250
Dual economy, 8, 254
Dynamic processes, 81-83. See also Central place theory; Range of central good

Economic activity: and product differentiation, 96-97
Economic advantage, 3
Economic base, 296-97
Economic growth: and discontinuities, 266; and innovation, 32, 264; and input-output, 299; and money, 267; and problems, 269; and skill, 237
Economic man, 26
Economics. See Spatial economics
Economics of community: and discontinuities, 266; and dual economy, 254-60; and energy, 242; and firm's decisions, 251; and inputs, 242; and location, 136; and money, 267-69; and prices, 245; and shortages, 243; and spatial theory, 67
Economic system, 23, 289
Economic units, 3, 28. See

Index 329

also Households
Economies of scale. *See* Agglomeration
Economies of size: and change, 245; and growth, 249; and promotion, 249; and specialization, 249
Economy: local, 37; closed, 39; open, 44
Education, 218
Elasticity: and advertising, 202; cross, 201; income, 201; and local demand, 94; and nonlocal demand, 94; and price, 94, 200
Employer discrimination, 272-89
Employment projections, 311
Enclaves. *See* Discrimination; Economic system
Endogenous relationships, 4, 37, 45, 270. *See also* Multipliers
Energy: definition of, 227; and production, 242; and space, 323. *See also* Inputs
Engel curves, 202
Equimarginal principle, 198
Exchange, 3
Exogenous: activities, 38; relationships, 4, 37, 270. *See also* Basic income
Expenditures. *See* Public expenditures
Exponential curves, 308
Exports, 5, 54, 298
External economies of scale, 116. *See also* Agglomeration; Urbanization economies

Factors, 37
Firms: and community, 252; and decision making, 251; and innovation, 250; managers of, 251; multiunit, 251; as productive units, 251
Flows, 5
Freight rates, 96, 105. *See also* Transport costs
Functional relationships, 308

Goals and subgoals, 184, 253

Gompertz curves, 309
Goods, 152-56. *See also* Public goods
Government action: development by, 253-54
Graphic extrapolation, 308
Gravity, 91, 304-6
Growth, 276

Home production, 207-9. *See also* Beutler-Owen model
Households: and community strength, 318; location of, 140; and production, 208, 316; problems of, 317; role of, 315. *See also* Von Thünen (Wingo) model; Yamada's model
Housing, 17, 289
Human-nonhuman: equilibrium, 231, 318; resources, 209; units, 207
Human resources: deepening of, 234; and information, 210, 234, 318; investment in, 284; nature of, 210; and production, 227. *See also* Information and human resources; Population

Imports: and exports, 5; and labor, 277; and raw material, 25; relationships of, 63; replacement of, 63
Income protections, 312
Income taxes: and dividend policy, 178; and equity, 169; and government, 169; and inhouse financing, 178
Indifference functions, 199
Industrial process, 74
Industry: distribution of, 70; location, 71; structure of, 248
Information, human resources: and attitudes, 212, 213; and discrimination, 282-85; and intelligence, 210, 215; and migration decisions, 219; and skills, 211-14
Information, location, 130, 135, 136, 140

Information base, 8, 210, 229-37
Information revolution, 323
Inheritance tax. See Property taxes
Innovation: and community interdependence, 264; and efficiency, 265; and growth, 264; and industry, 248; and monopoly, 248; and regional center and hinterland, 265; and rural communities, 265; and transportation conformation, 265
Input-output: and disclosure, 48; and Hawkins-Simons conditions, 46; and microunits, 47; model of, 39, 41, 298-302; relationships of, 5
Inputs: coefficients of, 41, 46; and propensity to buy, 46; and shortages, 243; and technical vs. local, 37; and technology, 243. See also Complementarity; Energy; Labor; Raw materials; Semifinished goods; Services; Substitution
Intercommunity: impact of, 64; models of, 63; relationships of, 31
Intergovernmental transfers, 170
Intermediate goods, 41, 198
Internal economies of scale, 114, 116. See also Agglomeration
Intersectoral: patterns of, 26, 28, 31, 37
Intracommunity: relationships of, 25, 31
Inverse, 54
Isodapanes, 75, 83
Isovectures, 83

Labor: characteristics of, 27, 218, 318; coefficient of, 74; export of, 9, 277, 320; import of, 277, 320; and obsolescence, 232; orientation of, 74; as resource, 8. See also Information base; Inputs; Location; Migrant characteristics; Migration; Population

Lancaster model, 203-6
Land: community ownership of, 180; and primitive society, 24; and production, 227; and profits, 147; rent of, 69; as social resource, 179; and taxes, 167. See also Property taxes
Law of market areas, 100, 102-4
Leakage, 42, 49
Linear programming, 302-4
Linkages: backward, 39; development of, 38; forward, 39; in monetary terms, 36; as multipliers, 36; in production, 266. See also Input-output
Location: and business firms, 146, 168; and decision, 130; and households, 140; index of, 71; and labor, 74; and prices, 74, 94; and quotients, 297; and trends, 11; and triangle, 70, 71
Locational index, 119
Locational patterns, 87. See also Spatial order
Logistic curve, 309

Manufacturing, 7
Marginal costs and benefits, 15, 156
Marginal revenue product, 246
Martinal utility, 162
Market: context of, 100; overlap of, 105-6; as place, 101; types of, 107. See also Nonspatial market; Product differentiation; Spatial market
Market analogy, 155
Market areas: arbitrary delineation of, 105; law of, 100; shape of, 87, 88. See also Demand cone; Spatial economics
Marketing: and barter economy, 23
Market principle, 77-79, 90. See also Central place theory
Markets: export, 39; local, 39; services, 76

Market size, 76
Maximum social gain, 184
Metropolitan patterns, 91
Migrant characteristics, 220-21. *See also* Labor; Migration; Population
Migration, 8, 219, 317; causes of, 219; retiree, 321; rural, 220, 321; urban, 220. *See also* Information; Labor; Migrant characteristics; Population
Money: and barter, 33; and change, 247; circulation of, 5; and counting, 34; and imports and exports, 34; price of, 247; and price system, 34; and resources, 247; and specialization, 34; and trade, 34; turnover of, 38
Moses model, 118-31
Multiple nuclei, 139-40
Multiplier concept, 43
Multipliers: advantages of, 44; calculation of, 39, 42; defined, 5; disaggregated vs. aggregated, 37; economic base model, 296; in enclaves, 289; input-output model, 298; limitations of, 44; overall, 54, 298; sectoral, 54; use, 44, 55, 63. *See also* Input-output; Turnover

Natural resources. *See* Raw materials
New communities. *See* Planned communities
Nodal points, 97
Nonspatial market: and imperfect competition, 108; and oligopoly, 108-9; and perfect competition, 107; and perfect monopoly, 108

Obsolescence, 240
Optimization, 199

Payroll taxes: and unionization, 170
People: characteristics of, 198; as consumers, 198-206; as consumer-producers, 207-10; innovative, 264. *See also* Home production; Human-nonhuman; Human resources; Labor; Migrant characteristics; Migration; Population
Planned communities, 270-72
Pollution, 12; and growth, 269; and regulation, 193; and solutions, 12; and spillover costs, 177
Pollution control, 193-94
Polynomials, 308
Population: age of, 216; density of, 8; growth of, 322; and pollution, 12; projections of, 307; and racial and ethnic differences, 217; sex of, 216; socioeconomic characteristics of, 218. *See also* Migration
Poverty: and housing, 18; and population growth, 322; and productive capability, 233
Preference revelation in communities: and budgets, 164; and natural monopolies, 157; voluntary, 157
Preference revelation in households: Beutler-Owen model, 209; characteristics, positive desire for, 204; completeness of, 204; continuity of, 204; quasi-ordering of, 204; strict convexity of, 204; transitivity of, 204; utility, maximization of, 204
Pressure groups, 157, 159, 163, 164, 253
Price changes, 199, 245
Price controls: and black market, 192; economics of, 191; and marginal cost pricing, 192; and rent control, 191; and utility prices, 193
Prices: differences in, 74; FOB vs. CIF, 69, 89, 94; and freight costs, 94; and multipliers, 62. *See also* Elasticity

Private morality regulation, 189
Problems: and economic growth, 269; and opportunities, 315; and rural communities, 7; and urban communities, 9. *See also* Crime; Dual economy; Housing; Location, trends; Pollution; Transportation; Unemployment
Product differentiation, 96
Production: definition of, 226; frontiers of, 238-39; and intangibles, 226; and intermediate goods, 226; processes of, 234; and sets, 235; and space, 235; and tangibles, 226. *See also* Capital; Human resources; People; Raw materials
Production function: definition of, 228; and frontier shift, 238; and quality factor, 228; and resource use, 237; and simple economy, 228-29. *See also* Human-nonhuman
Products, 324
Program budgeting: as information source, 165; multiyear planning of, 166
Projection, 307
Property taxes: and inheritance tax, 179; and labor costs, 179; and local revenue, 168; and penalization, 179; and regressivity, 168. *See also* Land, taxes
Public expenditures, 182-83
Public goods, 153-54, 290
Public ownership of business, 158
Public sector: and spillover, 176, 178, 183, 193. *See also* Costs and benefits; Public expenditures; Taxation
Public services, 17, 18

Queuing: economics of, 195; and pricing, 16, 160; and rapid transit, 16

Range of central good, 82-83
Rapid transit, 16
Raw materials: imports of, 25; and production, 242. *See also* Inputs
Regional differences: and change, 213; and productivity, 214; and utility functions, 214; and workers, 214
Reilly's law of retail gravitation, 147
Resources: allocation of, 161; and expansion, 237; and goals, 253; indivisibility of, 249; and money, 247; and planning, 272; and resource differences, 97; and services, 249. *See also* Human resources; Natural resources
Revenue: for communities, 167. *See also* Debt financing; Income taxes; Payroll taxes; Property taxes; Sales taxes
Richardson's equilibrium model, 146-47
Rural communities: agricultural, 6; and distance, 6, 7; and diversification, 7; and inmigration, 321; mineral based, 7; problems of, 7, 8; and urban, 276

Sales taxes, 168-69, 180
Samuelson model, 160-61
Sectors: definition of, 25; at Catal Mound, 29; and linkages, 28; endogenous and exogenous, 49
Sector theory, 138-39
Semifinished goods: production of, 242. *See also* Inputs
Semipublic goods: payments for, 160
Separation principle. *See* Administration principle; Central place theory
Services: as exports, 270; as inputs, 244; and production, 245; and products, 244; public, 155
Shortages, 243

Single nucleus, 139
Social structure: and class, 212; and discrimination, 213, 281; and extended family, 212; and geographic proximity, 213; and land ownership, 212; and poverty, 214
Space: new uses for, 323
Spatial cost curve, 122-26
Spatial economics, 102. *See also* Law of market areas
Spatial market: equilibrium of, 101; and imperfect polypoly, 109; and oligopoly, 110-12; and perfect polypoly, 109
Spatial order, 87
Spatial structure: and cost decisions, 136. *See also* Concentric zone theory; Sector theory; Single nucleus; Multiple nuclei
Specialization, 3; measures of, 306; and size of, 249
Spillover effects: and bidding, 183; and crime, 9; and housing, 18; and large companies, 266; and private activity, 176; and subsidies, 177. *See also* Public sector
Standard of living: and pollution, 12
States of nature, 131-32
Statistical techniques, 310
Subsidies, 159, 253, 268
Substitution: and community economies, 243; principle of, 84; and production, 242; short and long term, 243
System: economic, 3

Taxation: and communities, 178; and development, 253; and equity, 181; and individuals, 178. *See also* Income taxes; Property taxes; Sales taxes
Taxes. *See* Revenue
Technologists and growth, 239
Technology, 82; appropriate, 232; and capital, 233; and innovation, 31; and input, 243; and Lancaster model, 203
Town settlement, 86-87. *See also* Agglomeration, economies of
Trade area: boundaries, 307
Trading: and value standards, 25
Transfer economies, 113-14
Transfer payments, 5
Transportation: and choice of materials, 72; and distance, 68; and industry orientation, 72; and land rent, 68; urban, 14; and weight, 70
Transportation principle, 80, 91. *See also* Central place theory
Transport costs, 82, 85; absorption of, 94-95, 105; and plant location, 117; and rent, 147. *See also* Freight rates; Transfer economies
Transport networks, 113
Transport nodes, 85
Transport rates: and market structure, 102; nonuniform, 73; and optimal location, 73
Turnover: and integration, 38. *See also* Linkages

Ubiquitous inputs, 117
Unemployment, 9, 319
Urban communities: definition of, 9; problems of, 9; and rural, 276, 320; and suburban, 9. *See also* Labor; Problems
Urbanization economies, 116, 320
User charges: and public goods, 159
Utility function group. *See also* Collective

Value: and sectors, 36. *See also* Goods; Money
Von Thünen (Wingo) model, 140-43

Weber's general law, 74
Widening productive units, 239

Yamada's model, 144-45

6247